BANNER

by the Wayside

BANNER

by the Wayside

BY SAMUEL HOPKINS ADAMS

RANDOM HOUSE · NEW YORK

IN MEMORIAM

BANNER

by the Wayside

Foreword

My GREAT-AUNT Sarah remembered to the end of her days the banner of the Thalia Dramatic Company as she first saw it flaunting from the inn balcony at Geneva. She would describe the eager York-Staters thronging into town in gigs, ox-wains and hay-wagons, disembarking from sloops, flat-arks and dugouts; tramping sturdily in from farm, sheepfold, mint-meadow, and hempfield to forget in an evening of enchantment the rigors of their hard, frontier life.

That queer Mr. Quinn, who was not Mr. Quinn at all, flew the flag whilst singing a comical song for the edification of the idlers below. It was something about a frog, with a lifelike imitation at the end of each stanza "Jug-o'-rum! Jug-o'-rum!" He then made a little speech, extolling the superior quality of the troupe. Seats, two shillings.

The company arrived that afternoon with their scenery in Conestoga wagons. Starved for the higher culture, the farmfolk in particular flocked to the performances, three nights and a matinee. At the sensitive age of twelve Aunt Sarah was taken to two of the plays, the family being broad-minded, though Presbyterian. With the rest of the audience, she was contorted with mirth over the risible antics of Mr. Tim Baggo as the philosopher, Doodle, in *The Magic Pie,* and moved to ecstasy by the charms of Fair Luna Wayne who recited a poem and danced a hornpipe with inimitable coquetry.

The final performance, at which the Moving Melo Drama, *The Foundling of the Forest,* was rendered, was marred by the irruption of several young Corinthians from Geneva (now Hobart) College who had been banqueting. From their front benches, they

1

called out improper solicitations to the females of the cast until Aunt Sarah's father, the redoubtable Colonel Samuel Miles Hopkins, rose in his seat to rebuke them in round, Miltonian phrase, as "sons of Belial, flown with insolence and wine," which reduced them to respectful silence.

Not everywhere did the troupers fare so well as in hospitable and generous Geneva. Like most road companies, they fell upon evil days, playing hamlets with names since vanished from the map —Lennox, Watercure, Jerusalem. Ten years after, Aunt Sarah saw again and recognized by the faded ghost of the big T against a once white background, the Thalian emblem. Stained to pokeberry red, it had fallen to the base uses of advertising a farm vendu.

1

SNOW clung wetly to the high-gabled roofs of that thriving city, New York. Thin smoke from the night's banking of fireplaces rose into the chill March air. A belated hautboy rattled over the cobbles, the garbage gatherer on his high seat saluting with a respectful flourish of his whip the substantial householder who stood regarding with disfavor a file of retreating footprints in the spread of white on his steps. Overhead the sign of his prosperous trade swung and creaked.

PEARL STREET BOOKERY

Works of Piety & Edification.

Literature, Stationary & Notions.

ADAM P. ANDREWS, PROP'R.

The tracks marked the furtive and permanent evasion of the shop apprentice. Proprietor Andrews shrugged. The loss was by no means irreparable. He would insert in the *Evening Post* a paid notice, offering two cents and a bucket of ashes for the return of the fugitive and warning all and sundry against harboring him, since the undersigned would be responsible for no costs thus unwarrantably contracted.

Apprentices were easy to come by, a thankless and shiftless crew. But no more boys for the Bookery. A good, stout hussy would be competent for the light demands of the Literature, Stationary & Notions trade. Mr. Andrews inked out a neat placard which he affixed to the windowpane with four ass-skin wafers at the corners.

GIRL WANTED

He went comfortably to bed as the watchman cried ten.

At seven the next morning when he went out to take down the shutters, another line capped his.

HERE SHE IS

Beneath it was a wicker, warmly lined.

"Well!" said Mr. Andrews. "Hell!" said Mr. Andrews. "What's this?"

A placid coo issued from the woolly nest. Mr. Andrews cautiously displaced a fold of cloth and encountered the calm gaze of a pair of eyes.

"Hello, mite," said he. "What'll I do with you?" He looked at the sign board above the lintel. "You're no Work of Piety and Edification. Not if I know my New York. Come in."

Picking up the willow-work in gingerly fashion, he carried it inside and placed it on the counter where he stared at the contents in perplexity. There being no children of his household nor, for good and sufficient reasons, likelihood of any, Mr. Andrews was at a loss how to proceed. He must, he supposed, consult Mrs. Andrews, but she was likely to prove unco-operative if not worse, since they had not exchanged a spoken word for sixty-two months and five days. Outside of that they got along evenly in an atmosphere of mutual hatred.

Still, she would have to know. Mr. Andrews rang a bell and sat down. In her own good time his wife would appear. She did and looked coldly at the new arrival, still more coldly at Mr. Andrews. She then picked up the pad which was kept always at hand for essential communications, and wrote in firm script:

"No."

Mr. Andrews' wavering mind was instantly made up. Taking over the tablet, he wrote with equal decisiveness:

"Yes."

She who had long since ceased to be the wife of his bosom snorted wordlessly.

"Take care of your by-blow yourself, then," she wrote.

He blinked. "No by-blow of mine," he scrawled hastily.

"Liar," wrote his wife and would have left in triumph of the last word had he not intercepted her.

"How old?" he inquired through the written medium.

4

"One year," she concluded after examination.

He calculated rapidly from the previous March, counting back nine months and adding a tenth for a possible slowdown in the processes of nature. The mathematics reassured him.

"I was in Europe then," he wrote. "Your suspicions do you small honor."

She grimaced, unconvinced. "Ships still sail from Europe," she pointed out by pencil, and pranced out with an obscene and irritant giggle.

That settled it in Mr. Andrews' annoyed soul. Since Mrs. Andrews objected to the child, the child should stay. He sent for a nursemaid, and made an entry in his daybook.

March the 20th, 1817—Deposited on my doorstep in the course of the previous night, an infant, female, circa one (1) year; of unknown condition and unidentified origin, whom I purpose to rear in a manner and according to my own theory of proper upbringing.

Name? The child must have a name. But none of the slinky, sloppy, wishy-washy virtues should be attached to her—Faith, Hope, Charity, Patience, Piety, Obedience . . . A mincing lot! Endurance! He hit upon it with triumph. It might apply equally to boy or girl. It would set the keynote to the character he intended to mold. And she will need endurance, he reflected, if she is to be brought up beneath the same roof with that hellicat. By which injurious term he meant his life partner.

Thus there grew up to girlhood a grave, alert, silently observant little creature, who, at the age of six was beginning to manifest a clear-cut individuality. By virtue of some latent strain, she was possessed of a sunny and stubborn optimism and a calm self-reliance.

In that peculiar menage she lived a peculiar life. Without open rebellion she succeeded in foiling the mistress' attempts to make a kitchen-malkin of her. Her chief interest in life was helping about the shop. Toward Mrs. Andrews, who conscientiously hated her, she was respectful and indifferent. Toward Mr. Andrews, she was comradely, though, with his lined face of a discontented man of forty, he seemed to her very old. She became a household convenience as a substitute medium of conversation when the writing pad was not handy and the embattled couple wished to communicate.

"Ask that female if she intends to go out upon the public thoroughfare wearing those unseemly gewgaws," from Mr. Andrews.

"Tell that fool I do," from his wife.

"Inform her that her costume is an offense to decency."

"Apprise him that I value his opinion no more than a brass pistareen."

On Saturday evenings the Andrews played a match of seven games of cribbage with envenomed intensity, Mrs. Andrews wearing net gloves against the contamination of the cards which her opponent had handled. When she lost, she wept while he gloated. When he lost, he blasphemed while she simpered intolerably. Their original quarrel, from what Durie could make out, was over mutual allegations of cheating. At the age of seven, she expressed an opinion.

"I think it's silly."

"Leave the room," snapped the couple, for once in accord.

Whereupon little Durie repaired to the shop in contentment.

To the regular customers she became a familiar figure, a grave, wonder-eyed midget, browsing among books from which she was likely to derive more confusion than illumination of mind. Before she had reached the age of ten she had definite if not precisely orthodox views upon predestination, sanctification by grace, and adultery.

The child's status in that house of strife was anomalous. Mrs. Andrews treated her as little better than a servant; Mr. Andrews, as a member of the family. For years it puzzled Durie that in speaking to her of Mr. Andrews, the wife used the form, "your father," always with a sneer. Durie did not seek explanation. Personal questions were not encouraged by either of the couple. The child early formed the unchildish habit of reticence.

Durie took her meals with the pair, and afterward aided the "help" to clear away and wash up, after which she was free to go back to the books. Her growing independence of spirit brought about a crisis which shattered the long family silence. Mr. Andrews, drawn from his counter by his wife's voice raised in shrill recrimination, ran upstairs to find the child at bay over a shattered teapot while Mrs. Andrews menaced her with a sawed-off broomstick representing corrective discipline. He made a vain grab. The stick landed with a sound thwack across Durie's shoulders. Mr. Andrews addressed his wife for the first time in five years.

"I'll break your goddamned neck!" he said, and set about doing it.

Neighbors intervened before the point of fatality was reached. Mr. Andrews was haled before a magistrate who fined him five shillings for assault and ten for profanity. The latter, he paid, but repudiated the former, preferring principle and jail. When he came out, the couple resumed vocal relations with such vivacity that both were cited before the Baptist elders for impious and ungodly language. Mrs. Andrews recanted, expressing the fervent hope that her husband would stand by his principles and fetch up in hell. Mr. Andrews was read out of meeting and became a Free Thinker. Presently both took to drink, and the Literature, Stationary, & Notions trade began to suffer from neglect, the more so in that little Durie was sent to school at Miss Bartram's Refined Academy for Young Girls of Established Families, far north at Yonkers. There, it was expected, she would become adept in such appropriate accomplishments as French for Beginners, the Piano Forte, Floral Discrimination and the Chinese Crayons.

Such was the proper upbringing of a girl. Durie stoically bore with but did not approve the regimen. She much preferred the education received at the hands of her foster-father, which was of a hardier and less ladyish nature. On Sundays, while Mrs. Andrews was at church piously praying for the damnation of her spouse's soul, the two truants were abroad, shooting snipe in the Chelsea marshes, catching smelts off the Battery wall, casting for salmon along the banks of the Haerlem, or hunting foxes and raccoons on Weehawken Cliffs with due heed to the copperheads which swarmed in every rockpile.

Vacation time always found Mr. Andrews sobered up. Clad in his puce-colored coat with ruffling at the cuffs, he coached it to Yonkers to fetch the girl. Two bundles were left at the booking office while he presented himself at the Academy and politely listened to Miss Bartram's account of Endurance Andrews' proficiency. The school teacher had but one complaint. Was Mr. Andrews aware that his daughter professed familiarity with forbidden romances and poems? The profligate Robert Burns, and even, she feared, that notorious rakehell, Lord Byron!

"Not in my bookshop," asserted the dealer in Works of Piety & Edification.

But he thought uneasily of a private library which he kept under lock. Therein he was wont to revive his soul nightly from the dull limitations of churchly literature with a bottle beside him to sharpen his appreciation. There, too, he kept the neat manuscript of his magnum opus against wedlock which he hoped one day to publish, since he was sure that nobody else would. Suppose Durie had come upon that! How certain was he that he had always locked the treasure house of the forbidden? And there were Smollett and Fielding and some of the more private philosophies of the sage Franklin, and even the outrageous Rochester. It would be inadvisable, he felt, to mention such possibilities to Miss Bartram lest she swoon away.

He promised to supervise the girl's reading more carefully in future.

Once beyond the bounds of the school, Durie's extra-curricular education proceeded. The bundles at the coach office were retrieved and carried to an adjacent woodland where she changed into a serviceable boy's suit and Mr. Andrews into the rough garb of the wayfarer. From that moment her life became that of a boy rather than a girl. She was taught every wile of the open. Together the middle-aged man and the young girl ranged the hills and forests and fished the streams. Durie learned to row, swim, shoot, wrestle, tie and cast a fly, defend herself with stick or stone, weave a shelter, dress a wound, cook in the open or, where cookery was impracticable, live on the country; make and strike camp, and to be afraid of nothing animate or inanimate. Once her foster-father beat her for running away from a berrying bear.

Her whole training was addressed to the end of making her self-protective and self-sufficing. She must unflinchingly live up to the name he had given her, Endurance. Thus she acquired proficiencies and absorbed philosophies never contemplated in the correct regimen of the Bartram school. She became wise in the eccentricities of animals, the meannesses of insects, and the treacheries of innocent-appearing vegetation. At twelve years of age she was thoroughly competent to look after herself.

That was a typical chapter in her education when she awoke on the forested edge of a wild-cranberry bog in Southern New Jersey to find herself alone. On a curl of white birch bark was scrawled:

> I have gone home. Follow.
> A.A.

Five days later she emerged on the Palisades, found a log and, prudently taking that for support, swam the river. Her foster-father's greeting when she entered the Bookery was:

"You're a day overdue."

Nevertheless he approved her feat. From that time they became full comrades. No demonstrative affection was ever manifested between them. They understood one another. He told her that he had a strain of Indian blood. It was one of the few confidences he ever made her. It explained much.

Naturally Mrs. Andrews was excluded from these activities. But she, too, undertook to share in the child's upbringing. Her contribution was on the feminine side. At what she judged to be the appropriate time, the frigid and disillusioned wife delivered herself of a treatise upon the nature, phenomena and detriments of wedlock, with a mingling of venom, prejudice and incomprehension which rendered her a far from informative mentor. To the wide-eyed, serious-minded girl, it was more of a mystification than a revelation.

"Men want just one thing of women," expounded Mrs. Andrews, and was explicit upon the unpleasant nature of it.

"Is that what marriage is?" asked Durie.

"That and nothing else."

"Then why do people marry?"

"Because they're fools."

"The romantic tales don't say that. They say they married and lived happily ever after."

"Romancers are fools, too. Or worse. You'll find out."

"I don't want to find out."

"Well, you will. You're the sort that does find out, one way or the other."

"What's the other?"

"You'll find out," repeated her instructress. "You have harlot eyes."

"What's 'harlot'?"

Mrs. Andrews was expansive.

"I don't think I should like that any better than marriage," reflected Durie. "What do girls do it for?"

"Money. The same thing they marry for. You'd better marry—if you can find a big enough fool."

"Wouldn't I have to be a fool, too?" Durie had a logical mind.

The petty little face of the wife contorted itself into a mask of malice.

"Thanks to my dummergung of a husband, you think yourself half a boy. Don't you?"

"I'd rather be a boy than a girl."

"Well, you're not, as you'll discover one day. You're a girl—a wench—a woman now. It's in every line of that wicked young body of yours. Who knows what vice is simmering in your hot blood! Bastard that you are, you'll be the mother of roadside babies."

"I like babies," remarked Durie.

"You'll get 'em. You're going to have beauty of a kind; I grant you that. The sort of lewd beauty that tricks fools. Sell it in the best market; that's my word of wisdom to you. A rich old man is best; he won't pester you for long. But get the ring on your finger before you crawl between the sheets." She grinned evilly. "And take your pastime outside."

Durie pondered. "Does one have to do that to have babies?"

"Don't you understand anything of what I have been telling you?" snarled her mentor.

"Not very much. Why haven't *you* had babies?"

Mrs. Andrews cursed her foully and withdrew to find comfort in the bottle. The subject was never again referred to between them. One phrase of it stuck in Durie's mind with the persistence of unsatisfied curiosity. She took it up with her foster-father.

"Dad Andrews, what's a bastard?"

"Why?"

"Am I one?"

"Who says you are?"

"Mrs. Andrews."

He reflected. "If anyone else ever calls you that, blood their noses well for 'em. That's what any young blade of spirit would do."

"I'm not a young blade of spirit. I'm a woman, so Mrs. Andrews told me."

"Humph! Well—damn!" He sighed. "I suppose it had to come. What else did that hellicat say to you?"

"Something about being beautiful," said the girl indifferently.

This startled him. "Maybe you are."

He gravely considered her as she stood before him, straight, lissome, already delicately rounded. She was medium tall and strong, but so cleanly proportioned that she seemed less than average, an illusion to which her swift grace and suavity of line and curve, whether in motion or at rest, lent validity. Her face was puzzling. The eyes, of a sultry brown, were wide, grave and heavy lidded. The mouth, too, was grave; the chin almost too firm; the cheekbones solid supports for a wide brow, and above all, soft, bright-burnished ruddy hair sweeping upward with a sort of bravado which informed the whole face with gayety and spirit. Yes, he concluded, she might grow into beauty; beauty dangerous to herself and others.

But how much did she know? How much ought he to tell her? How much had his wife told her?

Had he asked, Durie could have given out only confusion from a confused mind. Indeed, her notions of love were a hodgepodge of romance from the private library, qualified by the surmises, guesses, reluctances and alarms which the venomous and neurotic communications of Mrs. Andrews had inspired. Upon this point the neophyte was clear; marriage was an institution revolting to any female of delicacy, and love an abhorrent persecution of woman by man. Explicit though the instructress had meant to be, Durie, while curious up to a point, was unreceptive. Her chief reaction to the diffuse and distasteful revelations was discomfort.

Nor had Durie's uncertainty been relieved by a note in Mr. Andrew's handwriting which she had come upon in the cashdrawer.

Love in its manifestation of wooing is to women like a habit of strong drink. Its fatal indulgence once established, it becomes a requirement of existence. Or the simile might advantageously be varied to state that objective love is, for a woman, a warm, soft perfumed swaddle in which she comforts her vanity and keeps her soul in cattish contentment. She yields to the necessity of being cherished. If the new essential to her well-being be snatched from her, she will pay the price of recovering it, even the price of herself. Hence marriage. For this is the pristine strategy of man, the pursuer, to surround the woman with adoration. His peril in such tactics is that, in privation of worship suddenly withdrawn, the inamorata may seek other warmth. Philosophers have long recognized that women do not crave love so much as they crave to be loved.

On suspicion that she might have seen it, Mr. Andrews used it as a strategic approach. Standing beside her as she was closing the shop and covering the books one evening, he asked:

"Have you ever happened on my monograph upon wedded life?"

"I read something," she answered evasively. "The rest was tied up. Will it be a published book?"

"Some day, God willing. When I can afford to turn printer."

He lifted the work from its place. The title page was inscribed:

THE MAZE OF MARRIAGE
A Diatribe
BY
ADAM PERSONIUS ANDREWS
"Love is the False Pruritus of the Spirit."

She glanced at it. "Why do you hate women, Dad?"

"It's safer to hate than to love. You'll know that when you've read my book."

"It hurts to hate."

"It hurts worse to love."

"Do most people think so?"

"Most people are fools."

"Then are wise people like you lonely?"

"Lonely is a coward's word. Don't ever fear to be alone."

"I don't."

"Do you want to go back to Miss Bartram's?"

"No."

"What do you want to do?"

"Attend college."

"College!" he echoed, dumbfounded.

"Your college. You attended Harvard College, didn't you?"

"Yes: but . . ."

"I should like to be a young gentleman. Wouldn't Harvard teach me to be?"

He began to laugh. "A girl in those classic halls! I'll warrant you'd stir the shades." His mirth subsided to a sardonic grin. "Our virgin Alma Mater privily conceives an alumna. But the four-year gestation period? No, no! The girl would get caught at it. Still, there's nothing to stop our having a look. Get your bundle together. Andrews, Class of 1800, and his promising young son, Endurance, will attend commencement. And may God protect the Yard!"

Blare and glare and clamor; voices raised in song, in laughter, in dispute, in greeting; dust rising from the shuffle and tramp of feet to dim the fierceness of the August sun; chaises, gigs and coaches, both private and public, pouring fresh accessions of humanity from the teeming Menotomy Road upon the overcrowded campus; elegant marquee tents exhaling rich odors of food and drink from the borders of the grassy plot; bright apparel of girls, bonneted, beribboned, befrilled, the gayer by contrast with the sober garb of the students, limited to gray, dark blue, or black on pain of fine; march and counter-march of parading militia behind their bands; sheriffs' posses of two counties stationed at strategic points to forestall too gross a breach of the public peace and safety; movement, color, jubilation everywhere.

Commencement at Harvard College.

Two wayfarers, who had come neither by coach, chaise, or gig, stood observant in front of Holworthy Hall. Their heavy and battered footgear, the bundles and staves which lay at their feet, attested them as foot travelers. But their pantaloons were correctly cut, their coats and shirts of the finest material, and their bearing that of prosperous and confident folk. The elder was gaunt and dark, with a saturnine cast of feature. His companion, much smaller and younger, was ruddy of coloring and lightly supple of carriage. The face, still chubby with youth, was firmly molded, sensitive and lighted by luminous eyes.

The senior waved his hand toward the dormitory which displayed a coarse crocus banner inscribed Lottery Lodgings in impious reference to the financing of the building.

"The sportive academic mind, Durie," said he. "Youth is changeless."

"Did you live there, Dad?"

"Yes." He waved his hand. "I give you the freedom of the Yard," he continued with that cheerful confidence in her capacity to look after herself which she fully shared.

Durie strolled contentedly out upon the sward. A sound of faint music attracted her. Flat upon his back beneath a secluded shade-tree lay a fashionably clad young man with a small and exquisitely inlaid guitar resting upon his chest. At first sight, he seemed constructed upon a somewhat haphazard pattern, long, thin, and casual-jointed. His face, also, was long and thin with a solid jaw and broad-set, reflective eyes. He was trying out soft harmonies, humming low as he explored new combinations. Across the burnished belly of his instrument was inscribed a legend in gilt-Gothic lettering, *Laus Deo*. It was not, however, praise to God which the strings gave forth but a livelier measure with the vocal overtone providing such secular rhymes as "eyes" with "sighs" and "heart" with "part."

A string slipped. He tightened it and, as he did so, caught sight of the intruder.

"*Ave, puer!*" he greeted.

"Good day," she replied courteously.

"Do you bear a message for me?"

"No."

"Do I know you?"

"I've never seen you until this moment."

"Then go away."

"Why must I?"

He considered the candid face above him, now showing a shade of disappointment, and his own relaxed in a slow, friendly smile. "Upon reflection, why, indeed? Harvard's precincts are hospitable. To what do I owe the honor of your attention?"

"I like the music. Why has your guitar that motto on it?"

"In my father's day it dispensed long-meter piety from the Congregational Church choir loft. In mine it seeks harmonious arrangements for the Glee Club."

"Are you a member of the learned faculty?"

"Dear God!" ejaculated the young man, getting to his feet the better to observe his questioner. "Here, indeed, is prime innocency!

You behold in me, my young pinkling, the very wrack and detritus of a liberal education, an outcaste of the classic world, remaining in its shades only upon sufferance."

"I think your speech is beautiful," said Durie gravely.

"Some hold that there is a plethora of it," returned the young man with equal gravity.

"When does the Glee Club exhibit its music?"

"If you are out of your bed at the unholy hour of seven, young innocence, your straining ears may pluck a far echo. And so good day to you for I must to my studious desk and notate my harmonies."

While she was still wandering about in admiration of the ancient buildings, she rounded the corner of Holworthy and came upon her foster-father in the company of a portly, chuckling gentleman of his own age whom Mr. Andrews addressed as Hey-Hey Jacobs. Upon learning that the supposed youth was his classmate's son, Mr. Jacobs assumed a future at Harvard for him, and raised a lusty voice.

"Peery! Peery Potter!"

An amiable face with a feathery whisker protruded from a second-floor window.

"My respects, Uncle."

"Come down, my boy. Experience Potter, my sister's young hopeful," he explained.

"What's up, sir?" inquired Potter.

"A candidate to be put through his paces."

"Sorry, sir, I'm busy. But here's Quinny. Quinny's your man."

"And who may Quinny be?"

"Jans Quintard, Esquire, of the Class of Thirty-one."

"Or not," amended a voice which made Durie lift her eyes, "as the case may be. Probably not."

"Shut your clam," admonished his classmate. "Are you sober enough to perform the ritual?"

"Soberer than you are," was the uncompromising reply.

The voices debated the matter in murmurs. Young Potter's head appeared again.

"He says he prefers to sing dirges and tell sad stories of the death of kings. He says let Macel Ayrault do it."

"What's Macel Admiral of the Royal Navy for if not for this?" demanded the other voice argumentatively.

Both young men began to shout at the top of their register, "Ayrault! Ayrault! Navy, ahoy!"

The door of Holworthy swung wide to emit a handsome viking of a young fellow with an empty face and an impressive swagger. Mr. Macel Ayrault affected the martial style with mustache and aspired to be a colonel of militia and a devil of a blade with the females.

"What's on the tappy?" he demanded.

"A suckling candidate." Peery Potter threw wide the window draperies, revealing the guitar player with his instrument, angled into the embrasure.

"Admiral Dumpf takes command," announced Jans Quintard. "The Royal Navy holds authority over all high jinks and low japes of the campus."

Durie lifted an eager face, expecting a word of recognition. The lordly Mr. Quintard was not even looking at her. But the viking was, with a portentous frown.

"Is this the candidate?" Ayrault thrust his grossly masculine countenance close to the smaller face which remained calm and watchful. A gentle diapason sounded from the window. Was it encouragement? The little hearer hoped so.

"Young didapper!"

"Yes?"

"Yes, *sir.*"

"Why?"

"Respect to your elders and betters, damn your impudence!"

"Sir."

"That's proper. Do you ambition to join the honorable forum of the Collegium Harvardiensibus?"

"None of your apothecary's Latin, Mace," protested the guitarist.

"Well, do that part of it, yourself," said the big fellow good-humoredly. "Damn the Latinity, anyway! I never could abide it."

The voice addressed Durie. "What class? Thirty-five, shall we say? Or a belated Thirty-six?"

As she did not know, Durie asked, "Does it matter?"

"Oh. sapient though beardless youth! Hold that for your device and you shall go far. Education doesn't matter. Culture doesn't matter. Wealth, poverty, meat, drink, wine, women or song don't matter, nor yet virtue or vice. What, then, does matter to Wisdom and Philosophy, my philosophic spratling?"

"Alma Mater," said the Honorary Admiral and contorted his big frame with mirth.

"Macey's turned wit!" said Jans in accents of stupefaction. "Laugh, spratling."

"I don't think the jest so risible," said the spratling.

Aggrieved, the big fellow brandished a flat hand above the unsmiling face. But the face was not there. Swifter than the slap, the lithe form had leaped backward.

"Not in the ritual," drawled the guitarist. "Proceed, worthy Admiral."

"Age?" Ayrault barked.

"Fourteen."

"Freshman-ripe. Where born?"

"I don't know."

"Why don't you know, stupid?"

"I wasn't born. I was found."

The catechist goggled. "A foundling seeking entrance here? A bastard?"

"Fair words, damn your blundering soul!" The voice from the window had lost its languor.

"Would that make any difference?" asked the candidate interestedly.

"No harm done, lunkhead," said the voice, bored again.

The viking did not take the epithet amiss. He was one of those who take nothing amiss. "Right you are, Quinny, my lad. We might have him at the Med. Fac. tonight to blood him properly."

"Not a bad notion. Who's our initiate?"

"Haven't got one yet. We'll pick one up. Seven o'clock at the three elms. And the youngling can fetch along his sponsors."

Durie whispered, "Dad, do I know enough to matriculate?"

"And more, if that were all. Be off with you now, while Mr. Jacobs and I pay a few festal visits."

They climbed the stairs where young Potter welcomed them at the door. The guitarist emerged from his perch and bowed.

"So you are a Quintard," said Mr. Andrews.

"I had an uncle in your time, sir."

"Sparks Quintard. I remember him well. He and two other blades attended the President's soiree astride of sawhorses, saddled and bridled."

"We have always ridden our hobbies hard, sir."

"And yours is?" asked Mr. Andrews, amused and interested as most older people were by this young fantastic.

"Had I taken fewer drinks, sir, I could expound. As it is, I can but say that, while I am vague upon the subject, I have a mild, impersonal interest in universal education. In fact, I presented a disquisition upon the topic which was very ill-received by the academic authorities."

The two alumni exchanged glances. "I should think so!" observed Mr. Jacobs.

"I claim no merits for my argument," said the young man modestly. "In fact, I prefer to drink. Gentlemen, a welcome awaits us in the tents."

"A moment," interposed Mr. Andrews, eyeing the guitar skeptically. "Do you profess yourself a scholar, Quintard?"

"The best of our class," put in Potter warmly. Quintard shook his head with a deprecating smile.

"I sustain my tests unevenly, sir. In Greek I am an adept of no mean pretensions. My Latinity, sirs, is classic. But in mathematics I confess myself a zero. In logic I am a false syllogism, and my deportment fails to find favor with the authorities. I am fined out of half my allowances," said the young man lamentably. He brandished his arms in an expressive gesture. "What avails it to make a shine in Greek if, the next hour, one does a barney in calculus? There have been times when, in sheer disgust, I have bleached my classes for a week on end. For my political heresies, expressed in prose and verse and exhibited in oration and discourse, I have been degraded, suspended and rusticated until today I do not know whether or not I am still an alumnus of this honorable institution."

"Who," inquired Mr. Jacobs mildly, "solicited you to exhibit an oration upon yourself?"

"It is my favorite topic," replied the young man. "But perhaps I overdo it."

While her elders passed from marquee to marquee in pursuit of the lavish hospitality afforded to all alumni, Durie strolled happily about in exploration. Back near Holworthy again, she gave ear to a roaring chorus from an upper window where the glee club were loosening their voices in preparation for the evening;

Tagrag, merry-derry, periwig and hatband,
Hic-hoc-horum, genitivo!

A guitar twanged. An impatient voice said, "Oh, let's be done with this piffery and sing something."

Silence fell. A rich chord sounded, and grew to a swelling harmony. The little listener below held her breath in sheer delight. She had never before heard secular part-singing. The voices trained to the strait control of the hymnbook were like prisoners released. They blended with a fullness, a suppleness, a passionate fecundity of sound that stirred her to uncomprehended and frightening sensations.

"Faintly as tolls the evening chime
Our voices keep tune and our oars keep time."

The robust maleness of it possessed her, pulsed in her veins, weakened her limbs with languor.

"Row, brothers, row; the stream runs fast;
The rapids are near, and the daylight's past."

A baritone rose above the chorus, which now subsided to a harmonic support.

"Saint of this green isle, hear our prayers!
Oh, grant cool heavens and favoring airs."

So, thought the rapt hearer, must the seraphic leader of celestial choirs have sung. Like one under mesmeric control, she moved forward to the choral beat.

"Blow, breezes, blow! The stream runs fast
The rapids are near and the daylight's past."

A hand fell on her shoulder.

"Here you are!" said Adam Andrews. "Listening to the juvenile minstrelsy?"

"It's cruel sweet," she breathed.

"Damned caterwauling!" said Adam Andrews.

"It does something to me, inside."

He stared. "Oh, it does, does it? Well, don't let it."

"I've never heard split-voice singing except in church. It isn't the same."

"Not quite," yawned her foster-father. "You'll get no good of such fah-doodle."

The gleemen came out in a body and scattered.

Prompt upon the stroke of seven a cowbell jangled. A harsh medley of horns sounded the summons to the faithful. Mr. Andrews handed Durie her waystaff, observing that one could never tell when a ready defense might be needed. They were joined by Mr. Jacobs.

The space around the three elms was occupied by some fifty students and half as many older alumni. A door of the building was flung open and three gowned undergraduates led forth the candidate for honors.

"Why, it's poor old Billy-Pickles!" said Mr. Andrews, identifying the campus vendor of egg pop.

The old fellow, ludicrously crowned with a tin coronet, looked terrified.

"Are they going to hurt him?" Durie asked apprehensively.

"Perhaps you'd better send the boy away," Hey-Hey Jacobs suggested to his classmate.

Durie dissented vehemently. This was a part of Harvard life and she wanted to see it. Her foster-father supported this attitude.

At first the proceedings seemed to Durie only dull and meaningless, full of gibberish and bad, unfunny Latin. Then, with the announcement of the Accolade, the sport began. The old fellow was battered to and fro, a helpless shuttlecock for the antics of the Med. Fac. roysterers. Blood trickled from beneath the tin crown. He began to bleat for mercy. The Magister inverted a stone jar of beer over his head. Billy-Pickles went down in a heap.

"Coward!"

It was a quavering pipe, but fiery with contempt and wrath.

"What *homunculus* have we here?" demanded the astonished Magister, glaring into Durie's wrath-contorted face. *"Fratres,* another candidate for our honors."

He stretched out a thick hand and reeled back as Jans Quintard's blow caught him full on the chin. Both went down. The crowd surged forward, yelling, and as lively a little riot as Harvard Yard had seen for many a year was on.

Using his stout ash staff, Mr. Andrews fought his way toward the center to the aid of Quintard and of Potter, who had joined in. Hey-Hey Jacobs, in his day a stout fellow and eminent ruffler, followed, making play and wreaking devastation with an egg-pop bottle, until he was brought to earth by an adroit trip from the rear. Mr. Andrews fell over him. Only then did the small figure which had squirmed out from under the fringe of the fray, plunge in. With a Valkyrie shriek she worked her way to the Magister, half-scalped that astonished combatant with an expert whirl of the knobbed end of her staff, stopped the on-rushing Ayrault short with a pretty poke in the midriff and was grabbed and hurled to earth just as a shrill cry of alarm rose and spread.

"Cave! Ca-a-ave! The procs! 'Ware proctors!"

Durie wriggled out from beneath a knee on her shoulder, and found herself in the grip of a gowned official. At the same moment she became aware of a serious rent in jacket and shirt and the coolness of night air on her skin. An astonished ejaculation from the proctor struck her ear. His grip relaxed. She wrenched loose and ran.

The rioters melted away with an address born of long practice. Durie rejoined Mr. Andrews in the rear of Holworthy. Rubbing a lump over his nose, he chuckled, "That was a fine brawl you got us into."

"I hate cruelty."

"Lads will be lads. I feel like one myself."

"Are you going to drink any more?" There was no accent of criticism in the question; it was purely for information.

"A few choice spirits are gathered at Massachusetts Hall."

"That means you will be at it till morning."

"If I had you disposed of . . ."

"You needn't concern yourself for me, Dad. If I can look after myself in the woods at night, I'm not likely to come to harm on a college common," was the composed reply.

From the dark shadow of a distant tree sounded a succession of chords. A supple, sensuous baritone rose, hovered, sank.

"H'm!" said Mr. Andrews. "That's a devilish voice, a dangerous voice."

"Dangerous?" she murmured. "How, dangerous?"

"You wouldn't know, being a boy," he jeered.

"Oh!" said Durie thoughtfully.

Mr. Andrews reflected. "If you need me, look for me in Massachusetts. Otherwise at six-fifteen tomorrow I'll be under the college pump. We take the road. Sure you'll be all right?"

"Sure." She gave him a smile of perfect self-confidence.

She strolled across the yard, lifted her face sensuously to the caress of a cool waft from the Charles, and paused before an unfinished warehouse whence issued voices in stress. A banner wavered torpidly in the breeze. Its once-white oblong was bordered with blue and offered for device a large letter T in flagrant crimson.

3

EARLY in the 1800's a mighty hunger of the spirit possessed and stimulated the lusty and culturally ambitious young nation. People yearned to go to the show. Drama was in universal demand.

The appetite found ready satisfaction in centers of population, where theatre, museum and forum vied in weekday popularity. No less than six hundred plays, all open to piracy, were in print. Trivial and fustian though most of them were, reflecting no phase of life honestly, they nevertheless held out to their prospective audiences the vision and the enchantment of a more radiant world. Established companies fared more than well on the eager patronage of the cities.

For the outlying districts, no less avid, there was scanty theatrical fare. Half a dozen itinerant troupes wandered abroad in the land by turnpike, canal, lake and river, flying their distinctive emblems from tavern, ballroom, barn loft, storehouse, horse shed, or improvised platform in meadow or grove. They were composed of a mixture of ambitious youth and broken-down virtuosi of the past, the cheerful dregs of the profession, bearing illusion and delight to the dark fringes of civilization.

Often these invincible troupers were broke, for their clientele was both poor and frugal. Sometimes they were hungry. They knew the rigors of the chase with themselves as quarry and the sheriff, an unsatisfied judgment in his pocket, as hunter. Hazards of travel were rugged; they must fulfill their schedules at peril of storm and flood, of accident, fever and venomous nature, both animal and vegetable. Where the banner flaunted by the wayside, there must they meet their appointments. This was their honor; the faith pledged to their public. Their lot was hard. Bitterly they bewailed and jealously they loved it.

"We could hold the curtain."

"And have the patrons clamor for their money back? Don't we get enough of that without extra incitement?"

Notwithstanding, the curtain was delayed until almost eight o'clock. There was exactly eleven dollars in the house. An ominous word from the management was issued by Mr. Passerow:

"Fill up on breakfast."

It was familiar formula, meaning that the troupe would slip away in the morning, leaving the tavern bill unsettled and that the next meal would be a matter of opportunity and ingenuity.

As the curtains parted upon Mr. Tim Baggo's pallid grin, the exchequer was improved two shillings' worth by the arrival of a very young patron who carried a staff and advanced hesitantly to a bench well forward, tenderly fingering a red and contused chin.

After parting from her foster-father Durie had strolled until she sighted the banner and, beneath it, the playbill. She studied it with fascinated misgivings. Only by seductive hearsay did she know of the theatre. These masques of Satan were anathema in her Baptist home environment. No such consideration would have deterred her; Mrs. Andrews' watchfulness was the effective hindrance. Consequently it was with a pleasurable thrill of guilt and defiance that the adoptive of that restricted household now paid over her silver piece and entered upon the forbidden ground.

From that moment she was a transported creature.

Half an hour of world-lost ecstasy was all that she had for her money. While Act 1 was still in merry progress there was a turmoil at the entrance, followed by an anguished yelp in the voice of Jack Ambide.

"Help! Robbers! Constab—— *Oof!*"

The assault had captured the moneybox for purposes of its own. The forces marched in, keeping the close order of the Royal Navy and singing a folderol chorus behind the leadership of Admiral Macel Ayrault.

> *"Dingee spotten-dotten,*
> *Ballio otten-dotten,*
> *Dingee rotten-cotten;*
> *Who dere?"*

27

The affrighted audience fled. They had had previous experience of Harvard culture. Only Durie remained, prudently withdrawing to a corner. A reveller closed the curtains, stepped out in front, and announced, "Decks cleared. None injured. I hereby take over this playhouse in the name of the barber, the gun and the hole-in-my-coat. We will presently offer an approved Diabolus."

A puff of sulphurous smoke heralded the parting of the curtains. The spectacle of gentlemanly academes arrayed as devils, harrying other academes in the garb of the clergy with inflated pig's bladders for bludgeons, afforded Durie little entertainment after the glamor and the humor of the professionals. But an interlude by the glee club held her to her seat, and again she was left tremulous as the lovely and tender "Ballad of Wapping Old Stairs" died into silence. Impromptu acrobatics followed, after which the Master of the Ceremonies tooted his horn and called for silence.

"For our closing proffer, shipmates of the Royal Navy, our comrade in arms, Mr. Jans Quintard, will exhibit a portion of his meritorious and admired oration, 'Masques and Mummers,' which the learned faculty of our Alma Mater, to their eternal shame, refused to countenance for delivery upon the rostrum (hisses and boos). I bespeak your respectful attention to Shipmate Quintard."

Slightly unsteady of gait, Jans came out, bowed, and said, "I should prefer to sing."

"No, no!" "Later!" "Speech, speech!"

"Or to render a genteel selection upon Laus Deo."

"No music!" "Speech!" "Give us the Diatribe *Contra Facultatem!*" "No, no! 'Masques and Mummers.'" "Speech!" "Quinny! Quinny! Hooray!"

Jans bowed lower. "Flasks out! Gentlemen, I give you the Thalians." He proceeded:

"These simple folk whom tonight we have ousted from their endeavors merit rather our support and respect. Lowly though their estate be, they are the bearers of a priceless message." Launched now into the midst of his rejected disquisition, Jans spoke with quiet fervor. "Their livelihood is harsh and precarious, their consideration among men, humble. Yet, once upon the boards, these vagabonds and players illume the outer darkness with the radiance of a sublime art, for they dispense the enchantments of a brighter world.

28

"Yon shabby mummer of the taproom, let him but step before the backdrop into that light that never was on sea or land, as saith the poet, and how magical the transformation that renders him a monarch, a hero, a knight of legend! This slattern of the weary roads is, in her brief hour of witchery, Venus *victrix*. Under her soft compulsion we behold Anadyomene rise from the moon-kissed waves. Phryne, Helen, Perdita enchant the vision and seduce the soul; their spell transports us from the humdrum of daily pursuits to the illimitable realms of fancy. *Lampadia echontes*. Bearing the torch, they cast its lucid ray into far shadows. Time shall not stale nor custom wither them; their insubstantial pageant fadeth not.

"And now, shipmates," the speaker went on with a shift to briskness of tone, "we have the pretension of being gentlemen. Let us act in accordance with our estate. We have dispersed these toilful play-folk and wasted their meager funds. I propose an offertory and appoint myself chairman of a committee to kick the unworthy fundament of any member so niggardly as to hold his hand from his purse." (Applause, conscientious rather than effusive.)

A cheer, solo, from the lobby punctuated the acclaim. The intrepid Ambide, after comforting his bruises with arnica, had returned to salvage whatever remnants might be left in the money-box. The remainder of the troupe had returned to the tavern or were hiding in the adjacent shadows. Manager Passerow was full of muttered threats about summoning the sheriff. It was all palaver. The prescribed show-tax had not been paid. To appeal to the law would be to invoke a fine on top of their other woes.

As delivered to Mr. Ambide, the collection came to three shillings above twenty dollars. The Thalian Dramatic Company could now honor their bill and digest their breakfasts in the heartening consciousness of solvency.

Durie loitered outside. By twos and threes and boisterous groups the Royal Navy sailed out into the open. But not the figure for whom she waited. A rumor of idly plucked strings impelled her to go back into the building. Jans Quintard's lanky six-foot form was disposed lengthwise along a bench, his back propped against the wall. A moon-ray illumined his highboned face. His eyes were closed. At the sound of light footsteps he opened them.

"Eh? What's this?" he said sleepily.

"It's me."

He peered at her so intently that she feared for the secret of her sex but reassured herself with the reflection that much drink would have dulled his perceptions. What would he be like when sober? Being of a forthright disposition, she put the query.

"Eh? Sober?" He appeared shocked. *"Absit omen!"*

"Aren't you ever sober?"

"Oh, frequently. Painfully, I may say. Not at commencement time, however. It dims my resistless charm. Are you sensible of my resistless charm, spratling?"

"Y-y-yes."

"Therein the learned faculty lack your appreciative intelligence. Go your way now, my sprat, and vex no further the sorrows of a mournful philosopher."

"Why should you be mournful?"

"'Why should the children of a king go, mourning, all their days?' Resolve me that, oh, spratling. Or, if unable, hold your peace that I may cogitate."

"Please don't cogitate. I want to talk to you."

"What about?"

"Entering Harvard College."

"Nil obstat. What's to hinder?"

"Dad Andrews. He flouts the idea. Will you advise me?"

"I? God save us! When was ever a Quintard that could guide his own destinies, let alone tamper with alien fates!"

"Dad said something about the Queer Quintards and about dreamers and drinkers."

"Ah! President Mather fastened that word upon us when the first Quintard came to Harvard and it has come down the generations. 'Drink and dreams are the Quintard curse.' Is that what you heard?"

"Yes. Like poetry."

"More fact than poetry. Though I versified upon it once and got no further than the end of the ballade."

"How can one get further than the end?"

"There wasn't any beginning," he explained. "That's the way we do things, we Quintards. But the end was not without merit."

"Will you repeat it to me? I like poesy."

"Oh, do you! I'll try." He closed his eyes and recited dreamily:

> "Out of the womb of chance we came,
> Reckless of deed, spendthrift of purse.
> Some for lucre and some for fame
> Saw the better and followed the worse.
> Ever our fate attends our name;
> Whether we travel by horse or hearse,
> Still shall the ending be the same,
> Drink and dreams are the Quintard curse."

"I think it's mortal beautiful," she said. "And so sorrowful I could weep!"

"Shed no tears for us, little crocodile. We survive."

"I heard your address," she said shyly.

He waved a lordly hand, dismissing it as not worth comment.

"Did you believe it all, or was it only a—a dissertation?"

"Oh, I suppose I believe it enough," was the careless reply. "Why?"

"I should admire to be an act——" She had almost said "actress" but caught her errant tongue in time. ". . . to go on the stage," she substituted.

"In preference to the sacred grove of Harvard College?"

"Couldn't one do both?"

"Hardly compatible. My own dramatic endeavors, humble though they be, have been frowned upon by the *curatores*."

"You've acted? On the real stage?" she asked, wide-eyed.

"While out of favor with the authorities and therefore rusticated I have contributed my talents upon the Bowery boards."

"Oh-h-h-h-h! How dicty!"

"Less dicty than you flatteringly assume. My roles were inconsiderable. But I have learned my medium. One day I shall write a drama."

"What about?"

"Princes, princesses and courtiers, if I would be in the swim. Or the noble Indian. But I have little taste for the fashion in plays. I shall write about common folk, the *profanum vulgus* disdained by Quintus Horatius Flaccus, and so cover myself with discredit."

"May I come to witness it?"

"When you've grown a beard, my fervent didapper."

"Will it have music in it? And will you sing?"

"Hullo!" Once more his eyes were intent, also amused. "Have we a budding *tenore* here for future glee clubs?"

"No. Dad Andrews doesn't approve music. He says it is unmanly."

Jans chuckled. He swept the strings of Laus Deo to a humming harmony and sang:

> *"Over the mountains*
> *And over the waves.*
> *Under the fountains*
> *And under the graves.*
> *Over seas that are deepest*
> *That Neptune obey,*
> *Over rocks that are steepest,*
> *Love will find out the way."*

Her hands went to her breast in a gesture that might have betrayed her had his eyes not closed again. Years before she had found the whole poem scrawled on the flyleaf of an ancient book and had conned it by heart. And once she had heard a street minstrel render it to an unforgotten melody.

"It's a brave song," she managed to say.

"An old thing that has come down, *viva voce,* through generations of Quintards."

"And nobody else knows it?" she asked cunningly.

"So says the family legend."

"Isn't there more?"

He fixed her with an eye suddenly reproving. "Why do I squander the precious hours of night upon an unfledged didapper when I might more profitably be drinking? Away, inconsiderable item, and trouble me no more."

"Yes, sir," said Durie.

Tucking Laus Deo beneath his arm, he strode forth.

"Love will find out the way," hummed Durie under her breath.

Old Kathie Morse, head sweeper of Hollis, checked her limping progress across the flat, her gnarled and weathered face screwed up questioningly as a tousled apparition confronted her.

"What does the likes of you do on Harvard Plain this hour o'night?"

"I'm looking for a lodging," Durie explained.

"By the look of your clothes you must lodge in a hayrick."

"I've been in a fight."

"Aha! The Med. Fac. ruckshus." Kathie knew all the campus news, current and for thirty years past. "You'll be Merry Andrews' young un."

"Yes."

"And it's time to doss." Kathie made an expansive gesture toward the dormitory. "My inn. Private and decent."

"I want a *clean* room."

"Them as I caretake is bunkum clean. There'll be Jans Quintard's chamber on the second floor. His linen was freshlaid only yesterday. You can't say fairer than that for tuppence."

"How do I know he won't come in?"

"Jans? Before sunup? Never at commencement. But if you're squeamy you can bar the door so as the holy faculty itself couldn't make entry."

The tuppence duly paid, the lodger entered. Light from an amethyst glass lamp illumined a scene of luxury; wing chairs, a tester bed with embroidered canopy, a deep, rich divan, a well-stocked liquor cabinet, and shelves lined with books both curricular and profane. A rope was coiled in a cushioned window seat beneath a hand-lettered placard:

ESCAPE IN CASE OF FIRE OR DUNS

Durie yawned and stretched upon the bed, intent upon getting her tuppennyworth of sleep.

Cockcrow roused her. She heard uneven footsteps on the stairs, a joyous voice raised in song. Leaping up, she unbarred the door, dropped the rope, and expertly swarmed down it. A near-by thicket afforded concealment.

Jans stumbled into his room. His bed was rumpled, but the room was untenanted. His eye, observant still through the mists of drink, noted the dangling rope. He peered down upon the dim yard. Nobody in sight.

He unslung his guitar, tuning it with unimpaired exactitude. In his brain was still ringing the brave ditty which had come down, lip to ear, through long generations of Quintards, Maitlands and Isaacs. He sang:

> *"You may tame the eagle*
> *To stoop to your wrist."*

"Fist," corrected a voice from the outer darkness.

"Huh?" ejaculated Jans, stopping as if from the impact of an elbow in his midriff.

"Fist, not wrist," repeated the voice persuasively. "Try it."

"Well, I'll be . . . ! Sing it yourself."

"I'll try," said the voice doubtfully.

> *"You may tame the eagle*
> *To stoop to your fist."*

The rendition was husky, uncertain, but informed with a warm loveliness.

"*Bis!*" said Jans. "Again!"

There was a lilt of soft laughter.

> *"Or you may inveigle*
> *The Phoenix of the East."*

Jans leaned from the window. "Who are you that knows 'The Great Adventure' better than I do?"

No reply.

"Man, woman or child? I charge you, speak."

Unbroken silence.

"Would you lay hold on my soul with sweet, deceiving lips?"

The sweet, deceiving lips giggled.

"Retro Sathanas!" said Jans with dignity. "Powers of Darkness, avaunt! Temptation, begone! Lorelei! Circe! Echo, the Disembodied, I defy your spells and snares. Riddle me this:

> *"Some think to enclose him*
> *By keeping him confined."*

The lines were confidently capped:

> *"Some do suppose him*
> *Poor fools! to be blind."*

Jans' baritone was a flung defiance:

> *"But howsoe'er ye wall him,*
> *Do the utmost that ye may . . ."*

The challenge was completed with a jocund lift, an assurance that laid hold upon the heart:

> *"Blind Love—if so ye call him—*
> *Still will find out the way."*

Jans leaned out. "Wait for me," he said.

"Echo waits for no man."

"Echo is a bodiless shape. But you are flesh and blood—and woman. Wait!"

It was a shade in enshrouding dimness that moved and fled lightly. He called after it, "Don't think to escape me. Whoever you are, I shall know you. Wherever you go, I shall follow. However you hide, I shall find you. Do you believe me?"

Far, soft laughter was wafted back to his ears.

A lank, haggard man spluttered out from beneath Stoughton pump, the handle of which was vigorously operated by a slighter figure.

"Breakfast on the road," prescribed Adam Andrews.

Durie nodded.

"Still for your matriculation?"

She turned color. "I can't."

"Wise conclusion. What leads you to it?"

"The blackgown who picked me up after the fight. My—my jacket was torn open. He saw."

Adam Andrews took up staff and packet, sighing. "We shall have to make a lady of you. A woman! Damn all women!" said he, thinking of one.

"It'll be mortal strange," murmured Durie.

From far across the plain sounded a wave of minstrelsy. All·

night revels had roughened the throats of the gleemen, but the
voices still blended unerringly, still stirred an urgency, incom-
prehensible, all but intolerable in Durie's young blood.

> *"I sent thee late a rosy wreath,*
> *Not so much hon'ring thee."*

She stood, entranced, ensnared, her hands pressed tight together. One voice rose and soared alone, striking to her heart with
its potent masculinity.

> *"But thou thereon didst only breathe*
> *And sendst it back to me."*

Adam Andrews shook his charge by the shoulder. "What's
wrong with you, Durie? Are you mazed?"

She looked at him with wide, bewildered eyes.

"Dad?"

"Well, Durie?"

"I'm not so certain any more that I want to be a young gentleman."

"No?" He regarded her intently. "What's changed you?"

"I don't know," said Durie.

4

GRIM and formidable, the live-stone mansion stood watch above the populous flats of the Mohawk River. A reverberant hum of industry rose from the mills over which it presided. Here dwelt State Senator Vryling Lovatt, proprietor of the Little Falls Fabric Mills, in widowed, but not wholly inconsolable grandeur. He was known and esteemed from Albany to Rochester as an unreconstructed Federalist and aristocrat, a sportsman, and, at the advanced age of forty-three, still a bit of a Corinthian and a devotee, within reason, of the bottle and the Sex.

A decrepit, black, woolly freedman was sluicing down the steps. He straightened up and stood, attentive, as the gate-latch clicked. A tall young figure strode up the path, which was bordered with peonies and the ornamental tomato.

"Hey, old Nicodemus!"

The aged face brightened. "Howdy, Mist' Jans."

"What's the Honorable doing?"

"Studyin' on his accounts, I reck'n."

"That's bad. Was there a post this morning?"

"Yassuh. I fetched it to him."

"A long, important-looking envelope with a seal?"

"Yassuh. He done rip 'er open an' read 'er."

"How did he take it?"

"He cussed."

"I expect so. Tell him the bad penny has returned. I'll be waiting in the library."

Word came back; Mr. Jans was to report himself at once.

Senator Lovatt stood before the fireplace of the great, high-wainscoted room, switching the beribboned fire-marshal's wand which he habitually carried in lieu of a cane, like a feline tail. He was a small, plump, alert, handsome man, ramrod-stiff in his costly broadcloth coat and embroidered beaverteen waistcoat, with a cameo brooch in his neckcloth like Mr. Daniel Webster, whom he vastly admired. Beside him on a stand lay a letter embossed with the seal of Harvard College. Senator Lovatt hammered it with the flat of the wand.

"What does this mean, sir? What does this mean?"

"Good afternoon, Uncle Vryling."

"Answer me. What does this mean?"

"Not having read it, I don't know."

"Shall I tell you what it means, sir?"

Jans bowed resignedly. A "No" would have been not only useless but provocative. The Senator was obviously resolved to expound the significance of the letter with all the considerable arts of oratory at his command. Casting the wand from him, he set his left hand in the hollow of his hip-joint, extended his right hand to its full length, massaged his jaw for action, and proclaimed in a voice at once formidable and mellifluous:

"It means disgrace, sir. It means mortification. It means the wreck and ruination of a once-promising career. It means the diversion of a life from its proper and appointed channels into the ebbs and shallows of—of—of . . . Look you, sir!" he barked, switching to the direct attack. "I squander riches upon you, sending you to the university of your choice, which would never be mine—never, sir!—and how am I repaid? Do you dedicate the midnight oil to studious pursuits? Do you devote your talents to the acquisition of the mathematics and allied branches? No! You contumeliously spurn the offerings of Science, absent yourself from your classes, insult your instructors"—he cast a side glance at the letters—"kick a football through the window of the Hall of Philosophies, whereby a charge of one shilling, ninepence" —another side glance—"offend the night with loud and unseemly noises upon a stringed instrument"—marking his place on the manuscript with a finger—"perpetrate upon the reputation of your tutor an epigram of very foul import in a corrupt and false meter . . ."

"Who says the meter was false?"

"Tutor Hawkes." -

"He's unqualified to judge, sir."

"Is that a reason for your casting doubt upon the legitimacy of his birth in Greek pentameter?"

"It was a neat couplet."

The Senator hammered the desk until his handbell fell jangling to the floor.

Nicodemus tottered to the door.

"Was you wishin' something, Mass' Vryling?"

"No, dash you! Yes, damn you! Fetch a julep."

"*One* julep, sir?" protested the young man.

"Yes, one. Haven't you drunk enough at your precious Harvard commencement?"

"No more than the others, sir."

"Am I to suppose that everyone was befuddled?"

"President Quincy, when I last saw him, appeared quite sober, sir."

The starchily elegant little man threw out his arms in a gesture of desperation. "Why did God ever give you to me as a nephew, and the courts for a ward!"

"I can't answer for the Deity, sir, but the courts, I suspect, didn't know what else to do with me."

"Nor do I." He flipped the tails of his claret-colored broadcoat like the wings of a perturbed rooster. "Nor do I, sir, and what is this about your embroiling yourself with one of the Honorable Body of Overseers?"

"Merely a small matter of politics, sir."

"Politics! Who are you to bandy political words with your betters?"

"He did the bandying, sir. He called President Andy Jackson a whoreson rabble-rouser."

"And so he is, sir! So he is! Don't think to propose your weevilly Bucktail sentiments in my house. See what they have brought you to." This time it was the letter upon which his fist descended. "Bastard Harvard Latinity to apprise a sorrowing uncle that his nephew and heir, God save the mark! is dismissed in disgrace."

Vryling Lovatt had the cultivated New York Stater's supercilious attitude toward Harvard and, indeed, all the New England colleges whose graduates, in his opinion, were not only ill-grounded in the humanities, but also talked through their noses. He was, himself, an alumnus of Union and now expressed regret that he had not insisted upon his nephew going to that institution, or to more adjacent Hamilton, whose godly Congregational standards set a pattern for reckless youth.

"Six A.M. chapel?" Jans murmured. "My delicate health couldn't have withstood it."

"Very good. I leave the election to you. Harvard and exemplary deportment henceforth, or the place which you must eventually assume, in any case, at the mills."

"Would you have me join the Sober Society, sir?"

Uncle Vryling brought out an oval snuff-box beautifully enameled in color design of faun and nymph engaged upon a somewhat sensational courtship.

"No, no!" he said, tapping out a delicate modicum upon the back of his hand. "Nothing excessive. Nothing fanatical. I ask only that you accept the responsibilities of your status as a gentleman."

"Have I failed in them, Uncle?"

"None of our blood," answered the Senator testily, "cheats at cards or brawls with low characters or despoils virginity. Thus far I can trust you not to dishonor our standards. But your political sentiments are not reassuring, and there is that in the Quintard blood which breeds misgivings in my mind for your future."

"Mine, also, sir," Jans replied gravely, declining a pinch of Brown's from the box.

"Experience in the world of commerce would settle your vacillating purposes, perhaps."

"I don't think I should like it in the mills."

"Why not? Tell me that, sir. Why not?"

"The mechanics don't look happy," blurted Jans.

"Damn and bitch me!" said his astounded uncle. "Why should they look happy? Let 'em attend to their jobs and thank God they have 'em."

"Or healthy," Jans pursued. "Particularly the children. It's the factory life, I suppose."

40

"Factory life? Damme! What does the young zany mean? Look you!" He lapsed insensibly into his instinctive forensics. "Our hired hands are loyal, industrious and contented. Our females, young and old, are suitably housed in quarters where they enjoy all the domestic comforts and advantages without the cares of a home. Their health is supervised, their morals carefully guarded." He checked his eloquence and advanced a stock boast of the contemporary mill owner. "Our bastardy rate is sensibly lower than that of the town and county. How do you account for that, sir?"

"Too tired, probably," suggested Jans.

"You are a blasphemous young sprig!" thundered the Senator.

"Uncle," said Jans pacifically, "I think I'd better go back to Harvard."

"Why, very good! You'll be none the worse for improvement in the mathematics when you assume your responsibilities here. Now, at your age, I . . ." And he launched forth into extended and eloquent reminiscences with great satisfaction to his ego.

Back of the rhetoric was the perturbing impression that he did not understand this nephew of his. Who could reckon on the damned, uppish Quintard blood, anyway!

5

COMPARED with the stir and clamor of Harvard, the Troy Academy for Females was the very abode of decorum. Durie did not like it. Before she had been there a month, she reached two convictions: first, that the school had little to impart to an apprentice of the Bookery and an adept of the Open Road under the tutelage of Adam Andrews; second, that its regulations were not so administered as to hamper unduly an adroit strategist.

Mrs. Ammidon, the lady principal, a stern and mustachioed widow, conscientiously labored, with the help of two spinsterish aides, to mold the young charges into the pattern of their own correct and sterile minds and the mode of their unexceptionable behavior. Miss Endurance Andrews did not take kindly to the process. It soon become apparent that she possessed an incorrigible mental independence.

She troubled her virginal teachers by asking questions about life which they were quite unprepared to answer. She refused to accept as authoritative the established tenets of religion. No fault could be found with her comportment toward authority; she was unfailingly courteous and attentive in class, ready in recitation, and at the head of her class in most tests. Yet she diffused an atmosphere of tolerant skepticism, as if she were doing it all not because she deemed it worth while, but simply to avoid trouble.

Nor was her moral character beyond suspicion. She was heard singing in the garden a ditty of presumptively lascivious import with a refrain of Love finding out the way, to which her husky contralto lent a strangely provocative quality. The voice, quite as much as the song, brought down upon her the principal's censure.

"It is," said Mrs. Ammidon darkly, "an improper organ."

"Why?" asked Durie.

Not for worlds would the widow have admitted that echoes of the song had troubled her slumbers.

"Do not presume to catechize me, Endurance," said she sternly. "Return to your lessons."

Had the authorities known of Durie's more secret activities, they would hardly have suffered her continued presence. For, unable to endure the confinement of the strict boundaries, she prowled by night in the masculine garb which she had secreted. The servants, who adored her, became accomplices of her nocturnal evasions, always ready to leave a door unbolted or a window unlatched for her safe return. Her roommate lived in a state of mingled admiration and agitation over these exploits.

"What do you *do* when you're out?" she fluttered.

"Oh, I find out things," said Durie.

"What do you want to find out? Don't you know enough now?"

"I know a mortal lot," admitted Durie. "But there's always something else. Look, Patty. How would you like to attend this?"

She spread out a heavily printed broadside which she had found on the garden path.

Mr. Archbold, now with the Distinguished Thalia Theatrical Group begs leave to impress upon the memory of his friends and the public the notorious fact that his Benefit is fixed for Monday, the 14th inst. Mr. Archbold from the most untoward and unforseen circumstances, has been driven from the heights of respectability to look for support for himself, wife, and family to a resumption of his personal appearances upon the stage, and will appear on the above date as Admiral Franklin in *Sweethearts and Wives,* a drama which, in other localities has been attended by the most fashionable and moral with avidity exceeding our most sanguine anticipations.

Towners' Tavern Ball Room

Pit 2 shil's—Gallery 1 shil.

Tickets Procurable at the Bar.

"Oo-oo-ooh!" breathed Patty.

"Haven't you ever attended the drama?" asked the superior Durie.

"No. My Pa is a Methodist. Methodists don't hold with worldly play-acting."

"I've been."

"Is it very wicked?"

"It's noble," said Durie, delicately licking her lips. "It goes through the marrow of your bones like—like soda water."

"How I'd admire to go!"

"I have decided to attend tomorrow's performance," said Miss Andrews grandly.

"How can you? It says seven o'clock. We have Elegant Posture till eight."

"That will be time enough."

Patty had the double chamber over the rear door to herself most of that night. So silently did her practiced roommate enter, via the porch roof, that she did not awaken. Before rising time, however, she became aware of an unusual activity. Durie was smirking and gesturing before the mirror. Patty hopped from bed as the 6:30 worship bell rang.

"Did you like it, Durie?"

"All I saw of it. And I talked to one of 'em afterward."

"You *didn't!* An actor?"

"Well, an actress. I confided to her that I ambitioned to join the troupe."

"Oo-oo-ooh! What did she say?"

"She said she would ask the manager to see me," answered Durie in a rush of words. "Then my tongue tricked me and I asked if she thought I'd make a great actress, and she laughed and said I'd better remember my pantaloons and stick to being a young gentleman when I accosted Mr. Passerow because there are better opportunities in the profession for young gentlemen than for young females. I'm to see him tomorrow night."

Manager Passerow sat in a corner of the taproom conning dourly the evening's receipts of $13.75, of which one shilling was a palpable bogus and one dollar a particularly uncurrent note. The fortunes of the little band were still precarious. They were now desperately facing a winter of hardship. It was, at best, a forlorn hope that had led the management to venture a Troy engagement, since the busy river city was a cut above them. But Mr. Passerow had hoped for a response to the past prestige of Mr. Archbold, now fallen from his high estate of ten years before, when he was joint proprietor of the Lyceum Company. Unhappily, Troy had evinced no loyalty to the past.

The manager switched his attention from the disappointing receipts to a column of more promising figures in the local press. He was an ardent devotee of Lady Fortune in her deceptive guise of the lottery.

Someone spoke his name from the doorway. It was Fair Luna Wayne. She had a young boy in tow. What the devil did the wench mean by interrupting his business pursuits? Then he remembered. She had spoken to him of this aspirant, whose clothing was of superior material and genteel cut, indicating prosperity. There might be transactable business here. He beckoned the youth forward, winking at Miss Wayne to retire.

"So, young sir," he rumbled heavily, "you are interested in the arts of Thespis."

"Yes, sir," Durie replied, though with a sensible diminution of thrill. Offstage, Mr. Passerow with his sagging jowls, his pouched eyes, and his large, sluggish figure, was unimpressive.

"Good voice, pleasing aspect, graceful carriage," the manager commented approvingly. "Any experience?"

"No, sir."

"That can be acquired. Upon terms, of course, upon terms."

"What sort of terms?"

"Let me explain. Wherever we appear we are beset with applications—supplications, I might say—from the most superior members of the community who wish to tread the boards in association with artists as notorious as those who compose my troupe. Only those of exceptional natural accomplishments are acceptable. For these we fix a rate."

"You mean that I'd have to pay?" asked Durie.

"A moderate, I may say a nominal honorarium."

"Does Miss Wayne pay?"

"Miss Wayne is a professional, an artiste. Our rates apply only to amateurs. For a mere walk-on, young Mr. Whittlesey of Herkimer paid us two dollars and professed himself well satisfied. Two of the most dashing blades of Utica offered a ten-dollar rate to alternate for a week as page-boy in *Rosario*. When we made a ten-pistareen-per-appearance charge in Albany, we were overwhelmed with solicitations. Old Mr. Vryling Lovatt, rich though he is, is proud to accept the humblest part and pay five dollars into the money-wagon."

Though the manager was exaggerating grossly, there was a core of truth in his representations. But for this shabby expedient of profiting by the vanity of amateurs, such an aggregation as the Thalians would have been hard put to it to get from one stand to another.

"I, myself, will take you in hand," Mr. Passerow continued benignly. "Shall we say ten shillings per appearance?"

"I don't want to do it that way," protested the disillusioned Durie. "I want to become a professional."

"Ah! By indenture, then. With your parents' consent you could be inducted into my Thespian School of Dramatic Art." (A nonexistent but hopeful project of his immediate imagination.) "Honorarium for the entire season, fifty dollars."

Durie forgetfully dropped a curtsey and withdrew. It might be that this way of life was worth the price stipulated, but fifty dollars was a considerable sum. She thought it unlikely that Dad Andrews would advance the amount for any such purpose.

A recurrent obsession disturbed the dreams of Mrs. Ammidon. Into her slumbers intruded occasionally the figure of a burglar in the woodshed. Nothing would dispel the vision but personal investigation. On the early morning of Durie's theatrical venture, the dream-burglar appeared. Carrying a candle and armed with a hatchet which she kept handy for such occasions, the intrepid schoolmistress descended the stairs and opened the side door. The apparition of the long-expected malefactor rose from the shadow of a lilac. Mrs. Ammidon leaped back with a shriek. The next moment she recognized her pupil.

"What means this calumnious disguise?" she demanded, pointing a bony finger at Durie's breeches.

Durie stated the self-evident. "I've been out."

"On what graceless errand?" said the Mistress, and added hastily, "Remain here until I return."

Durie meditated flight for home, but abandoned the idea as impracticable on the three shillings total capital in her pocket. While she was still seeking alternatives, the grip of discipline fastened upon her ear, and she was led to the penitential study.

"Now, young lady, where have you been?"

Durie disliked lies. She considered them cowardly, complicated, and difficult to defend.

"Out," she repeated.

"I asked you where. The truth, you brazen baggage!"

"I'm not a brazen baggage, Mrs. Ammidon."

"Do you presume to controvert me, Miss?" The schoolma'am peered into the candid young face, her own eyes hot with suspicion. "You've been meeting a *man!*"

"It was on business," said Durie calmly.

"Satan's business!"

Doubtless Mrs. Ammidon would consider the stage Satan's business. Having nothing useful to say, Durie held her peace.

"Doff that indecent garb, and to bed with you," pursued the schoolmistress. "A week's diet of toast and tea will cool that hot blood of yours."

"My blood doesn't feel hot, ma'am," she protested.

"Silence!"

In her room the girl removed the offending garments and hid them away, hoping that they would be forgotten as, in the stress of the moment, they in fact were. Later, she sneaked them into the attic. Sentence was passed before the whole school. For recalcitrant and contumacious conduct, Endurance Andrews was to be confined to her chamber for twenty-four hours, and to the house for a week. Any further misbehavior would be visited with a public whipping and expulsion.

The culprit spoke up resolutely, "You can expel me if you want to. But if you try to ferule me I'll kick your stomach."

After that only the hardiest of the pupils spoke to Durie. Even the faithful Patty regarded her with the sorrowful awe accorded to a lost soul.

The week's regimen of tea and toast reduced the prisoner's energy, but not her spirit. She obdurately refused to enlighten Mrs. Ammidon as to her nocturnal excursion. The schoolmistress dispatched a pained communication to Mr. Andrews.

Meantime, he had written to his ward, "By obligeance of gentleman, bearer, herewith," a letter which left her uneasy rather by its vague implications than by its facts which were sufficiently explicit and unfavorable. The Literature, Stationary & Notions business was on the rocks of bankruptcy. Mrs. Andrews had money of her own to which she was welcome and the devil give her good of it. Durie need not look to her for anything, for certain reasons which would presently appear. Nor could he, himself, be of help to her beyond the $50 in notes current "herewith enclosed, for which bearer will take receipt." He hoped that the school would have prepared her to find some genteel position suitable to her sex and capacities, though, indeed, he deemed her better fitted for man's pursuits than woman's. There would be no more monies for tuition forthcoming after the present semester.

For myself, (he wrote in his neat and literate hand) I would leave you my blessing, if I thought that an endowment so dubious would advantage you in this world or the next. Discredit your mind of one notion which it may have harbored. I am not your natural father. I can truly say that I wish I were. If you were a boy, I should have few misgivings for your future. You are adroit, courageous, and of a shrewd if indisciplined mind. You have, for one of your years, some learning, both practical and in the realm of books. Such an equipment would serve to establish any youth. But this is a hard world for an unguarded female, and you, I fear, will find yourself with the dangerous dowry of beauty. Marriage, recklessly reputed to be a sanctuary for such, may well prove the entry to Hell. Because of my personal experience, I confess that I lack a balanced judgment upon this painful subject. As to the alternative to wedlock, I believe it to be hazardous and therefore inadvisable for your sex. Upon this point I can do no better than refer you to the amplification in my treatise, on the sage and pertinent reflections of the incomparable Benjamin Franklin with which you are perhaps unfamiliar.*

*Unfortunately only fragments of the Andrews manuscript survive. Collateral evidence, however, suggests that the passage referred to is contained in a letter of Poor Richard's, as follows: "The posture is ridiculous, the pleasure momentary, and the results lamentable."

Whatever your lot or your pursuits, persevere in your reading. Treat all folk fairly, but expect no such equity from them. Most lies are needless; where the truth will not serve, silence is best. The underdog is usually in the right; but, right or wrong, he needs your help. Let neither man's love nor woman's hate move you unduly. When fools bicker over religion, politics, or philosophy, do you pass by on the far side. Trust no man closer than arms' length, nor woman beyond the range of vision. If any put to you unwarranted questions, look him in the eye and answer with firm courtesy that it is no concern of his. Above all, look to it that you preserve your independence, for this is the chastity of the soul.

So, wishing you well, I subscribe myself,

Your faithful servant,
ADAM PERSONIUS ANDREWS

A reperusal of the letter impressed her with its ominous and puzzling note of finality, of farewell. When the explanation came in the form of an item in *The Mirror,* headed RASH ACT, it was more a shock than a surprise to her. Adam Personius Andrews had carried his prejudice against matrimony to its logical conclusion; he had cut his wife's throat and shot himself.

White of face, the schoolmistress summoned Endurance to her study and broke the news. The girl received it with tremulous lips but steady self-control.

"What can have driven him to so desperate a deed?" cried Mrs. Ammidon.

"Marriage," said the girl.

"You seem strangely unmoved. Reprehensibly so, I may say. Have you no affection for your father, unnatural child?"

"He was not my father. And he did not wish affection."

"Not your father? I had heard some such rumors. Did he—er —leave an estate?"

"No. When must I go?"

"I have not said that you must go." Mrs. Ammidon was of chilled sensibilities, but she was not inhumane. "Arrangements might be made to retain you in some domestic capacity. Contingent, of course, upon your prudent behavior."

"I don't think I should like bed-making."

"What else can you do, thrown upon the world at your tender

age, an ignorama in all its wiles and wickedness? Has the prospect no terrors for you?"

"No, ma'am."

Durie spoke the simple truth. She was not in the least dismayed. She had an intrepid attitude toward a world of which she deemed herself to possess a practical, working knowledge. The Andrews training had inspired her with a calm self-confidence. What problem could seriously disturb an experience as comprehensive as hers?

"You appear assured of your capacity to maintain yourself," Mrs. Ammidon pursued. "How?"

"I might go on the stage."

Mrs. Ammidon uttered a pious shriek. "Hell yawns for virgin souls in that light companionship."

"I'm not afraid, and I don't believe in Hell."

The eyes behind the octagonal spectacles goggled. "You—don't —believe," said Mrs. Ammidon faintly. Then with resurgent vigor, "Unhappy and abandoned child! I can no longer harbor one who holds sentiments so vile, lest you corrupt the thoughts of your innocent mates. One might believe that you have been reading that disciple of Satan, Tom Paine."

"So I have. May I leave my trunk?" asked the unmoved Durie.

"You may. At your command and without cost." So far Mrs. Ammidon relented.

Early the next morning the figure of a young lad closed the garden gate after it. But it was not a lad's rich-throated contralto that reduced the first meadow lark to envious silence with its song. Mrs. Ammidon turned on her uneasy pillow as the final echo reached her, faint and valorous:

"Love will find out the way."

6

TRADE was brisk at the State Street Book Mart. Of Albany's 25,000 population, more than half could read English and another quarter Dutch, and the Benjamin Blairs were profiting mightily by this literacy. So much, indeed, that they were in need of extra help, and had advertised to that effect in their window.

To Mrs. Blair's discriminating eye, the slight figure patiently waiting on the doorstep was not promising material. Still, a few questions would do no harm.

"Come in," she said when business slackened at the dinner hour. The applicant entered.

"I had in mind an older boy," said the proprietress.

"Wouldn't a girl do?"

Mrs. Blair blinked, peered, then frowned. "Why this disguise?"

"It's easier when you're traveling."

"Can you read?"

"Yes, ma'am."

"What is your reading?" She had in mind the common-school texts.

"I've read everything."

"Bless us!" said the startled shopkeeper. "Where?"

"Wherever I could find it."

"Hm! References?"

"Must I have references?"

"How do I know you won't rob the till?"

"Do I look thievish?"

"One can't tell by looks. Any trade experience?"

"Yes, ma'am. In the Pearl Street Bookery, in New York."

Mrs. Blair's shrewd lips formed a silent "Oh!" She went to the rear room where her husband, a handsome man who led a sportive life on the proceeds of the store which his wife conducted, was smoking and meditating upon his conquests.

"Adam Andrews' girl is outside," she informed him in a whisper.

"What! The by-blow?"

"Yes. She's seeking a job."

"Is she well-favored?" he asked, preening his whiskers.

"I made no mind of it. She seems knowledgeable."

"Let's have a look." His scrutiny, with eye to a crack in the door, satisfied him. "If you can get her cheap enough," he said.

Returning, Mrs. Blair informed the applicant that if she was smart and willing, a chance would be offered her. The work, she added, would be practically nothing: Open shop and fetch out signs, clean windows and sweep steps, dust shop, take off covers, lay out bargain books, run errands, deliver sales, refresh memory of forgetful debtors, make herself handy with the customers, close shop, cover up, and sleep in to answer the watch when he knocks. She would have a warm blanket and snug quarters under the counter. To each item Durie nodded gravely. So far, so good. There remained the matter of wages. Generous, said her prospective employer: $1.50 a week, and found. And she would have an afternoon off every fortnight.

"I can start at once," Durie said.

The terms struck her as being less than munificent. But it mattered the less in that she had no intention of sticking to the book trade. The theatre was her goal.

Most of her scanty time off was spent in patient and futile endeavors to get a foothold in the profession. Her respectful letters to the local managers went unanswered. Nor did repeated personal calls get her beyond the stage doors of the two legitimate houses. Her ambitions descended a peg to the museum business. If it was not precisely the theatre, it might afford a side entry. She took to haunting the Knickerbocker where Mailzell's Cosmorama and Phantasmagoria Including the Burning of Moscow flourished under the management of Mr. Thomas Tallinger. There she spent shillings and hours in rapt contemplation of the mighty canvas composed by Mr. Robert Fulton, professionally regarded as a renegade from the arts since he had abandoned a promising scenic career to tinker with steamboats.

52

She did succeed in waylaying Manager Tallinger who vaguely indicated that there might be something later in the winter. Durie professed herself ready to do anything, however menial. She clipped and kept in her bodice a bit of lofty rhetoric from *The Argus*.

We would advise all to go and see this most exquisite exhibition. The *Automata* are the most perfect of *Androides* and are exhibitions of skill and mechanism quite inexplicable to the beholder. To do justice to the effect would require a pen of light dipped in all the coloring of the rainbow and guided by the hand of the most inspired genius.

Nor was the Cosmorama all that the patron got for his two shillings. There was Mailzell's Invincible Automatic Chess Player —Defeats All Comers for Any Stake, an Egyptian Mummy Seeress, a ventriloquist, and the bewitching female marionette who danced upon a tightrope, uttering at appropriate intervals the ejaculation, "Ooh la la!" in the most lifelike manner and an unimpeachable French accent.

Though arduous, the shopwork was seldom irksome. The only distasteful feature was being sent on the rounds with duns which the patrons seemed strangely reluctant to pay. One of these documents was inscribed with a name which recalled to her a vivid event in her life—Mr. Experience Potter. Being out when she called, young Mr. Potter brought to the shop the bill which she had left and the cash in settlement. With him was a college friend with whom he consulted as to the purchase of some rollicking choruses in leaflet form for a Harvard dinner to be held in the winter holidays at Crittenden's Tavern. Durie, unobtrusively listening, learned with excitement that Jans Quintard would be there with Laus Deo to lead and accompany the music. She instantly decided to attend. Her breath quickened at the thought of hearing again those stirring young voices in the unforgotten harmonies which had thrilled her with such sweet pain on the Harvard campus. That was all, she told herself, that she asked.

The vicinity of Crittenden's Tavern was well suited to her project. Adjacent bushes and trees afforded opportunities of concealment, and there was a small shed near the banquet room from the roof of which the proceedings might advantageously be viewed. So much Durie determined from a scouting expedition.

While her plans were still maturing, Fortune beckoned. It came in the unprepossessing shell of Mr. Tallinger of the Mailzell shows. Up went Durie's expectations when he entered the Literature Mart of a frosty afternoon; down they sank when she learned that he had come not to enlist her services, but to buy a book. He sought data upon fortune-telling, dream interpretation and allied mysteries. He could have consulted no better authority than the little salesgirl, who had read deeply upon the subject, though with more interest than conviction.

"Is it for your own use, Mr. Tallinger?" she asked.

"No. For the show."

"We are offering a very fine *Dream Dictionary* with interpretation of more than five hundred dreams and visions," said Durie, all business woman now. "Only three dollars."

"Don't cover enough ground."

"Then here is a most respectable work," she went on, holding it up. *"Divinations, Vaticinations, and the Use of the Rod, Together with Astrological Charts and Interpretation of Occult Messages."* She pressed it into his hands.

"Five dollars," he demurred. "Too costly. Besides, the footnotes are in a furrin tongue."

"They have secret virtues," Durie assured him, "and are very pompous when properly read."

"The old hag can't so much as read English."

Durie's eyes turned shrewd. "The Mystic Egyptian Seeress?" she asked.

"Yes. Have you been to her?"

"I wasted sixpence. A very fustian cheat."

"There's been complaints," he said gloomily. "That is why I am seeking new matter for her."

"You might better seek a new seeress," said Durie.

"Where am I to find one?"

Durie looked cautiously about to make sure that no Blair was within earshot. "Here," she said, poking her breastbone with an indicative finger.

The manager stared, then laughed. "You, you spindling?"

"I could make up to be Methuselah's wife," she said eagerly. "Besides, it's very dark in the booth."

"But you don't know the patter."

"Listen, Mr. Tallinger!" She intoned solemnly:

> *"Dies irae, dies illa;*
> *Solvet saeclum in flavilla;*
> *Teste David cum sybilla."*

"What's that?" he asked, impressed in spite of himself. "The Hebrew?"

"Mystic tongues."

He made some swift calculations. "I've been paying old Sal—um —er—Princess Sakurabi—three dollars and a tithe of the take." (He had actually been paying her twice that.) "A beginner wouldn't be worth so much to me."

"I'd take half as much."

"You'd have other duties; helping with the androides and such."

"I'm cruel handy. Your figures need a touch of the paintbrush. I could do that, too."

Mr. Tallinger was favorably impressed. His seeress had been manifesting an inordinate susceptibility to rum, of late. Business had suffered. As the girl wrapped up his purchase, he said cautiously: "I don't say I'll take you on. And I don't say I won't. You work up the patter and drop in, come January first, and we'll see."

Durie's elation was mitigated a few days later by the first toothache she had ever suffered. Business was too brisk to permit of her absenting herself in working hours; she knew her place too well to proffer any such extravagant request. The left side of her face swelled grotesquely, but she minded that the less in that it relieved the pain. She hoped ardently that she would not be incapacitated for her informal attendance upon the Harvard festivities; in fact, she intended to go anyway, and next morning, which was her half-day off, look up a cheap dentist.

That evening was exceptionally mild for the time of year. The streets were quaggish with mire and slush, the board walks gleaming in a drizzle which presently dissipated in moonlight. Clad in her boy's suit, Durie spent several happy hours on the shed roof where, through the open window, she heard much praise of Alma

Mater and joined, *sotto voce,* in many a heart-melting harmony; also she listened to the interchange of taproom tales with more curiosity than comprehension, which was doubtless just as well.

When the watch cried four she slipped down, the entertainment having slackened, with the intention of getting back to the Mart, catching a couple of hours sleep, and changing clothes for the dentist. The tooth was mercifully quiet, though the distortion of her face had reached the point of disfigurement.

Durie never saw her under-counter bed that night. The fault lay with the Albany Common Council.

In the previous year His Honor, the Mayor, homeward bound from a levee, had spent an uncomfortable and indignant night in the Reverend Mr. Condit's outhouse, besieged there by a band of the semi-wild pigs who roamed the streets at their sweet, nocturnal will. He attended the Council next day with a bill to have the animals impounded at a release fee of two shillings a head. A councilman raised the pertinent question: if we impound the pigs, who disposes of the garbage? The objection being unanswerable, a motion to appoint a swine-warden was passed and a gentleman chosen for that honorable, if not over-remunerative, post who was henceforth known as Pig Baker. The bands continued their garbage-collecting and night-roaming, unmolested.

Having stopped over in Albany, en route to Little Falls, for the purpose of attending the college jamboree, Jans Quintard put in a pleasantly busy day. He dined liberally at two o'clock, lost four shillings to Mailzell's Automatic Chess Champion, yawned through that sadly dull farce, *The Canal Barge,* at Nosey Phillips' Alhambra, relieved his ennui with a hearty supper of frankfurters, that fashionable and toothsome specialty of the well-known Mr. Welch's Connecticut Coffee House, corrected an uncomfortable distention of the chest with copious draughts of Congress Mineralized Water from the State Street Spring, applauded the panorama of burning Moscow and the graceful footing of the French marionette who cooed, "Ooh la, la!" in his ear, purchased drinks for and swore eternal friendship with several admirable characters whom he had never before seen, including two constables and a night watchman; bought a dog, a watch, and a walking stick, reported on time at

Crittenden's supper room, whither Laus Deo had preceded him by messenger, and with the aid of that tuneful instrument, became the center of the night's kantikoy.

Toward dawn he became possessed of a desire for fresh air and solitude. Leaving his guitar in charge of a friend, he assumed hat, greatcoat and walking stick, untied his dog and set forth. At the crest of the hill he found himself contemplating with interest a sycamore in the low crotch of which a boyish figure was propped.

Jans Quintard stood on his head, righted himself, and was able to take three steps without staggering. This is a useful test.

"I have been drunk at times," he mused, "and drunker at other times, but I have never fallen asleep in a tree."

He looked at the newly purchased watch, which, having no works, still pointed to 11:15, the hour of its acquisition. He hammered upon the tree trunk with his stick. The dog barked. Jans hailed:

"*Ave, puer!*"

A sleepy voice from above answered, "*Et tibi, ave!*"

The form in the tree leaned forward upon a cross-limb. The posture subtly but unmistakably altered its outlines. Jans altered his form of address to match.

"*Ave, puella,*" he said.

"How could you tell I'm a girl?" came the voice, in an aggrieved tone.

"*Status quo stas.* Your attitude."

He grinned. She drew her weight sharply back from the support which had betrayingly outlined her breasts.

"You don't mind being addressed in Latin?" he asked courteously. "I am always moved to exhibit my Latin in a certain stage of drink."

"No, I don't mind."

"Why should you, since you understand it? A marvel. A paragon. *Quae nunc abibis in loca?* as the Emperor Hadrian pertinently inquired. Or, in the vulgar tongue: Where are you going, my pretty maid? Though, indeed, that is not precisely what the old Caesar meant."

"I'm not going anywhere and I'm not pretty." She caressed her distorted face.

"That is yet to be determined. Descend."

"Have they gone?"

"Who?"

"The pigs."

"What pigs? I see no pigs."

"You can hear them." There was, indeed, a chorus of faraway squeals.

Jans struck a noble attitude. "Fear not. Descend. Come down." The figure slid to earth. "Why did you stand on your head?"

"To determine the degree of my sobriety. I distrusted my vision. Why do you sleep in trees?"

"I don't. The boars chased me, and Pig Baker asked a shilling to call them off."

"Who's Pig Baker?"

"The municipal swineherd."

"If they come back here, we'll take care of 'em," said Jans, making his stout cane whistle in the air. "Won't we, Towser?"

The mongrel barked again.

Half a dozen small, evil tuskers appeared, snouting along the open sewer.

"At 'em, Towser!" shouted Jans.

With a howl of joy, Towser stampeded the pigs and vanished into the mists with the official Mr. Baker lumbering and cursing in pursuit. Jans sat down and waited, but the dog did not come back.

"Here am I," he ruminated, "a young gentleman of parts, means and education, diddled like a lummox at a shell-and-pea table into buying a dog with no heart and a watch with no bowels, and presently have on my hands a young female who inhabits trees and whose face, now that I observe it, seems strangely misproportioned. Is it my fancy or your face?"

"I have a burning tooth."

"Then you should consult a dentist."

"I tried the temporary one in South Street, but he said go away and not come back till he was out of bed or he'd warp the skin off my back."

"A dishonor to his profession. Lead me to his haunt."

Near the South Market a shop with a sleeping-loft above displayed a large plaster molar with unsightly roots, swinging from a sign.

DR. S. BLISS
SURGEON DENTIST
Fair Treatment—Low Prices—Pain Relieved
at All Hours.

Jans hailed. There was no reply. A handful of gravel thrown against the upper window produced results in the form of a round face with a square whisker.

"Come down," said Jans.

"Go away," said the face.

" 'Pain relieved at all hours,' " Jans quoted.

"Let it wait on my breakfast."

The young man reached upward with the crook of his walking-stick.

"Down you come or I'll extract your false tooth and push it through your window."

The face yawned, groaned and said, "I'll come."

Presently its owner was poking and prodding not urgently at the hollow molar.

"I counsel a sound job of repair."

"How much?" Durie asked doubtfully.

"One dollar."

She thought of the hoard at her waistband. But this she had sworn not to touch except for extreme urgency. "How much to have it out?"

"*Extractio dentis,* sixpence."

"Draw it, please, sir."

Dr. Bliss sighed. "It goes against my gorge to break into the finest mouth of teeth I've seen in a twelvemonth. Six shillings."

"Repair it," said Jans in a lordly tone. "At my expense."

"Oh, no!" protested Durie. "I couldn't be beholden."

"Repair it. Do your best dollar job. Here is your full pay."

Further possible objections were checked by a wooden plug inserted between the patient's jaws. Briskly massaging the gum with ether paint to the point of blistering, the expert went swiftly and thoroughly to work, grinding the harsh burrs down with his powerful fingers until the cavity was clean enough to satisfy inspection through his magnifying glass. When the filling and tamping was over without so much as a groan from the taut figure in the chair, he said, "Brush your teeth night and morning, and tell all and sundry that Dr. Bliss is a friend to the poor."

In clogged accents she tried to thank him, and also her benefactor, but was cut short.

"Did it hurt much?" asked the lordly young man.

"No," said Durie.

"You *are* a solid one. I'd have cursed like hell. Where are you going now?"

"Back to the shop where I work."

"I'll escort you."

"I'd rather you wouldn't."

"I should be a poor gallant to leave a lady unprotected in the streets."

"I'm not a lady." She spoke with difficulty as the ether exercised its paralytic influence upon the muscles.

"Are you beautiful when unswollen?"

"No, I don't suppose so," said Durie, after devoting some consideration to the question which rather surprised her.

As the cool air reduced the swelling, her companion was contemplating her with increased interest and curiosity. The atmosphere was serving a double purpose, since it was also sobering him up.

"Where have we met before?" he demanded.

She wriggled away. "Nowhere," said she, in panic. All that Harvard visit had taken on a taint not only of regret and frustration, but of shame. She wanted nothing better than to forget her venture into thwarted masculinity: all of it except Jans Quintard, his shrewd, weary, humorous face, his voice that had the power to move her strangely, uninterpretably.

"Nowhere," she repeated earnestly. "You must give me your address, so that I may pay my debt by post."

"My address only? Not my name?" he asked, smiling.

Durie flushed. "Your name, too. I will post it as soon as I have the money."

"Post it when you please. Post to Andy Jackson. Post it to Jemima

Wilkinson. Post it to Professor Peter Popple. Post it to Pig Baker or President Quincy or Black Dan Webster. I've no need of it."

She mounted the shop steps and reached for the latch. "Good night," she bade him softly. "I shan't forget. . . ."

"Don't," he said.

". . . the dollar," she finished and popped inside.

But not before a female voice, half querulous, half railing, made itself heard.

"So here you are, you vagrom wench! And with a follower! And it nearly seven o'clock with breakfast hot in the oven."

Late on the following afternoon, Jans Quintard entered the Mart to buy a book. Mrs. Blair served him. He inquired for the young damsel with the toothache. Smiling and obdurate, the proprietress assured him that there was no such person about the place. Jans passed a hand over his face.

"But I was in command of my faculties. Surely this is the shop. Surely you know what I mean, ma'am."

"Too well to further you, young sir."

"Is there any impropriety in my inquiring after a painful tooth?"

"Look you, Mr. God-knows-who. You're a gentleman. This is a working lass and, to the best of my ken, decent and virtuous. Though it be not in the indenture, I mean to keep her so."

He made her a bow. "Your sentiments do you much honor."

"Can you say as much for your own? Take your purchase and be on your way."

Jans was not so easily dissuaded. "She asked my address. Shall I leave it?"

"With the cat. Ten shillings. Correct. I thank you and bespeak your further custom, sir—" she glanced pointedly at the lift-bar dividing the shelves from the public—"so that you keep your side of the barrier."

Saluting, he withdrew in good order. Mrs. Blair summoned her apprentice.

"So, hussy," she began with rancor.

Durie waited.

"Your pursuer was here."

"My pursuer?"

"The young blade you were night-farin' with."

"It was morning," said Durie demurely.

"Night or morning, you'll get small good of *him*. He's a come-and-goer; one of the nothing-better-to-do tribe. Look at that phiz of his!"

"He may not be comely," conceded the girl, "but . . ."

"Not comely!" broke in Mrs. Blair, looking at her pityingly. "There's more damage to maidenhood in a face of his kind, with that romantical, melancholious look on it, than in a boxful of scented pretty-pinks."

". . . but he's a kind young man and I owe him a dollar," finished Durie.

"He's the Devil's whelp with the Tempter's own grin for a wile, and a way of speech that'd wheedle a bee from a balmweed. The only safe place for a maid to be meetin' his like is at the head of the First Presbyterian Church aisle."

So, reflected the employer, the child was becoming a woman, with a woman's allure, unconscious of it though she might still be.

Not long after, Mrs. Blair had displeasing confirmation. Durie came to her with troubled eyes.

"Mrs. Blair, why does Mr. Blair come into the shop nights?"

"Does he?" said the wife sharply. "When?"

"After you're asleep. Last night again. He said he wanted to talk with me. He said not to tell you."

"Oh! Did he so! What then?"

"He pinched me."

"Eh? What? Where? The apostle's pinch?" Mrs. Blair snapped. Durie flushed. "No. Just my shoulder."

"What did you do, girl?"

"I bit him and he went away. So I think I'd better leave."

"So do I," agreed her employer. Compunction stirred within her. "But what will become of you, poor child?"

"Oh," said Durie complacently, "I'm going on the stage."

Mr. Tallinger had finally notified her of a job keeping in condition the one hundred and twenty-nine wooden soldiers that marched in the Mailzell-Fulton cosmorama.

7

Perched on the Knickerbocker Hall thunderbox, Miss Endurance Andrews studied the outline of the new panorama. She had been with Mailzell's Exhibition for three months and had proved herself worth every cent of the ten shillings a week which the management grudgingly paid her.

"Slickest little mink with her hands I ever hired," Showmaster Tallinger said.

In that time the Burning of Moscow had gone stale. Patronage fell off. Mr. Tallinger purchased and was preparing to substitute The Grand Spectacle of the Burning Mountain Vesuvius, Pleasure Resort of Pompeii, and the City and Bay Adjacent Thereto, in Panic Dismay.

Durie studied the production chart with rapt attention. It would, she foresaw, entail extra work for her since she would be expected to transform, with her handy paintbox, the French soldiery of the Russian campaign, one hundred and twenty-nine strong, into togaed Romans. But she was prepared for that if only she might secure a speaking part in the spectacle. It would be no more than offstage reading, but still a real start upon the dramatic career that she craved with all her eager little soul. Mr. Tallinger had as good as promised it to her. She read:

A finely toned bell strikes distinctly the hour of ten. Rumbling of an earthquake is heard at a distance with two or three slow echoes.

No trouble about the bell. Earthquake rumbles? Larger stones in the thunderbox with the bass drum for echoes. She skipped to:

Loud thunderclap (Iron plate in the thunderbox). Curtain rises; lightning and thunder. Volcano roars. (That could be managed with the wind-maker; couple of sheets of tin fixed before it, not too loose.)

63

Bells, wild, rumbling noises, explosions, noise of alarmed crowds. Music of procession afar. Beggars and lazzaroni appear in flight.

"Mortal awesome," the intent student approved. She continued to read:

Music, bells, drums, pipes, wind, murmurs of sea, cannon-like explosions—ships pass—one founders—one blazes—volcano spouts fire (that would be the hell-machine)—smoke, lava, red-hot stones roll—houses and palaces prostrated as the earth shakes—shrieks of wounded.

This was where Durie figured herself in. Forgetting her environment, she tried a modulated shriek, was pleased with it, and repeated in full voice. An oath responded.

Durie clutched her lips. She had violated professional courtesy. The furious face of Mr. Hart, the Celebrated Fire Eater, appeared, spat a hot word at her, and vanished. Mr. Tallinger's patter, onstage, reached her ears.

"Ladies and Gentlemen, this marvelous example of digestive invulnerability dines upon a platter of burning coals with as much *sang froid* as would an epicure upon a dish of turtle soup, and draws a plate of heated iron across different parts of his body as if he were made of tempered steel."

The manager came back.

"Take a look at the Amusing Little Bass Fiddlers, will you, Durie?"

"Yes, Mr. Tallinger. What's amiss with them?"

"One of 'em creaks."

Called back from dreams of glory, Durie set herself to the endless task of repairs. So completely had she performed her job for these last three months that she was now established as dresser, repair-drudge and general lackey to the whole troupe of inanimate actors. Because every detail, however menial, was touched with the glamor of stagecraft, she devoted herself to the labor with a passionate resolution.

Ten shillings a week was a respectable wage, though after her healthy appetite was satisfied, there was little left to bank in her waistband. Lodgings cost her nothing. She slept in the traveling casket of Ooh la la, the slack-rope beauty. For toilet facilities she had only to run around the corner to the inn stable-yard, where there was a free pump and outhouses.

Anything that nobody else had time to do fell to Durie. She greased the rollers, tested the mechanism, restored the thunderbox with new rocks when the old ones shivered, operated the bellows for the twelve-mouthed trumpet machine, tidied up the androides, freshened the paint on Ooh la la's cheeks, ran errands (mostly beer) for Herr Schlumberger, who was the moving spirit behind (and beneath) the turbaned chessmaster, trimmed the lamps and polished the reflectors on the lampboard under the fire curtain, tended the torches and fuses, kept the watering-pots filled, prepared the charcoal sieve which blew up the Kremlin with a profusion of black smut, maintained inventory on the properties, and practiced the art of the piano forte upon that masterpiece of mechanical instruction, the chiroplast.

One day of early spring, the showmaster said to his wife, "That Andrews girl is a trove."

"Too sightly," sniffed Mrs. Tallinger.

"She hasn't found it out yet. And I am going to put her where it won't be noticed."

"Where's that?"

"In the black hood."

"The magic booth? Is old Sal quitting us?"

"She and Schlumberger are on the raree three, four nights a week. He could play in his sleep, but she's no good next day. Little Andrews is a knowledgeable one. I'll bill her as an aged Romany Queen." He meditated. "With help from me I think she might handle old Lovatt."

His wife looked up. "The Senator? What d'you want of him?"

"Money for my plans, woman. Did you ever hear tell of Chang and Eng, the wonderful Siamese Twins? What a bill they'd be! And I've my eye on Signor Valdenci's live twenty-foot python, nine feet long, rigged on wires so that nobody can tell the difference."

"The Honorable Lovatt cares nothing for fortune-tellers or snakes," objected Mrs. Tallinger. "All he comes here for is the chess."

"Precisely the point. I've got my ideas," said the manager darkly. Sakurabi's prophesied downfall was a resounding crash. Under the influence of a hangover, she read the tea-leaves for an elderly female client, and advised her (a) to buy the Erie Canal as an investment, and (b) to prepare for the advent of twins. As the customer was the Governor's spinster aunt, the repercussions were considerable.

On her early morning return from a house-to-house itinerary, distributing advices of the Sweet Swiss Bellringers Special Engagement, Durie received the management's offer. She accepted with confidence, but suggested a raise to five dollars a week. A compromise was effected at three-fifty.

Her former routine was now abated, but only in part; she was drudge by day and seeress by night. She found no difficulty in filling the role. Her instinct for drama helped her in the tastier role. To her it was a delightful game. Her spare moments were devoted to planning for Vesuvius and her debut in the shrieking part.

Senator Vryling Lovatt took his legislative duties seriously. He attended all sessions, made frequent speeches mainly directed to the recalcitrancy of the working classes and the vice of democracy, and entertained handsomely in the mansion he rented on Albany's fashionable State Street. His amusements were many, varied and discreet. He was a prop of the theatre, both in the pit and backstage. His intellectual fad was chess. Three evenings a week he patronized the Mailzell exhibit, where he had a season ticket, and played chess with the Wonderful Automaton, a stiff-jointed wooden Turk in a silk robe and white turban with long green feather who held a pipe in his hand, nodded pensively over his moves, and with jerky, unhesitant precision, built up his game to the inevitable checkmate.

Nothing could persuade Vryling Lovatt that he was not a better man than the Turk was a manikin. He would stand in rapt contemplation of the announcement above the board, maturing fresh tactics.

> Chess is pure mathematics. Every move is corrigible by a countermove. So perfect is this mechanism that the mere pressure of a pawn upon a square sets in motion the springs and wires resulting in the proper, ordained and invincible retort.

It might be so, but Senator Lovatt refused to believe it. Shilling after shilling did he contribute with rising exasperation, but no diminution of his self-esteem. Some day he would diddle that wooden scarecrow.

But not this Wednesday. Other matters were troubling his mind to such confusion that he lost his queen by a heedless interposition on the seventh move, and went home in a passion to have it out with his erring nephew, once more rusticated and paying him an unsolicited visit.

Summoned to the presence, Jans found his uncle in the library, his hands extended to the steam radiator which was hissing and clacking and making more fuss than Mr. Peter Cooper's Model Locomotive Engine on a two per cent grade. Convenient to the Senator's elbow stood a glass of rum punch based upon goat's-cream, a potion authoritatively recommended for the maintenance of virility.

"So, sir," he began. "In disgrace once more. Sequestrated. For how long this time?"

"Permanently, I fear, Uncle Vryling."

"Never say that I failed to warn you, Jans," said the Senator mournfully. "I commend to your prayerful perusal, my boy, that sterling opus of the learned Dr. Benjamin Rush, *The Effects of Ardent Spirits upon the Human Mind and Body.* You will find a copy at your bedside."

"Yes, sir," murmured Jans. "But it wasn't ardent spirits."

"Don't contradict me, sir. What else should it be?"

Jans assumed an expression of airy innocence. "A trifling conceit of mine, no more than a jingle."

"Well? Out with it!"

"It was about a girl."

"Oh! Ah! Very well. No harm in that."

"A ten-year-old girl . . ."

"Eh?"

". . . who worked in the mills."

"What mills?"

"Any mills . . . Well, in this instance, the Lawrence Mills."

"Whose proprietors have made handsome endowments upon vour Alma Mater."

"That's the point, sir. The faculty said my little ditty was indecent."

"Uh! Er! Fie upon you, my boy! What was the indecency?" asked the Honorable Vryling with a gleam in his eye.

"The song suggested that the faculty go on a fourteen-hour shift like the mill mechanics."

"Disgraceful!" thundered his uncle.

"And so, here I am, sir."

"Here you are, indeed! And what do you propose for yourself now?"

"I should like to look about a bit and see what my country is like."

"It's a very affording country for folk with money, a harsh one for those without. What, may I ask, are your financial avails?"

"Counting my next month's allowance . . ."

"I shouldn't."

Jans stared. "Are you cutting me off, sir?"

"Sixty dollars a month is not penury. You have but to enter our establishment to earn it."

"I could borrow against my inheritance."

"Not due until you have attained the age of twenty-three. And not legally pledgeable without your guardian's consent. Which you will not secure."

"I might make my way as a trader," suggested the youth.

"Without capital?"

"Oh, I've a few dollars left. And, I flatter myself, a natural bent for trading. Last semester I swapped myself into a horse, a basso horn, and a disquisition on the Greek aorist which I lacked time and interest to write for myself. It's the Jewish blood in me, I suppose."

"Your great-grandmother, Esther Isaacs, sir, was a fine lady of American lineage as old and honorable as the best," said Vryling Lovatt impressively. "You need not blush for your Israelite strain." He used the term which gentlefolk preferred in speaking of the race.

"I don't," said Jans cheerfully. "I've a notion for the stage, too."

"Well, bitch me! Bitch my bones!" Uncle Vryling glared at him.

"My nephew a Thespian! A stroller! A vagabond! What put that crotchet into your empty head?"

"But I thought you a patron of the drama, sir?" said Jans with a significant side glance at the restorative drink on the mantel. "Wasn't there a Miss Wayne, a Fair Luna? Or do I err in the name?"

"Hum! Haw! Damn your impudence!" said Uncle Vryling, vastly pleased. "Whence had you that—er—baseless report?"

"Ex ore equi," smiled Jans.

"More likely from his tother end," returned the ribald Senator. "Anyway, what's the lady got to do with it? Not the same thing at all, sir."

"The difference between the amateur and the professional point of view," Jans murmured.

"And by what warrant do you conceit yourself to be a professional?"

"I don't as yet."

The Honorable Vryling smiled patronizingly. "Doubtless a couple of walk-ons at some local house. What did it cost you?" He knew all about that from long experience, but had no intention of betraying himself and so answered his own question. "A dollar an evening, I presume. For which honorarium you spoke one line, perhaps two. 'Milady's carriage awaits.' 'Gentlemen, the King.' Harmless enough, in a spirit of sportiveness."

"A little more than that with me, Uncle." He hesitated but went on apologetically, "The summer I vacationed in New York, I worked backstage at the Bowery Theatre."

"Worked? For hire? My nephew? What for?"

"Experience. I studied the methods of the most accomplished artists—Mr. Booth, Mr. Kean, Mr. Placide, Miss Fisher, Mrs. Austin and their like."

"And now you wish to go bogueing about the back roads, yourself a vagabond and player?"

"Only as a means to an end. I thought one day to try my hand at a drama."

"Play-writing?" The worthy gentleman was thunderstruck.

"Yes, sir."

"A vulgarian and ignoble ambition. Letters, sir, are the pursuit of

a gentleman's leisure. To demean them to the earning of a livelihood is the conception of a huckstering mind. Nobody of respectable position takes money for the trumpery business of pen-
pushing."

"Mr. J. F. Cooper? Mr. Washington Irving?" Jans suggested
mildly.

"A mere by-blow with them, not arising from any vulgar itch for
gain or cheap repute. They are and remain gentlemen despite these
eccentricities."

"I can't argue with you, Uncle."

"Then don't try," advised the Senator, his good humor temporarily restored. "Not that I regard your grotesque project seriously.
You'd be back, hat in hand, within the month."

"Make it a year."

"Good God! He is serious. I appeal to your family feeling, my
boy. You have not done well in college. Ought you not in fairness
to give the mills a trial before embarking upon this shameful
course?"

Jans sighed. "I can see nothing shameful in it. But since you put
it that way, I have no alternative. Am I to start at once?"

The uncle relented. "No, no, my boy. You shall pay me a little
visit first. Meantime, the Harvard authorities may be persuaded to
overlook this alcoholic indiscretion of yours. After all, excess is
natural to the spirited youth."

He had convinced himself now that he must contrive a method
of saving the boy from a drunkard's grave. The device which he
subsequently adopted, however, derived not from his own cogita-
tions but indirectly from the designs of Manager Tallinger upon his
purse.

That astute schemer encountered him two days after Jans Quintard's arrival, and two minutes after his seventeenth consecutive
defeat at the wooden hands of the Turk.

"Senator," said he, "you have not yet patronized our Magic
Booth."

"Flummadiddle!" retorted Mr. Lovatt. "That withered hag, by
what I hear, derives her vaticinations from the almanac and the
rum-puncheon."

"We have a new one. Very mystical. Of the true Egyptian breed."

Mr. Lovatt exhibited a gleam of interest. "A Romany?"

"Of unblemished line."

"I will afford her opportunity to prove herself," said he with affable dignity. "Shall we say tomorrow at this hour?"

Assenting, the schemer went to find Durie and give her explicit instructions. She was to flatter the patron, prophesy great achievements in the political realm, compliment his courtly and pompous manners and dandy appearance, and, as opportunity offered, subtly hint at a great fortune awaiting him in a theatrical venture. Having gained his confidence, she could then lead to the subject of chess, and advise him how to defeat the Turk.

"But I don't even know the moves," she protested.

"Follow directions. I will make all arrangements with Schlum—— with the Turk."

The general plan was worked out, the German being now so conversant with Senator Lovatt's methods that he could pretty well lead him into any course of play.

A full half-hour's sitting with the seeress was arranged for the Senator. The groundwork having been laid, Durie had no difficulty in stimulating her client's interest by suggesting that he lay a five-dollar wager on the next contest.

"That Turk always beats me," objected Mr. Lovatt in aggrieved tones. "I believe he's inspired of his master, Old Scratch, himself."

"Victory shall be yours."

"How do I know that?"

"Faithfully follow the instructions of the Mystic Powers."

"Let's have 'em," said the Senator.

"Once and only once. On the seventh move . . ."

" 'The seventh move,' " he repeated as the voice paused impressively.

". . . of the queen's gambit, which you must pursue . . ."

"It is a formidable tactic of mine."

". . . advance your queen's bishop to queen's second," read Durie from her directions.

He shook his head. "It sounds paltry to me."

"Follow the directions and you shall win your wager."

That was a glorious day in the career of the Honorable Vryling Lovatt when the *Albany Argus* published a local paragraph, announcing the first defeat ever suffered by Mailzell's (hitherto) Invincible Automaton. The Senator strutted for a day. Then he was back in the booth, presenting a grave face to the black-shrouded figure. A plan had occurred to him.

"Seeress, I bespeak your aid."

"The Mystic Powers are responsive. What is your trouble?"

"My nephew. He's a randydandying young fool. A mad Quintard."

He did not see in the dimness the slight start of the shrouded form.

"I want him scared."

"The Mystic Powers do not . . ." she began, at a loss.

"The Mystic Powers can warn him that he's hell-bound for ruin unless he mends his ways. Through your voice. He won't listen to mine."

"What is his vice?"

"Drink."

"And you desire me—us to convert him to sobriety?"

"If he can't be converted, he can perhaps be frightened into reasonable behavior."

Durie's impression was that Jans Quintard would be an extremely difficult person to frighten into or out of anything, but this was no time to say it.

"Fetch him to the Presence," she directed with professional solemnity.

"I'll have him here before the week is out," promised the Senator. "Pitch it to him strong on the drink question. Don't let him laugh at you. It's no matter for mirth. One of his Quintard uncles is in an Institute for Cachexic Intemperates. His grandfather died of spirits. It's wild in the Quintard blood. I don't want the boy to go to the dogs," he added with feeling.

Senile decay was Jan's first thought when his uncle broached the subject of the Magic Booth. But since the old boy was so earnest about it (and had put up the coin) he acceded with a good grace, and duly presented himself before the shrouded and coiffed figure, mildly amused, mildly bored and wholly skeptical.

The interview began in a hollow whisper and according to formula.

"I bear a message."

It was not in Jans Quintard's nature to show discourtesy to anyone beneath him in station, least of all to a poor old crone struggling to maintain herself in a precarious trade.

"I shall be glad to receive it," he said politely.

"You tread a perilous path. Have you considered whither it leads you?"

"Would I be the wiser for inquiring, do you think?" he asked in confidential tones. "I have always considered that the less I thought about myself, the better."

Momentarily at a loss for her next move, Durie said, "Beware!" in a raucous whisper, but hastily got back upon the track. "I behold a broad common. It is flanked with stone buildings, very noble, very pompous. Many young gentlemen traverse the space. I hear glad voices. They sing."

"What do they sing?" Jans was attentive now.

"Songs of youth, of love, of gallantry."

"Can you repeat them?"

"One among them plucks at a stringed implement," pursued the voice, ignoring the question. "It has a motto gilded upon its body. I cannot interpret it."

"Look you, madame," said Jans, beginning to be interested. "When have you told *sortes* in Harvard Yard?"

"Harvard?" A pause. "I know it not."

"Nor I, henceforth," muttered Jans with a pang.

"Another motto impends in letters of mist above the player's head."

"What does it say?"

"It is dim. It brightens—pales—it flames with the fires of doom. Wait! I have it!" In measured accents she intoned: "Drink and dreams are the Quintard curse."

"Well, damn my eyes!"

"Hold your peace, rash man. Hearken to the fates, speaking through my mouth. I behold you lightheartedly speeding to your ruin. I behold bestial orgies of liquor, shame, degradation, perhaps death. I behold barred sunlight upon a besotted face, the pattern of a prison window that falls across your prone figure, blighting your career. I exhort you, young sir, turn aside, turn aside from the paths of evil."

Thus far Durie was giving a very sound performance. But in her fervor, she forgot to control her voice which rose from a whisper to soft appeal. "Oh!" she breathed brokenly, movingly, "you have so much to live for! Don't spoil everything."

"Damn!" repeated the young man softly. "Reach out," he commanded, holding up a silver sixpence.

Professional instinct impelled her response. The hand that stretched across the barrier was firm, smooth-skinned, and shapely. He pressed the piece into it, holding the wrist.

"How old are you?"

She came back into character sharply. "One hundred years and more have passed above this head," she replied in the patter.

"They've dealt lightly with this hand," he observed, and leaning over, set his lips to the warm flesh of the wrist that pulsed sharply under them.

The seeress uttered a little moan of astonishment and dismay. Once before in her life she had felt something of that same shock: when she experimented with the two handles of Mailzell's Electric Pleasure-Box (Delicious Shock—1 penny.) which was the special delight of schoolboys and Indians. Though this was subtly different.

The sixpence fell to the floor.

"Now, shall *I* tell *your* fortune?" he bantered. "This then, is my sortilege. You are not aged and withered, but young and warm and sweet, and, I think, beautiful. Can you deny it?"

She was silent.

"Then shall we prove it or disprove it?"

Still silence.

"Shall I cross the barrier?"

She found her voice. "No," she breathed in panic.

The curtain rattled harshly on its rings, dividing them. His laughter came lightly to her ears.

"Banished from paradise. But, O, Venus Victrix! Your pulse leaped under my lips. By that token I know we meet again. Farewell, sweet witch."

She went to her knees and groped until she found the sixpenny piece.

74

8

WINTER passed and spring exhaled from the streets of Albany in a stench of dismaying vapors. Wistful for the woods, Durie grew restless. She still loved the toilful glamor of her work, but the monotony of city life depressed her spirits. Often she brooded upon her traveling staff. It would hardly have surprised her had it put forth shoots from the sap stirring within its pith as the blood stirred in her veins.

Then it was in her hand. She was in her easy, familiar garb of the road, skirting the banks of a swift stream and wishing for a rod, for there were betraying circles in the quieter pools.

If she lacked the means of profiting by them, another did not. He stood casting from the opposite bank, a beautiful youth, hardly beyond boyhood, clad richly in a velvet jacket with nacre buttons and a chain of beads. Everything about him was costly; his tasseled boots, his doeskin shortclothes, his long and over-heavy greenheart rod. Respectful in the background, a blackamoor servant bore two other rods and a gun.

While the youth's accoutrement was impressive, his skill was not. Durie disapproved to the point of disdain his swiping, full-arm whirl, designed to project the fly into a promising backwater. The expected happened. An overshot fixed the hook in a low-growing willow. The fisherman tugged inexpertly and cursed expertly. He noticed Durie.

"Lout!" he called.

Durie grinned and made to touch the coarse mechanic's cap which confined her bright hair.

"Cast loose my hook."

She scrambled through the brush and freed the fly, a beautifully finished hackle.

"Catch!"

A silvery gleam clove the air. The York shilling embedded itself in the earth. She pried it out and pitched it back. But as she bent, a treacherous twig loosed her cap, and when she straightened up, a gust of wind sent it sailing. Bright waves fell to her shoulders.

One look was enough for the young angler. Beckoning the black to follow, he ran lightly upstream, forded a shallow to his knees, and stood before her, a figure both gallant and impudent, sweeping a bow with his glossy beaver below his knees.

"Mister Guy Ayrault, at your service, Madame."

What elegance! thought Durie. With a view to matching it, she said, "I am Miss Endurance Andrews, of Mailzell's."

His eyes widened. "The show place?"

"Yes."

"An actress?"

"Ye—es."

"I'll come and see you. What do you do?"

To reveal that she was the Egyptian seeress would have been unprofessional. She said, "I turn the roller for the figures and play the chiroplast and care for the androides and the Parisian danseuse, and I am rehearsing to be the cries of the injured."

"Huh!" he commented, losing his gallantry in his disappointment. "I wouldn't call that being an actress."

Mortified, Durie found no response to the injurious words. She watched in disapproving silence while he made several more maladroit casts. Unable to repress her feelings over another snagged fly, she said, "Let me show you."

"You? Show me? How to angle?"

"You're a very preposterous angler," said Durie firmly.

"Prove that you can do better. Give her a rod, Enos."

The grinning black obeyed, and winked as she carefully chose and attached a fly. Young Mr. Ayrault's respect was restored as he observed her skillfully placed, long, looping casts. It swelled to admiration when, after a dozen or more essays, she had a strike and nonchalantly landed a fine two-pounder. Maybe she was a real actress, after all, or on the way to being.

Anyway, with her warmth of color, her unruly hair, her lustrous eyes, and the rounded young figure, she was a delight for any male vision. What a tale he could make for his elders of this rencontre with a fair young Thespian! It was very much in the fashion of the day for young gentlemen of position to air their liaisons (generally fictitious) with frail charmers of the footlights. Better still, he could perhaps exhibit his conquest—so far had his callow ambitions already progressed—to his companions.

"Come and dine on the boat," he invited.

"What boat?"

"My brother's. She's in the Lower Basin."

"Is he a packet captain?" she asked, a little awed.

He laughed that off scornfully. "He *hires* captains. The *Merry Moment* is the dandiest Durham on the Erie. We're laying up for a few days on our way to the Hudson and New York to visit the theatres. The *real* theatres," he elaborated. "A party of Harvard men."

"Not *you!*" said Durie incredulously. That derogatory "real" had annoyed her. "You're only a boy."

"I'm almost fourteen," he said, ruffled. "I shall enter next year. And I'd have you know that I'm an accepted Corinthian. Will you come to the boat?"

"No, I can't. I must get back to my duties," said she importantly. "We bespeak your kind patronage and that of your friends and families and you may keep the trout."

Reimpressed with this exhibition of stage lore, young Guy evolved a very creditable tale for his older companions of the *Merry Moment.* He bragged incontinently of the beauty of this girlish houri whom he had so romantically met in the woods, and lightly hinted at further and hopeful pursuit. Huge Macel guffawed at him, big-brotherly.

"You, infant? Why, you're not dried behind the ears. Let me deal with this pretty bonaroba."

"She's no bonaroba," said the lad with sulky dignity. "And I'll thank you not to poach on my ground."

"Ho! Our designs are amorous. We are coming fast. Presently we shall sport a whisker." Macel complacently stroked his own militant mustache.

"Were you older when you had your first bedding, Mace?" asked Mark Richards.

"Oh, I! I knew my way about at his age."

"Then give the lad his chance."

"I'll do better than that. I'll further it. We'll all go to Mailzell's tomorrow evening and look over this dainty bit of flesh. Does that meet your approval, my gallant Corinthian lads?"

There was no opposition. Mynderse Verplanck spoke up.

"Mailzell's? Isn't that where the chess player holds forth?"

"Beats all comers," confirmed Macel Ayrault.

"My New York cousin, Gulian Verplanck, says he isn't a machine. He's a man."

"How does he know?"

"A friend of his named Poe told him."

"Who's Poe? Never heard of him."

"One of those printer fellows. A pen-pusher. He investigated when the Mailzell Turk was in New York, and says there's a man cooped up in the box under the Turk. He says he's going to print it."*

"No! Is there?" Macel's round eyes brightened. Like so many lusty and stupid men, he was an inveterate practical joker. "We could have a shivaree out of that."

"How?" Half a dozen voices asked.

"Leave it to me. Anyone here play chess?"

None volunteered.

"Jans Quintard's uncle, Senator Lovatt, plays there and always gets checkmated," said Experience Potter, who was dining aboard.

"That old goat!" said Penuel Lummus, with his horse laugh. "Better look out, youngster," he warned Guy Ayrault. "If your wench is comely, he'll be after her."

Macel reached for his castor. "I'll step around and spy out the field," he said.

When he reached the hall, the Turk was playing a slow game with a thoughtful young Dutch baker named Pruyn whose queen was already trapped. The manikin, Macel observed, was well guarded behind a brass rail, six feet away from the public. The dais upon which the board was set was roomy enough to harbor a hunched-up human. It was covered with a rich Oriental drape,

---

*This was a preliminary report and inconclusive. The final publication was not issued until four years after and did not include the Albany engagement.

78

which was unfavorable. But if this fellow Poe's suspicions were correct, there must be an opening for air, presumptively at the rear. There would be the point of attack.

In a corner a few yards away was set up the Magical Gas Machine with its nervous bearded operator, "warranted a Medical and Chemical Professor of the Highest Attainments," and its overhead sign:

> Nitrous Oxide or Exhilarating Gas Which Produces the Loftiest Sensations of Pleasure in Those Who Breathe It and the Greatest Wonder and Surprise in the Spectators of Its Operations.

Carrying in his mind a general ground plan, Macel visited a local smithy whose proprietor was also a veterinary, and made a purchase. Thence he went to the tobacconist's where he bought a large jar of Burpee's Titillating Snuff: Extra Quality. His next concern was to secure a ladylike outfit for his Sophomore boat-guest, little Dick Salisbury, that excellent singer in the falsetto. Dick tried on the costume and accepted with confidence the role assigned to him.

Prepared for his regular contest with the automaton and, as ever, fiercely hopeful of the outcome, the Honorable Vryling Lovatt was gratified to find himself in a circle of youthful admirers, several of whom he recognized as friends of his scapegrace nephew. They were respectful and complimentary and presented him to the seemly young damsel who accompanied them. Macel Ayrault stated that they had brought cash to bet on him.

"Oh, Senator! I'm persuaded that you will win," trilled dainty Miss Salisbury.

"I shall be inspired," declared the Senator gallantly.

Attracted by the placard on the wall, the supposed young lady strolled over and, after some chaffering, paid sixpence and prepared to undergo the gaseous experiment, as the Honorable Lovatt approached the chess board.

The automaton jerkily raised his long pipe to his lips and waited. Macel Ayrault, his greatcoat bulging untidily at one side, edged along toward the curve of the rail.

Senator Lovatt drew the white. "What shall I open?" he mused.

"The Ruy Lopez, I think. Yes, decidedly the Ruy Lopez. That best develops my genius for bold attack."

The game started at a brisk pace, the android, as usual exhibiting no hesitation in his mechanical placements. After the twelfth move, the challenger slowed down. Furrows appeared upon his statesmanlike brow. He caressed his chin with nervous fingers.

"Um!" he said, communing with himself. "Hum! The queen's knight's pawn to . . . No, no! Let me consider." The spectators, now augmented to more than thirty, distracted him. "A trifle more space, if you please, good people," he said petulantly. "Now, if I interpose . . . Good God!"

A hair-raising shriek rent the air. The pretty young damsel performed a wild contortion that overturned the gas machine, flailed the air with wild arms and toppled to the floor in a most convincing heap. Everyone pressed toward the place. There were calls for a burned feather, for hartshorn, for a surgeon to bleed her. In the turmoil, Macel Ayrault, with an adroitness very commendable in one of his bulk, slithered under the railing and noiselessly wormed his way beneath the side curtains shrouding the flank of the dais. There he crouched, unnoticed.

The swooner was borne to the outer air, artfully moaning. The spectators became quiet. It was still the Senator's move. He swept a bishop across the board and glared defiantly at his opponent.

From behind the curtains issued a dull, metallic sound, as of a plunger, twice descending. The Turk's left hand advanced, hovered, retreated. Senator Lovatt entered a claim.

"You touched that piece. It must be played."

The hand dropped. The curtains moved in agitation. A formidable sound issued from the bowels of the dais.

"Arr-rrc-rr-rrch! Gott-ver-sch-choo!—dam! Schwein—schoo—oop!—hund! Tausendteufel wheesh—choopp—schloo-oo-oo-oo—HOOPH!"

Turk, dais, and chessboard were rocking as in a mighty sea. The huge Ayrault emerged. In one hand he held the veterinary's implement from which he had discharged the snuff, in the other, the still-convulsed frame of the objurgating Herr Schlumberger, once, e'er the passion for drink had overcome him, champion of Prussia, Bavaria and the Low Countries.

Bedlam broke loose. The show folk and house mechanics descended in force, led by Manager Tallinger. Senator Lovatt, storming, denouncing, demanding his money back, was hustled to the street together with all the other patrons, the Merry Momenters fighting all the way, until the doors were barred behind them.

Thus it was that the gallant young Guy Ayrault was balked of seeing again his damsel of the bright hair, tawny skin and lustrous eyes. He had to content himself with inditing a romantic letter which she did not answer.

Outraged both in pride and sense of legality, the Honorable Vryling Lovatt instigated proceedings. He made a ringing speech in the Senate. He laid the matter before the Mayor and the Council. He wrote a letter to the *Argus* which the printer of that respectable journal had to edit line by line to make it fit for publication. He hired a lawyer.

The wretched Tallinger gave up. Gone forever his hopes of extracting any money from the rich legislator. Gone, too, his fair repute as a showman. He was done for in Albany. He vanished into the limbo of show business and was no more heard of by his one-time utility slavey.

So Durie lost her job. All those sedulously practiced shrieks gone for nothing. Oh, well! She had begun to doubt whether the panorama business was the likeliest portal to the legitimate theatre for which her soul yearned. Moreover, the itch for change had been irking her nerves. She had a twitching heel. The road called. Somewhere out beyond, so she had heard in the waif gossip of the trade, the banner of the Thalians was flying for custom. With luck she might find them. At worst she would be seeing the world.

9

DURIE sat on an up-ended and discarded gin-pipe, solicitously massaging her feet. It was her second day out from Albany. She was feeling fit, free and happy. Back of her rose the busy hum of thriving Schenectady. Before her passed the unceasing human parade that used the Erie Canal towpath as highway for its unlicensed travels.

An odd figure, passing, gave her a glance, paused, twisted a burnished red head for another look, and backtracked with the swinging stride of the road folk. The girl was coarsely but trimly dressed in breeches and a crocus shirt with a gay silken ribbon at the throat. Her face was shrewd and blithe, her glance both merry and knowing.

"Hello," she said.

"Hello," answered Durie.

"Westbound?"

"Yes."

"On your lone?"

"Yes."

"Want to step along of me a bit?"

"How far are you going?"

"How would I know till I get there?"

"You're a girl, aren't you?"

"Certes." She touched the ribbon at her throat. "So are you."

"How could you tell?"

"By the way you set. Started to spread your britches like a skirt. Got your fee ready?"

"What's that?"

"Tuppence for a draught of ale to make you free of the towpath."

Too roadwise to balk at an established point of etiquette, Durie said, "Where?"

"Sign of the Hungry Pike. Next lock. Have a chaw?" She proffered a quid.

"What is it?"

"Lickrish and pukeweed. Keeps quickrot from your teeth."

"No, thank you."

"Suit yourself."

They fell into step together. "What's your name?" inquired Redhead.

"Dick."

"Going to stick to your britches?"

"If I can."

"It's lumpy going for a wench unless she knows the world," said the other sapiently. "But you can get more free lodgings if you stay a she. I ain't paid for a bed since I left Haverstraw."

"Is that where you live?"

"If you call a brickyard shack living. I left with my hoof in my hand and sat on the dock. When the up-river boat pulled in, there was I, smiling to myself like I knew something good about the world. Two gentlemen bespoke me from the deck, and we all had a drink and the dice. And that's how I traveled to Albany in style."

"I don't think I understand," said Durie.

"They cast dice for the honor of my company," explained the other. "The Dutch gentleman won. Damn all the Dutch, say I. They're sluggards in love and with their shillings. So," she rattled on, "I burked my gentleman in Albany and here am I, back on the path."

"You've been on it before? I never have."

"Then you've plenty to learn and I'm a proper teacher."

She led the way beneath the wooden sign of a huge pike with jaws distended into a dim taproom where a mustached man was wiping down the bar with a foul rag.

"Two foamers," she ordered.

"Hullo, Reddy," said the tapman. "Cash or trade?" He winked and leered.

"Cash, you hunks."

"Is that your new sweetikins?" He set out the drinks. "He doesn't look to have much pith."

"You keep your observations to yourself," advised the girl loftily. "Give him fourpence, gal. I mean Dick."

The barkeep looked up quickly and grinned. "Trouble you for a fip," he said. "Barrelage has went up."

"Go kiss a pig," retorted the girl. "Fourpence and not a stiver more." The barkeep, grumbling, tilled the coin.

Redhead raised her pewter ceremoniously. "Here's Gypsy Vilas' respects."

Observing the liquid doubtfully, Durie took a swallow, gagged, and ran to the door.

"Wassa matter of you?" demanded the barkeep indignantly. "That's prime brew."

"The ale is all right," commented Gypsy. "Down with it."

"I c-c-an't," quavered poor Durie.

"Baby! Haven't you ever had a drink before?"

"No."

"Anan! I was drunk before I was fifteen. And you're on the path! I reckon I got a contract of indenture, looking after you! Go back to your Sabbaday class."

"Leave her with me," suggested the tapman with a wide smile. "I'll learn her."

"Yah!" retorted Gypsy. "You'd learn her what she couldn't forget. Cripus! What's that?"

From a corner a voice had quavered a wheezy and broken yodel:

"Ooolie-oolie-aylie-oo!
Oolie-ayley-oo!"

"Bully Suggs's hoggee," the tapster said. "He's a nacheral. He got hurted."

"Why, blow me down and lay me low!" ejaculated Gypsy, peering. "If it ain't Looby! What's come to you, lad? Hoss kick you?"

A woefully thin youth lifted a bloodied face from the bench where he had been stretched. The tremulous grin of the underwitted quivered on his lips. He looked to be all of twenty, which was old for a towpath driver.

"No," he quavered. "It was Captain Suggs."

"A son-of-a-muckworm if there ever was one," said she cheerfully. "He tried to take me once and I gave him the knife. Ain't you got a sticker?"

"I wouldn't dast," said the hoggee. He sat up, pressing his hand to his temple.

Gypsy whistled, looking at the raw gash. "That's a nasty clout."

"Let me see," said Durie. She examined the wound. "Fetch me a pan of water from the pump, will you, Gypsy?" she said and busied herself cleaning the place with a square of cloth from her pack, while the barman sniffed scornfully. All that fuss over a hoggee! Gypsy watched with interest.

"Kinda handy, ain'tcha!" she observed approvingly.

Durie got out a swatch of fresh linen and put on a workmanlike bandage. Two open sores on the youth's neck attracted her notice. There were scars of older sores around them.

"Canal pus," explained Gypsy. "Comes of eating the muck they feed these punks on the cheap freighters. Don't touch it."

But Durie was already pressing in light-fingered exploration around the angry area. The lad winced and whimpered. Under Durie's direction, Gypsy threw out the water, rinsed the pan, and poured in the unconsumed ale from the beaker.

"A cupful of raw oatmeal," ordered Durie.

"Penny," said the barman and took the price.

"Where can I boil this up?"

"Kitchen."

She carried the pan in, set it on a stove, and stirred in the oatmeal. A door on the far side opened. There stood the barman. He had sneaked around to the other entrance and now invited Durie with a seductive leer and his fingers on his lips. She scowled and turned her back. Too late when she felt his hand over her mouth, she realized her mistake. Strong and agile though she was, she could do little against that grip from behind. But as she was being dragged she lashed out with one foot and upset a table full of crockery which came down with a loud crash.

The door flew open. A fury darted in, snatched a fallen knife from the floor and attacking from the rear, gave the assailant a jab that wrung a yell of pain and anger from him. He dropped Durie to turn upon Gypsy, but the long, sharp blade dissuaded him.

"The drinks are on you, Pete," said Gypsy.

His sheepish grin admitted it. He returned to his bar.

"Get on with your doctoring," Gypsy directed Durie. "I've cooled him off."

Apparently it was all in the day's work, the sort of thing that a girl must expect, reflected Durie, as she stirred in the oatmeal now swelling in the seethe of the ale. Making a rich paste, she summoned her patient and bound it firmly above the boil, bidding him leave it for twenty-four hours to draw off the poison.

In no wise discountenanced by his failure, Pete set forth the drinks, generously adding one for the hoggee. Durie took sweet-pop.

"What are you going to do now, Looby?" asked Gypsy.

"Go back to the *Water Witch*," he mumbled.

"After the way you've been treated?" said Durie indignantly.

"I ain't got my ten dollars hire-money yet."

"That's a season's pay," explained Gypsy. "I reckon Captain Suggs has screwed many a poor lunk out of his year's hire by beating him dozey or some other dirty trick."

"I hate cruelty," said Durie fiercely.

"You can't be a softie on the path," warned her mentress.

"He gimme this"—Looby pointed to the damage—"when I ast him for two bits for boil medicine."

"You'll get nothing out of that old skeezicks except what you take," opined the worldly-wise Gypsy. "So you better take it."

He gawped. "How kin I take it?"

"Suggs'll be drunk tonight, won't he?"

"I reckon."

"Know where he keeps his rhino?"

"Yes'm. Hid under a loose board."

"Good boy! Slip in and get your money and run like hell. Ten dollars. No more, no less. Savvy?"

"Yes'm." He tried haltingly to express his gratitude to both girls and limped out, chanting his lamentable:

> *"Ooolie-oolie-aylie-oo!*
> *Ooolie-aylie-oo!"*

"It'll be murder if Suggs catches him," said Gypsy. "Well, the poor lout couldn't be worse off dead. Where'd you learn your doctoring, Dick?"

"In the woods."

"You're peart at it. But you don't know much otherways. You need looking after. I guess we'll make do together, you and me." She lifted her mug. "Here's to path and berm and free passage west and may our roads never spread wider apart than a spinster's knees. Let's hit the dust."

They set out at the loose-limbed, four-mile gait of the experienced "roadee," the cheery Miss Vilas exchanging repartee, not always of the most delicate, with the hoggees and helmsmen of passing craft. At the end of an hour she developed a limp.

"Drat these boots! Cost me a hard dollar not a month back and the off-foot sole is wore through already. It's blistering me."

"Take it off and I'll have a look."

"Later. Squatty-vouz, as the Frenchies say. We're going to make a charter."

"On a boat?"

"Not for your big sister! Too much to pay." She winked. "The rafters are better."

"Why?"

"You're always in the open," the experienced traveler explained. "You can yell for help or jump for land."

"Isn't it mortal slow?"

"Two mile an hour, and bubbles in your wake," Gypsy trolled. "What's your hurry, gal?"

So well and favorably known was Gypsy that the pair had no difficulty in getting free passage. Toward noon of their second day they were sunning themselves on the deck of a tamarack logger when the steersman, with an alarmed look astern, crowded her close in upon the bank.

"Hey!" said Gypsy lazily. "What you trying to climb the berm for?"

The rafter pointed to a fast craft overhauling them. "That's the *Water Witch.*"

"What of it? You got as much right on Erie Water as she has."

"I don't want no to-do with Bully Suggs. He'd as soon run you under as look at you."

The Durham drew abreast. Captain Suggs' broad and vile face thrust upward from mid-deck. A stream of curses issued from it, directed upon all canal-clogging rafts in general and tamarack loggers in particular. At sight of the two passengers his color deepened from crimson to purple.

"Hey, you red trollop! Where's my hoggee?"

"How would I know?" returned the girl coolly.

"You put him up to thievin' my box," he yelled. "I heard about you colloguin' with him at Pike's. I'll have a reward onto both of you."

"He only took what was his own."

"I'll get it back. And I'll see all three of you in jail yet."

"When your wife foals a shoat."

"Stand by to repel boarders," Durie warned, grabbing for her staff as the captain set foot on the rail.

A gleam of bright steel in Gypsy's ready hand cooled his evident intention of leaping upon the raft. The Durham swept past, Suggs still spluttering filth.

Presently the raft basined to cut out a delivery of timber and the girls continued their journey afoot. Gypsy's chafed heel slowed their progress. She called frequent stops, scanning the eastern vista hopefully, but there were no more rafts. Short of Amsterdam, a neat roan tandem hove in sight, handled by a hoggee so comfortably clad and so sleek-bellied with good food that he was a phenomenon in that ill-used calling. Gypsy cupped her hands.

"Peace ahoy! Peace!"

A hail came back from the boat. "And to you, peace."

The craft drew on until Durie could read, blue-lettered on the bow, the legend:

PEACE-ON-EARTH

"What are you going to do?" she demanded.

"Freight on a stretch."

"I thought the boats weren't safe for girls."

"This one is. Deacon Gildersleeve's the piousest captain on Erie

Water. He freights rum, whiskey, pickled eels and pork between Albany and Utica."

A small, neat figure, soberly clad for a canaller, stood at the rail. To Gypsy's self-invitational gesture, he responded with a meek smile, tooted twice on a tin horn for the hoggee to halt, and nosed the boat into the bank.

"Can we come aboard, Cap?"

The Captain nodded.

"Not very conversational, your friend," whispered Durie.

"He's a dummy. Used to be the meanest cusser on the route. Lord struck him wordless one night and he's never spoke since. Joined the church, too. Shake hands with him."

They went aboard and were courteously received. Some recondite motions on the Deacon's part were gravely observed by the helmsman, who translated:

"Divine service forward at two o'clock."

"Now," Gypsy informed her friend, "we pay our scot. Want we should neat up a little below?" she asked the commander.

In response he opened a cubbyhole from which he took broom, mop and pail. Filling the pail overside, Gypsy handed it to Durie and led the way below. They banished a plump and sallow young man to finish his weekly shave on deck, fell upon the bedding which they turned out to air, and in two hours of intensive work gave the place such a scrubbing as it had not known for months. As Gypsy sat down for a breather, ear-high to an inner window that gave upon the freight-hold amidships, a singular noise gave her nerves a jerk.

"Spsst!"

"What's that?" she demanded.

"It's me, lady," answered a voice from the dark.

"Who's me?"

"Looby, lady. Cap'n Suggs' boy."

"Stowaway?" she asked quickly.

"No'm. The Prayin' Cap'n tooken me in."

Gypsy whistled softly. "He would!"

"I got my money," continued the frightened voice.

"So I heard. You better get away from Erie Water. Suggs'll jail you."

"Where'll I go, lady?" sniveled the unfortunate. "I ain't got no other trade, only hosses. Would you take me 'long of you?"

"Yes," said Durie instantly.

"What'll we do with him?" objected Gypsy.

"Find him a place somewhere. We can't leave him on the path."

"Softie!" jeered the other. But there was no unkindness in her tone.

A bell rang sharply, followed by four rusty tootles on the horn.

"'Sound the loud timbrel,'" said Gypsy. "That's for service. Go back and hide," she bade the invisible youth.

"No, lady. I gotta go up. Deacon Gildersleeve won't leave nobody stay that don't come to the meetin'."

When the helmsman prayed lustily for deliverance from the powers of evil, the fugitive cast apprehensive looks ahead and astern and sniveled into his sleeve. Before the concluding hymn was fairly finished, he had ducked back into retirement.

"This place," Gypsy announced as they drew into the lock at Little Falls, "dries up my gullet."

"Why?" her companion asked.

"Mill dust. I used to work here. In the Lovatt factory."

"Was it good employment?"

Gypsy sniffed. "A slave-pen. They kept the girls in nights. Leastways, they tried to. Old Ruffleshirt Lovatt was hell-set on morals for everybody but hisself. Let's go to the inn and wet our whistles."

In the tap, she became reminiscent over her ale. "I didn't last long at the looms. But I remember one good day." She grinned. "It was a sizzler of a week and young Quintard, the old boy's nephew, was back from college—him and a friend. The Senator was away. Even the old hands were dropping from the heat. The two young buckos came out of the big house, drunk and singing like buglehorns. They locked the overlooker in the bolt-room and turned us all out to go swimming in the Mohawk. That's the first bath some of 'em had in a month, I warrant."

"Was that Jans Quintard?" Durie asked.

"He's the lad," answered Gypsy, looking curiously at her. "Takes his riches from the mills and don't go near 'em any oftener than he has to. Too high-toned. But he's a good un in his toploftical way. When old Lovatt found out about the holiday he docked all hands half a week's pay for it. Up pops our young cockerel and makes up the payroll out of his own pocket. We'd-a went hungry but for that. They say there was a fine stink-and-brimstone turn-up betwixt him and the old ruffleshirt. But by that time I was on the hoof again. Mill work is too confining for me delicate health."

She took a second foamer, which Durie declined, not being too well inured, and suggested that they go out by the front where the inn hoardings displayed their notices.

"Might's well have a look," she said.

"For what?"

"Looby. Suggs may have posted him."

Sure enough, there it was. Durie read aloud the heavily inked card attached to the notice board.

STOP THIEF ! ! !

Reward. Reward. Five—$5.00—Dollars Reward
Paid for Apprahension of one, Thompson called
Luby or Looby. Twenty Years Old of Weak Mind
and Evil Nature, a Theeving Rapscal. Above
Reward will be Paid by Me.

Wм. Suggs, Captain *Water Witch*.

"Dirty work!" Gypsy snapped.

"Can't he keep hidden?" asked Durie.

"With his oolie-aylie-oo?" Gypsy shook her head. "He ain't got the gumption. The black-hunters'll get him, sure. They'll search the boats."

The *Peace-on-Earth* having wharfed for the night, the girls slept on deck. At earliest light, Gypsy went below to rouse the derelict.

"Looby, you gotta shove off."

"Whaffor?"

"There's money out on you."

"How much?"

"Five dollars."

He groaned. His sheep-like eyes goggled. "Where'll I go to?"

"Just as far away from Erie Water as ever you can get."

"What'll I doo-oo-oo," he whimpered. "I don't know nothin' but canawlin'."

"Hire out in the back country. Farming. Trapping. Logging. Anything but the towpath. Now pack."

Durie gave him a dollar as he went overside, weeping, and vanished into the brush.

Short hauls interspersed with leisurely hoofing took the young vagrants to Manlius, famous for good merchandise. There they went shopping. Gypsy borrowed ten shillings and bought a pair of stout new shoes, a hat, a dollar's worth of gewgaws from Tinkham's Jewelry Palace, and, to Durie's surprise, a flax-hook.

But Durie gave her companion a greater surprise. She bought a book—*Kenilworth,* by the author of *Waverley.*

"Ten shillin' for a book!" marveled the redhead. "What in god-'lmighty for?"

"To read."

"Reading for *fun?* Look, gal: I can read if I got to. And I can write if you give me a big goosequill and plenty of time. 'Course I wouldn't let on to any of my pals about my book-learning. They'd think I was highty-tighty. But I never seen anyone pay out hard coin for reading. How much education you got?" she asked wistfully.

"Some. You know a lot of things I don't."

"Some of 'em wouldn't do you no good. And some of 'em might. Here's a present for you." She handed over the keen, curved blade well set in a horn handle.

"That's mortal handsome of you. Thank you, Gypsy. But what do I do with it?"

"You might get you a job in the flax-patches out around Lyons or Palmyra," said the other. She patted the flax-hook. "But whether or not, it fits slick to the body. And it's likely to come in handy."

"For what?"

"For your kind."

"What's my kind, Gypsy?"

The young towpather fiddled with the knife. "Mind if I ask you a question?"

"No."

"You don't know much about men, do you?"

"Why, yes. Plenty of men used to come to the shop."

"Oh, hell!" said Gypsy. "That ain't what I mean. You're a virgin, ain't you?"

"A what?" Durie was startled.

"A virgin. A gal that ain't never done nothin'."

"Oh! Why—why, yes."

"Aim to stay that way?"

"I hadn't thought about it. Yes, I do."

"Well, tastes differ," said Gypsy tolerantly. "So tonight I learn you about the flax-hook."

Her instructions with the wicked, little scimitar-like blade were explicit and technical. Quick of eye and hand, Durie was an apt scholar.

"That'll hold off any man," said the instructress. "Just don't let 'em catch your wrist if they corner you. When I was only a sprat of fifteen," she added meditatively, "they near had me up for murder, only the man didn't die. But I don't reckon he bothered the gals much afterward. Think you got the hang of it?"

"I think so."

Though they were footing it a good four miles an hour in the morning, a high-riding boat drew up on them from the rear. The *Merry Moment* was a Durham-type sixty-footer, slim and trim and decked out with bunting, "like a hoor at a fair," observed Gypsy, casting a disparaging glance backward. Even the draft horses were perked out with metal trimmings and the hoggee's whip had ribbons interwoven with its thong leather.

"Isn't she pompous!" said Durie in admiration.

"A party boat." Gypsy's tone suggested light contempt. "They're at it now."

Sounds of music floated to their ears from between decks.

"There's many a filly lost her maiden rating in that cabin. That Macel Ayrault's a limb of hell," said the girl, wagging her head.

"Macel Ayrault? I know him."

"Anan! Where?"

"I've seen him," she corrected herself.

A haughty-looking boy, beautifully dressed, waved languidly to them from the deck.

"That's young Guy Ayrault," said Gypsy. "He'll be going the same way as his brother when he's old enough."

"I *do* know *him,*" said Durie. "He wrote me a letter."

"What kind of a letter? A love letter?"

"I don't know. I never had one like it before."

"I know a gal got fifty dollars for one."

"This one isn't even spelled right."

"If it says 'Darling, I love you,' it's worth money," said the practical Gypsy. "Spelling or no spelling."

"It doesn't—not exactly," said Durie, not in the least understanding this.

"Aren't you going to speak to him?"

"Do you think I should?"

"Certes. We could get a freight. But don't go below."

Durie hailed, "Hello, Guy! Have you caught any more trout?"

He started, stared, then made a running leap to the path. "It's the little actress from Mailzell's!" he cried, and swept them a magnificent bow.

"And this is my friend, Miss Vilas," said Durie, in her best Elegant Academy manner.

"I've heard of Miss Gypsy," returned the boy, trying for a man-of-the-world effect.

"Aren't you going to offer us a freight?" asked Gypsy pointedly.

A shade passed over the sightly face. "I don't know," said he doubtfully. "My brother—the men—I mean, the fellows—they're pretty drunk," he blurted.

"Then I reckon the path's good enough for us."

"Did you receive a post from me?" he whispered to Durie, blushing.

She nodded. Gypsy had the tact to fall back.

"I asked you not to forget me."

"I haven't."

"But I want to see you again. Where are you going?"

"Westward. I don't know how far."

"Have you quit the stage?"

"Not permanently," said Durie, hoping that it was true.

"When shall we see each other again?" he persisted.

"Sometime," she smiled. Then, seeing his face drop, "I'll let you know when I have a position." She nodded toward the boat which had now pulled ahead. "Is Mr. Jans Quintard of your party?"

"Jans? No. Do you know Jans?" he asked jealously.

"A little."

"He's gone."

"Gone? Where?"

"Nobody knows."

Her eyes widened. "I thought he was to return to the mills."

"He did. Just a couple of days. There was a big whoobub over something—I don't know what—and the Honorable Lovatt turned him from the door, so they say. He'll be all right. You can't kill a Quintard, drunk or sober."

"Are you joining us or going on with the Durham?" put in Gypsy, pointing to the boat which was out-distancing their relaxed pace.

He made his good-byes, crying eagerly that he must see them again, and set out at a run.

"A seemly boy," commented Gypsy. "If you set your trap right I'll warrant you could marry him."

Durie stared. "Why should I? I don't want to marry him. I don't want to marry anyone. I don't hold with wedlock."

"You don't hold with wedlock! And you aim to stay a virgin! What a life you got before you!" said the prophetic Gypsy.

Near Syracuse they spent the night in an abandoned barge and breakfasted over a chatwood fire.

"We'll be crossing paths again," said Gypsy abruptly.

"Are we parting?"

The elder nodded. "I'll be trying for a trick in the saltbeds. Rough work, good pay. You'll do all right alone now."

"Surely," said Durie with confidence.

"Keep away from the hemp pickers. Those bunkhouses wouldn't do for you. Same with the shearing. Mills, factories, all right for the short shift. Same with choring on the small farms, but not just for hay-pay. Stores, too, if you're town-minded. What do you really want to do, gal?"

"Get back on the stage."

"Don't blame you. It's a life. I was with a medic show once. Got any connections?"

"I had a sort of promise from Passerow's."

"That lot? They're on the corduroys somewhere east, traveling by conniewagon," said Gypsy, who was a repository of road-lore. "Maybe they'll catch you up."

Durie made a mental note of it.

"Well, good-bye, Durie. Luck follow your feet. We'll hear of each other by the tow-line." She spoke with assurance. The word-of-mouth news which followed the canal was a comprehensive and not too inaccurate record.

"I hope so," said Durie cheerfully.

She headed westward along the path and presently vanished into the fluctuant and unquestioning world of the vagrant and the casual.

10

HAVING persuaded his nephew back to the mills, the Honorable Vryling Lovatt thought it only right to return and see how the lad was doing. He found out promptly.

His informant was that prime example of factory management, Mr. Undriel Barnes. Hat in hand and plaintive of speech, Mr. Barnes presented a list of grievances as long as his thick arm, the culmination of which was that young Mr. Quintard was a violent fellow with no respect for law, order, or profits.

"Give you my affy, Mr. Lovatt, I'm fearful of my life at his hands."

"You're bigger than he is, by a stone," returned the Senator, who actually had little love for the blustering, though efficient, superintendent.

"You don't know him, sir," said the other lamentably. "You don't know him in anger."

"Very well," sighed the mill-head. "I'll talk to him, Barnes."

Summoned to the library where justice or what passed for it in the senatorial mind was decreed, Jans regarded his uncle with a weary and rueful smile.

"I was afraid it wouldn't work, sir," he said deprecatingly.

"And why shouldn't it work?" demanded the Honorable. "I purpose to be reasonable in this as in all matters, sir. But bitch-and-damme, am I master in my own properties or not? Answer me that, sir."

"No," said Jans.

"Eh? What?" roared his uncle. "What in Hell's fiery flames do you mean by that?"

"You leave everything to Barnes. Barnes," said Jans judicially, "is a bastardly skunk."

"Barnes is the most profitable overlooker in York State."

"Yes, sir. You've told me that before. Dirty profits."

Senator Lovatt exhibited the tense calm of extreme rage. "Explain yourself."

"He fines the help without cause. It's cheating."

"Guard your language, sir," shouted the uncle. He rallied his forces to a stock defense. "Those lazy louts of mechanics," he set forth, "waste my very substance what with malingering and shift-footing. Don't meddle."

"Sorry, Uncle Vryling. But if I'm to handle the help I've got to protect them from what is no better than thievery."

"Thievery? *Thievery!* Let me out!" choked Senator Lovatt. "I can no longer breathe this festering air." He caught his hat from the hook, seized his beribboned baton, then, abruptly changing his mind, tossed the insigne of authority into a corner, hurled the beaver upon the floor, kicked it after the baton and, pointing a tremulous finger at his nephew, "In a moment," he warned, "I shall lose my temper."

"Perhaps I'd better give up the job, sir."

"So do. So do. All Quintards are born with swivel knees," mourned the afflicted uncle. "Thwart their least whim, and they turn and go and be damned to you! Under that smooth exterior, what black pride and pigheaded self-will! Blunder ahead. Never explain. Even when you're wrong you won't admit it any more than when you're right." (Uncle Vryling was getting a bit mixed.) "Why should I waste further breath on you? I'd rather deal with a badger in a hole. Be off with you!"

The Senator marched out. Nicodemus had his orders to help the young master store his belongings, pack his carpetbag, and speed him on his way after breakfast (at which the disgruntled Senator would *not* be present) with a note of farewell.

My dear Nephew:

While Stricken to the Heart by Your Ingratitude and Revolutionary Sentiments, I cannot Steel myself against the Claims of our common Blood. Know, then, that this Mansion remains for you a Refuge in your Time of Need, where you may Claim a Welcome so long as you remain Faithful to the Requisitions of an Honorable Lineage. Though well Persuaded that, unless you Mend your Ways, you will End your days in Gaol, I still Cherish the Hope that your Malfeasances may be Stained by no Dishonor. Should you Persist in your Mad Ambition to join your Lot with Thespians and Vagabonds, I suggest that you change your Name out of Respect for your Forebears.

In closing, I solemnly Warn you against the Excessive Use of Ardent Spirits and Remind you of your inherited Quintard tastes. This alone will never alienate you from my consideration. But if ever you turn Back upon the Standards of your Blood and Breed, you are no longer Kin of Mine and would be well Advised to Cut your Throat.

I subscribe myself,

Your affectionate Uncle,
VRYLING LOVATT.

Carpetbag over shoulder, Laus Deo snug in a deerskin weather proof strapped beneath his arm, and his fund secure in his pocket, Jans was ready for high commercial emprise.

Schenectady occurred to him as a propitious town for his uncertain venture. Schenectady, "Crossroads of York State." Surely opportunities would be found there.

Two days earlier Mr. Bassford Pilkington had arrived in Schenectady on a scouting expedition of sorts. For reasons of his own he had been living very private through the late winter and early spring. This precaution was connected with a transaction in horseflesh, the legality of which was a moot question, Mr. Pilkington holding one view, a Pennsylvania sheriff, the contrary. The sheriff was a scant half hour behind, on a crisp January evening, and the desirable goal of the New York State line a long six miles ahead, when the animal in question went inopportunely lame. Mr. Pilkington left the high road on foot and, guided by cheery voices, joined a party of skaters merrymaking around a bonfire.

North and south stretched the wild Susquehanna, a reach of black ice.

The stranger was welcomed with hot rumbullion and no questions asked. After a couple of drinks, he mentioned modestly that he enjoyed some slight repute in his native place as a fancy figure skater.

"Where's that?" someone asked.

"Montreal, Canada."

"I never yet seen the Canuck I couldn't best," boasted a wiry young fellow, the local ice champion.

"I got no skates," the supposed Canadian pointed out.

"Somebody lend him a pair."

They were strapped on, tested, pronounced satisfactory. "Now gimme another set," requested the alien.

"What for?"

"My hands."

"Your *hands?* Whaddaya going to do with your *hands?*"

"I'll show you."

Anyone, he explained, could maneuver on a pair of skates, but quadrupedal skating was a special knack and if some kind friend would fix the second outfit to his palms, he would prove it.

Full of skepticism and curiosity, the Pennsylvanians obliged. Outlying skaters from up and down river were whooped in to enjoy the marvel, thereby clearing the field for the performer. He explained that he would retire to the far bend, start back at a moderate pace, and when within a hundred yards of the fire, cast himself prone and come in at full speed doing a graceful outer edge on alternate left and right. (Approving shouts and jeering laughter.)

Waving his shod hands jauntily in the air, he took his leisurely course to the turn a quarter of a mile up-river—and kept right on going, but no longer leisurely. He was a mile away when the spectators awoke to the annoying fact that they had been neatly gulled. Half an hour later, secure on the New York side, Mr. Pilkington slept in an inn where, in the morning, he left the skates with a polite message of thanks.

As the disputed horse, now permanently disabled, belonged to the sheriff's brother-in-law, there was more hue and cry than usual in such cases. Mr. Pilkington found it expedient to strike rapidly north and find himself a logging job under an assumed name. Upon his return to civilization he found that his exploit had made him a legendary figure. It gratified his vanity, but complicated his career. He was still maintaining a precarious incognito when business brought him to Schenectady.

Jans strolled up into the busy town, to scan the inn billboards for possible employment. Toward the foot of the river slope he heard a hum of activity from the Givens House. He pushed open the door and entered upon a scene of minor riot. Politics appeared to be the chief issue. Curses, threats and wagers were freely exchanged. Incredibly peaceful in the clamor, a stout fellow slept in a corner, his hand thrown across his eyes. His distinguishing feature was the large, pinkish goiter on his neck.

A fight broke out at the bar and spread. The tapster sallied forth with a whiteash baseball bat for a dissuader and was joined by a peace officer wearing a star and wielding a truncheon. The combatants surged back, throwing Jans off balance. He stepped on the sleeper. The man came to his feet, agile and ready as a bobcat.

"Wanta fight?" he said. It was not a challenge, but an inquiry, directed toward the melee, which was free to any who chose to enter.

"No," said Jans.

"Neither do I. Let's get out."

He heaved up a window and let himself down into the coach-yard. Jans followed. In the comparative quiet of the yard, he scrutinized the stranger with interest, deciding that he had seldom encountered an odder person. The man was squat and muscular, his thick barrel supported on bow legs. He looked to be a mature and hardened thirty; his face was seamed and pocked. A tight mouth, stained at the corners, formed a straight line above a blue chin. His eyes were small, slightly protuberant, and very bright. Two tusks were conspicuous between his lips. The general effect, grotesque but not unpleasing, suggested a character resourceful, alert and insusceptible. He eyed Jans up and down.

"Collegian?" he asked abruptly.

"How did you know that?" asked Jans, amused.

"Cut o' yer jib. Don't like 'em." He spat. "Weedsaps. They're soft."

"I'll wrestle you for the drinks," offered Jans.

The other held out his hand. "Shake."

But Jans knew the trick of the shoulder-turn. He advanced his left hand, with right leg braced. The man grinned sourly, brushing the hand aside and straightening.

"Know a thing or two, don't yeh?" he commented. "Lookin' for work?"

"Yes."

"What line?"

"Music, drama, and the classics," said Jans without batting an eye. He foresaw amusement.

The man spat again. "Can't use 'em."

"What can you use?"

"Muscle."

"What line?" asked Jans in his turn.

"The lake trade."

Jans' heart jumped. The romance, the adventure, the risk of smuggling!

"I can sail a boat," he said.

"Sail my rump! Shift ballast. Dollar a night and found."

"Night?"

"D'jeh think we unload in the daylight? Ever hear tell of the revenoo cutters?"

Expectations of adventure on the broad waters of Ontario faded. Still, it was something new and untried. Landing contraband on a wild and lightless shore with perhaps a revenue cutter on the prowl outside would not lack for thrills. And the pay was generous.

"Where and when?" he asked.

"That's business," the stout man was pleased to approve. "Oswego. Cagg's Cellar. Tuesday, week."

They had a drink to bind it, and several more before the stranger turned away with the curtest of farewells to round up, as Jans suspected, further recruits for the enterprise.

How Jans reached Oswego he never clearly knew. Through a pleasurable mist he traveled by boat, by land, by boat again and at the end of the journey found himself in a town of neat frame houses, church spires and a lighthouse with white sails in the offing against a wide blue lake.

Cagg's Cellar was a foul, smoke-heavy joint beside a wooded backwater on the edge of town. There he found the goiterous man engaged in accepting invitations to drink from all and sundry who addressed him as "Pilk." Someone handed Jans a large glass of whiskey.

"Cagg's three-cent Sudden Death."

Jans accepted and, at the finish of the drink, found another automatically standing in its place. It inspired him to offer a song. Great applause.

Huddled over a table at one side was a group who had little part in the fellowship, except for a grossly pimpled fat man with a jews-harp and a mellow, basso voice. Jans regarded him with affection. They sang a duet. Uproarious applause.

Alcohol always stimulated the Quintard benevolence. Jans felt himself becoming the Friend of Humanity. He would buy a round of drinks for the table. He would buy two rounds. They were his brothers in song. He beckoned Pilk over, and that saturnine drinker lurched across and sat heavily down. All drank. All sang. All drank again.

Jans asked Pilk if these fine fellows were the lake-trade men. Pilk said he didn't know and didn't care. Neither did Jans. Mists accumulated in Jans' brain; rosy mists through which pulsated unearthly harmonies. The group at the table rose and went out, followed by an ominous growl. Evidently they were in ill-repute. Jans could not understand why. He was sorry for them. They should not be left friendless in that town. He would stand by them. So would Pilk. Gruff though he was, you could count on Pilk. And here was a wagon. . . . What wagon? A freight wagon. What had a freight wagon to do with the lake trade? And what was in it? He was. And Pilk. And the others. What else? He was sleepy.

A savage jolting roused him. The horses were running away. There was a crash—shouting—a swathed figure rolled from the over-burdened vehicle, and Jans was sick with horror. A vague horror connected with something ghastly which loomed white against blackness and toppled from the parapet of the bridge against which their wagon had smashed. He could not make out what it was—nor why he was running—nor what vengeance was pursuing him. It didn't matter. Nothing mattered. He was tired—so tired—so sleepy. . . . If they'd just let him alone he'd be all right and sober in the morning. Nothing mattered but sleep.

Snores, heavy and rhythmical, woke him. He sat up on the mud floor, aching. A pang transfixed his skull. Three-cent rotgut. Sudden Death. He was almost prepared to wish it had been. By the dim, pre-dawn light, he could see five other men in the strange quarters. One was a lank rag, slumped across the raw-wood bench.

A second lay half-curled around the wooden slop-bucket which, with the bench, made up the room's furniture. The jews-harp artist was propped in an angle of the wall. He looked dead but did not sound so. One of the chinless men was whimpering and picking something out of a bare thigh. Birdshot!

The sun, lurching drunkenly over a hilltop, cast a barred pattern on the far wall. Jans stared at it, his mind working like sour yeast. What had that gypsy girl in Albany warned? Something about his waking to barred sunlight on a wall. Something about disgrace. "Drink and dreams are the Quintard curse." Was it a dream that was weaving and gnawing in his brain? Or a memory, vague and dreadful, too dreadful to interpret?

To what brink of disaster had the curse brought him this time?

Pilk jerked and gurgled in his corner. Staggering across, Jans shook him awake.

"Where am I?"

Jans pointed to the barred window.

"Jail! What for?"

"God knows!"

Heaving himself to his feet, Pilk pressed his hands to his temples. His face, cleared of its stupor, was suddenly convulsed.

"Oh, Jesus!" It was not an oath, but a gasp of agony. Jans knew that he was remembering. But what?

Raising himself to the high window, Pilk peered out. Hardly was he back on the floor before he had thrown off coat and shirt and unwrapped a circle of stiff wire from his body. With this he started operations upon the heavy lock, muttering feverishly, "We don't oughta be here. We don't oughta be here at all. We gotta get the hell outa here."

The lock creaked and clicked. Pilk cautiously peered from the door.

"All clear," he said over his shoulder. "Comin'?"

"What about the others?"

"I hope they rot in hell!"

11

THE two jailbreaks stepped out, free, in a day of sunlight and gathering wind. Pilk set the pace at a trot. Still too muzzy to act for himself, Jans followed. At this edge of town nobody was astir but a wench with a piggin and milkstool. She smiled and waved them a greeting. Evidently, then, thought Jans, however sinister the events of the night which had stirred his hardshell companion to such repugnance, they could not yet be matter of general knowledge. Otherwise the herd-hussy, instead of being sympathetic to a couple of overnight drinkers, would have raised a hue and cry upon them.

A church bell pealed. Jans caught up with the swiftly lumbering Pilk and panted.

"Is it Sunday?"

"No. It's us."

He dived into a copse, with Jans at his heels, threaded it, and came out on the far side a few rods short of Cagg's Cellar. Bare masts thrust upward beyond the building. Pilk whirled and seized him by the shoulders.

"You said you could sail a boat."

"Yes."

"Run up sail on the blue hull."

"Is she yours?"

"You ask too many goddamn questions."

Jans hesitated. Thus far his escape had been semi-automatic, but now the stubborn Quintard streak asserted itself.

"I don't like running away," he protested.

"Doncha?" retorted the other with a feral snarl. "Doncha, my fine bucko? Didja ever hear tell of Judge Lynch?"

Jans made for the backwater.

Stealing a boat was a step beyond anything that he had undertaken in the wildest of college pranks. But the older man's white and deadly serious face, and even more, the insistent clangor of the bell were sharp incentives. He hurried down the back of the creek. Pilk vanished into Cagg's.

There was no difficulty in identifying the blue-hulled craft. Jans inventoried her with an expert's eye. Her lines were trim; he judged that she would be fast beating up and easy downwind. The sails looked foul but sound. He wished he were as sure of the mainmast which showed two dozey patches. The running gear, too, was gray with age. As to the hull, he could only hope; there was no time for inspection. Evidently the *Mary Belle* (he could just make out the name in damaged lettering on the prow) had seen little recent service and that, by the smell of her, in the fishing trade.

Further examination was not too encouraging. Her visible equipment consisted of one boat-hook, one oar, a bucket, an anchor with a rope that Jans wouldn't have trusted to lead a pig to market, and no spare canvas. Hardly an outfit to pit against the frequent rages of stormy Ontario. A foot of bilge sloshed about in the gentle roll from the harbor. Outside, that roll would be far from gentle. Jans hauled up the sails to dry and set about bailing.

He was hard at it when Pilk appeared, heavy-laden. A huge wicker held a ham, bread-loaves, beans and other provender. Two demijohns protruded their necks. But Jans could hardly believe his eyes which showed him an almost new shaker broom, worth a shilling of any man's money, stuck down the burdened man's back.

Heaving the supplies to the deck, Pilk produced a stout cord with which he clumsily spliced the broom to the bowsprit, casting quick, apprehensive glances back over his shoulder and quivering when the wind gusts exaggerated the clamor from the church steeple. His queer task finished to his satisfaction, he cast off and clambered aboard.

"Get her goin'."

"Where to?"

"Canada."

"In twenty-two feet of deal box?" said Jans. "No, thank you."

"Scared, huh?"

"So would you be if you knew any seacraft."

"Genesee mouth, then," said the other with an ill grace. "You're such a cock-a-hoop sailor-man, maybe you could make that."

Jans eased around in the backwater, and with sails flapping to keep down speed lest he run upon a shoal in this unmarked water, headed downstream. As the boat swung into the current, two men appeared at the crest of a rocky height, gesticulating and shouting. One fired a fowling piece, but the charge fell short. Pilk leaped to the gunwale and shook his fist, cursing foully and triumphantly.

The *Mary Belle* gathered speed. She answered to handling like a trained pony. Beyond the river mouth whitecaps were tumbling. Once in the open lake, Jans would have his hands full if, as he suspected, his shipmate was a lubber. While the going was still easy, he wanted to find out more about this. He cleated down the mainsheet, eased off the foresail and turned to the older man.

"What are we running away from?"

Again Pilk retorted, "You ask too many goddamn questions."

Jans studied the solid chin, the somber eyes, the straight, hard level of the lips. He would get nothing out of that face until its owner was ready to talk. But why this secrecy? With a shock, Jans wondered whether it was all natural foul temper. Whether, rather, his shipmate was not meaning to do him a kindness in concealing the events of the night.

Just the same, he was not going to endure any bullying. He had the easy temper of indifference. But not beyond a certain point.

He let the sails fill again. The *Mary Belle* heeled and slid along the first of a parade of smooth rollers, not yet breaking over. A dash of spume sprinkled the faces of the two men. Pilk flinched. Three minutes later, he was sitting in the bottom of the weaving craft, his features distorted between fear and fury.

"Keep her steady, cancha, goddamn ya!" he snarled.

Jans had been waiting for this.

"Take over," he said mildly.

"Huh?"

"If you think you can handle this boat better than I can . . ."

"Who the hell said I could?"

"Then suppose you let me give the orders."

"And me take 'em, huh?"

"We'll make better weather that way."

"All right. But I'll hammer the guts out of you when I get you ashore."

"That's as may be," replied Jans, exhibiting no signs of apprehension.

Now they were heading due west. The sloop sped like a joyous wraith through the sportive seas. There might be doubts of her staunchness, but of her speed there could be but one opinion. Nothing in sail or, as long as that weather held, under steam would be likely to overhaul her.

Toward sundown Pilk resigned himself, with no special reluctance, to die. Last night's dregs were being violently wrenched out of him, and with them much of his pugnacity. In melancholy tones and between empty retches he cursed himself for a fool and demanded that Jans put him ashore anywhere; it didn't matter where if only it was solid land. Looking at the unbroken line of wilderness, Jans shook his head.

"We're nowhere near any settlement."

The wind became milder and more puffy. Pilk grunted his relief but Jans uneasily eyed a mass of thunderheads, banking up in the northwest. The breeze crept around behind them; the whitecaps smoothed out; the little schooner slid along gently before the favoring waft. It would not be long in their favor, Jans knew, since a thunderstorm always approaches against the wind which whips around at the last moment, bringing the rain with it. How much violence there was in those bellying curves of massed blackness, he could only guess. They looked formidable.

What had preceded called for no more than ordinary seamanship. What was coming might well be serious. The *Mary Belle* would need all she had of seaworthiness. From every indication she would have to keep clawing off a lee shore. Even the slight wind surface of the strange embellishment on her bowsprit impaired her balance. Jans addressed his companion:

"What's the broom for?"

"Hexes."

Jans knew the Pennsylvania Dutch defense against witches, but had seen it only on barn peaks. He grinned.

"There are no hexes out here."

"Oh, ain't there!" retorted Pilk.

He sat up in the ominous calm that had fallen and turned his ear to the oncoming storm. A faraway, prolonged note, like the moan of a tortured giant, rose and died.

"*Ain't* there!" he repeated in bitter contempt. "Djever hear of the carcagne?"

Jans had. The carcagne is a storm hag with bat wings and a borrowed wolf's head, generally held accountable for such ships as put forth on Ontario and Erie never again to be reported. The distant moan rose to a howl and again sank into silence.

Jans eyed a dark line, racing across the water toward them.

"Cut that broom loose," he ordered.

"Go to hell."

"All right, then, I'll do it. But if she broaches to you'll have to swim for it."

"I can't swim," yelled Pilk.

"That's your bad luck."

Cursing and moaning, the landlubber crawled forward and hacked through the cord. "There goes the luck and the life," he muttered, as the protective broom went overside.

The gale struck almost dead ahead. This was no sportive breeze. There was evil in it. With no help from his cowering shipmate, the navigator soon found that he could not handle the boat up-wind.

"Drop the mainsail!" he shouted above the clamor.

Pilk only cowered.

"Cut the halyards then, damn it!"

Pilk stared at the knife in his nerveless hand and let it fall. Not daring to leave the tiller for so much as a second, Jans could only pray for a lull. A mighty gust hit the foresail; the frayed sheet parted; the sail rose like a clumsy bird to drape itself around the mast, which, unable to stand the strain, snapped a foot above the deck.

"Oh, God help my poor soul!" howled Pilk and beat his head on the gunwale.

There was now but one course to follow. Jans must take the risk of abandoning momentarily the tiller. Swiftly he jumped to the main halyards, lowered the canvas to a few spare feet of sailing surface, cleated down again, and was back at his place of control before the *Mary Belle* had shipped more than two combers.

Lashing curtains of rain now obscured the shore toward which they were driving. Under the unbalanced impulsion of one sail, the craft yawed hideously, but did not ship enough water to endanger her. Huddled in the bottom, Pilk wept for his past sins.

The rain moderated. The wind rose and drove them, full of hate. In the lessening light, Jans made out a low reach with rushes. It looked like a creek mouth. Craftily he maneuvered the boat to a point almost direct to windward, dropped his fragment of sail and let her scud under bare poles for the shallow stream which opened out, "Like a banner with Welcome printed on it," as Pilk poetically remarked later. The prow slithered gently in soft, harmless mud. The pair waded ashore, Pilk bearing a half-gallon jug from which he took a long swig before handing it to his companion. When he spoke, it was grudgingly.

"I reckon you saved my life."

"Damn your life! I was thinking of the boat."

Pilk chuckled. "Lad," he said, "you got gristle."

Jans lifted his brows.

"I didn't take to you first-off with your dandy clothes and your tol-lollish way of speech. I was wrong. I can't say handsomer than that, can I?" The taciturn and bristly little man was becoming not only loquacious but positively genial.

"No, that's fair enough," admitted Jans.

"Then you just curl up and have a snooze, whilst I build a fire and cook us some vittles. You must be wore out."

"I could sleep," confessed Jans.

Pilk took another snooker, carefully corked the demijohn, and shook his fist at the clearing sky.

"Fooled yeh!" he crowed.

"Look out," warned Jans with a grin. "You'll make the carcagne mad again."

"She'll never get another crack at me," declared the other. "What sailin' I do from now on'll be on the Ee-rye-ee Canal."

"Aren't you going on with me?"

"In that wreck?"

"This is no wreck. We'll cut a tamarack sapling and step as good a mast as you could ask for."

"Not me, boy, not me! I don't want no smarter hand at a boat than you be. But I'm a landsman. Good earth is what I need under my feet."

"There's a lot of it between here and the nearest settlement." Jans stared at the high, black, unfriendly wall of the forest.

"It's solid footin'," said Pilk. "That's all I ask. Gimme b'ars. Gimme cattymounts. Gimme rattlesnakes or wolves or any kind of woods meanness and I'll face it. But them waves!" He gulped windily in recollection, and took another swig. "You can sail her alone, can't you? I don't reckon you need me."

"No, I don't," admitted Jans.

"'Cause if you did, I'd stand by. I'm never one to quit a pal. And that's what you are, lad, a pal and a staunch one and any man says no to that has got Bassford K. Pilkington to fight."

"Pilkington?" Jans said. "Not Four-Skate Pilkington?"

"Heard that name before, huh?" said its owner, pleased.

"Who hasn't!"

"That's me. The old Four-Skater, himself."

He launched into autobiography, starting with the Pennsylvania exploit and passing on to other deeds which varied in their degree of morality but stopped short of criminality or what, in the narrator's elastic code, would be so classed. Jans listened, fascinated. The extreme of Harvard undergraduate license was lusterless and puerile beside such a career. As Bassford K. Pilkington's historical muse was unhampered by modesty, his saga was a record of brilliant achievements without a failure.

"That's me," he repeated with innocent pride. "I'm a sharpshooter. I'd diddle my own brother in a trade. But I never go back on my passed word or my sworn pal."

"Have you been keeping dark on account of the Pennsylvania business?" Jans asked.

"Well, I figure that's about played out." Pilk's face darkened. He agitated his goiter. "And now comes this goddamn business."

Jans took a resolution. "Pilk," he said quietly, "I want to know what happened."

"Sure, lad?" The adventurer's tone was gentle, compassionate.

"Yes, I'm sure. I remember gunshots. Was it a killing? If it was, I'd rather face it."

"They were shootin' at us."

"What for?"

Filling a cup full of the potent corn, Pilk handed it over. "Drink that," he said.

Jans drained it. His fingers were constricted on the tin. Pilk stared into the embers. His lips twitched, opened, closed, barked out a single word.

"Anatomy."

"*What?*" The grasp on the tin cup became nerveless. It fell and rolled, rattling into the coals.

"That's it," said Pilk tonelessly.

"Pilk! Did you *know?*"

"Beforehand? Whaddayeh take me for?" growled the other. "I wouldn't touch it if cads* fetched a thousand dollars apiece. Not in my right mind."

"Then why—how—?"

"That whipbelly rotgut they gave us. I was as sozzled as you was."

"The men at Cagg's?"

Pilk nodded. "Resurrectioners for the medical-school market. Sweet bastards."

"Pilk, do you—can you remember any of it?" Jans asked fearfully.

"The stink. And the hogshead bustin' open and spillin' a couple of the cads over the bridge. That's when they took after us."

A question stuck in Jans' constricted throat. "How much did we have to do with it? The—the digging?"

The other opened out his gnarled hands. "Look at your palms," he said.

Jans did so.

"Any blisters?"

"No."

"Neither have I. We didn't handle."

Jans fetched a deep sigh. "That isn't so bad. But it's bad enough, God knows. How will I ever sleep again?"

*Cadavers.

"You'll sleep, lad. You're young. You'll forget. That's the way life is," said Bassford K. Pilkington profoundly.

They put in the better part of the morning selecting, felling and fitting a hackmatack sapling which Jans stepped in place of the broken foremast. All was ready by noon. The two friends had a final drink together, with Pilk giving the toast.

"Quick forgotten, soonest mended."

He vanished into the forest with a jerky nod for farewell. Jans pointed west with a favoring wind. He decided upon Sodus Bay for his landing point. There he would take the road.

The Saratoga Springs post brought the letter to the Honorable Vryling Lovatt.

Dear and Respected Uncle:

That you have had no word from me these several weeks speaks ill for my duty but marks no diminution of my loyalty and affection. Owing to unfortunate circumstances with which I will not burden your forbearance, I have determined to adopt a course once suggested by you, and change my name. Until further advices then, sir, I shall make my way as plain J. Quinn.

I beg further to inform you that I have taken the Minister's Oath* and shall faithfully adhere to its provisions. In conclusion I beg to subscribe myself,

Your very respectful and obedient nephew,

Jans Quintard.

"The Minister's Oath, eh?" Uncle Vryling said thoughtfully. "Well, well!"

More could hardly be expected from any young blade of spirit.

---

*The affiant to this formula pledges himself to get drunk no more than four times a year; at Christmas, Muster Day, Independence Day and Sheep Shearing.

12

TEN years in prison is a sour prospect for a young man with his
life before him. Though his conscience absolved him from guilt,
Jans suspected that in the eyes of a jury, he would appear, at best,
an accomplice. Anatomy was a particularly unpopular crime at the
moment. So scarce were cadavers that medical-school professors
were resigning their positions for lack of material to teach with;
so high the price that there had been an epidemic of grave deliv-
eries and the authorities were taking stern measures against the
resurrectioners. It behoved Jans to become inconspicuous, at least
until he could find out whether he had been identified in his proper
person.

Financially he was secure enough. There was nearly six dollars
in small paper and specie in his wallet besides a five-dollar current
note for which he could account in only one way. At the first
opportunity he unobtrusively dropped it into the poor-box. He
wanted none of that money!

Without his guitar, which he had sent back for safety, he felt
lost. It would be waiting at his call in the Potter mansion. Albany
was not the safest place in the world for him. But he had raised a
fine obscuration of whiskers and thought he could risk it. Peery
Potter was reliable. So he made a quiet call, retrieved the instrument, and prepared to join the westward current of the towpath.

But first he had another errand. He wanted to see or, at least,
speak with the Hundred-Year-Old Egyptian Seeress, and hear that
warm, vibrant, young voice, and tell her how near to fulfillment
her dire prophecy had come, and inform her of the Minister's
Oath. All nonsense, of course. Why should she, a professional, be
interested in the outcome of a shilling's worth of mechanical for-

tune-telling? Mechanical? No, it had not been wholly that. There had been some inexplicable emotion in her warning. He found himself wondering warmly whether her lips would quiver beneath his kiss, as had her hand.

Decidedly he must have his shilling's worth of magic. He made for the Knickerbocker Hall.

The hoardings were unpropitious. Here were exploited Prof. Zaharamath the Wonderful Ventriloquist; the Grand Solar Microscope with a Magnification of 5,300,000; The Halian Phantasmagoria or Optical Illusion, Ending with Dance of Multiplication of Witches; Galvin Edson, the Living Ghost—45 Years, 45 Pounds; and Chauncy Johnson's Miraculous Musical Clock, Pronounced by the Most Competent Judges to be Altogether Unrivaled by Anything in the World; also a Six-legged Calf.

But nothing of Mailzell's and its appurtenances. Jans bought the ticket man a drink and made inquiries. It was sixpence ill-spent. The show had busted. Some sort of row. The Egyptian Seeress? Couldn't say. Every show had one. Gone back to her tribe, most likely, if she was a true one and not a bogus. Thanks for the drink.

With guitar and pack, Mr. J. Quinn, vagabond, set about trading his way westward, and for several self-supporting weeks led a varied life between profit and loss with a general balance in his favor. He found himself, on a soft summer morning, well rested from a comfortable night in a barn loft, awaiting a towpath lift. He was superbly attired in the green-white-and-red uniform of an artillery major in the militia, and adequately disguised, so he hoped, by a set of loosely dispersed whiskers. The call of lock-ho! a few rods away attracted his hopes to a smallish, trim Durham.

The boat eased out to the lower level, riding high. The lock-gate closed slowly behind it, and the lock-keeper, having pocketed the toll, waved a dignified godspeed. A small, thick man with a broken nose moved forward along the deck until he stood above the lettering on the prow, *The Barter Boat*.

"Tail on," he shouted to the hoggee, a wizened goblin of fifteen. Jans waved to him. He saluted.

"Day to Your Honor."

"The like to you, Captain."

"Can I sell you a handsome broadcoat?"

"Not this summer day."

"Can I sell you a stuffed anaconda?"

"Wouldn't know what to do with it."

"Can I sell you a harmonious jews-harp or a bottle of sure-cure for the you-know-what?"

"Don't play the one and don't need the other."

"Can I sell you a glass eye in case you got into a gouge-fight and lost one of yours at the end of a thumb?"

"Keep it and I'll keep mine. I'm in the trading line, myself. Can I sell you this uniform?"

"Might, if it was navy. Where'd you get it?"

"From a muster-outer in Stone Arabia. You can have it cheap."

"I'll swap my anaconda for it, evens, and no questions asked."

The young man reflected. "Stuffed ones are slow on the market, I judge. What's your price, cash?"

"Six dollars."

"If I sell it for you for five, what'll you allow me?"

"What are you asking?"

"Free passage through the Black Snake."

"Done, if you'll lend a hand with the boat."

Jans climbed aboard. The anaconda, picked up at a bargain from a stranded medicine show was a sorry specimen of serpent, sagging at the seams, and flaking the paint from its burlap skin. While Captain Byles, as he introduced himself, tied in at the Utica wharf, Jans disembarked and studied the notice board at the entry to Baggs' Tavern. Presently he was ashore for the second time, burdened for business. The spectacle of a major of artillery in parade uniform with an anaconda coiled about his shoulders, attracted some pleasurable attention in the busy little city. Admiring crowds attended his martial tread up Genesee Street.

By sunset he was back, shabby and minus the snake, with notes and specie which he handed over to the captain.

"You *are* a sharpshooter," said that trader, in admiration. "Who'd you sell to?"

"The Reverend Belazeel Jenks for his lecture on the Evils of Strong Drink."

"We'll have one on that. Where's your uniform?"

"Sold."

"Gawshamighty!" exclaimed Byles. He eyed the substitute clothing. "Where'd you find the slops?"

"Fairlee's Basement. Two dollars. I got ten for the uniform and seven for the snake."

"I be damn!" said Byles. "Some trader! Howdja like to buy into a partnership?"

"No capital," said Jans. "But we might work out a commission deal, say on a twenty percentum basis."

Captain Byles squawked his indignation. Five, he proffered, would be a fairer figure.

"I'd be cheap at twenty," argued Jans. "If I haven't swelled your trade by half the first week, I'll take only my board and keep. First of all, I'll show you how to pick up a bit of passage money."

He retired below decks and presently emerged with a cardboard placard neatly lettered in paint, which he had found in the trade room.

DECK PASSENGERS ACCOMMODATED
1 Cent per Mile

The captain's skepticism was dissipated when no fewer than fourteen fares occupied his space between Utica and Rome. West of the latter town a lone passenger boarded by the simple but athletic process of a running take-off from the path which landed him neatly on the rail. This was the more of a feat in that he was burdened with a small pack and a fowling-piece in a bandolier. Giving Jans' placard a scornful glance, he seated himself at the prow and from time to time studied the landscape through a spyglass. He was richly dressed, flashily handsome with curly, black hair, lambent, restless eyes, a saturnine curve to the red lips, and a figure as lithe and tense as a bent bow. Jans, roping the tiller since the captain was below and he was steering, approached, gave the newcomer a civil good day, and asked where he was for.

"That's as may be," said the passenger indolently.

"As far as Manlius?"

"Tell you when we get there."

"That will be four bits."

"Soap it on the glass," said the other in round, taproom terminology.

"This is a cash boat."

"Are you the captain?"

"No. Captain's below."

"Fetch him up."

"Fetch him, yourself," suggested Jans equitably.

"You looking for a fight?" asked the man softly.

"No. Fares."

At this moment of tensity, Captain Byles appeared. He greeted the stranger with an obsequious smirk.

"This is Lucky Seven Smith," he explained to Jans. "He's a puke."

Mr. Smith confirmed this characterization. "Yes, I'm from the great state of Missouri, where," he added, staring at Jans, "they shoot first and talk afterward." His speech and manner were those of an educated man gone to seed.

"He hasn't paid his fare," said Jans to the captain.

"That'll be all right," put in Captain Byles hastily. He drew Jans aside. "D'you want a sticker through your weasand, you young fool? Go back and steer."

Jans shrugged and obeyed. Having brought a drink from below to Mr. Smith, who continued to scan the landscape, Byles rejoined his steersman.

"I don't like your friend," said Jans bluntly. "Who is he and what does he do?"

"He's one of the swampers from Nine Mile. There's a whole nest of pukes there. Hunters."

"What does he hunt?"

Byles lowered his voice. "Black game, mostly."

Jans gave an exclamation of disgust.

"White, too. Jailbreaks. Indentured men or gals. Anything with five dollars on their head. No small fry."

"A dirty trade," said Jans.

"Well, I don't hold with it, myself. But you got to treat them pukes perlite. They're an active lot. Carry a knife under one coat-tail and a jackeroo under the other. Club, knife, or shoot you—they don't care."

Near Manlius Jans had an opportunity of seeing the manhunter in action. A small group of boys were plodding along, and, limping after them a few paces in the rear, a gangling youth with a vacant look. This fellow the foredeck passenger studied with attention through his glass, then drew from his pocket and consulted some notes. He shouted to Captain Byles, "Hold the boat."

With an agile leap, he gained the berm and ran swiftly toward his prey. Jans observed with astonishment that he did not have his gun. The vacant-faced youth sighted him, gave a shriek, and tried to run down the bermside but was caught and tripped. At this the group in front turned and stood, uncertain.

"Name of the law," snapped Lucky Seven Smith, and slowly oscillated the jackeroo, a heavy-loaded sandbag which he had drawn from his rear pocket, over the fallen quarry.

He had courage; that much Jans was forced to admit in spite of his disgust. Yanking the captive to his feet, he propelled him toward the *Barter Boat,* which Captain Byles had obligingly halted, and thrust him aboard. There he trussed him like a chicken and laid him on the flooring.

The youth kept sobbing, "They'll put me in Obbun. They'll put me in Obbun. I'll never git out."

"Not for ten years, you won't, my lad," said Lucky Seven. "This is Captain Suggs' hoggee that robbed his till," he explained to Byles. "I'll collect my five dollars at the next jail and leave him there for the constable. That's no more'n cornshucks to me but I've got a hundred-dollar nigger on my list, if somebody else doesn't pick him up first."

Sick with loathing and pity, Jans walked up to the hunter.

"Are you an officer of the law?"

The other smiled with easy malevolence. "What's that to you, punk?"

"I'm asking about your right to take this boy without a warrant," said Jans.

Lucky Seven caught up his fowling piece and pointed it at Jans' belly. His face worked with fury. "Here's my rights!" he shouted. "D'you want to test 'em?"

"Don't shoot! Don't shoot!" gibbered Captain Byles. "For cri' sakes, I don't want no murder aboard my boat. Let him go, Mr. Smith." He turned upon Jans. "Git off my boat! Git off! I don't want no troublemakers here."

"I'll get off," said Jans through hard-pressed lips. He said to the hunter, "You wouldn't come ashore without that gun, would you?"

Smith laughed contemptuously. "Haven't got time today, punk. But we'll meet again and I'll kick your backsides through the roof of your mouth and choke you to death on your own pantaloons."

It was open country where the enforced debarkation took place. There was no difficulty in finding a hospitable farmhouse where, for the haypay of a few chores, the wayfarer was made free of the barn accommodation. He got a dawn start next day, and, by afternoon, was in Syracuse, sniffing the air for the scent of trade or, better still, employment. He was deacon-sober and had every intention of remaining so.

Fayette Street stretched, broad and prosperous, between neat stores and smoking factories. A hand-inked playbill, fluttering on the inn's notice-board, caught Jans' eye. He sought out the proprietor.

"Are Passerow's Thalians stopping here?"

"Not them! This is a first-class house."

"Where could I find them?"

"Tenting it among the bugs in Bernard's Marsh just beyond town limits."

Jans studied the bill carefully, after which he sat down to a mug of ale and spread out before him several clippings from his capacious wallet. Selecting two, he conned them over, set them apart, finished his ale, and took his departure.

A short distance out on the Old Salt Road which stretches three hundred miles from the sodium beds to tidewater, Jans located the encampment. From one of two shabby Conestoga wagons a woman's querulous voice upbraided.

"And what was our take last night? Fourteen dollars."

"I know, my dear," replied a deep, theatrical bass pacifically. "Consider the competition. The Temperance Lecture, Illustrated, free. The School Exhibition, charity. The town already papered with the Angevine Circus broadsides. And at best, Fayetteville is a languid town."

"Not for a well-conducted show," was the acrid retort.

"I do my best, my dear."

"Fourteen dollars," lamented the female. "And less than sixteen the night before. How long can we survive such vicissitudes, Mr. Passerow?"

"This town will prove better."

The manager emerged, flapping hopelessly at the gnats, and was accosted by Jans.

"You present as your first offering the tragedy of Bellario, with Mrs. Passerow as Celeste, I observe, sir," he began elegantly.

That lady, who had been listening through a loosened flap, thrust forth her head.

"You have seen me—us?" she simpered.

"I have not had that happy fortune as yet, madame," replied the visitor. "But I have seen the handbill and ventured to adapt a slight poetic testimonial."

"Oh, do recite it! I dote upon poesy."

Jans obliged.

> *"Earth's bosom seems with pain to swell.*
> *What wand'ring spirit tolls that bell?*
> *Celeste! Is this thy virtue's knell,*
> *That dooms thee to catastrophe?"*

"I think it's cruel lovely," the lady declared.

"Not bad," Passerow grunted.

"We could attach it to the notice, Mr. Passerow," his wife said.

"Payment," Jans suggested. "I would accept a pit seat for the evening's rendition."

Grumbling, Mr. Passerow disappeared into the wagon. He returned with a pass. An insinuating murmur in Jans' ear said, "Couldn't you write something tasty about me?"

Turning, he saw a pretty young woman in her early twenties, with a buxom figure, a shallow, languorous, and invitational eye, and a ripe-fruit mouth.

"The Fair Luna, Miss Wayne, our accomplished singing chambermaid," Mr. Passerow said.

Jans bowed. From a tent beyond the second wagon came the sound of singing, rich, low and husky.

> *"I've been roaming, I've been roaming*
> *Where the meadow dew is sweet."*

Jans lifted his head sharply. "That sounds like happiness," he said.

"I don't know what she's got to be so happy about," sniffed Fair Luna.

"She's attained her life's ambition in joining with us," said Mrs. Passerow.

"And I'm coming, and I'm coming,
With its pearls upon my feet,"

hummed the voice.

"Our all-purpose girl," explained Mr. Passerow. "Small parts. Hardly more than an aspiring amateur as yet."

"Billed as La Jeune Amour?" inquired Jans, drawing the handbill from his pocket.

"When she gets onto the bill at all, which ain't always," Miss Wayne sniffed.

"Surely I've heard that voice before," said Jans. "She sings as naturally as a bird."

"And as incorrectly," said Mrs. Passerow.

"I wonder if she's ever sung in Albany."

"Hul-lo, mister!" Fair Luna laughed. She called negligently, "Hey, Durie, come out! You got a follower."

"Tomorrow," said the unseen. "I'm studying."

"Wouldn't you honor me by sharing a drink at the tavern after the close?" invited Jans.

"I would," said Fair Luna promptly.

"Hast Lethe's potion for a harried heart?" inquired the tent.

"That's her!" jeered Fair Luna. "Always conning her silly lines. What's she know about acting? We picked her out of a hedgerow. And she thinks herself a star already. Tomorrow! Is that polite deportment for a civil invitation?"

"Tomorrow and tomorrow and tomorrow
Creeps in this petty pace from day to day. . . ."

chanted the tent.

Jans capped it:

"And all our yesterdays have lighted fools
The way to dusty death."

"Why not allay the dust with a timely drink?" he pleaded.

"What manner of man is this who would vex with mirth the drowsy ear of night?" demanded the tent.

"It's a young gentleman," Mrs. Passerow explained.

"I don't know any young gentlemen. Good night, sweet prince."

"That's all you'll get out of her," Fair Luna warned. "Sot as a farrowed sow, she is. I'll see you after curtain, mister."

With no hankering whatsoever for Miss Wayne's company, Jans was too courteous to dishonor a social obligation. He escorted her to the Syracuse House taproom where the ale-brew was famous. There they sat until closing time in conversation which lacked stimulus for the young lady since she was unable to hold it to the fascinating subject of herself and her talents. Egotist though she was, however, she had the professional virtue of loyalty. From this angle and for reasons of her own shrewd reckoning, she did her naive best to interest young Mr. Quinn. When they parted, she had no satisfactory assurance that she had succeeded.

Waking early in the conniewagon, which she shared as road quarters with La Jeune Amour, she reported, "That's a queer one, that young mister."

"Is he?" said Durie uninterestedly. "Why?"

"I sat next to him through four tall ales and he never so much as tweaked my knee."

"Why should he?"

"Why shouldn't he?" retorted Miss Wayne angrily. "Ain't he human?"

"How should I know?"

"Meaning you don't care. Well, he asked a lot of questions about you."

"Perhaps he saw me act in Utica," surmised Durie complacently.

The ingenue snorted. "Two sides, of five words apiece," she said. "You two carried on like you were on-stage. 'Tomorrow and to-morrow and today,'" she mocked. "'Good night, sweet prince.' Yah!" She changed her tone. "If you was to ask me," she ruminated, "I think he's got the dibbs. He don't look it and he don't act it, and, God and my grandmother knows, he don't dress it."

"What makes you think so, then?"

"I can smell it on him. It's a gift. When I was born, the midwife pressed a shilling into my little rump and left a print. And Mr. Slowpoke Quinn carries the sweet scent of the rhino with him."

"Is that his name?"

"J. Quinn. He sports a whisker and uses a heap of long words. You'd never call him sightly; too long in the beak and the jawbone. There's something about him, though, but what it is I couldn't tell you, not if my backside was on a griddle. Maybe it's the polite way he bespeaks you, like as if you was a lady. You think *you* can sing. You'd ought to hear him when he plays on his little stringbox with gold letters across its front."

Durie shot upright in bed. "Gold letters! Latin? Laus Deo?"

"How would I know? Funny letters."

"I thought I'd heard that talk before," murmured Durie, and lay back.

"Getting notional about him? You *do* know him," she accused.

"I think perhaps I do."

"Is he rich?"

"I think perhaps he is."

"Then how," said the practical Miss Wayne, "do we tap his kick?"

"Why should we?"

"Look!" said her companion with vigor. "We ain't making hay-pay. You ain't only just joined, so you don't know how long it is since the ghost walked. What this show needs is a backer. You play your cards right and you could toll him in and make yourself solid with the management. I'll warrant he'd support a benefit for you if you played the cards smart."

Durie shook her head. "I don't believe I'd be apt at that sort of thing."

"Pfui! What are you a female for?" retorted the disgusted Moon Maiden. "Or ain't you?"

Durie had joined on at Victor where the company banner was out for a three-day stand. She studied the billboard at the grocery whose loft served as a makeshift theatre, and recognized the names with a thrill of anticipation: Miss Wayne, Mr. Archbold, Mr. Baggo and, most important to her, Mr. Passerow.

Sonorous voices overhead apprised her that rehearsal was in progress when she arrived in town afoot. She retired to a thicket, a travel-worn youth, and presently emerged, a trim, demure and determined maiden. She intended to get that job.

"May I solicit a moment of your time?" she asked the manager when he emerged.

He gave her a professional frown. "My time is much compromised at the moment. Be brief."

"I wish to join your troupe."

"As do thousands of others," he returned with a flourish. "What experience have you had?"

"Three months with Mailzell's."

"The panorama? Hardly a preparation for the legitimate stage. In what capacity?"

"Responsible utility." Durie was stretching it a bit.

"No opening," he said. But his glance, lingering with instinctive approval upon the lissome figure, gave her hope.

"I ask only for a trial."

"There's no time to try you out now. And we have no vacancy. But if you choose to call after the evening show . . ."

"Where?"

"Starker's Grove on the main pike."

The site had been chosen, Durie guessed on inspection, because it was rent-free. Nobody would pay money for occupancy of such a low-lying, swampy, miasmic meadow, buzzing with insect life and noisy with the song of frogs. The soiled and bedraggled tents of the camp were speckled with mosquitoes and early moths, already active when Durie strolled out in the evening. Tethered to ground-pegs, the livestock threshed and whinnied unhappily beneath the persecution of the winged pests. A sullen fire smoldered. Scenery, hastily unloaded, leaned against the sides of the wagons or lay flat on the grass. The visitor thought that she had never seen so slack an outfit. She thought further that she could readily find a sphere of usefulness here, though it were not precisely on the scale of her ambitions.

The Thalians straggled in at ten-thirty, a discouraged crew, with the Passerows bringing up the rear. Hardly had they separated for the night when a turmoil broke out among the pestered animals. The roan mare was wrenching her peg loose. She kicked wildly at the manager who ran to the spot, whirled, and was trying to bite him when a firm hand on the halter rope and a soothing voice in her ear checked her.

"Who's that?" demanded Mr. Passerow, peering in the dim light.

"Endurance Andrews. I applied for a position this afternoon."

"You've got a handy way with a beast. Don't let that mare loose."

"The bugs are driving your bestial mad," Durie pointed out.

"Don't I know it!" he said surlily. "What can I do about it?"

"Give me someone to help me and I'll show you."

She spoke with such assurance that, after a moment's consideration, the manager shouted, "Ambide! Jack Ambide!"

The utility man lumbered up, growling. He bestowed a glare upon Durie and said he'd be damned if he took orders from any hedgerow wench; he'd quit the poxy job first; he was ready to quit anyhow, and where was his wages? Mr. Passerow cursed him and was doubly objurgated in return. The high voices brought Tim Baggo and young Rapalje to the spot. They volunteered to help, the buffo observing that the damned bugs wouldn't let you sleep anyhow. Under Durie's direction, they filled a pig-kettle with water and set it over the camp fire to boil while she gathered a barrowful of husks, brown and withered, from beneath a clump of walnut trees. These she dumped into the kettle.

When the water came to a boil a pungent odor rose and filled the camp. Such mosquitoes as were caught in the fumes departed in disgust. Presently the stew spewed up a greeny-brown scum which turned thick and viscous as the mixture cooled. Durie deftly skimmed it off, mixed it into a heavy paste with flour for a base, and smeared the horses with it. That ended the insect feast. When the sun rose and the stabbing deer-flies gathered, every animal was protected as by sheet armor.

Meanwhile a cot in the smaller wagon had been prepared for the successful experimenter. In the morning she was summoned by the Passerows.

"While there is no vacancy," the manager said cautiously, "a place might be found for you, if you can offer any qualifications."

Her reply gave him the surprise of his life. "I can cook, mend, paint and repair scenery, handle livestock and properties, pitch and strike a camp, provide game, concoct simples, and bind up injuries. Do you need my services?"

"My God, *yes!*" the manager ejaculated.

"I shall expect wages and instruction in the art of acting."

"Let Ambide go," whispered Mrs. Passerow in her husband's ear.

"What wages?" inquired the manager.

"Five dollars a week."

"Take her," said Mrs. Passerow, who needed the help, interrupting her husband's automatic, "Too much." Later she reported upon the neophyte's professional capacity.

"She knows nothing."

"Can she be taught?"

"She's quick of apprehension. And she can work wonders with a silver-eyed blunt and a spool of packthread."

"Give her all the odd jobs and fend her off the stage work."

Thus Durie became nominally a Thalian. So useful did she prove herself in the incidentals of theatrical life that the Passerows conveniently forgot the stipulation that they were to train her in stagecraft. At the end of a month, she felt secure enough to advance her claim to a part, however small. Mr. Passerow reluctantly assented and composed a programme name for her, having a pretty conceit in that line.

What was her thrilled gratification upon beholding for the first time, in Syracuse, the legend in Mr. Passerow's flourishy handwriting on the *Tailor in Distress* handbill:

Polly, the Scullery Maid——*La Jeune Amour.*

13

The drama! Light of innocence and truth.
The scourge of vicious age, the friend of youth.
The stage! Vast field where stormy passions pass
In bold review as in a prescient glass.
The stage! Where Virtue her fair form may see
Vice shrink before his own depravity.
Patrons! The Thalian portals open wide;
Your smile our hope, your favor still our pride.
The Drama here shall dignify the stage,
Amuse, instruct, while it amends the age.
     J. Q.—*Adapted with kind obligeances to* Mr. Lawson.

Affixed to the taproom mirror, this specimen of Mr. John Quinn's adroitness at adaptation—though appropriation would be a fitter term—met with its sponsor's approval as he stood, reading it for the fourth time. Pretty pat for bespoke verse, he flattered himself. It could hardly fail to enhance the sale of seats. The company ought to be grateful to him.

Looking in the glass, Jans became aware of an ill-favored fellow seated alone at a table, glowering thoughtfully at him. The object of this reflected scrutiny stood it for a while, then turned and said, "Good day to you."

The stranger did not return the greeting. "Your name begin with J. Q.?" he asked brusquely.

"It might be," said Jans.

"D'you play a fiddle with gold letters?"

"Guitar," corrected Jans.

The man clenched his fist and placed it under his jaw, a grotesque but vivid suggestion of a goiter.

"Know a fellah like that?"

"Pilk!" exclaimed Jans.

"Clam it!" barked the man. "I've a word for you."

Jans moved over and sat down.

"The case is tried."

"What happened?"

"Ten years."

"Good God! Were we involved?"

"Not by name. 'Two individuals to the court unknown but believed to have been unwitting participants.' Some lawyer gab like that."

Jans drew a deep breath, fingering his whiskers of which he was wearied. "The times I've felt a grip on my shoulder!" he said. "Now I can be rid of these."

"He says you better lay low for a bit yet. The reward's still out."

"Where is he?"

"Not knowin', can't say."

"Does he think I'd better move on?" asked Jans uneasily.

"If I can find you, what's to hinder others?" snapped the stranger, and, rising, he clumped through the door without so much as a backward look.

It occurred to Jans that the canal route with its immense current of human traffic was, in the circumstances, an unpropitious environment for a person of interest to the authorities. For aught he knew there might be a reward upon his head and Pilk's, and they be prey for the Lucky Seven Smith type of manhunter. A thought which had been mulling within his mind since Monday, took more positive shape. The Thalians were striking off from the towpath southward. Why not join their fortunes?

He found Manager Passerow glooming over a solitary drink in the taproom and made his application, stating his experience. The manager was impressed by his three months in the famed Bowery Theatre in New York; less impressed when Jans admitted his histrionic activities were comprised mainly in tinkering and shifting scenery and contributing a deep-voiced "Aggrhh!" to Off-stage Voices Raised in Anger. No, there was no place for young Mr. John Quinn's talents in the Thalian company. Mr. Passerow broke out upon the theatre-going or theatre-abstaining public in general and Syracuse in particular.

"A scurvy town. A paltry town. Fit for one-act Moral Exhibitions and nothing better. We shall do well to get out of the place with a dollar in the till."

"Have you cash for your fee?"

"What? What's this? What fee?"

"The sheriff came home today. He'll be around with his requisition for the play-tax."

"Play-tax!" cried the manager wildly. "Nobody told me of that. A bilk! A mulk! An outrage! How much?"

"Two dollars per diem."

Mr. Passerow turned bile-pale. "My God! The night's takings will be hardly more when the lighting and rent are settled. We're pawked! Dunkled! Slubbered! Done for!"

Jans' quick and provident mind had been turned to a memory of a tale told over the after-theatre rumbullion by the great Mr. Placide; a tale of old corduroying days and an expedient more ingenious than ethical.

"Mr. Passerow," said he, "if I get you out of this, will you take me on?"

"Young man," said the other solemnly, "perform this miracle and you are one of us."

He went so far as to order a drink over which they went into private conclave.

The evening performance found Jans ensconced back-stage with a borrowed watch in his hand. Out front in two center seats with special cushions sat Sheriff Willigus and his deputy, the latter with the requisitions in his pocket with wafer and seal, backed by a writ in case the tax were not satisfied. The writ would not put them in jail. But it would distrain upon their properties and end their tour.

Sheriff Willigus was all smiles and high good humor. Sheriff Willigus had dined with the management and met the charming ladies of the troupe, with which he was to have supper after enjoying the performance from the free seats presented to him. Sheriff Willigus had amiably agreed to wait until the night's receipts were in hand before presenting his stamped and formidable document. There was perhaps twenty-five dollars in the house, a poor enough showing for the double bill. For, in the Sheriff's honor, the management was supplementing the popular *Black-Eyed Susan,* with the Risible Burletta: *Tom Thumb.*

Seven-thirty, the opening hour, wore on to nearly eight. The curtain was late, owing, as the manager apologetically explained, to the change of bill. Meantime Fair Luna Wayne would entertain them with a Refined Terpsichorean Act. Miss Wayne did so. The Sheriff was charmed.

"Eight-ten," said the watch-bearer, and the curtain parted.

Black-Eyed Susan's romance was played with every embellishment that ingenuity and long practice in ad-libbing would provide. Between the acts, Mr. Tim Baggo, the buffo, sang two comic songs.

"Nine-fifty," reported Jans. "For the Lord's sake, slow it up!"

Halfway through the second act he got a shock. The Sheriff was yawning. They had to speed it up again. Mr. Passerow appealed for patience between the two shows. Three of the artists, while the scenery was being shifted, would contribute specialties which had been greeted with éclat by press, pulpit and the President of the United States. Sheriff Willigus was applauding again.

"Ten-fourteen," reported Jans. "An hour and a quarter to go."

That is a rare burletta which plays an hour, and *Tom Thumb* ran in a thin vein. Gallantly did the actors pad and gag and improvise. The hour had barely passed when the end only too obviously impended. Jans, Mr. Passerow and Tim Baggo were in excited consultation while the curtains were slowly conjoined and the dramasated audience rustled to its feet. It was stayed by Manager Passerow's impressive form, uplifted hand and mellifluous voice. As a final and very special farewell treat and in gratification of appeals from ardent admirers of his comic genius, Mr. Tim Baggo would terminate the evening's entertainment with that rib-tickling ballad and monologue, "The Boston Post Office."

Bone-weary but game to the core, the buffo nerved himself to the task, Jans accompanying him on Laus Deo.

"Oh, what a town the Bostonians have to talk about!
There's the bank, the theatre, the church, and the exchange!"

He mouthed and stumbled on to:

"Oh, what a place the Boston Post Office is!
What a place of bustle when iliction once begins."

131

"Five minutes gone. Hang to 'em," encouraged Jans the time-keeper.

A hoarse croak checked the song. Jans banged out some gallant chords. Tim got a breath and swung into the patter.

"Pray, sir, does the iliction come in today? Who's to come in, pray? What name? Pat Mahony . . . What! Half a crown for my letter when I can nayther read nor write? Sell it to someone else. The iliction now? So Nibble-em has got in. Well, I've lost a cheese. . . ."

"Time!" from the triumphant Jans.

"And so good night," gasped the buffo and staggered off.

The Sheriff came back at once, attended by his deputy.

"A very bunkum entertainment," said he heartily. "And now, Mr. Passerow, our little matter of business." The tax form appeared.

"I regret to inform you, Mr. Sheriff," said the manager with elaborate courtesy, "that in the present depletion of our cash balance, it is impossible to satisfy your claim. But I will be glad to give you my note for the sum."

"Not my claim—the law's. Your note is not acceptable. Come sir, fork up," said the official gruffly.

"I lack the wherewithal." This was true. At the curtain-draw he had hurried out to pay the other bills.

"Tarker, the writ," said the Sheriff.

"Mr. Quinn, the time," said the manager.

"Twelve-sixteen," said Jans.

"Of a Sunday, I believe," said Mr. Passerow to the Sheriff, waving away the document which the deputy was pressing upon him. "Writs are unenforceable on the Sabbath in York State. And by Monday we shall be safely out of your county."

"Diddled!" said the Sheriff lamentably.

"Have a drink," invited the chivalrous Mr. Passerow.

Jans found himself the lion of the moment. The gentlemen of the troupe pressed forward to shake his hand; the ladies kissed him effusively; Miss Wayne, languishingly. Only the young girl who played the responsible utility role—in this instance the juvenile and unimportant daughter of the family—took no part in the amiable exercises. To Jans Quintard's experienced eye there was a palpable difference between her and the others. It was inherent in her bearing, her detachment, even in her dress. Though the material was worn and tarnished, she had cleverly garnished the defects so that the high chemisette of clear cambric accentuated the gracious promise of the young figure. The skirt fell in pliant folds from the slender waist. A saucy cap, bordered with blond lace perched jauntily on the lustrous brown of the hair. Rouge, artistically shaded, brought out the warm ruddiness of the skin and the tawny glamor of the eyes. Altogether a figure of witchery, Jans thought, and somehow vaguely familiar.

Throughout his anxious vigil, Jans had slanted a frequent look at her, haunted by that elusive resemblance to someone seen before. Once or twice he thought that she was regarding him with an interest in which there was nothing either coy or furtive. As she would not come to him, now that the ordeal was over, he went to her.

"We spoke last night," he began.

"Yes."

"But I never pictured you as looking like this."

"No?"

"'Yes.' 'No.' Have you no other conversation?" he mocked.

She smiled.

"Where have I seen you before?"

"Said the cat to the mouse."

His laughter had no tone of discomfiture. "It was not wholly a trap. And you are no mouse except in your quietude. You have secret eyes."

"From thinking, I expect," was her placid answer.

"About what?"

"Everything."

"Will you think about me?"

"Perhaps."

"Kindly?"

"Don't you think kindly enough of yourself?"

"Vixen!"

"They're calling you."

It was a summons to another round of drinks, this time at the bar. When he returned to find the girl, she was gone.

Soon the others melted away. To get safely beyond the limit of the Sheriff's writ before their grace expired, they must pack up at once and take the road by daybreak. Only Tim Baggo, the hard-working buffo, remained in the taproom to pamper his besetting vice, which, indeed, had brought him down to the present level. Still sober, he hailed Jans.

"Welcome to our honorable company."

"Thank you."

"What's your opinion of us?"

Jans hesitated. His standards of judgment, formed upon the best New York performances, were hardly a fair criterion applied to a struggling road company.

"A mongrel crew, eh?"

"Why, no," protested Jans. "I thought your own performance meritorious."

"Oh, I! But it's a sorry come-down for one who"—he lightly tapped his meager chest—"once teamed it with the great Lafayette, Prince of Mirth."

"Have you played with Mr. Stepanfetchit?" asked Jans, interested.

"In my day. Before unmerited reverses befell me."

"I should be interested in your own opinion of your fellow players," Jans said with flattering attention.

"Low, low. But which?"

"Well, Mrs. Gorham, for example."

"Capers and snorts like a she-ass in a pasture."

"And Mrs. Alwyn?"

"Heavy as a cold battercake."

"You can hardly say that of Mrs. Passerow," said Jans, amused.

"That quivering mammal! If she were not the management's wife . . ." He dismissed her with a gesture.

"Well, Miss Wayne, then?"

"The Fair Luna has the rudiments," Mr. Baggo conceded. "We play well together. I have trained her not to steal my laughs. Under my tutelage, she may go far. She has an elderly admirer—no bad thing for an ambitious young actress. A rich politico: name, Vryling Lovatt."

"I've heard the name."

"I doubt that he has had his reward yet. He dangles. She keeps him so. Smart. He will doubtless join us later in the tour."

Devoutly hoping that he wouldn't, Jans led the conversation back into professional channels.

"Ah, yes, our troupe," said the obliging Mr. Baggo. "Item: poor old Archbold. A broken tragedian. Preserves the great tradition. But the fire is gone. A dingy relic of the past."

"I saw him when I was a child," said Jans.

Mr. Baggo dismissed the has-been with a flirt of his fingers. "Item: Flavel Crosbie, our leading gentleman. A pretentious ass. Conceives all the females to hanker after him. Item: Ripley Rapalje, juvenile comedy, God save the mark! a blundering study who throws all of us out on our cues. The eternal amateur. Booms like a basso podunker in a marsh. As for the others: trumpery, trumpery."

"What about the young girl who plays bits?" inquired Jans with an affectation of carelessness.

"La Jeune Amour? That is French and means young love," explained the obliging buffo. He twirled his mustache. "Pretty as a pink with wings," he smiled. "Between you and me it may be that the Fair Luna is a bit miffed by my interest in our newest accession."

"I daresay," said Jans, regretting that it would be impolitic to kick him.

The comedian's expression became pensive and a little petulant. "A strange creature," he asserted. "Apparently impervious to the seductions of love. With all the appurtenances and allurements of femininity in—in what I might term a high degree, she exhibits none of the inclinations or responses proper to the sex."

"Strange!" said Jans.

"Isn't it!" said Mr. Baggo.

"It couldn't have anything to do with you?" Jans could not resist that.

Mr. Baggo exhibited surprise. "That's hardly likely. If you can make 'em laugh, you can make 'em love. Females are that way."

"Can she act?"

"Not a bit. And never will. Hasn't got it in her."

"Then what is she doing here?"

Mr. Baggo winked. "Stage-struck. Passerow gets her cheap—as he'll try to get you. By the by, if you haven't got him on stamped paper, you'd better see to it sharp."

"I'll go out there now," said Jans.

On the way, Mr. Baggo advised that he try for a salary of three dollars a week and found. Modest enough, Jans thought. But Mr. Passerow, stony-faced and stony-hearted in all matters of finance, would not hear of it. Five dollars a week, and Mr. John Quinn was to feed and bed himself; such was the management's last word. For this Mr. John Quinn was to help with the livestock (he had uncautiously mentioned that he was familiar with horses), take his turn at driving, set the stage, handle scenery and lights, play incidental music on his guitar, learn small parts, carry and plant the banner in advance, and understudy Mr. Baggo against such time as that gentleman might decide to treat himself to an alcoholic vacation. In his leisure hours he could check on the receipts and accounts; take it or leave it. Jans took it, speculating upon where the leisure time came in. Matching his specified occupations with the twenty-four hours of the day, he could find no vacant spaces.

As he walked out into the busy darkness fitfully illuminated by flares, he saw a light in the near-by tent, and within a shadow moving. He approached and called softly, "Jeune Amour!"

The shadow stood, alert and graceful. "Who is it?"

"You haven't thanked me yet for saving the show."

"There were plenty to do that."

"Who are you?"

"You have forgotten?" said the voice teasingly.

"What was there to forget?"

"I have sung your songs. I have fought your fight. I have foretold your fate. I have slept in your bed. . . ."

"What! Drunk or sober, could I forget that?"

"You were not there."

"Riddles!"

"All this you have forgotten," accused the voice. "And for that, Mr. Jans Quint——"

"Not that name!" he broke in.

"As you will. And one more prime event which even the most faithless memory should recall," the voice pursued.

"And that is?" said Jans, eager for the clue.

"I owe you a dollar," said the voice.

The light went out.

136

"Under a name not my own?"

"Actor people always do that."

"True. But that isn't my only reason." His face darkened. "We won't talk about it. Only, please remember that I'm John Quinn."

"Yes, Mr. Quinn. But that doesn't explain why you're here. You must be after something."

"Hasn't it occurred to you that it might be you?"

"I don't like that talk," she replied calmly.

"It's true—partly."

She shook her head. "You won't tell me what you're really seeking?"

"Suppose I said—reality?"

"Wasn't life in college real?"

"How could it be? What did we ever do?"

"The factory, then."

"That was real enough. But it was the wrong sort."

"I wouldn't think that you'd come to a world of make-believe in search of the right sort."

"I'm planning to write another play."

"Oh! Have you written plays?" She gazed at him with respect. Or was it only curiosity?

"Yes. I entered one for the five-hundred-dollar prize offered by Mr. Forrest of Albany."

"Did your play prevail?" she asked politely.

"It came back in the ribbons it went out in."

"What will you do with it now?"

"Rewrite it."

"Would there be a part in it for me?"

"The professional attitude already! There might be."

"You've seen me act. What do you think of me?"

"I think you're lovely enough to witch a man's heart out of his body," he said fervently.

At this she frowned, shaking her head a little, as if in perplexity. He set his hand over hers, but swifter than his clasp she caught it away and thrust it into the bosom of her blouse. He knew what that gesture meant, and wondered pityingly what desperate expedients of resistance had trained sense and sinew to that instant revulsion. He smiled at her.

"Is that the hand I kissed in the Egyptian Seeress' booth at Mailzell's?"

She made no reply, only looking straight at him with those small wrinkles of uncertainty between her brows.

"Are you afraid of me, Durie? Don't be."

"Then don't touch me," she breathed.

"Do I revolt you so deeply?" He laughed a little. "What manner of woman have I fallen in love with?" he said lightly. "Is it the voice in Harvard Yard, the girl at the Bookery"—he puffed out one cheek in extravagant travesty of the swelling—"the witch who warned me, or the little vixen who would cut my heart out with her deadly flax-hook?"

"I don't want to cut your heart out. And I don't want you to be in love with me," said downright Durie.

"Why not? Are you in love with someone else?"

"No. I don't even know what it means." She lifted her brows. "Why are you looking at me so?"

"I was wondering whether you are telling me the truth."

"I hate lies. A lie is a corpse, heavy about the neck of the liar like a dead fowl bound to a chicken-stealing dog."

"Who said that, Miss Wisdom?"

"Dad Andrews. In his book."

"The truth or nothing, then. You don't know what it is to be in love?"

"No."

"Or to have someone in love with you?"

"Oh," she answered negligently, "one gets cupidities. All actresses do."

"Cupidities?" he queried.

"That is what Mrs. Passerow terms them. Amorous missives. Sometimes by prepaid post. More often sent in by messenger. Even Mrs. Passerow gets them. With ribbons and Cupids on the corner."

"Do you answer them?" he demanded jealously.

"Mrs. Passerow answers them for me. She says it is good business for the show."

"What do they say?"

"Some say 'I love you' and some say 'Will you be mine?' and some say 'Fly with me' and some, 'May I have the honor of your company to supper?' One asked me to marry him. That was that silly Mr. Ayrault."

"Macel? Look out for him," warned Jans, flattering himself that he was being innocency's protector. "He's been up twice in breach-and-seduction cases already."

"It was the other one," she explained. "Mr. Guy."

"That little shaveling?" he snorted. "He's hardly out of panta-lettes."

"What does it matter? I'm not going to marry him or anyone. Wedlock is for fools."

"Where do you get such doctrine?"

"Dad Andrews' learned book on it." She quoted: " 'Wedlock is a bore to woman and a gyve to man. Between the altar and suicide, Wisdom repairs to the drugshop for arsenic.' And Mrs. Andrews told me that marriage is the horrid persecution of women by men. They were married folk, so they must know."

"I'm not a marrying man, myself," said Jans, quite the Corinthian now. The cult was fashionable at Harvard.

It was just as well, he thought, to let this strange, bewitching, independent young creature understand where he stood. After all, she could hardly be so innocent. . . . She couldn't be so ignorant as at times she seemed after sharing the free and easy life of the way-faring theatre. Jans was no militant seducer like Macel Ayrault. But, neither, he told himself, was he a bloodless anchorite, and Durie was a vision to stir any pulse. Well, he had given fair warn-ing. *Caveat puella* was the motto of the Corinthians.

He studied her as she sat relaxed among the cushions, strong and lithe and lovely, the softness of the full-lipped yet delicate mouth offset by the firmly molded chin, the slight flare of the nostrils be-neath the strong, clear-cut bridge of the nose, the questioning lus-trous eyes, and beneath them the faint darkening of the skin, sign of latent passion. And a line from a little-known poet named Shelley framed her with romance: "Tameless and swift and proud."

"So we are of like mind on marriage," he said smoothly. "But we might differ on the tender passion. Or perhaps you are ignorant of that."

"I know all about it," she said importantly, "from the romantic tales."

"Do you like reading romantic tales?"

"Not as much as high emprise and gallant adventure."

"And where they are mingled as in the old songs? Do you like that?"

"I don't know," she answered uncertainly.

He took up Laus Deo from the corner where he had carefully deposited it. "Shall I sing you one?"

"Yes."

He brushed his hand across the strings in a brief succession of chords.

"No," she said with a quaver. "Not that."

"Then you haven't forgotten." He plucked the strings with a firmer authority and sang, in half-strength:

> *"Where there is no place*
> *For the glow-worm to lie."*

"Don't."

"Why not?"

"I—I don't like it."

"Don't you, Durie?"

"It makes me feel—queer."

"Like cures like, says the great Hahnemann. Sing it yourself."

"Oh, no!" Her lips were parted, her breath fitful.

"Sing," he urged, and the stringed harmony pulsed in the air and enfolded her.

As if mesmerized, she forced her troubled breathing to steadiness. The contralto, fresh and rich and clearer now than when he had heard it in Harvard Yard took up the refrain.

> *"Where there is no space*
> *For receipt of a fly."*

He sang in his turn:

> *"Where the midge dare not venture*
> *Lest herself fast she lay."*

"Now, together," he said, and his soaring baritone carried the counter to the swell and lift of her melody:

> *"If Love come he will enter*
> *And will find out the way."*

As the chords died into silence, she sat tense, motionless. Her eyes heavy with question, gazed past him into some unexplored distance. She murmured something too low for him to understand.

Jans set the guitar back of him. It toppled and fell in a jangle of sounds; a string snapped. He reached down and took her nerveless hands, drawing her into his arms. Her eyes closed slowly, heavily; her lips parted beneath his. As their voices had blended together, so now his breath and hers merged and became one in the tide of passion. He felt the lassitude creep along her surrendering body. She gasped once. Her eyes opened. She set her hands against his breast, pressing herself back from him.

"I don't know anything about this, Jans," she murmured wonderingly.

"You don't have to know, darling." His own voice was not quite steady.

"I'm dizzy," she complained.

Heavy footsteps approached. "Who was that singing split-parts?" called Mr. Passerow.

Jans caught up Laus Deo. "Experimenting," said he.

The manager climbed the three steps to the roost and pushed open the door.

"Not without merit," he said, with patronizing approval. "But stiff. Wooden."

"Stiff?" repeated Jans.

"No roulades. No flourishes. Dull. Folk like their love ditties more graceful and twiddly. You've got a musical knack, young man. Set a bit of frillery to that, if you take me, and we might put you two on as a special request number. Try it again."

"My instrument lacks a string," said Jans, after a glance at his companion's face.

"Ah, well! Some other time. There's an odd-job in the taproom inquiring for you, Miss Amour."

"For *me?*" Durie asked. "Who could be looking for me?"

"I understood her to tell Mr. Baggo that she was the Queen of Sheba," he answered from the steps outside. "She has red hair on her head and red pepper under her tongue."

"Oh, I know!" cried Durie and made to follow. Jans put out a hand to her.

"Durie," he said softly.

"No. Don't, Jans. Let me go."

He stood aside. "But we've got to do the song again for Old Passerow."

"Not that song," she replied breathlessly.

"You still don't like it?" he teased.

"I never want to hear it again."

"Something else, then. Will you?"

"I don't know, Jans."

"Meet me after the show and we'll talk it over," he pleaded.

"Tonight?"

"Yes."

"Where?"

"I'll find a place."

"I'll come," she whispered. Her consent was that of a person under a spell.

She hurried out and in the hallway collided with Gypsy Vilas.

15

H EY—o, wench!"

"Oh, Gypsy, I *am* glad to see you. How did you know I was here?"

"Folks with pointed ears get to hear everything. Who you running away from?"

"Nobody."

"Prr-rrt!" commented Gypsy. "What makes your eyes look so queer? A body might think . . . Where you been?"

"In the fiddler's rest."

"Who with?"

"Mr. John Quinn."

"Don't know him."

"Yes, you do. It's Jans Quintard. But you mustn't tell."

Gypsy whistled untunefully. "And what were you doing in a fiddler's rest with Mr. John—Jans Quintard?"

"Singing."

"Not hymn-tunes, I'll be bound. Come in here." She led Durie into a vacant parlor. "Now tell Gypsy all about it."

Her ingrained reticence relaxed by the emotional shock she had undergone, Durie reported on the encounter. It was an unclear recital, but it told the sage little vagabond more than the speaker, herself, realized.

"Meet him after the show, huh?"

"Yes."

"Want to?"

"N-n-no, not exactly."

"Going to, though?"

"Yes."

"Why?"

"I don't know."

"Keep on and you'll find out. I expect you've found out a few things already, ain't you?"

"What things?"

"That you're a female, f'rinstance."

Durie stared at her, slowly changing color.

"You was bound to find it out sooner or later. But I don't reckon that romantical-voiced young guitar-tinkler is the safest teacher you could pick. Better keep your flax-knife handy."

"I always have."

Gypsy scrutinized her hard. "Hasn't anybody told you *anything?*"

"Fair Luna Wayne tried to. I wouldn't let her. I don't like to talk about those things. It makes me feel shamed."

"I think I'll have a parlyvoo with young Jans," said Gypsy importantly.

She found the utility man patching scenery—one of the dozen routine chores of his day.

"You wouldn't know me, Mr. Jans Quintard," she began. "I worked in your Number Two one summer."

"I'm John Quinn and I do know you. You fought the forewoman."

"She was an old ingler," Gypsy said. "What are you doing tonight after the show?"

"Packing up. And so to bed."

"Who with?"

Jans laid down his hammer, removed the last of several brads from between his lips, and observed the girl with calm speculation.

"Is this an invitation?"

"No. I'm no Molly Turnover, mister."

"Why, then, the flattering interest?"

"Not in you, my cocky."

"Let's have it."

"You're a gentleman, ain't you, for all your fusty clothes?"

"As you see me, Johnny-on-the-job. Willy-of-all-work. What's all this leading to?"

"Where are you taking her tonight?" said Gypsy bluntly.

"You know too much," he growled.

"Suppose you get her up Queer Street? What then?"

"I mean no harm."

"Said the fire to the flax."

"It's true," protested Jans.

"You never mean anything, you gentlemen. But things happen that nobody means," said the little wiseacre. "You leave that gal be, if you know what's best for both of you. Love ditties!" sniffed Gypsy. "Romantical tiddley-ums on the Spanish guitar. No more of your split-parts around here, if you please."

"Oh, hell!" said Jans. He picked up his hammer again. "All right, Gypsy, I'll be busy after the show. You tell her." He smiled. "You're good wood, young Gypsy."

She contemplated that smile and shook her head. "Well, I don't know as I blame her," she admitted. "Reckon I didn't get here none too soon."

"So you're going to be guardian of the sheepfold?"

"Yes, Mister He-wolf."

"I wonder just why?"

"I ask myself! Maybe I wisht I was a virgin again and so want to save little Durie."

"Are you so certain of her?"

"*I* am. But it would take a wedding ring and stamped paper for you to make sure," she gibed.

In the best Corinthian manner he said, "I'm not a marrying man, Miss Gypsy."

"Nor is she a marrying girl. So she says. But I'd sooner trust the pair of you in a church than a haystack. So good-bye to you, my songbird."

Durie was unresentful when her friend bore the message from Jans. She even felt a relief, as from some inner pressure. Now she wanted to know about the returned wanderer.

"Are you in work, Gypsy?"

The other nodded. "With a couple of birthdames." Noting the incomprehension in the other's face, she explained: "Midwives. We'll probably hitch onto you folks. I'm their telltale."

"I don't know what that is, either."

"It's this way. Wherever there's a crowd, like at circuses or fairs or corduroy theatre companies like yours, the Smyzer Sisters tail on with their wagon. My trade is standing at the entrance and watching for ladies with big bellies. I get their dates and sign 'em up and when there's a good enough list we swing around the circle and birth the brats. Three dollars a birth, five for twins. It ain't the slickest trade in the world, but I eat and sleep. Didja hear about Looby?"

"No."

"One of them swampmen got him for the reward. A bastard named Lucky Seven Smith."

"Oh, poor Looby! Where did they take him?"

"Jail. I dunno where. When does your show hit the logs?"*

"Tomorrow. For Ithaca."

In the morning a small, hooded wagon, carrying Gypsy and two fat, homely, and placid females of middle-age took the road behind the two-wagon outfit of the troupers. Jans soon had to pull out to let them pass, Gypsy waving him a derisively friendly signal from her driver's seat.

Roadfaring was a stern ordeal, particularly over the log-supplemented turnpikes of swamp and lowland, without which half of the Central New York towns would have been isolated in time of rains. They were inconceivably rough and hazardous. Even the best coach lines with genuine steel springs often delivered their passengers with broken ribs or dislocated shoulders; and at every stop the fares limped forth to ease their racked joints and comfort their bruised muscles. Pregnant women were banned. In the wet spells, schedules were abandoned.

But theatrical companies which depended upon their own motive power must "make town" or go hungry and bedless. And their ancient Conestogas, slung in leather straps, were worse than the poorest public coach. Fortunately for Jans, his four-horse equipage, cut down from six, was held to the pace of the smaller rig, which, being ox-drawn, was good for no more than three miles an hour under forced draught. His conniewagon, tattered, shabby of paint, leaky of cover but still staunch, was a carrier of scenery and props and a dormitory for the ladies of the troupe in emergency. The

*A reference to the corduroy roads.

150

other was a hybrid contraption, bearing the treasury—no great burden—the trunks, and three or four emergency hammocks.

When the weather was too foul to face, everybody piled into one or the other, and hung on for the dear life. Woe to the incautious who dozed off!

La Jeune Amour was one member of the troupe who seldom rode. Impervious to weather, by virtue of her long experience on the roads, she strode blithely along, well in advance of the lumbering cavalcade, coming back to lend a hand and contribute shrewd advice when something bogged down. The sight of her was the one mitigating feature of the route to Jans, precariously perched upon the lazyboard, a white-oak plank projecting from the near side of the wagon. It was about all that he did see of her for a week of one-night stands where there was no rest between unloading, performing, reloading, and taking the road again. Jans could not even say that the girl was avoiding him. There was simply no opportunity for their being together.

The same did not apply to Gypsy Vilas. She made opportunity. Relinquishing the reins to one or the other of the birthdames, she would amble nonchalantly alongside the big conniewagon and gossip, or, when the roading was smooth, cling like a small and impudent bird—a redheaded woodpecker, thought Jans—beside him on the lazyboard. Gypsy's gossip was a compendium of the itinerary's news. Before she had been with them a week, she knew more about the company's internal relationships, factions, jealousies and cross currents than Jans and Durie together would have discovered in a year. All this was at Jans' command, who found it a relief from the tedium of the way. The news would come out piecemeal, such as:

"Old Passover (her irreverent soubriquet for the manager) hit the Lit-Lot (the Literature Lottery which, though outlawed, continued to advertise and conduct its business openly) yesterday for twenty-five. He'll be soft as soap for a week."

Or, "Tim Baggo is readying for a sozzle. You'd better work up his part in *Tailor in Distress.*"

Or again, "Fair Luna's jealous of Durie."

"Why?" said Jans.

"Too comely. Or maybe on account of you."

"Me! Fair Luna? You're daft."

"Luny thinks you're rich. And she knows who you are. Anyway, she suspicions."

Jans frowned. "How did she come by that?"

"Not knowing, can't say. *Are* you writing a play?"

"And how did *you* come by that?"

"Tow-rope news," replied Gypsy, employing her accustomed formula, equally useful for explanation or evasion. "Luny'll be after you for a part."

"She's got the possibilities of a good actress," said Jans thoughtfully.

"Anan! She turns my bile when she simpers."

"Nonetheless with proper coaching she could do something." He was quite positive about that. "She's nobody's fool, the Fair Luna."

"She doesn't know as much as Durie and she ain't half as well-favored," declared Durie's friend jealously.

"Durie's beautiful. But she's an amateur."

It was no surprise to Jans when, as he was furnishing the set-up for the next performance, Miss Wayne approached him, addressing him with the formality which the members of the troupe expected from one another.

"When is your play to be exhibited, Mr. Quinn?"

"It is hardly more than outlined as yet," said Jans.

"Will there be a part in it suitable to my person?" she asked with an upward glance from melting brown eyes.

"What kind of part would you prefer?"

"Romantical Indian maidens are much the fashion now."

"Like *Metamora*, the prize play? Or Mr. Cooper?"

"I've never seen Mr. Cooper act. I like a plot where I would save the life of the handsome officer."

"Like Pocahontas."

"Mm. Yes. I suppose so," said she doubtfully.

"And you'd be wedded and live happy forever more?"

"But there'd be a lot of diverting matter first," she said vivaciously. "Combats and captures and a fair and false temptress trying to seduce the officer's affection from me. Mrs. Alwyn has fine black hair; she could play that. And you could put in a laughable part for Mr. Baggo, and a dignified chieftain for Mr. Archbold, and—and

". . ." she broke off, laughing self-consciously. "Anybody would think I was writing the play, not you."

"I'm not," said Jans. "Not that kind of play."

"Why not?"

"It wouldn't be true."

Her eyes widened with genuine astonishment. "Who wants a drama to be true? They want it to be transporting, like the *Wept of Wish-ton-Wish.*"

"I shouldn't like to set myself up against Mr. Cooper," said Jans modestly.

"What kind of play are you composing?"

"Would you really like to know?" He swung a chair into position. "That's a mill."

"A *mill?*"

"Yes, a factory. You can hear the looms clacking inside."

"Who can? I?"

"The audience. You can, too, of course. You're sitting on the hillside back of the mill."

"Am I the rich mill owner's beautiful daughter?" she asked hopefully.

"No. You're an operative."

"A working girl? I won't play any such three-line part," she pouted.

"It's the lead."

"The *lead?* A mill-hussy the lead! Dressed in coarse, horrid crocus, I suppose."

"Something like that."

"And what am I doing?"

"Crying."

"What for?"

"You think you're going to lose your job."

"Why?"

"Because you're going to have a baby."

"On the stage?"

"Of course not on the stage."

"I mean are you putting it in the play that I'm supposed—well, that the lead is supposed to be in that nasty condition?"

"Yes."

"I think it's crazy," she asserted.

"Things like that do happen."

"Not to the lead. Whose baby is it?"

"The mill owner's son's."

"Oh!" She brightened. "Then I'm secretly married to him."

"No, you're not married at all."

"Oh, fie, Mr. Quinn!" said Fair Luna archly. "What do you want to write a play like that for?"

"Because nobody's ever done it."

"And nobody ever will. If they did, no artist would play it. And if anybody was fool enough to, nobody'd pay money to see it."

"Probably not," agreed Jans. "But I'm not interested in Indian maidens, and I never met any royal kings or even dukes so I can't write about them. I can only write what I know."

"That's mortal dumb of you," said the girl fretfully. "You'd better throw your silly mill wench away and earn your keep by writing a nice, poetical posy for my testimonial."

"Something in the 'Peep-peep, Sweet Bird,' measure?" he asked slyly.

"More spirited. I'll speak to Mr. Passerow about it."

Plainly there was nothing profitable to be had from this young sprout, in the professional line. But she held to her original theory that he had money. It was worth trying. True, she was practically certain of being able to finance her testimonial from another quarter. But there was no harm in having two strings to one's bow.

"Our third evening at Geneva is to be set aside for my benefit," she informed him.

"May it be all you deserve," said Jans politely.

She glanced at him, sidelong. "Geneva is a costly town," she murmured.

"All the better, isn't it, if they are used to spending freely?"

She sighed. "I was thinking of the cost to me. I don't really know how I am to meet it."

"Why should there be any cost to you?" asked Jans, puzzled. This was a phase of the profession that he had not yet encountered.

"You *are* a greeny! On eight-a-week can I afford the testimonies?"

"Testimonies?"

"Floral wreaths. A goblet. A cup," she explained, impatiently. "Maybe a richly embellished scroll: 'Tribute to the Superior Art and Beauteous Charms of the Accomplished Miss Wayne from her Admiring Public.' That kind of thing."

"Doesn't the admiring public do that?"

"Maybe in New York. Not here. We have to buy our own."

"I'll speak to Mr. Passerow about it."

"No! No! No! Stupid stock!"

"What do you want me to do?"

She moved close to him, so close that he could feel the warmth of her thigh, the stir of her breath. "Just a few shillings," she murmured. "Twelve or fifteen. You wouldn't miss it; you with your rich uncle."

"My uncle and I are not on terms," he said stiffly.

She flounced away from him. "Johnnie Stingygut! I know where I can get more dollars than you ever saw in your penny-pinching life."

Nose in air, she made a haughty exit to the bar to borrow quill, ink and letter-sheet (a penny the lot) and concoct a letter of pathetic appeal. Unless the Kind & Generous Sen'r. Vryling came to the aid of the Writer, now in a state of Finansial Dissmay, her Gala Testimonial in Geneva, N. Y. would turn out a Mournfull Calamitty. Could he now find it in his Benevolents to meet her there Wensday Week on which occasion he could be Assured of a Warm Wellcome?

"That'll fetch the old buck," Fair Luna told Durie who had acceded to her request to correct the orthography. "It ought to be worth ten dollars on the benefit silver and, like as not, wine for supper." She yielded to an impulse of generosity. "Would you like to sup with us?"

"No, thank you."

"He's rich. And mortal fashionable."

"Are you enamored of him?"

"Fiddle-faddle-foodle!" said Miss Wayne. "He's an old man. Forty and better, I wouldn't wonder. But mortal dandy. A regular old beau."

She was confident enough to notify Manager Passerow, who ordered a poem from Jans. But the poet's muse declined to work for

Fair Luna. Several promising starts took a turn wholly inapplicable to Miss Wayne's pert charms. Durie kept getting between the lines. Unable to exorcise her, Jans surrendered to his wayward and unbusinesslike fancy, and in a week of odd hours snatched between jobs, produced and polished a lyric which, he felt, could be translated into the very expression of La Jeune Amour's young loveliness.

But could she personify its light and dainty spirit? Every rendition of hers, under Mrs. Passerow's heroics-school tutelage, had been stilted and hifalutin. The part of the debutante-coquette conceived by him called for simplicity and directness. He could see himself rehearsing an unwilling and perhaps stubborn pupil and striving to make her unlearn most of what she had been taught.

Opportunely, Mrs. Passerow came to him with a request. She had several difficult parts to learn for the Geneva engagement of a full week. Would Jans relieve her of part of La Jeune Amour's coaching? Jans said that he would, provided the young lady made no objection.

Durie was serene when she came to him. There was an unspoken question in her eyes. He caught, now and again, a covert glance, as if she were speculating upon what manner of creature he was, harboring what potentialities of disturbance or harmfulness. But this was business and the best way to ease her mind, he shrewdly judged, was to ignore what had passed between them and proceed upon a strictly professional basis, for the present.

He put her through her minor roles with growing discouragement. She had her lines pat for she was a quick study. But to him, schooled in expert rendition of the metropolitan productions, everything was on a false note. At the end of a trying half hour, he said, "Rest." Then: "I've found something for you."

"To publish in the bills?" she said, expectantly.

"No. To perform. But I don't know whether you can do it."

"Why shouldn't I be able to do it?" she asked with that candid glance of hers which he had already found himself awaiting with a quickening pulse. "I could exhibit it at my testimonial."

"What testimonial? Are *you* going to have a testimonial?"

"I suppose so. When my turn comes around. Young Mr. Ayrault said he would attend and fetch all his friends."

Jans, with his new-gained knowledge concerning this sort of entertainment, frowned. What would young Mr. Ayrault expect in return? It was not the sort of question that he would put to her—not until his puzzlement as to her character was resolved. He handed her his script. She read the title: "A Dismissal" and continued through the first stanza, her lips silently forming the words:

> *The leading of apes is a story*
> *Of days and of dames that have vanished.*
> *A damsel is ne'er in her glory*
> *Before thirteen lovers are banished.*
> *My Washington cousin had twenty*
> *In the reign of good Mr. Monroe,*
> *And surely they now are more plenty.*
> *So I'll love you no longer. Oh, no!*

"Oh!" she breathed through parted lips. "I think it's dicty! I could wear an embroidered muslin with ribbons and carry a striped parasol."

"Doubtless. But you might better be considering your lines," said he with a touch of grimness. "Let's begin. Make your entry."

She walked off and pranced on, head tossing and neck arched like a high-schooled mare. Jans groaned.

"Now whinny," he said.

"What?"

"You've done everything else like a horse."

"I think you're very disobliging," she said with dignity. "Mrs. Passerow taught me that."

"I know. 'Enter bridling.' We're in a ballroom, not a stable. Try again."

After several repetitions he allowed her to read the stanza, but only to the end of the second line when he broke in. "Keep your hands down."

"Can't I gesture gracefully?" she said, aggrieved.

"I'll tie your hands back of you if you try," he threatened.

With a conscientious effort at restraint she read as far as the final line, maintaining a reasonable degree of quietude. But at the conclusion her dramatic instincts surged up victoriously and she deliv-

157

ered the finale with the embellishments which she deemed proper to the sentiment.

"So" (simper and sidelong glance of coquetry) "I'll love you no longer." (hip-waggle) "Oh, no!" (slump)

"Oh, my God!" said Jans.

"Don't you like it?" she demanded, disappointed.

"When I want you to do the Rutland Wriggle, I'll inform you," he snapped. "Here! I'll show you."

He went through the stanza. She conscientiously tried to imitate him and looked anxiously for approval, which she did not get.

"Don't simper. Don't twist your waist. Don't, for God's sake, look coy! Try to forget the antics of Miss Patty Pouff."

She set the manuscript down, went to him, and looked up into his eyes.

"Why are you being unkind to me?"

"I could be very much kinder."

"I don't want you to be. Not that way."

"Why not?" he asked fatuously.

"It's—it's dangerous. Gypsy says . . ."

"Damn Gypsy!"

"If you do it any more I can't work with you."

"Would you mind that?"

"I do think you're severe. But you can teach me what I don't know."

"If you admit that, it's a start," he retorted.

At the next rehearsal Durie was docility itself. Jans began to entertain hopes of her as a possible entr'acte recitalist, though nothing more. Her voice, with its faint hint of huskiness, its provocatively feminine undertones and its flexible cadences was charming. She could look the very incarnation of youthful innocence. She even showed signs of getting into the spirit of the sprightly little poem. He drilled her with loving patience. Each time she would thank him sweetly.

"I do so want to be a good actress. Do you think I shall be?"

"Yes," lied Jans.

16

THEATRICAL life Durie found to be largely chores. Half her
waking hours were given over to odd jobs. There were costumes to
be refreshed, scenery to be painted, harness, running gear, tents,
provisions, playbills and tickets to be looked after. Anything that
others had no time to do was passed over to her as handymaid. She
bore with it patiently for the sake of the golden hours when she
was transformed into La Jeune Amour. This was her presto change
into enchantment.

Even rehearsals were glamorous. The company was always rehearsing—before and after performances, at wayside stops where a
stable or a granary might serve as substitute for a theatre, in the
open when nightfall caught them on the road. Bills must be
changed frequently, sometimes at the last moment because a stage
was too small or a set had been damaged in transit or Mr. Baggo
was drunk or Fair Luna had the vapors, or merely to suit the vary-
ing tastes of Owego which wanted song-and-dance farce or of
Lockport which leaned to heroics. Durie had no private life and
little time to miss it.

Already she had taken on the coloration of her environment. She
was a good trouper. That the demands were often harsh, the career
always precarious mattered nothing to her. Inexperience saved her
from realization of the company's status. Nothing told her that her
compeers were shiftless adventurers, improvident and, for the most
part, incompetent human remnants, the tattered fringe of the profession; that the plays in which she acted her multiple and always
minor roles were the mutilated remains of cheap balderdash, rudely
trimmed and adjusted to the exigencies of an insufficient staff,
tawdry scenery and makeshift stages. She had no standards

whereby to measure the deficiencies, as had Mr. John Quinn. For her it was the enchanted realm of the Drama. She was of the glittering, the uplifted confraternity of Thespis. The light that never was on sea or land shed its luster from the sooty flare of the footlamps. She loved it all.

That was a proud and hopeful day for La Jeune Amour when Mrs. Passerow, more out of kindness than confidence, gave her some leads to understudy. Her delight was mitigated when she learned that her training, hitherto fitfully administered by the manager's wife, would be transferred to Mr. John Quinn. That amateur of Harvard Yard!

"What can he teach me?" she asked.

"My dear, he has acted at the famous Bowery Theatre."

"Walk-ons," said Durie.

"Association with the aristocracy of the profession cannot but leave its mark," Mrs. Passerow replied. "Mr. Passerow thinks well of his knowledge."

"He's a paltry actor."

"It is true that he lacks the divine fire and exhibits little sensibility," the older woman admitted. She sighed. "I cannot comprehend this modern tendency to subdue emotion to a dead and dull level, as I am told, they do in Philadelphia and New York."

Naturalism had, indeed, begun to assert itself in the higher ranks of the profession. But the Thalians and their ilk still tore a passion to tatters by the rant-and-roar method. Besides Jans, only Mr. Passerow and perhaps Tim Baggo had an inkling of the new art.

Durie sought out Jans.

"Mrs. Passerow says that you are to rehearse me."

"I'd like that if only because it would give me a chance to see you once in a while," he said. "Would you like it?"

"I'm not sure. I want to learn all I can of my profession."

"But you don't believe that I have anything to teach you?"

A frown wrinkled Durie's candid brow. "Your instruction might be better than none at all," she reflected. "At least I'd be learning my lines."

"There might be a difficulty, though."

"What?"

"If I'm to rehearse you, it must be in my way, not yours."

"I'm not very biddable," she admitted.

"How could you be, with that chin!"

"Never mind my chin. And I wish you wouldn't look at me that way. It makes me feel queer."

"Me, too," said Jans cheerfully. "That's why I do it."

"About rehearsing: in cases where I was sure I'm right . . ."

"You always would be, wouldn't you?" he said mildly. "Not right. But sure."

"Never mind," she returned, with dignity. "Shall we try the passage from *Marinetta* where the British officer makes his evil advances? I'm quite proficient in that."

"Let's hear."

"You can be Mr. Passerow—Colonel de Lacy, I mean."

"Suppose you run through your part first."

She did so, following Mrs. Passerow's method in general, but improving upon it by pitching it several tones higher in emotional stress. When she reached her lofty defiance of the villainous Briton, Jans put his hands to his ears.

"Whew!" he said. "Ease down."

"But I must be fervent," she protested. "The part calls for maidenly sensibility."

"It doesn't call for yelling like Damsel Davis, the Voice from Dublin."

"I don't yell."

"Let's see. I'll try it with you as the Colonel. I approach with a libidinous leer."

Durie thrust forth both arms, declaimed, "Unhand me, ruffian!" and performed some complicated calisthenics.

"What's that?" Jans inquired.

"I'm repulsing you."

"You'll split your bodice and then where will you be?"

"I don't think you're delicate."

"Try it again."

"Unhand me, ruffian!"

"Don't be a windmill."

"Oh, dear! You've thrown me quite off my lines. . . . Oh, yes . . . What do I see? Heavens!"

"Omit the hand to the brow."

"Heavens! T'is hee-ee-ee-ee-ee!"

"Haw!" said Jans.

"Oh!" said Durie.

"This is no use," Jans muttered.

"That's the way Mrs. Passerow reads it."

"I hope she goes on reading it."

"You don't want me to have the part?" Her eyes reproached him.

"God knows, I don't! For your own sake."

The small chin set firmer than ever. "You wait, Mr. John Quinn."

"Too much John Quinn. Too much La Jeune Amour. Couldn't we be Durie and Jans again?"

"I think it's better this way," she said calmly.

"But I like you better as Durie. If our life is to be divided into compartments like this . . ."

"Our life?" she interrupted.

"Into compartments," he insisted. "Work and—us. I prefer us."

"This isn't rehearsing, Ja—— Mr. Quinn."

"No, this is real life. Are you afraid of reality, Durie?"

"I don't want it to be a reality," she said with a quick, indrawn breath.

"That's past prayer," he retorted. "For both of us."

"It isn't! It isn't! Oh, let's rehearse again."

At the end she asked, "Is that any better?"

But he could only shake his head despondently.

La Jeune Amour's big chance came at Auburn, a week after that first drill. In his capacity as courier, Jans had advised against the town as being sophisticated, superior and a touch cynical, only to be overruled by Mr. Passerow. They were to open with *The Gambler's Fate!!!* (always play-billed with triple exclamation points to emphasize the horridness of the fate), and follow with the heroic American drama, *Marinetta.* On the morning of their arrival, Mrs. Passerow appeared with reddened eyes and nose, complaining of a running rheum. In vain did her solicitous husband lay out a shilling in leeches and medicaments; she did get through the evening performance but was almost voiceless next morning. Mr. Passerow and Jans put their heads together in consultation. Durie's hopes rose.

She walked up North Street toward the burying ground, conning her lines, when a familiar hail from a lodging stoop halted her.

"Hey-o! Wench!"

"Hello, Gypsy. When did you get here?"

"Couple of nights ago. What d'you think of Auburn?"

"It's a dicty place."

"It's a handsome town," Gypsy allowed, "but the men are a slack-backed lot."

"Are they? They look stout enough to me."

"Not as husbands. There aren't three big bellies out of a hundred wives," complained the practical Gypsy. "I got only two prospectives in a day's work. No wonder Rochester's got the pace of 'em. What you doing between now and curtain?"

"Nothing special."

"Let's go visit the model prison."

"What for?"

"To view the jailbirds. Everybody does. It's the pride of the town."

"I can't bear to see caged things. Not even animals."

"Oh, come on," Gypsy urged. "Don't be so mollycoddly. They say it's a rare sight. I got a friend there."

Against the judgment of her heart, Durie yielded. Gypsy's friend, whom she had encountered at a vendu the day before, proved to be a youngish keeper, spruce enough in his uniform, but with avaricious little eyes which he kept fixed upon Gypsy. His name was Gospel. No sooner had the visitors paid their sixpences at the gate than Durie regretted her weakness. First they were taken to the cell tiers to inspect the accommodations on which the prison authorities prided themselves. Each cubicle was seven feet long, four feet across and seven feet high. It was furnished with a basin, a slop-bowl, and a two-foot plank, raised four inches above the dark floor. This served as a bed, with two unclean cotton blankets as bedding. A small barred opening in the door admitted light which was little better than darkness and air which might have been wafted from a cesspool. A sick prisoner eating salted mush from a wooden bowl with his fingers, no utensils being permitted, was the sole occupant of this tier. Gypsy spoke to him, but he only shook his head.

"They get flogged for conversation," their cicerone said with a grin.

In the refreshing air of the courtyard the girls looked about them with modified repulsion. Listless figures were moving around in the lethargy of the ill-fed, performing casual jobs under the lax supervision of a guard. Their escort took Gypsy over to meet the fellow and the three were presently engaged in lively converse. Durie wandered idly toward an open window. From within, the clacking of looms was the only sound, as the inmates wove patriotically designed blue-and-white coverlets for the trade.

A rod away a lumpish fellow dabbed listlessly at a window casing with a dirty rag. A faint, unmelodious hum reached her ears.

"Ooolie-oolie-aylie-oo.
Oolie-aylie-oo."

Durie's head jerked up.

"Pss-ss-sst!" It was a warning signal.

"Looby!"

"Don't speak," he said almost soundlessly out of the side of his loose mouth. "Move along."

She tried to make her approach seem casual.

"I didn't know you were here."

"Seven years," he said brokenly.

"Oh, how dreadful! Isn't there something I can do?"

"Got any chawin'?"

"No, I'll send some in."

"The keeps'll prink it. You gotta fetch it, yourself. Pss-sst! They're comin'."

Gypsy was strolling toward them with Mr. Gospel in close attendance. She stopped abruptly. Durie heard her say, "There's a fella I know."

"Which one?"

"Yonder by the window."

"That poor zany? He's kinda tetched in the wits."

"Born that way," she said. "Could we have a little gab with him?"

"It's against the rules. But for you, Miss, I'd do that and more." He hailed, "Hey, you—Two-naught-five! Don't hardly know his own number," he interpolated as Looby slowly turned his cringing body to the call of authority. "Move on to the corner window." The convict obeyed. Where he now stood, an angle of the wall partly concealed him.

"The P.K. comes around on the hour," Mr. Gospel said. "You got a good five minutes. Talk low. I'll watch." He lounged around the corner.

Looby began to cry. "I'll die," he babbled. "I'll never get outa here alive."

Scanning the ravaged and vacant face, Durie thought it more than likely. He began plucking gingerly at the back of his shirt, groaning as he loosed it. Gypsy peered down the neck.

"All scabbed up," she said with indrawn breath.

"They whup me two, three times a week."

"What for?" Durie demanded angrily.

"'Cause I can't keep lockstep," was the listless response. "And they whup me 'cause I forget and sing."

"Much you got to sing about!" Gypsy said.

"You gotta sing or something or you go crazy and butt your head on the stones. Cancha get me out?" he implored.

The girls looked at one another. "How?"

"There's ways. Four fellas got away awhile ago."

"I heard something about that," said Gypsy to her companion.

"Time's getting short," the keeper warned, thrusting his face around the angle.

"Mr. Gospel, do prisoners ever escape?" Durie asked in an insinuating tone.

"Why, yes, yes. There was an evasion last month."

"How did it happen?" she asked, looking straight at him.

"I heard they had friends outside."

"And did the friends have money?"

He grinned. "Must have, I guess."

"How much money?"

"Hundred dollars. That's what I heard tell."

"Meet us for supper before the show. We'll talk it over quietly," Durie said.

"Quiet's the word." He winked.

Outside the high stone wall, Gypsy asked, "Have you got a hundred dollars, Durie?"

"No."

"How much you got?"

"Fifty."

"That's the fifty you been saving for hard luck."

"Yes," Durie gulped.

"Don't you do it, gal."

"We can't leave him to die there, Gypsy."

"No, I guess we can't. I'd pay half, but I'll never see that much rhino."

"Do you think he'll take fifty?"

The girl's lips tightened into the line of resolution. "I'll see he does."

Mr. Gospel came to the rendezvous conspicuously scented for conquest but with the money-gleam undimmed in his ferret eyes. Two to one, the girls beat him down from his original demand of one hundred dollars to seventy-five, and thence by bitterly argued fives, threes, and ones, to sixty, where he dug in.

"And I wouldn't do that for my own sister," he averred pathetically.

"I ain't your sister," Gypsy said.

"That's the point." He ogled her and she played her trump card.

"Harky, my bucko. If we talked it over tonight, private-like, would you listen to reason?"

"All night?" said Mr. Gospel.

"Gypsy! No!" Durie cried.

"Sixty stands, then," Mr. Gospel said sourly.

"How else we going to get Looby out?" asked Gypsy reasonably.

"I'll borrow the money. I'll—I'll take up a collection. I'll get an advance from Mr. Passerow." Gypsy giggled derisively. "I'll do something." She fumbled in her waistband for her little current hoard, turning out three bits and some odd pennies. Gypsy profited by the diversion of her attention to wink at Mr. Gospel.

"Oh, hell!" he said gallantly. "I'll take the fifty."

Durie handed over the amount. "When will he get out?"

Within his limitations, Keeper Gospel was an honest man. "I want to play fair with you ladies," he said. "It ain't so much the getting out; that's easy. It's the keeping out. We can cut him loose next week. But there'll be a reward on him. And by my guess, if the sheriff don't get him, the marshmen will."

Through tight lips, Durie said, "We've got to give him his chance."

"Tell him to get word to us," Gypsy added. "We'll look after him."

Durie left them over a final drink and went to study her lines. Upon reporting at the theatre, she was told that Mrs. Passerow was going on, ill though she was.

From the rise of the curtain, the performance ran into foul weather. The whole cast was shaky on the lines; the improvisations were clumsy. Halfway through the first act, Mr. Crosbie forgot and put in a passage which Jans, whose business it was to know and defer to local prejudices, had carefully cut out, declaiming with effect the lines:

> *"Stone walls do not a prison make,*
> *Nor iron bars a cage."*

Though marked, the effect was not what the actor had expected of his exalted rendition. For Auburn, having swapped its chances of the Erie Canal for the solider State's Prison and got the worst of the bargain, was sorely sensitive on the subject and prone to scent insult at the slightest allusion. The hoots and jeers which greeted the Crosbie eloquence ruined the scene and so discomposed Mrs. Passerow that she collapsed. The curtain was rung down and La Jeune Amour rung in.

Before a less experienced audience, the neophyte might have won through. But Auburn was used to the best; it had applauded Kean and Booth, been thrilled by Clara Fisher and Mrs. Austin, and contorted its sides over Yankee Hill and the inimitable Mr. Placide. The opening of *The Gambler's Fate!!!* had been received with bare tolerance. Now the small and skeptical house was not improved in temper by the Crosbie *faux pas*. Nevertheless the first impression of the understudy, her youth and loveliness and the husky charm of her enunciation won modified favor over her awkwardness and too statuesque posturing. Jans, watching from the flies where he was contributing his useful services as off-stage music, noted with approval her growing confidence, with misgivings her obvious self-satisfaction. Presently she began to let herself go.

"Keep it low. Keep it low," he cautioned.

The advice won from the elated actress only a patronizing smile. She felt that she was doing very well. Her big scene was coming;

she would show the superior Mr. John Quinn what she could do with that.

"Unhand me, ruffian!"

The first effect of her whoop of defiance was to disconcert the musical accompaniment, resulting in a wild quaver on the flute and a melancholy discord from Laus Deo. This, however, was hardly noticed in the more sensational sequel. In the fervor of her rejection of the military lecher's advances, La Jeune Amour forgot the strength of her trained muscles. Her thrust in defence of her threatened virtue was less a maidenly gesture than a solid one-two to the midriff. It brought from the surprised Mr. Passerow a realistic grunt of quite startling volume. The lethargic audience showed signs of awakening interest.

"Poke him again, pretty!" called an encouraging voice.

La Jeune Amour lifted her stressful tones above the applause. She warmed to the realization that she was stirring them from their languor. With a start so violent that it enlisted the co-operation of every muscle in her body, she clapped both hands to her brow.

"What do I see? Heavens, 'tis he!" she chanted.

A jocose patron in the fifth row caught the rhythm and carried it on.

"Fiddle-de-dum! Fiddle-dee-dee!"

"A penny a peep through the wonderglass," piped a neighbor with a very creditable imitation of a street hawker.

Durie faltered, her complacency shaken by the ensuing laughter. Jans' steady, comforting voice threw her the next line, adding warningly, "Play it down! Play it down!"

Poor Durie stumbled desperately on with contributory but unhelpful lines from in front. The curtain left her white and shaking. Jans put out an arm to comfort her.

"Steady, Durie. Don't show them you're scared."

"I'm not. I'm infuriated."

"Shall I put on Emma's costume and understudy you?"

She forced a forlorn grin.

"You can do it, Durie. Take it quietly. Play down."

"You're always telling me to play down."

"And you're always overplaying."

With a resentful determination to show him, Durie did play down throughout the remainder of the drama. The result was colorless and dreary. Jans sweated and fumed over his guitar. Out front the audience rustled and coughed and yawned. Five disgusted patrons walked out. The other actors tried to compensate for La Jeune Amour's insufficiency by overplaying, which served only to point glaringly the incongruity. The final curtain was drawn upon hoots and groans.

"Teapot acting!" barked Manager Passerow as she came off.

"What does that mean?" Durie asked miserably.

"You stick your arm out like the spout and mutter like the steam."

"I don't care," she retorted, stung to defiance.

"Two dollars fine," the manager snapped.

Durie turned upon Jans. "So much for your playing down!" she said wrathfully.

"You were no worse at the end than at the beginning."

"Are you deliberately trying to be injurious?"

"I'm telling you the truth."

"He is, Durie." Gypsy, having paid her way in to witness her friend's triumph, had come backstage. "A fine whoobub you made of it."

"I did as he bade me," returned poor Durie, "and it cost me a fine."

"I'll pay it," Jans said shortly.

"I'd scorn to accept it at your hands."

"You're behaving like a pampered child."

Criticize a woman, wrote Adam Personius Andrews, and she asks herself not *Is this true?* but *How can I best confute the calumny?*

It was one of the passages which Durie had often pondered, but in reference to others. In the middle of the night, she awoke, recalled it, and with a painful effort applied it to herself. She sought out Jans in the morning.

"Will you rehearse me again?"

"Not as Emma, I'm afraid. The bill is changed. I'm sorry."

"I knew it would be," she said bravely. "Perhaps I'd be better in something else. Could we try over your poem again?"

"Come up to the stage."

She went through the opening stanza. The throaty richness of her voice had a quality of physical enticement. By itself it would have undermined his power of criticism. But she could not restrain herself from appropriate and expressive gestures. He contemplated her with a thoughtful frown, then stepped back into the wings and emerged behind her.

"Hands at your sides," he ordered.

She obeyed.

He looped a cord around her several times and drew it tight.

"I can't recite when I'm trussed like a fowl," she complained.

"Nothing else will keep you from waving your arms like a pair of flails. Second stanza. On the last line you may shake your head twice, not more. Slowly and thoughtfully. On 'no longer' and 'oh, no!' And just breathe the 'no'."

She moved her arms uncomfortably, sighed (with no effect upon his resolute austerity) and began:

> "I saw you at Madame Geroni's
> Gallanting Lavinia Larme."

"Halt!" from Jans.

"Can't I even move?"

"Why should you?"

"I can't stand stick-in-the-mud while I'm rendering my part."

"You can in this part."

"I don't believe it's right, Jans."

"Shall I try Fair Luna in it?"

She wrinkled her nose at him, wriggled a little to ease the pressure of the cord, and resumed:

> "I saw you at Madame Geroni's
> Gallanting Lavina Larme
> Like a tame, promenading Adonis
> With his goddess tucked under his arm.
> If I waltz with a chargé, you're worried
> Although I'm but sixteen or so.
> If I flirt with Fitz Herbert, you're horrid.
> So I'll love you no longer, oh, no!"

"Gee-ee-ee!" It was a long exhalation of wonder from offstage. Gypsy stepped forward. "What you got the gal hogtied for?"

"I'm going to sell her in the Baltimore Slave Mart," said Jans. "What am I bid?" He loosed the swathings.

"He won't allow me a gesture," said Durie, fluttering her hands. "I think it's tepid."

"It ain't," said Gypsy with conviction. "But," she added more doubtfully, "it ain't much like acting."

"It isn't meant to be," Jans said.

"Then what am I an actress for?" demanded Durie.

"Oh, Lord!" said Jans.

"Harky, Quinn. Can't I get a job with the troupe?" Gypsy asked.

"Do you, too, aspire to be a queen of drama?"

"I was with a medic one summer."

"That's a preparation," he said politely.

"Wager I'd be as good as Durie."

He examined the pert little face with its careless eyes and loose, humorous mouth. "I daresay you'd be better."

"Why?" demanded Durie.

"She knows more and thinks less," a reply which was little to the taste of either girl.

"Act or not, I'd like to go along to be near my pal," continued Gypsy, "and to keep an eye on you, my bucko."

"I haven't the disposal of positions," Jans said. "But I doubt if Passerow would accept that as a qualification. However, I'll try him."

Manager Passerow was not interested in adding to his troupe and so told Jans in explicit language.

Apprised of her rejection, Gypsy said easily, "I'll hang on for a while. One breeding-pen's as good as another for my old milkers. Something'll turn up."

17

THAT whimwhamsical fellow, Mr. Tim Baggo, was sipping his
morning antifogmatic at the bar of the Farmer's Hotel in Geneva
when he sighted a fellow player busy with pen and ink at a
table.

"Hah!" said he. "Genius labors." He struck an attitude and
declaimed:

> *"Attend, my muse! Inspire me with a rhyme.*
> *My belly tells me it is breakfast time."*

Jans, just up from free lodgings in the clean and fragrant
stable-loft, grunted. The buffo strolled over and began, "Have
you heard the one about . . . ?"

"Yes," said Jans.

". . . the blackamoor wench, all toggled out in new finery . . ."

"I know. She'd been ruint. But I've got to fix this up."

Mr. Baggo peered over his shoulder. "Dotch me if it ain't for
the Fair Luna! Is she going to exhibit it at her testimonial?"

"Not unless you let me alone."

"She'll have little time to con it today," observed Mr. Baggo
comfortably. "Her aged but loving heart is arriving post-haste.
The Honorable Senator Lovatt." He hummed the refrain of a
popular ditty, "A Kind Old Man Came Wooing."

"This morning?" asked Jans, lifting his head.

The comedian nodded. "They'll be merchanding for silver
goblets and wax-flower wreaths. So you may as well join me in
a snifter."

"Not here, he won't get no drink," interposed the sour-faced
tapman.

172

"Hel-lo! What bug has bit your bum?" inquired Mr. Baggo inelegantly.

Jans grinned. "Our friend, Mr. Clonny, got careless with the ticket receipts and some of 'em dropped right into his open pocket."

"It's a damn, dirty lie and I'll be evens with you for it," growled the barman with a malevolent glare.

"We'll have a fat house tomorrow night," prophesied the buffo. "The Senator's taken fifteen pit seats for Fair Luna's benefit."

Reverting to his toil, Jans found time to speculate upon his uncle's probable attitude toward himself. Would he be treated to an outburst of forensic denunciation? Or would the Honorable loftily ignore the exsistence of a insignificant John Quinn? For preference Jans would have chosen the latter.

At high noon the inn yard cobbles rang to the hooves of a spirited pacer and the steel-rimmed wheels of a brilliant-hued gig, blue upon white with crimson running gear. Senator Vryling Lovatt in a bottle-green greatcoat with large nacre buttons, relinquished the ribbons and hopped nimbly out while his traveling groom unstrapped a studded and initialed trunk, shouldered it, and made an impressive entrance. Mine Host David Wilson trotted forward to welcome the important guest.

"Would you wish an arrangement of rooms, sir?" he inquired, with an effect of being very confidential and discreet.

"Tomorrow, tomorrow," responded the plump and dapper traveler. "For tonight your best chamber will suffice."

"Already reserved for Your Honor. We are strongly patronized just now and sleeping sixpenny standees in the halls, but the arrangement shall be at your commands." Too tactful to wink, he did not repress a perceptible twitch of his left cheek.

"And the banquet. Do not forget that."

"Everything of the primest," the hotel man assured him.

Swiftly the glad news spread that on the night of Miss Wayne's testimonial Senator Lovatt was feting the entire company and bringing his own special wines.

Routine duties in the wings occupied Jans most of the afternoon. He had two small parts for the evening and was returning to his airy lodgings to perfect himself in them when he ran full upon the Honorable Vryling Lovatt in the entry. To his unbounded surprise the Senator greeted him jovially.

"So here you are, you young rascal!"

"Yes, sir," admitted Jans, groping for a clue to this inexplicable geniality.

"Sly dog! Sly dog!" chirped the holidaying legislator.

Repressing a temptation to respond with a "Bow-wow," Jans grinned feebly.

"I perceive now the reason for your pretended interest in the Drama," pursued the old Corinthian. "Blonde, brunette or ruddy, you young rogue?"

So that was it! Fair Luna had been chattering and, accepting her gossip for truth, the Senator was more than reconciled to his nephew's adventure; he was ready to approve it. By his standards, to join a theatrical enterprise as a working member was disreputable. But to use his work as a pretext in furtherance of amorous pursuit—that was quite in the tradition of the gentleman-sportsman.

"Sly dog!" said the Honorable once more and dug the supposed Don Juan in the ribs. "You shall present me to your pretty plaicer."

Mumbling something noncommittal, Jans pleaded press of work, but the uncle blocked his escape.

"I am offering a little jollification to the troupe after tomorrow evening's performance," he announced. "As a member, you will, I presume, attend."

"Afraid I'll be too busy, sir."

"Nonsense, nonsense! Busy at what? Your little inamorata will be a guest."

"Considering my relationship to you, sir, mightn't my presence prove embarrassing?"

"Nobody knows of that except Miss Wayne, and I've stopped her tongue." (Jans took leave to doubt privately an assumption so optimistic.) But the Senator did not insist when Jans stuck to his declination.

Having conned his sides, Jans strolled down Main Street, stopped short in front of a sign designating the premises within as Mrs. Lilligate's Fount of Delices, and contemplated a group at the soda counter. Two fashionably attired young blades were concentrating upon La Jeune Amour who was daintily sipping a flavorsome vanilla. The bigger young man, glancing up, caught sight of Jans.

"Quinny, by the great Lord Hawkins!" he cried and, rushing out, dragged the spectator in. "You know my young brother, Guy. And this is the fairest of the drama's buds, La Jeune Amour, fittingly named."

"Since when did you become learned in the French, Macel?"

"Never mind. What fetches you here?"

"Mr. Quinn is a member of our company," explained Durie.

"Hul-lo, hul-*lo!*" The quick, light-gray eyes shifted from the girl's serene beauty to Jan's annoyed face. "Mr. Quinn, eh? A Thespian, our Quinny! Don't seem overpleased to see his old college pal, either. I can guess the cause of your grout, my boy." He preened his mustache, quite the conquering male. "It's a fair field and room for all comers. Hey, lovely Amour?"

Durie smiled vaguely and addressed her attention to the refreshment. Jans said, "I'm John Quinn, Mace. Pleace to remember it."

"Mum's the word, eh, my boy? I always play fair."

"You don't," said young Guy peevishly. He had been regarding Durie with unhappy and adoring eyes.

Macel burst into boisterous laughter. "The youngster's nose is out of joint. Wait till your voice changes, pinkling. Miss Amour knows the difference between a child and a man, I'll warrant."

"What fetches you here, Mace?" asked Jans, declining the offer of a drink.

"The lure of beauty," answered the ladykiller with a languishing side glance at Durie who placidly ignored it.

"We're visiting our cousins," young Guy corrected his brother. "We didn't know Miss Durie was here until I met her on the street and"—with a look of resentment—"Mace attached himself to us."

"Never to be dislodged," added the big fellow with hand upon his heart.

"Seven o'clock curtain," Jans reminded the girl.

She rose and curtseyed. "My obligeances to both of you." Her angelic smile was quite impartial. "I'll return with Mr. Quinn."

"After the show, then, Madame," said Macel with a brisk, military salute.

Durie fell into step with Jans. "Don't you think they are very amiable young gentlemen, Jans?"

His response, though it could hardly be identified as language, distinctly conveyed disapproval.

"I don't think you were very mannerly toward them."

"Of course, it's no affair of mine," said he with an effect of disinterest.

"What isn't?"

"Your indiscretion."

"Is it so rash to partake of a vanilla-flavor soda water?"

"What about the supper invitation?" said Jans bluntly.

"Is that indiscreet?"

"Ask your friend, Gypsy Vilas."

"About supping with Mr. Ayrault? You think I shouldn't?"

"Ask Gypsy," repeated Jans doggedly.

"I might request Mr. Ayrault to invite her," said she brightly. "Do you think he'd do it?"

"I'm sure he would. He's a mortal kind young man. Shall I tell you something?" There was the little, husky catch in her voice that betokened excitement. She studied his face. "I don't think I will while you're in such a distemper."

"As you choose."

"Then I will. It's such pleasurable news that I can't keep it to myself. I'm going to have a testimonial, myself. Bigger than Fair Luna's."

"Here?"

"In Rochester."

"Rochester's a cut above this crew of mountebanks. We don't play it."

Durie executed a little skip. "We do. Mr. Ayrault has it all fixed with Mr. Passerow."

"The kind young man! What's he got to do with it?"

"He's going to fill his pleasure-boat with friends and cruise up the canal and all come to see me play every night. And at my benefit I will exhibit your elegant poetical composition. I will deliver it beautifully. Just as you tell me." Her soft, upward glance was like an unconscious caress.

"You'd better ask yourself a question, Durie."

"What question?"

"Why is Macel Ayrault doing all this for you?"

"Both the Misters Ayrault," she corrected.

"Pooh! Young Guy's a milkling."

"He composes a cruel pretty cupidity," she returned, chuckling. "He has sent me three, by post, all with posies. And his brother admires me so much as an actress that he says he will hire a play for me. . . . Are those bad words you're growling, Mr. John Quinn?"

"No. Congratulations," he snapped.

"Senator Lovatt has invited the Ayraults to the collation. But I could ask to sit by you if you'd like it."

"I'm not coming."

Her eyes widened. "Not to your own uncle's fête?"

"He's not John Quinn's uncle. Let me remind you of that."

"I don't see why you should mind. And why are you so cross-grained with me when I'm so happy?"

He forced a smile. "Because I'm a dunderhead, Durie. The Honorable Vryling doesn't consider it quite decent of me to be boguing about the state with a company of strolling actors."

Her dancing eyes steadied. "Doesn't he think us decent? Then why does he offer a benefit performance to Miss Wayne?"

"For the same reason that Macel Ayrault offers one to another female member of our troupe." Was there any use in trying to enlighten such appalling innocence? Or was it innocence? Uncle Vryling would have laughed at him. "Ask Gypsy," he said for the third time.

Gypsy Vilas came backstage between acts that evening to see Jans.

"That gal's got the stubbornness of Adam's off-ox," she declared.

"Have you been advising her?"

"She won't let me tell her anything. Just gets red as a turkey's wattle and says she doesn't want to hear about such things."

"She'll hear 'em from Ayrault," said Jans grimly.

"Not this evening; some other evening," grinned the girl. "I'm going with them."

"You're a good girl, Gypsy."

"Not me," chuckled Gypsy. "But she is. And she ambitions to stay so as fur as she knows anything about it, which ain't much. I don't trust that Ayrault lad any further'n a louse in a wig. And what about you, my buck?" She puckered her shrewd little face at him. "You got a warm eye and a dangerous one, and I'll be telling Miss Durie that one of these fine days. Unless you aim to marry her."

"She's not the marrying sort," evaded Jans.

"Meaning you ain't. Did she tell you she wasn't? She did!" Then, with scorn, "What does she know about it?"

Backstage cleaning-up kept Jans long after the final curtain. Coming down from the top-floor big room which was convertible into a theatre, he heard recognizable voices in one of the private parlors: Gypsy's free laughter; Macel Ayrault's booming basso; Durie's even tones with, he thought, more vivacity than usual, and young Guy's eager, uncertain chatter. Plainly they were having a friendly time, probably drinking. How far could he trust Gypsy? How far could he trust Durie? For that matter, how far could he trust himself?

Something was reconnoitering around the foot of the ladder leading up to his hayloft as he crossed the stableyard; something that slipped away and scuttled through the stalls. It was no more than a blotch of palpable darkness in the murk, but, as it emerged at the far end, Jans made out a figure suspiciously resembling the stocky form of Mr. Clonny of the taproom. What would he be up to, Jans asked himself, recalling the fellow's snarl and threat. Mounting the ladder to his sleeping loft, he found his belongings undisturbed. For the behoof of whom it might concern, he announced clearly through the open hay-gate giving on the yard, "I'll break the damned neck of anyone I find messing around my quarters."

He looked for no further activity on the part of the guileful Mr. Clonny that night, but thought it might be well to keep an eye on him for the rest of the stay. He slept well enough and rose to an unseasonably cold day with rain squalls intermittently sweeping in from white-flecked Seneca Lake. He saw Durie only once in the course of the day and then with no chance to talk· with her. But Gypsy, at an adjoining table for dinner, gave him an impudent wink and the grinning information in an undertone, "No damage done—yet."

Notwithstanding the weather, which grew fouler toward the evening of Fair Luna Wayne's special, success was in the air. The Ayraults had marshalled a contingent from Geneva College with instructions to render proper acclaim to the chief figure of the evening, but to whoop their heads off for La Jeune Amour. Having many friends in town, Senator Lovatt had no difficulty in distributing his tickets to receptive hands. It would be a crowded house. Manager Passerow beamed.

The play was *Husband at Sight,* with Miss Wayne as the provocative bride. She would, Jans felt sure, make the most of the role's blatant coquetries. The production was a severe tax upon his humble capacities as he was required to take three minor parts and furnish most of the incidental music with slight aid from Mr. Tim Baggo on the flute and Ripley Rapalje on the harmonica could provide at such rare times as they were not on the stage. Durie played two small characters with equal over-emphasis. At rehearsal Jans noted that his attempts to instil simplicity and naturalness had not gone further than the recital of his poem.

They played to the expected full house, a fattened money-box, and gratifying applause. The star of the evening bridled girlishly over her silver goblet (which she would sell back to the whitesmith before their departure for a twenty-five percent discount), gushed over the sumptuous floral wreath (its disposition was already determined by bargain with Mrs. Alwyn against that lady's coming testimonial), and delivered the poetaster's hifalutin verses rather better, as he admitted to himself, than they deserved. The one fly in the amber of Miss Wayne's satisfaction was the disproportionate éclat accorded to La Jeune Amour for each and every one of her insignificant sides. The Geneva College contingent was doing well by their friend's bewitching plaicer, as they naturally assumed her to be. The Fair Luna was displeased almost but not quite to the point of rescinding the responsible utility's invitation to the feast.

After the final curtain, the young blades swarmed backstage

with flowers and compliments, both charmingly artificial. Senator Lovatt, beaming with pride of possession, ordered unlimited drinks from the bar, the consumption of which with impromptu toasts consumed the time until the banquet was announced. With Fair Luna languishing on his arm, he led the way to the second floor. The performers were in stage costume. Durie, as a milkmaid, was attired in a profusely befrilled and beribboned garb which would have astonished the cattle of the most refined and elegant barnyard. For that presentment her faithful flax-knife had done duty as a feed chopper. She was flushed and lovely with her first taste of what she innocently believed to be artistic recognition.

Seated between the Ayraults, she found herself drinking a toast to the honor guest of the evening in an unfamiliar liquid which bubbled and fizzed sunnily in the etched glass and continued to bubble and fizz sunnily down her throat and up her nose and along her veins. Between laughing and choking and sneezing, she was not sure whether or not she enjoyed it. All doubts were dissipated by her second essay, the toast to the giver of the feast in which she participated only upon Macel Ayrault's assurance that to refuse would be a gross breach of hospitality.

Champagne wine, she now perceived, merited all that she had heard spoken in its favor. She had heard, also, that it was intoxicating, though she could hardly believe it of anything so delicately flavored. She wished that worldlywise Gypsy were there so that she might ask her. Macel Ayrault was quaffing it in repeated glassfuls, and he did not appear the worse for it; only very big and handsome and eager and—and near. She did not quite like that nearness. It was not like Jans Quintard's; not disturbing in the same way; not as alarming, either. . . . Why think of Jans now? As for herself, surely this was not inebriety, this singing of her taut and joyous nerves.

She noted that her costume, for all its ribbons, was fustian; by no means dicty enough for so elegant an occasion. Tomorrow night she would be a court lady in sarsenet. Well, any way, a fair imitation of it. Why not change into that more appropiate costume? It would be quick and easy, since the chamber which she shared with Fair Luna was but three doors away. Excusing herself temporarily to her protesting partners, she slipped out without disturbing the rhetoric of Senator Lovatt's thanks to his dear and valued friends of the Thalian aggregation of genius, and tripped lightly down the hallway to Number Ten.

The door was bolted.

No! She did not believe it. It couldn't be. It must be the champagne wine. She tried again. She rattled and shook and pushed. The barrier on the inside stood firm. Then, at the end of the passage she noticed a traveling-box. Her own traveling-box! She ran to it. Her spare clothing was heaped inside. She had been evicted. But not Fair Luna. There was but the one box. What did it mean?

Her roommate would surely know. Durie fled back to the banquet room. The honor guest was toying daintily with her glass and giggling at some witty sally of her host. Durie plucked at her sleeve.

"Miss Wayne! Miss Wayne! I can't get into our chamber."

"Shut up, you fool!" It was a rasping whisper thrown across the temporary star's shoulder.

"But some of my things . . ."

"Come out of this." Fair Luna staggered a little as she pushed the girl into the passage. "Now what ails you?"

"I'm locked out."

Fair Luna smirked. "You know why, don't you?"

"I don't want to know," Durie gulped. "That awful old man!"

"What do you mean, awful old man?" Fair Luna retorted. "He's a better catch than your slowpoke John Quinn. Go and ask him for a night's lodgment. Or your big, fat friend with the militia whisker."

"Mr. Ayrault?" said Durie stupidly.

"He'd accommodate you, I warrant."

Something had undermined Durie's habitual self-reliance— perhaps the champagne wine. She did not even resent Miss Wayne's cavalier manner. She stood aside with a confused mind as the singing chambermaid marched past her, nose in air, and tripped back through the doorway with a merry, on-stage laugh, to rejoin her host. Durie was left forlorn in the hallway. From below she could hear the snoring of the standees, asleep in their sixpenny corners. The hotel was chockablock. There would be no place for her anywhere.

Half an hour earlier Jans Quintard, having completed John Quinn's professional chores, passed the doorway back of which his uncle was expressing a grateful nation's recognition of the culture spread abroad by the dramatic profession in general and the Passerow Thalians in particular, when he met the night clerk wheeling up a festooned bowl of iced punch.

"Where's Clonny?" he asked the man.

"Off his chump. Took sick."

Jans was interested. "When did it hit him?"

"Hour or so since."

"Did he go to his room?"

"Nope. Went out for air."

This might be it, then, whatever the vengeful tapman had in mind. For one thing Jans suspected that his usual method of entry would not be safe. Anyhow, why take chances? Whistling to advertise his presence, he crossed the rain-shimmering cobbles, entered the main door, and ran his fingers across the boards at the foot of the ladder. Sure enough, sawdust. Careless work. Jans made an unobtrusive entry to his loft by the rear window.

His lantern was in place on the wall, but he dared not risk it. Cautiously he struck a locofoco, and instantly blew it out. One glance had revealed all he needed to see. That ingenious contraption known as a Neptune's Blessing was familiar to him as one of the minor diversions practiced by the Royal Navy of Harvard days.

Mr. Clonny had rigged a neat one. The heavy bucket, full of water, was delicately balanced on the brink of the opening so that the lightest twitch of the attached cord would trip it. The other end was fastened to the half-severed rung. Under pressure from a climber's weight, the rung would give way, the cord pull taut, and the cold douche drench the unfortunate below.

Several feed-bags were within reach. Selecting one, the lodger bore it to the well's edge. He uttered a shrill cry, as of a person falling, and dropped his burden. The convincing thud was followed by what he hoped was an equally convincing groan from his lips. He stood, expectant, gripping the bucket, waiting for Mr. Clonny. Nobody came. Well, he and Neptune were in no hurry. Settling back into the hay, he listened idly to the bursts of oratory which exuded from the open windows of the banquet room where the Honorable Vryling Lovatt was unweariedly speechifying.

Someone moving below, groping toward the ladder's base. Jans crouched, tense. He heard stealthily scuffling feet. He tipped the bucket. The cataract descended. So much for Mr. Clonny!

A yelp and a gurgle followed, but not in the tapman's rum-hoarse accents. It was quite a different voice that was raised in sorrowful protest.

"What did you d-d-d-do that to me f-f-for?"

"Hellfire and snake poison!" Jans ejaculated and precipitated himself upon the ladder, forgetful of the impaired rung. It gave way. He landed upon Durie, sending her flat on her face.

"First you drown me and then you knock me down," she lamented.

He crawled to his feet, dragging her up after him. "I thought you were Clonny," he babbled.

"Who's Clonny? I'm c-c-cold."

"Why have you come here?"

"They l-l-locked me out and put my box in the hall."

"Your box? Why? What for?"

"Fair Lu—— N-n-never mind. I'm c-c-cruel cold."

"Go up the ladder. Mind the missing rung. Take off those wet clothes," he directed.

"Before you?" she quavered.

"I'm going to fetch dry things from your box. Wrap yourself in my greatcoat."

Dashing through the rain, he gave a sharp order at the bar. "Hot buttered rum, double. Put it in a covered cannikin. Smoking hot."

There was no difficulty in locating the box. He did not pause for selection but scooped out such garments as seemed to meet the emergency and made a hasty bundle. Back at the taproom entrance he met Mr. Passerow. The manager's eyes blinked and narrowed upon the inapposite burden tucked under Mr. John Quinn's arm, but he made no comment. Jans tossed a coin upon the bar and burned his fingers on the tin.

Arrived at the ladder's foot, he first handed up the drink. "Take three slow swallows of that," he prescribed.

He could hear her teeth chattering against the rim, followed by a strangled gasp, a splutter, and a soft "Oo-oo-ooh!" of satisfaction.

"Here are your clothes." He thrust them upward. "Tell me when you're dressed."

"It's so dark."

"Feel along the beam near the hay-gate. You'll find a box of locofocos. There's a betty on the wall."

The light glowed and swelled. Presently she called, "Come up."

She looked entrancing in the dim flicker, though nothing that she had on seemed quite to match. Her soaked clothing was spread over a joist to dry.

"Warm now?" he asked.

"Almost."

"Take some more of the rum."

"Is that what it is? It makes me feel good all the way down." She tilted the cannikin for a long draught, followed by several sips. "It's more satisfying than the champagne wine," she decided.

"Hello! Had you been drinking champagne? You didn't tell me."

"Only two glasses. Perhaps three. Why?"

"Nothing." But he took the tin from her and set it down.

"I'm sleepy," she murmured.

"All right. I'll find a place for you if I have to haul somebody out of bed."

"Why can't I stay here?" she yawned.

"And I sleep in the passage with the standees?"

"No. Why should you?" she asked a little thickly.

Hot buttered rum on champagne, thought Jans.

"Are you warm now?" he asked again.

"Yes." The voice had grown very drowsy. "Sing to me, Jans."

"Laus Deo is with the props."

"I only want to hear you."

"What shall I sing?"

"You know." It was a caressing whisper.

"I thought you didn't like that song any more."

"I love it!"

He dropped beside her and began in half-volume. Thus controlled, it seemed to her, there was more of warmth and richness in his voice, and—yes, of possessiveness than any music that had ever soothed and thrilled her.

> *"You may esteem him*
> *A child for his might.*

"Are you asleep?"

Her eyes remained closed, but her lips parted for the counterpoint.

> *"Or you may deem him*
> *A coward for his flight."*

Jans' baritone soared to the tenor as the soft passion of her contralto took the lead.

> *"But if she whom Love doth honor*
> *Be concealèd from the day,*
> *Set a thousand guards upon her,*
> *Love will find out the way."*

It was as inevitable as the final harmony that their lips and bodies should meet in a long pressure. He heard again her broken murmur, "I told you, Jans, I don't know anything about this." Something deep within him warned—*That's the damnable part of it, Jans Quintard. For it's true, and you know it's true.*

She was leaning back from him now, her hand fluttering at her bodice. The feeble gleam of the betty-lamp glinted from steel. The flax-sickle, thought Jans; is she trying to knife me? With a wrench and a little sobbing gasp she hurled it away from her. He heard it tinkle on the wet cobbles below.

"Put out the light, Jans," said her voice, faint and sweet. "I want to go to sleep."

185

He moved over to the wall.

Rhetoric boomed in his ears; the noble sentiments of the Honorable Vryling Lovatt, rising above the plash and splutter of the storm. The orator had risen in praise of American womanhood. He was dithyrambic, ecstatic upon purity, modesty, the homely fireside virtues which, Mr. Speaker, have made this great nation of ours what it is. He was stalwart in defence of Maid, Wife and Mother.

It was the sheerest bombast, balderdash, foofaraw to Jans' long-habituated ears.

But through it spoke the imperative creed of the generations, the standard of tradition, of honor, an intangible, irrefragable barrier to his passion.

"American womanhood," boomed the orator, "the sacred trust of every man worthy of the name."

"Jans! Jans!" murmured the warm, dim voice below him, broken, seductive, assenting.

Jans blew out the betty, dropped down the ladder and fled into the night.

Durie slept, smiling.

18

SOMETHING was wrong with the digestion of the midwives' horse. Gypsy Vilas set out at early dawn with a bottle of Dr. Campo's Sure Stomach Cure for Man or Beast, to physic the animal. Crossing the inn yard she stumbled. Metal clinked beneath her foot. She stopped and picked up a gently curved blade, set in a bone handle.

Gypsy whistled between her teeth. No doubt as to whose knife it was. But where did it come from? And what did it mean?

Not a window was open on the hotel side. All were unbroken. Therefore Durie's weapon of defence had not come from there. There remained the hay-gate overhead, opening to Jans Quintard's roost. Gypsy whistled again more thoughtfully.

Having ministered to the horse and studied the surroundings she climbed a tree opposite the loft to reconnoiter. One glance, and she was down to earth, across the court, and mounting the ladder. The broken rung perplexed her, but this was no time for trivialities. She threaded the opening and stood above the slumbering Durie.

Alone. Well, that was something. An open tin on the floor exhaled odors. Gypsy sniffed at it.

"Well, I'll be spavined!" she muttered.

The sleeper turned her head without opening her eyes and smiled. "Jans," she murmured.

"Hell!" snapped Gypsy. "Wake up." She stimulated the operation with a nudge from her heel.

Durie sat up in the hay, rubbing her eyes. She regarded her friend with bewilderment.

"Here's your knife," Gypsy said.

Durie explored beneath her bodice. "Mine? Why! Where . . . ?"

"In the courtyard."

"How did it get down there?"

"You tell me! Did he wrassle it away from you?"

Durie's brow puckered. "No, I don't think so."

"It didn't hop through the door by itself."

"I—think it was me."

"How, you? Did you lose it?"

"I think I threw it away."

"What for?"

"It must have been the drink."

Gypsy gave the pannikin a kick that sent it hurtling through the opening. Durie protested, "Don't! My head hurts."

"Your head, huh? Is that all?"

"I don't know what you mean."

"Well, what happened next?"

"I don't know what happened," Durie answered slowly.

"Oh! You don't know what happened, Miss Mealymouth. Haying it with that young luster! D'you want me to tell you?"

"No!"

"Huh! Beginning to remember for yourself, are you?"

"I—I think I swooned."

"Some do," said Gypsy.

"My head doesn't think right."

"Hot buttered rum."

"I'd have frozen without it. I was so wet and cold."

"So you fetched a change of clothes," commented the other, staring at the garments laid out to dry. "Figuring on settling here, was you?"

"I didn't have any other place to stay." The events of the evening were coming back to memory now. She set them forth to her friend, somewhat raggedly but still intelligibly.

"That Fair Luna," said Gypsy judicially, "is a dirty, rotten, misbegotten, turkey-trodden slut."

"Then I came to ask Jans what to do and he poured water down my neck. . . ."

"Water, did you say?"

". . . and then he fell on me."

"Oh-oh!"

"He thought it was someone else. Clonny, he called him."

"It's all boggledybotch to me. What did you go up into the loft for?"

"To dry off. Jans fetched me my clothes."

"And helped you put 'em on, huh?"

"No. He went away. And when he came back we sang."

"What! Again?"

"I know. . . . No, I don't know. It just happened that way."

"And you that was going to be a permanent virgin!" Gypsy jeered.

"Don't talk like that. I—I don't feel any different."

"Tell me that six months from now."

Durie considered. "Jans wouldn't do anything to hurt me."

"What do you know about men and their pretty tricks? Champagne wine! Hot buttered rum! 'Come up into the hay with me, my dee-rie, we'll sing a pretty song.' My Gawd! So there you are, and too late to mend."

If Gypsy expected any symptoms of dismay from her friend, she was disappointed. The Andrews philosophy, deeply instilled into its sole disciple was that when a thing is done, it is done, and repining is but waste of time. "A shilling's worth of remorse is tenpence self-justification," the Maze of Matrimony put it.

"I wonder where Jans is," Durie said.

"Probably taken his hoof in his hand and off to the wars."

"Gone away? Why should he?" asked Durie, wide-eyed.

"So's he won't have to marry you, you zany."

"I don't want to marry him," protested poor Durie. "I don't want to marry anyone."

"The more fool, you. But if that's your lay, why not pick 'em richer? Big Ayrault is fair love-muddled over you, I hear."

Durie shuddered. "Oh, no! I never could feel like that toward anyone else. Wanting to be so—so near them, I mean."

"So! A one-man wench. Let's get you out of here before they find us. I'll stick your costume in our wagon till you get settled back in."

Since the dining room did not open until six, the two girls cooked a kettle-breakfast over an improvised fire. Gypsy laid out her stock for the day's peddling, a dozen bottles of Dr. Micajah Drake's Milk-Maker for Hopeful Mothers, $1.00 per bottle, on which she would touch a commission of a shilling per sale. While thus busied, she did some concentrated thinking, the fruit of which was Wisdom's Counsel to Inexperience.

"Durie."

"Yes, Gypsy."

"Spos'n Jans comes back."

"I doubt that he's gone away."

"What are you going to say to him?"

"Nothing," said Durie placidly.

"You're a cool one!"

"I suppose he'll say something, though."

"That's right. Let him do the talking till we see where we are. Then you tell Gypsy all about it."

"I know where I am."

"Like hell you do! If you did, you'd be scairt."

"Why?"

"Or sorry."

"I'm not."

Gypsy meditated over this. "Lookit, Durie. Are you honest in love with your young spark?"

"I don't know. I don't think so."

"Good Gawd! You'd oughta know, after what happened."

That was the difficulty; in spite of her friend's conviction, Durie was still unsure as to what had happened. Whether from the lurking fumes of the hot buttered rum or because of the confusing and undermining stress of emotions, she could not bring back clearly the final events of the night. She knew only that the music had irresistibly drawn Jans and her close together again, closer than her instinctively aloof spirit could ever be drawn to anyone else. At the end it remained to her as a compelling dream with Jans' song and Jans' kiss and Jans' passion matching and merging with her own.

What Gypsy surmised was perhaps true. How much it mattered, what it might mean in future, were questions for the future. For the present she felt no fear, no remorse. Why should she? Of one desire she was keenly conscious; she wanted to hear Jans say, "I love you."

Mindful of Durie's good name, Jans roused himself in the unoccupied stall where he had slept fitfully. He must get her out before she was discovered. Climbing the ladder, he thrust his head up through the well and called softly. No answer. He called again, louder. He still could not trust himself to approach and touch her. If she stretched out those strong and sweet young arms to him again as she had last night . . .

Still no response. He lifted himself higher and saw that his greatcoat had been tossed aside from the empty nest of hay. The betty lamp lay, overturned, but the girl was gone and her discarded costume with her. So much the better. Yet a pang of disappointment shot through him. He longed for the sight of her.

Preparatory to his watery joke upon young John Quinn of the Thalians, Mr. Clonny had fortified himself with several drinks of that potent concoction known to the trade as whipbelly-vengeance. Its effect was somniferous. Sleep overcame him before he had been five minutes at his vigil in the barn. A long feed-box served as his bed. Thus Jans' realistic thud-and-groan performance had been wasted. Mr. Clonny slumbered heavily through it. He did not waken until an insecurely tethered mare, foraging for fodder, bit his foot. Voices overhead came to his ears. Female voices. Two female voices. In John Quinn's quarters. The young rip!

Mr. Clonny reeled out into the dawn, prepared to tell the world.

Fortune had been treating Manager Passerow shabbily. The Literature Lottery had paid his number but once in a year, and that only a niggling prize. Fortune's Headquarters returned a dreary succession of blanks. Three Sundays before he had been certain of favorable results by virtue of an attendance upon church, on the offchance of enlisting the support of heaven. The preacher's text was Numbers, One-eighteen-twelve. Surely an omen! One-eighteen-twelve. He put all his spare cash together with what he could persuade from a skeptical wife plus a forced loan of rather more than was prudent from the company treasury, and invested it all with Lucky Draw. And what happened? A five-hundred-dollar prize fell to the very next number, One-eighteen-eleven. After he had put a shilling in the contribution-box, too. It was enough to turn a man atheist.

Mr. Passerow was in financial straits by the time Geneva was reached.

It would never have occurred to him, rising early after a troubled night, that Mr. Clonny of the Farmer's Hotel taproom would be an agent of salvation. But the barkeep, after a revivifying drink, babbled to the receptive ears of the manager. Two girls, eh? And one of them seemed to be reproaching the other with loose behavior. Who would that be? Mr. Passerow did not know. But, recalling John Quinn's burden of feminine apparel and the traveling-box outside the "arrangement of rooms," he had no doubt as to the identity of the rebuked one. Projects formed in his wily brain.

Five dollars, extracted from the waning treasury, persuaded Mr. Clonny to swear himself to silence. Playing for heavy stakes, the manager could not afford to be niggardly.

After breakfast he carefully drew up two documents. One was a contract between Miss Endurance Andrews, professionally known as La Jeune Amour, and Jonus Passerow representing the Thalian Dramatic Company. The other which superficially might be taken for a duplicate of it, was a legal release. The young lady was summoned to the managerial chamber and invited to read the contract terminating her apprenticeship and putting her on the permanent roster. She signed it and its supposed duplicate with a modest elation. She was getting on in the world of her choice.

Rising betimes—for he enjoyed the immunities of a drink-proof head—the Honorable Vryling Lovatt gave himself a splash with cold water to toughen his fiber. The companion of his revels was still asleep and, if the unromantic truth be told, stertorously so. Why, thought the Senator with regret, must pretty women snore? After rubbing himself to a glow, he carefully washed his head in a solution of copper sulphate blended with fourth-proof brandy, and worked in a couple of palmsfull of beef marrow. The hairs which adhered to his fingers from the massage, he counted with solicitude. Too many. Forty-four years old, he reflected with a sigh, as he diluted some brandy and applied it to his cheeks and throat until they tingled. He then shaved carefully and dressed with due heed to the details of material and color.

During the process he considered pleasurably the events of the evening. He had been a success; it would be stupid to deny it to himself. . . . That was a devilish pretty child seated between that big bullfrog of an Ayrault and his stripling brother. If she were the one in whose pursuit Jans had turned Thespian, he could but applaud the young blade's taste. He went down to breakfast alone.

Strong though his stomach was, it was unwise to overeat after late night indulgence. Prudently he eschewed the roast spiced ham and boiled pork and contented himself with a small fried eel, a plate of eggs and bacon, a nice slice of well-browned steak, a platter of wheat cakes, half a dozen saleratus biscuits with honey and molasses, two cups of coffee, and three fingers of corn whiskey from the table decanter. Thus fortified, and with a rich, thick Havana between his smiling lips, he could face the world with equanimity.

The first person he faced was a nephew disheveled, unshaven, and patently perturbed.

"Sit down, my boy, sit down," the Senator invited. "Have an eye-opener."

"No, thank you, Uncle Vryling."

"Best thing in the world after a randan."

"I was sober last night, sir," Jans said with intention.

"Don't tell me. You look powerfully seedy. This vagrant life has depreciated you. You might at least maintain the outward appearance of a gentleman."

"Vagabonds and players," Jans murmured.

"Fiddle-faddle! You're a Quintard. How long will you keep up this farce?"

"It is no farce. It's serious, I assure you, Uncle."

An expression of cunning contracted the fresh-hued face. "Ah, yes! It always seems so to ardent youth until the bird is snared. A pretty bird, too, you rogue. Dee—licious! I make you my compliments. But you must be a slow wooer, my boy. Or is she shy? Sly, more likely. 'Ware traps and pitfalls, Jans."

"There's no occasion. You'd better prepare yourself for a shock, Uncle Vryling."

"I'm staunch," the Senator asserted.

"I intend to marry Miss Andrews."

"Who?"

Jans corrected himself. "La Jeune Amour. The young lady to whom you have referred in terms which I find offensive."

"Marry her?" exploded the Honorable Mr. Lovatt. "Young lady! Bitch-and-damme, sir! Are you mad?"

"No, sir."

"You find my terms offensive, sir," spluttered his elder. "Well, I find your project monstrous, sir, monstrous."

"I'm sorry, sir."

"So marriage is her fancy, is it?"

"I haven't asked her yet."

The foxy look returned to the old boy's face. "Marriage is too high a price. Leave her to me."

"I think you'd better keep out of it, sir," said Jans quietly.

"Eh? What? I'm to stand by and watch my own flesh and blood shamelessly tricked . . ." He broke off, daunted by Jans' expression.

"There is no question of trickery. I give you good day, sir." Jans turned and walked out.

Dark humor descended upon the Honorable Vryling Lovatt. It was not lightened by a message from Manager Passerow, requesting an immediate parley with Senator Lovatt in terms which that gentleman found presumptuous. What the devil! Did the fellow think to presume upon his, the Senator's affability of the previous evening to improve the acquaintanceship? He sent back word that he was busy, but would give Mr. Passerow fifteen minutes in his second-floor parlor at two o'clock sharp. Then, to show how busy he was *not,* emerged into the inn yard and took his constitutional with a straw in his mouth.

Another incident was no more to his taste. He encountered La Jeune Amour on her way to the street, looking, he thought, a bit drawn, but still so pretty as to give a wrench to his jaded nerves. Gallantly doffing his light tan beaver, he gave her a breezy good morning and solicited the favor of a word.

"What on, sir?" she asked.

"The subject is Jans—Mr. John Quinn."

"Are you speaking for Mr. Quinn?" (Very self-possessed, this little slewer! Quite the lady, if one were easily fooled by play-acting.)

"In a manner. He is my nephew."

"Yes, I know."

"I'll be bound you do! Then you will comprehend the advantage to yourself of a private word with me."

"I cannot conceive to what purpose."

The Senator's rasped temper gave way. "Damn it all, girl, who are you to lift your nose in the air at me! Bitch me if I know what the times are coming to."

"I think you forget yourself, sir," said the girl and, with a stately bow, left him gawking.

This, reflected the Senator, promises to be troublesome. Very queenly! Wonder who rehearsed her in that part.

Prompt upon the stroke of two, Manager Passerow presented himself at the private parlor.

"Good afternoon, Senator Lovatt." His manner was portentous.

"Well? State your business."

"Last night, sir, you delivered some very praiseworthy sentiments upon the sanctity of womanhood."

"What of it?"

"I venture to ask you, sir, whether you are prepared to live up to your professions."

Senator Lovatt was thunderstruck. Had this fellow the impudence, the incredible insolence to be calling him to account for Fair Luna Wayne? The ribboned baton which accompanied his travels in lieu of a cane, twitched in his hands. For a brass bawbee he would lay it across his interrogator's shoulders. Better keep cool, though, until he could see his way.

"Be explicit, if you please."

The manager fumbled in his waistcoat pocket and brought out a newspaper clipping which he held between thumb and forefinger.

"Mr. Percy of Varick Street in New York," he stated, "was mulcted by a jury in the sum of twenty-two hundred dollars damages for seducing a virgin of thirty. The proof." He held out the slip.

Senator Lovatt waved it away. "And how is this germane?"

"In the case which I am approaching in my capacity as representative of despoiled womanhood . . ."

An uplifted hand stayed him. "Are you suggesting," said Senator Lovatt suavely, "that the lady in question is either thirty or a virgin? I should be equally surprised by both."

"Ask your nephew."

"Eh? What's that?" (Not the Fair Luna then! Worse!)

"The young man known as John Quinn. He is, I believe, your blood-nephew."

"Oh, admitted! Admitted!" said the Senator testily.

"Then on behalf of La Jeune Amour, toward whom I stand in —er—*locus tenants* (Mr. Lovatt snorted) I assert a claim of marriage upon your nephew."

"Assert and be damned to you."

"A financial composition might be made," said Mr. Passerow lowering his voice.

"It might," the Senator agreed, "if reasonable."

"In the Percy assessment the lady who was compromitted . . ."

"Not comparable in any degree. The lady was presumptively a virgin."

"What do you insinuate, Senator Lovatt?" puffed the manager.

"And in this instance, a Thespian. Thespian—Cyprian; interchangeable terms in my experience."

"Sir! You dishonor my profession. The girl is chaste—*was* chaste."

"I hear you say it."

"You shall hear me prove it in court, if you force us to the measure."

"I have no wish to have a scandal aired," admitted Senator Lovatt.

"Nor I to air it, if proper provision is made."

"What is your estimate of proper provision?"

"You have read what Mr. Percy of Varick Street in New York . . ."

"Damn Mr. Percy and his thirty-year-old virgin!" roared the Senator. "I'll pay you fifty dollars in full release."

"A thousand," said Mr. Passerow.

"I'll see you in fiery hell first, you conscienceless sharpshooter! I might go to seventy-five as my last word."

"Now, be reasonable, Senator. The poor girl's honor is despoiled. Make it five hundred."

They bickered and chaffered like a pair of hucksters at a cheap-john stand before reaching an agreement as to the market price of La Jeune Amour's chastity. At one hundred and fifty dollars, cash, they reached a level. Manager Passerow withdrew and returned with the signed document. It expressly released one Jans Quintard, bachelor, known professionally as John Quinn, from any and all demands, penalties, assessments or responsibilities arising from his carnal knowledge of one Endurance Andrews, spinster, known professionally as La Jeune Amour.

"All very well," said the Senator, "but how do I know this to be the wench's veritable signature?"

Therein lay the risk for Mr. Passerow. He was not yet prepared to let Durie know the nature of the negotiations. Who could tell but what she would cut up rough and demand marriage? Then the fat would be in the fire. He intended to play fair with the girl; to turn over her proper share of the proceeds, say two-thirds. Then there was that rich young Ayrault; something might be done there. Durie was a potentially profitable bit of merchandise; he must keep her good will.

Meanwhile that damned Senator must be satisfied. Mr. Passerow sought out Durie and gave her explicit instructions. Senator Lovatt wished to be assured of the genuineness of her signature.

"Why?" said Durie. "I don't like that old man."

"He's going to invest money in the troupe," explained the manager glibly. "So he has a right to inspect the contracts. You don't have to do anything but answer a couple of questions."

Durie liked the Senator even less than before when she confronted him in the parlor of the "arrangement." Why, she wondered, should he look so forbidding, as he stood, his feet apart, his handsome, rubicund face stern, the baton in his hand switching the air until its ribbons streamed.

"Young woman," he said, "is this your signature?" He held up the paper.

"Yes," said Durie.

"Have you read this document?"

"Yes."

"And you signed it with full knowledge of its contents?"

"Yes."

"Mr. Passerow is acting for you, with authority?"

"Of course. He's the manager. He acts for all of us." She spoke impatiently, having matters of more importance on her mind. Jans! Where was Jans? Why had he not come to her?

"That is all, young woman," the Senator barked.

"Thank you, Miss Amour," said the manager ceremoniously.

Senator Lovatt paid up and took receipt at the hand of Jonus Passerow. Between relief and wrath, he sent for Jans.

"A pretty penny you've cost me, my precious nephew," he began.

"How is that, sir?"

"You and your hayloft loves."

Jans colored. "Still I don't understand you, Uncle."

"You still purpose to marry that prettykin?"

"I've had no chance to ask her as yet."

"You needn't. You're free of obligation in that quarter. I've bailed you out."

"Don't you think, sir," said Jans through tightening lips, "that you could keep out of my affairs until you're requested to meddle?"

"Don't you dare talk to me of meddling, sir. Bitch-and-damme! Where would you be, had I left you to cope with that extortionate little harpy? Have you one hundred and fifty dollars in your pocket to satisfy her demands?"

"One hundred and fifty dollars!" Jans repeated, gaping.

"To the penny."

"You paid her that?"

"In negotiable moneys. The proof." With a flourish he extended the Passerow document.

Jans went through it slowly, his face pale and twitching.

"How do I know there isn't some trickery?" he demanded.

"She asseverated to me personally that she had signed the paper with full knowledge of its contents."

"The girl was never the worse for me, sir," Jans said with an effort.

"I can well believe you, my boy. None but an old hand could have diddled me so handsomely. I trust you had your money's worth," he concluded sourly.

"You misinterpret me, Uncle. For all of me she is *virgo intacta*."

"The more fool, you," roared the Senator. "Not that I believe you, my boy. Some misplaced notion of chivalry. But I can't have our name fouled in open court."

Jans was still staring at the release in a semi-daze. "I'd have married her gladly," he muttered.

"She prefers the cash."

Jans groaned.

"Why, I believe the poor lad is really love-stricken," said the Senator, not without feeling. "Grave error, my boy. Women are pretty playthings. Sometimes they get broken. But it is we men that suffer when we take them for more than that. Quit this foolishness and come home with me."

"I'm afraid you're right, sir," Jans admitted.

"We'll leave tomorrow," said the Senator.

It struck Jans that throughout the day and evening Durie was deliberately avoiding him, which confirmed his uncle's accusation. Still, covertly studying her face, he could not quite bring himself to believe it. Before the evening's curtain he wrote her a long, impassioned, pleading letter and tore it up, substituting a brief note which he confided to Gypsy. Without salutation it ran:

There is one thing I must know. It can be answered in one word. Did you sign the acknowledgment and release now held by my uncle— yes or no?   J. Q.

Expecting and longing for a word of love, Durie was chilled. And what a pother about a simple contract! First that stuffy Senator and now Jans. What was his interest? It occurred to her that perhaps he, too, was putting money into the venture. "Acknowledgment and release" meant nothing special to her; she had signed but one form, so this must be the one. Gypsy was waiting for her answer. She scribbled it at the foot of the paper:

"Yes."

"Have you seen him to speak to?" Gypsy asked.

"No."

"And he hasn't made occasion to say anything?"

"No."

"I told you so. What's in his note?"

"Nothing. Only company business."

"I told you so," Gypsy repeated. "He's going to lightfoot it. You'd better be seeing my birthdames one of these days."

"What for?"

"They might have something to tell you."

Durie reddened painfully. "It couldn't be. Could it, Gypsy?" she appealed.

"I've known it to happen to a cow."

"*You* ask them," Durie said.

"Me! *I* ain't the one that's been haying it. Never mind, gal. It'll keep."

19

To THE end of his life Jans could close his eyes and evoke the vision. She stood at the inn window overlooking the court. The play for that evening was *Mr. Wright Was Wrong* and she had dressed for her part as Hoyden of the Manse, before going up to the ballroom. In her bodice of bronze tabby she had fastened a single Gold-of-Ophir rose. The heavy, rippling watered silk was matched by the wavy hair that fell to meet it and outmatched by the radiance of the eyes the hue of an October oak leaf flecked by sunlight.

She saw him below and gave him a long, steady look, serene yet questioning with something in it of soft expectancy. He heard again in fancy that desperate whisper, "I don't know anything about this, Jans." A lie. An artifice. And he, the gull of a practiced trickster. He read again with the inner eye that damning "Yes," the response to his note. There at least, was truth; the cool and hardy admission of blackmail. Why was she regarding him now with that uninterpretable gaze? What more could she hope to cozen him out of? She smiled, and in that soft, husky, far-carrying tone of hers, said, "Jans!"

He hesitated. "I have nothing to say to you."

She leaned forward a little, her face at first incredulous and wondering, then darkening with comprehension.

(In the teeth of the sentimentalizers and of the over-sensible— Adam Personius Andrews had written—I aver that the man who takes his privilege of a woman and leaves her is justified in his escape from a prepared pitfall. Let none prate to me about the guilt of the seducer, the wrongs of the seduced. If advantage there be in that association, it is wily woman's.)

Is that what Jans is thinking of me, Durie wondered. The notion was intolerable to her pride. She recalled a romance in the insufficiently secluded literary hoard of the Bookery, the theme of which, only half understood at the time, was that when a man misled a maiden, he inevitably visited upon her his scorn and contempt. Such was Gypsy's idea, too. At least, she could and must disabuse Jans' mind from the suspicion that she had sought to entrap him.

"I have something to say to you," she said gravely.

"Very well. Say it."

"Shall I come down there?"

"No. I'll come up, if you wish privacy."

He joined her in the second-floor sitting room. They were alone there. Her costume lent the illusion of girlish inexperience, innocence, qualified by the radiant vitality that exhaled from her whole person. She said directly, "Are you worrying yourself about last night?"

"No. Why should I?"

"You have nothing to fear from me, Jans."

"Nothing further, you doubtless mean," he retorted with deliberate brutality. "And you have nothing further to expect from me."

The swift color flooded into her cheeks. He damned his eyes for finding her more beautiful than ever in her shame. Shame? He was speedily undeceived of that idea.

"I'd rather beg in the gutter," she said wrathfully.

"Hands clenched and stamp by the right foot," he suggested. Pretty neat, he thought it. She paid no heed.

"You're leaving the company, aren't you?"

"What is the source of that?"

"Senator Lovatt told Miss Wayne."

"You would like to believe it true, wouldn't you?"

"I don't see that I am concerned in it," she returned with spirit.

"Well, I'm not leaving. I've decided to wait and get my money's worth."

That ought to hit home, he thought. It was childish; it was gross; he knew it. Yet he burned to hurt her; to be even with her for his ruinous disillusionment; to appease the dark, ill-repressed, brooding anger, heritage of his blood, a vengeful faculty which lay like a sediment of poison at the bottom of the easy-going, negligent Quintard character.

She only looked faintly puzzled. Still playing innocence! He turned his back on her and strode away, humming airily.

He was young. And he had been hurt, badly hurt.

Gypsy intercepted him at the lower door.

"Wouldn't you offer a drink to a thirsty gal?"

He swallowed his reluctance. "Certainly. What shall it be?"

"Rumbullion, and thank you kindly," she said, following him into the side room of the tap.

He ordered two drinks. She smiled at him and said, "Colloguing again, mister?"

"And you? Eavesdropping?"

"You'll stand a bit of it. So will she."

"I should think her quite able to take care of herself."

"Quoth Fleetfoot, the Bachelor. S'posen you get her up Queer Street? What then?"

"That cock won't fight, Gypsy."

"Would you marry her? Not you. Take her to the gyppos. Purge her with tansy and seven-sisters. And if that don't serve, take your foot in your hand and the next seen of you is a dust-cloud on the skyline while little Durie listens to the cuckoo sing."

"So you're in on this, too. What's your interest?"

"I'm a friend of Durie's."

"Well, if there is anything of that sort in prospect . . ."

"I didn't say there was. There might be."

". . . she can look further for the father."

"Oh, you dirty pup!" said Gypsy and poured her drink into a convenient spitbox.

She thought it as well not to report the conversation to Durie.

Box-office returns held up well through the Geneva engagement. On the final night, Senator Lovatt summoned his nephew.

"Have you given in your notice?"

"Yes, sir. But I've withdrawn it."

"Damme! Why?"

"I have more to learn."

"Much," the Senator agreed. "Experience keeps a dear school, but fools learn in no other."

"I've had my experience, sir."

"And a pretty penny it cost! Cold baths morning and night are said to allay hot blood, though I never found them of much avail. Absence is better. Don't tell me that you're still besotted over the doxy."

"I despise her," snapped Jans.

"Unphilosophical, my boy, unphilosophical. She has behaved after the nature and tradition of her kind, the world over. You'll find a cure beyond range of those eyes of hers. We'll be off in the morning."

"Not I, Uncle. I ask your indulgence."

"Bitch-and-damme, boy! How many more amorous scrapes d'you expect me to bail you out of?"

"There will be no more."

"Not when I have you under my eye. You're to come home, and no more palaver about it."

"I'm like Mr. Webster, Uncle; a little hard to coax, impossible to . . ."

"You compare yourself to that great man, you preposterous oaf? As sure as your name is Jans Quintard . . ."

"You're talking to John Quinn, sir."

The Senator's neck swelled ominously. "I know no John Quinn. Not on my list. Does your intelligence grasp that?"

"Without effort."

"And henceforth no John Quinn may pretend to any association with me. Are you prepared to accept that?"

"Without regret."

"That's well . . . Eh? What's that? Are you making game of me, sir?"

"By no means, Uncle. Shall you extend your exclusions to the rest of the company? Miss Wayne, for example?"

He retired, grinning, before a storm of objurgations which left him unruffled. Uncle Vryling would be all right when he had cooled down.

Half that night was spent stowing scenery and props; the rest in the saddle exploring for the next flag-stop. His duties for a time brought him little in contact with La Jeune Amour except upon the stage, and so it might have continued indefinitely had not their route taken them through an insect-infested region where Durie's walnut-shuck decoction was much in demand for the livestock.

On the principle that what is good for beast should be good for man, young Mr. Rapalje, who was not overbright at best, sought relief from the pestiferous mosquitoes by a liberal application of the paste to face and hands. As the color, a smeary brown-green, was fast, he could not be cast for ten days in any part except the Leper of Sidi Bar.

Thus Mr. John Quinn, substituting as juvenile, found himself obliged to rehearse passages with La Jeune Amour. He was none too good and knew it, but he derived a grim satisfaction from the knowledge that she was considerably worse. No poker could have been as stiff as was she in the love scenes. Fortunately these were few and brief. There was a tacit understanding that communications between them were to be purely professional. Jans was illogically exasperated by the equanimity with which she accepted the status and even improved upon it. Yet both were conscious of strain. The harassed Mr. Passerow, rehearsing them, was equally conscious of it and righteously exasperated.

"Embrace warmly," he read from the stage directions. "Do you call that warmth? A couple of frozen fishes. Try again."

Someone called him offstage. Durie closed her eyes and shuddered. Jans noted the shudder with annoyance.

"Well," said he harshly, "come on, let's get it over with."

She came into his arms, rigid as a length of cordwood, and softened to tremulous, breathless surrender against his heart.

"Better! Much better," approved Mr. Passerow, turning back.

The spell was broken. Jans passed a shaking hand across his brow.

"Hellcat!" he muttered. He was not to be made a fool of twice, not Jans Quintard! Not by any female, however seductive.

Ever with an eye out for profits, the manager perceived a hope of building La Jeune Amour up, poor actress though she was, by casting her more frequently with John Quinn. There was always that prospect of her coming benefit, backed by the important Ayrault interest. Mr. Passerow had recently adapted a drama for which he had great hopes. La Jeune Amour had had a reading. He decided that John Quinn's efforts in the line of simplification should be utilized in the new part.

"That recital of yours, Mr. Quinn," he said one day between acts. "Is Miss Amour well practiced in it?"

"Yes," said Miss Amour.

"No," said Mr. Quinn.

"What's wrong about it?" the manager asked, addressing Mr. Quinn.

"I think it would be better suited to Miss Wayne's style and talents."

The look which La Jeune Amour directed upon him was a weird admixture of wounded fawn and incensed rattlesnake.

"No question of Miss Wayne. She has had her benefit," returned the manager snappishly. "I look to you to assure that Miss Amour's rendition is satisfactory in the poem. You are in charge." He left.

"Don't you wish me to recite your poem?" asked Durie.

Jans shrugged. "It doesn't matter. You or another. Question of where to interpolate it. What are you playing?"

"Cecilia in *The Misprized Wife*."

"Passerow's play?"

"Yes, do you know it?"

"I have read the script."

"It has a mortal fine female lead."

"It's foofaraw."

"You think nothing good but your own poesy, Mr. John Quinn."

He ignored this. "There are emotional passages in the play, false but difficult, that would try the powers of an experienced actress."

"Experience isn't everything," she returned defiantly.

"It's much."

"If the others can do it, why not I?"

"The others are actors. They may be bad actors, but they're actors."

She flushed indignantly. "I think," she said with dignity, "that we should proceed with the coaching, since Mr. Passerow wishes it so."

The rehearsal ended in a murk of mutual disesteem.

They tried out *The Misprized Wife* at Canandaigua with indifferent success. Jans' part was mainly off-stage music while he writhed impotently at Cecilia's heroics. The Passerows covered her ineptitudes from self-interest; Baggo, Archbold and Crosbie from tradition, but Fair Luna Wayne supported by the other women slyly knifed her with false cues, stolen situations, and tricky by-play to divert a rival from the path of possible success. Jans could have warned her but, in his bitterness, would not. His cautions would have gone unheeded. She was assured of a triumph preparing for her in Rochester, for she had received a letter in the sprawling, unformed hand of Macel Ayrault, telling her that his pleasure boat with a full complement of the Merry Moments Club would be on hand for every performance in which she appeared, and tactfully inquiring whether she preferred Gothic or Franklin lettering on her testimonial silver. The missive ended with amorous hints which its recipient did not bother to interpret.

The troupe was routed to Rochester by way of Palmyra and Pittsford. At Palmyra the cortege was hailed from the canal and the manager invited aboard a gayly bedizened boat for a drink. Mr. Macel Ayrault with his fellow Corinthians was on his way to meet his Rochester appointment. Mr. Passerow shrewdly fended off the swain's eager suggestion that Miss Durie Andrews join the festivities. Miss Andrews, he explained, would be much occupied in rehearsing her important and thrilling part. He had no wish to play his trump card prematurely. Let this big calf-face of an Ayrault wait and nurse his ardor.

While the prospective star was practicing gestures of despair and resignation before a mirror, Manager Passerow called the other principals together and addressed them sternly.

"No trickeries when we reach Rochester. The town is alert. We shall pack 'em in."

"Thanks to your partiality," whined Miss Wayne. "I had no such advertisement for my benefit."

"You brought in no such patronage," he pointed out.

"A favoritism," put in Mrs. Alwyn. "Those rantipoling young Corinthians from the Durham boat."

"Did anyone ever set eyes on such a craft!" said Mr. Baggo. "Beribboned like the you-know-who of Babylon."

"No foul language," snapped the manager. "And no foul play on my stage. Don't think I failed to see some of you trying to trip her heels at Canandaigua."

"She don't even know her lines," complained Fair Luna.

"Not when you throw her false cues. There'll be a shilling penalty for every one from now on."

"Can't you make her loosen that ramrod spine in the tender passages?" asked Crosbie. "I'm used to more ardor."

"You might inspire it if you played more like a man and less like a lillypuke," contributed Mr. Baggo, between whom and the lead no love was lost.

"Does this clown presume to learn me my art?" demanded Mr. Crosbie with lifted brows.

"Less quarreling and more attention to the script, gentlemen," prescribed the manager. "I have made some changes in the second act to which I call your attention."

"Tinkering, tinkering, tinkering," grumbled young Rapalje who was recovering his normal hue. "Are we paid for rehearsing a new part every other performance?"

"You are paid what many another actor would be glad to touch," retorted the manager significantly.

At which reminder of the slack times besetting the theatrical profession, the complaints subsided.

At Palmyra, they played to good business for three nights. Macedon, the next town westward, was hardly more than a wagon-stand, but Jans guaranteed it worth a night's stop. As it was only four miles distant, the start was set for late morning. With time on his hands after the pack-up, Jans strolled down to the water-side to look over the shipping.

One canal boat is much like another. Yet there was something vaguely familiar about the craft moored in the basin at an hour when most traffic was on the move. Amidships a royally lettered placard invited the public with the message that all were welcome. Jans strolled aboard and looked about him. A voice behind him croaked, "Low bridge. Ducker-down."

Jans whirled. "Pilk!"

"The old Four-Skater himself," confirmed the other. "Shake."

Jans lowered his voice. "What's the news up north?"

"Good. We're in the clear. Reward withdrawn."

"That calls for a drink."

"It calls for a lot. Come aboard, lad."

They faced one another, grinning, across a neatly set table supporting four different liquors.

"What are you doing with the boat, Pilk?" Jans asked after the first libation.

"Business, and plenty."

"Are you working on her?"

"I own her. Part way, anyhow. And I captain her, lock, stock and barrel.

> *"Oh, I got mun-nee,*
> *An' I ain't gonna work no more . . ."*

he chanted.

The visitor stared about him. The boat was clean, fresh-painted, prosperous-looking. A second placard announced:

MERCHANDISE BELOW
Cash or No Deal.

"Merchandise?" inquired Jans. "What kind of merchandise?"

"Notions, toys, games, knives and cutlery, drapes, ink and quills, pounce-boxes, powder, fancy bedding, whiskey, rum, pickled eels, medicines and books," rattled off Pilk, prodding his goiter into place. "You'd be surprised the market there is on books. Folks hanker for 'em. What they want to waste their time for reading I dunno. But if they'll buy 'em, I'll sell 'em. That's my trade mark."

"A very good one. Where did you find the money for all this?"

Mr. Pilkington winked. "Ask me no questions and I'll tell you no lies. I picked up a bit here, a bit there. It was honest. Honest enough," he qualified after consideration.

"This outfit couldn't be had at less than seven or eight hundred as she stands."

"Eight-fifty, she's appraised."

"And the goods half as much."

"All o' that. Ever hear of a feller called Lucky Seven Smith?"

Jans drew back. "If that's where you got your money . . ."

"Hold your horses, boy. Know another feller named Captain Byles?"

"Of course! This is his boat. I remember her now."

"Was his boat," corrected Pilk.

Jans waited.

"The three of us met up in Clyde Tavern and got drunk together like the jolly good fellers we are. Though, come to think of it, mebbe I wa'nt so much so as I looked. Mebbe, I say. So we sat down to a little game."

"Poker?"

Pilk nodded. "Cutthroat. When it was all over I had Lucky Seven's cash and a half-share in Captain Byles' boat. The hand is quicker than the eye."

Jans whistled. "I'm surprised Smith let you get away with it."

"I hit him first," admitted Pilk. "And mine was loaded at the tip."

"I should say you've done well for yourself."

"You ain't seen the half of it till you've been in my private room, as the Queen of Sheba told King Solomon."

He led the way to the forward hatch. A large sign indicated an Indian Museum. There were the usual bows and arrows, war clubs, fish spears, scalps, headdresses and wampum. Opposite was a closed door displaying the legend in discreet lettering:

MALES ONLY

"Little side-show," Pilk explained. "A picture. Ve-ry tasty. Agricultural subject."

"Not the Le Sueur pigs!"

Pilk nodded complacently. "Ten cents a look. Don't crowd, gents. Room for all."

All Central New York knew of the itinerant and improvident Frenchman's painting, forfeited to a Schenectady tavern on an unpaid bar bill, and there exhibited profitably until the church folk entered a protest and the sheriff descended. But "The Amatory Pigs," a barnyard scene, executed with great spirit and explicitness, had vanished. And here it was, doing business beyond reach of any county official, since Erie Water was a state highway.

"It's a mint," said its owner. "On Ladies' Evening, I charge two bits. You'd ought to see 'em sneak aboard." He studied his young friend. "Wanta come in as my partner?" he barked. "You're book-learned. There's money in that end."

"Thanks, Pilk. But I've got a job."

"What is it?"

"Theatre. The Thalian troupe."

"Jazes and blazes! Wandering Willie! You!"

"It's not such a bad pitch."

"I'll warrant there's a wench in it."

"There is not!"

"No need to yell, young feller. Where you headed for?"

"Rochester next week. Way stands in between."

"Some town, Rochester. Think all hell of themselves, they do. I'll say this for 'em, though—they got the cleanest jail I ever was in. Likely I'll see you there before you leave."

"The jail?" grinned Jans.

"No, spoopsy, the theatre. And I'll bopp an egg off your nose, if you ain't good."

Jans jumped ashore. Pilk saluted him, captain fashion.

"Think over that partnership when your show busts," he shouted after the retreating visitor.

"We aren't going to bust," Jans called back.

But he had his doubts.

20

ONE hundred and fifty dollars swelled the Thalian money-box to unprecedented richness. All of it was originally destined, in the manager's good intentions, to much needed restoration of equipment. One recurrent expense which had long grated on Mr. Passerow's niggardly soul was lighting by candle or oil, paid for nightly in addition to rental. This painful outlay he now obviated by an investment in Burnett's Highlight Illuminant for Theatres, Stores and Public Halls, a cheap, odorous and diabolical mixture of alcohol and spirits of turpentine, burned in special lamps. Vainly did Jans protest against the device as dangerously explosive. It was a money-saver; that was enough.

Other disbursements, which Jans did approve, were on the Passerow list. They were never made. For, the night before the troupe reached Rochester, the manager had a dream. Clear and bright before the backdrop of a Mint & Mine Lottery show window, the numerals 3—5—0 glowed, paled, glowed again, and burst into a profuse shower of golden coin. What man in his right senses could ignore such a portent? How could he lose?

In the morning, the dreamer took all that remained of the Vryling Lovatt windfall to the Mint & Mine office.

News exchange of the road had forewarned Jans against Rochester as a pernickety and stuck-up community, harsh in its judgment of theatrical offerings. Mr. Passerow declined to be impressed. He insisted in making reservations at the costly Exchange Hotel. Let the Rochesterians come or stay at home, the patronage of young Ayrault and his fellows would, of itself, insure a profitable week.

But when the Thalians arrived, there was no news along the basins of the pleasure craft, *Merry Moments*. Suppose they had

212

been delayed or diverted? Jans put it to Mr. Passerow. The manager scratched his head and consented to a substitute arrangement for cheap camping space at the Liberty Pole. They found the lot swarming with the followers of a newly arrived circus, a motley horde among whom he distinguished the midwives' outfit with which Gypsy Vilas traveled. Jans set down a small deposit on cramped space at the East Main Street angle and left the rolling stock there.

At the Carroll Street Theatre to which he accompanied Mr. Passerow there was cold encouragement. The factor demanded a three-day advance with the sour observation that the Thalians wouldn't last any longer, if that long. He sniffed at the richly typed sheet upon which the management, through the composition of Mr. John Quinn, had announced the coming of the troupe. After a dithyrambic eulogium of the company in general, it concluded with a special tribute to the youngest member.

This charming and dainty artist is equally mistress of allurement and risibilities. The toast of beaux and the despair of suitors, she has dedicated her talents to the drama in which, notwithstanding her tender years, she has already attained heights that are the envy of her rivals. It is expected that the young Corinthians of fashion and wealth will signalize the event of her benefit by a profuse attendance.

"La Joon Amour," the factor read superciliously. "Who's she? Never heard of her. Never heard of any of you except Old Archbold, and thought he was dead long ago."

Mr. Passerow explained in haughty offence, only to be cut short by a curt, "Twenty-five dollars down or you don't draw a curtain."

This would leave the treasury too depleted to meet the hotel bill. Somewhat dashed in spirits, the manager sent Jans to arrange the cancellation.

"That'll be a forfeit," the host said casually. "Shilling a room."

"I'll whistle and you levy on the tune," said Jans.

"You can't get blood out of a turnip," the host admitted. "One of your ladies is settled for, though."

"Which one?" Jans' first thought was that Uncle Vryling might be rejoining his light o' love.

"Naming no names. Mr. Macel Ayrault's account."

Jans scowled. "Cancel it."

"Huh?"

"The company is quartered at the Liberty Pole."

"I don't care if they're quartered at the North Pole. This room is already paid and entered on my books and so it stays. And who may you be, my bucko, to be giving orders?"

The question was painfully pertinent. What status could he assert in the matter of Durie's disposal? If she chose to play the cheap-and-easy doxy with Macel Ayrault, he couldn't stop it. Couldn't he, though! At least, he could try. He had the good name of the Passerow Thalian Dramatic Company to protect.

Back he trudged to the encampment. By this time Durie should be there. If not, then she was already established in Ayrault's quarters at the hotel and no more to be said.

During the long, hot walk out to the spot he proved to himself that he was animated by public spirit and not private interest. As he entered the grounds, he heard Durie singing and was furious at himself for the intensity of his relief. Gypsy Vilas met him at the tent-flap.

"Who fed you a pickle this fine morning, Mr. Sourmaw?"

"Is Durie with you?"

"Inside. Polishing her trophies. Want to see 'em?"

For an instant, as he entered, Jans thought to catch a flash of warmth from the amber eyes uplifted to his. If it was there, it was instantly gone. She welcomed him soberly.

"Aren't they pompous!" She indicated the gold-trimmed cup, the bracelet, and the wax wreaths upon which a pair of doves regarded one another with mild approval. "Mr. Ayrault had them sent up for my inspection."

"Very elegant." He looked about him with an affectation of superciliousness. "But out of place in these humble surroundings. They would be better displayed at the inn."

She made no comment.

"In an arrangement of rooms."

She set down the goblet she had been delicately polishing, and turned to face him in silence. There was nothing to be had from her by insinuations; he might have known that!

"Are you innocent enough to believe that you can accept all

this without return?" he burst out. "And are you fool enough not to know the payment expected?"

"Are you warning me? Of what?"

He made a gesture of surrender. "Why waste breath!"

"As a guardian of my virtue, you play a singular part, Mr. Jans Quintard," said she slowly.

"Marketed but not delivered," he snapped.

They stared at one another in wrath and incomprehension. The next move might have set off an explosion which would have cleared the air had not Gypsy, who had been pottering around with the guy-ropes, intervened.

"I never seen such a pair!" she averred. "Leave you together five minutes and you're either loving or fighting. What ails the lad! Jealous?"

"That would be strange," said Durie.

"Wouldn't it!" he muttered.

"You leave the gal alone," said Gypsy. "Ain't you done enough damage?"

"That account is settled and receipted," he snapped.

"Think he's a little tetched here?" Gypsy inquired, tapping her brown forehead.

"There isn't a doubt of it," Jans said somberly, and left.

At the canal front he found the Ayrault craft moored to the Fitzhugh Street Wharf. A round dozen of the Merry Momenters lolled on the deck, the rising generation of pioneer mid-state families: Averys, Skinners, Bristols, Van Inwagens, Sybrandts, Verplancks and Roses; all moneyed, all carefree and classroom-free and bent upon supporting their friend Ayrault in his pursuit of the young and lovely Thespian. Unless, of course, they could contrive to supplant him as each and every one secretly aspired to do.

Jans was welcomed and bidden to dinner. Nobody questioned him about his theatrical connections. They accepted this little fad of his as that proper Corinthian pursuit, the petticoat, though they considered that he was pushing matters to extremes in joining the company. He must be hard hit.

Someone handed him a glass of flip. The interrupted conversation was resumed.

"What's the signal to be, Mace?" Sennett Avery asked the host.

"A blast from Brass Betty," suggested Wilgus Sybrandt, patting the muzzle of the shining two-pounder.

"Or the lady's silk stocking displayed at the forepeak," amended David Verplanck.

Samson Bristol stepped upon the low cabin top and lifted high his julep.

"To La Jeune Amour. Delicious Durie."

"A torment to our dreams," added Cassius Skinner.

"A fillip to our hopes." This from young Peter Avery.

"Despair of our desires," added Kurt Van Inwagen sentimentally.

Wilgus Sybrandt cut a pigeon wing. He was a gross, bepimpled young fellow with a jaunty carriage and a ready grin.

"Despair be damned!" he chuckled. "A free field and no favor."

"Shilling in the pool?" young Bristol asked Jans.

"What's the issue?"

"How long it will take our sore-stricken friend"—he indicated the smirking host—"to prevail over the damsel's virtue. Pay your coin and name your date."

Jans set his drink down, untasted.

"Sore toes, tread craftily," cautioned young Verplanck in a quiet murmur.

Sybrandt, the humorist, was not to be diverted from his play. "I believe, on my soul, Quintard fancies himself as competitor. Who'll back him?" he roared jovially. "Two to one, the stallion on the inside track. Is our Macey to be cuckolded before . . . ?"

He ducked as the glass from Jans' hand whizzed past his ear to vanish beneath the canal surface with an inglorious "Glumph!" His lower lip dropped, abject, his face a mask of shocked surprise. Verplanck and Skinner pinned Jans from behind.

"Steady, Quinny," said Verplanck in his ear.

"All right," said Jans, mastering himself. "Let me go. I won't kill him."

"A word with you, Quintard," said Macel Ayrault. "Come below."

Jans followed him down the companionway.

"What's this girl to you?" asked Ayrault seriously.

"What's that to you?" retorted Jans.

"You've insulted one of my guests."

"He insulted one of our troupe. You all did, damn you! I won't have her name—their names bandied about like cheap Cyprians."

"Are you telling me that she is virtuous?" asked the other incredulously.

"Ask her and see what answer you get."

"I'm asking you."

"You're asking the wrong person."

"Look you, Quinny," said the big fellow with rising suspicion. "You haven't made a fool of yourself by marrying the girl on the sly, have you?"

Jans composed a face of perfect blankness as he met his questioner's eyes. It was as illogical as it was instinctive. Why should he attempt or even wish to protect the girl, who would doubtless laugh with her lover at his silly Quixotism? For there was no doubt of the interpretations which Macel Ayrault would put upon his silence. Macel's next speech confirmed this.

"Well, by God! So you're caught."

"You've no right to assume that." Jans' protest was mild.

"She's sightly enough," conceded Ayrault. "I wouldn't pay the price, myself, not being a marrying man. Yet, I dunno. Those eyes! And those lips!" He sighed stertorously. "Sybrandt's an ass," he went on in a brisker tone. "I'll make him apologize."

"Not a word to him or anyone else," said Jans sharply.

"You mean I'm to mum it?" inquired Ayrault, amazed.

"Until I give the word."

Ayrault began to laugh, clapping his huge thigh. "Am I finely diddled!" he cried. "Gold-lettered testimonies. Cooing-dove wreaths. A supper party promised with prime wines. I can smell my burnt money."

"You can withdraw them."

"And show myself a Sabbaday gull? Not big Macel! Why, they'd laugh me daft from the Four Corners to Hanford's Landing. No, no, Quinny, my boy. I'm properly bammed and I'll pay the scot. The cunning little minikin!" He laughed and swore in one breath.

Pleading an afternoon's work, Jans left the boat. What had he let himself in for by his headlong strategy? As far as revelation went, he thought that he could trust Macel if only on the ground of masculine pride; he knew that he could trust him in regard to Durie.

Easy though his standards were, Ayrault would be faithful to the tradition of his class; he would not pursue a friend's wife. As for Durie's finding out, that would come later. He would face it when it came. Damn the girl! She wasn't worth it. He'd made a fool of himself.

The Thalians were opening in Mr. Payne's farce, *Truth's a Lie*. Despite the success of his *Clari, the Maid of Milan*, with its song of "Home, Sweet, Sweet Home" now being plagiarized by scores of songstresses, the latter play had small success in New York. But it commended itself to Mr. Passerow as being easy and cheap to produce. The advance sale was still thin when, at four o'clock, Jans, having finished his set, rejoined the manager in the lobby.

"Where are the young ladies?" he asked.

"Hellicatting it in a coach with some of the canal boat bucks."

"Oughtn't they to be rehearsing?"

"That would be work," returned the sour-faced manager. "Not good enough for miladies. They prefer tol-lolling it at the sweetie founts. I hope they get the bellygripes."

"Durie's role is an easy one," reflected Jans.

"Lucky fip that it is! She mouths it like Lady Macbeth. I wish Wednesday evening were well over."

"Her benefit? It's a chance," said Jans.

"It's all that will save us."

They were working out estimates when the merry-making party arrived, Durie serenely beautiful, Gypsy flushed and laughing, Fair Luna coquettish, and the young men in boisterous spirits. Some of these they imparted to Mr. Passerow by bespeaking the entire center section of the pit. As the party entered the lobby, Durie glanced at the public notice board and stopped short.

"Gypsy!" she said in a low tone.

The older girl dropped back. "What's amiss?"

"Looby."

"Didn't he make his evasion?"

"Yes. Look. The reward's posted."

"That keeper-fella warned us."

"It's a hundred dollars."

Gypsy gasped. "That's a mort o' money."

"The broadside says he was westbound on the towpath when last seen."

"He would be, the poor zany!"

"He'll be looking for us."

"If Gospel gave him the word."

"Where would we hide him?"

"I dunno. We might ask Quinny."

"Do you think he's to be trusted, Gypsy?"

"I know what's on your mind. But there's many a man can't be trusted in a hay-loft that'll deal fair and square in the open," replied the oracular Gypsy.

"Let's wait and see if we hear anything," said Durie.

So perturbed was she over the problem that she gave a poor and listless rehearsal. Jans drove her with cold patience. She tripped, repeated, jumbled her lines, forgot every direction.

"Start again," said Jans.

"I can't. It's no use."

"You've got only two more days."

"I can't help it."

"Something on your mind?"

"No. Yes."

"Macel Ayrault, perhaps." He could not resist that.

Her eyes clouded with reflection. "I never thought of him. He might help." She spoke with animation.

"Mr. Quinn! Mr. Quinn! Mr. Passerow wants to see you."

Unthinkingly he put down the manuscript of the poem to answer the summons. Durie had recourse to it to aid her distracted memory. Her surprised glance encountered a new leaf. She read the verse with mingled feelings:

> *He's a fool who would pose as love's martyr.*
> *He has ventured his heart; let him pay!*
> *Since your favor is subject to barter*
> *I can laugh and forget it next day.*
> *You are practical; I but a dreamer.*
> *You're for settlements; I'm touch—and—go.*
> *So the worshipper bows to the schemer,*
> *But I'll love you no longer, oh, no!*

She held it out to him on his return. "Am I intended to include this?"

"Not meant for your eyes," he answered sharply.

"I doubt that I could do it justice."

"Since you've read it, what is your opinion?"

"It is as lame in versification as blind in meaning," she said primly.

"It means nothing to you?"

Her smile was malicious. "The touch-and-go line is misplaced. Let's get back to our work."

Truth's a Lie failed to thrill Rochester. Had it not been for the solid block of Merry Momenters and their friends, the reception accorded to the troupe would have been lukewarm, indeed. But this loyal contingent supplied a running commentary of applause and "Bravos!" to the performance. Every time La Jeune Amour made her entry, they rose and cheered, repeating the tribute at her exit, which was highly gratifying to her but annoyed the others and seriously impaired the continuity of the drama.

"We've a distinguished patronage," said Mr. Passerow to Jans complacently.

"I see Mr. Everard Peck, the printer," said Jans.

"And Colonel Rochester and wife, and the Dr. Ward family; Mr. Hamlet Scranton, Mr. Reynolds; half of the Ruffleshirt Third Ward is here."

"They don't seem very fervent."

"Spoilsport!" Genial for once, the manager smote him between the shoulders. "There's eighty dollars in the house. We move to the hotel tomorrow."

Scrutinizing the front through the peephole, Jans described two faces which lent no éclat to the assemblage—Lucky Seven Smith and, above him in the gallery, Bassford Pilkington. What was the Missouri puke doing in town? Pilk might know something; anyway, they'd have a dram together after the curtain.

"Have you got that puffery for Mr. Peck ready?" asked Mr. Passerow.

Jans took the manuscript from his pocket. As a rule, the press paid no attention to anything as trivial as the stage, beyond accepting the paid advertisements. But the redoubtable Everard was

220

a pioneer and spoke his editorial mind upon any subject that interested him. To give that mind a slant in the right direction was Manager Passerow's purpose in ordering an advance notice from the ingenious and serviceable pen of Mr. John Quinn. The manager ran through it with grunts of approval.

"I will present it for the printer's consideration," he said.

Ayrault and his claque gave curtain-call upon curtain-call at the close of each act, but, though many of the Rochesterians stayed through, they seemed to Jans ominously apathetic. The manager intercepted Mr. Everard Peck to hand him Jans' composition which was received with a curt nod.

Supper was offered by Ayrault and his fellows to the ladies, but Durie declined on the ground of duty. With Gypsy she set out for the camp while Jans joined Pilk at an adjacent bar.

"Seen the notice-board?" the Four-Skater asked.

"No. Too busy."

Pilk told him of the reward.

"Looby? I didn't know he was out," Jans said. "Think that's what Lucky Seven is here for?"

"Like as not. When was it you was in Auburn, lad?"

"Week before last."

"That's about the time," Pilk said thoughtfully. "The talk is that two young females pried him out of chokey."

"Good Lord!" Jans had remembered Durie's being late for rehearsal after a visit to the prison. "You don't think . . ."

"Naming no names," Pilk said with characteristic secretiveness where matters of the law were involved, and quaffed his ale.

Out at the Liberty Pole, Durie filled the betty-lamp with oil and lighted the wick. As it flared up, the other girl exclaimed. A long, white cord, curiously knotted and embellished, swayed from the ridgepole in the light current of air.

"What's that?" asked Durie, staring.

"Reckon it's a message." Gypsy fingered it lightly.

"Who from?"

"Deacon Gildersleeve's hymn-singing son," answered the other, after a scrutiny of the string's end. "Remember him?"

"The helmsman of the *Peace-on-Earth?*"

"That's the lad."

"If he's got something to say why doesn't he do it in a letter?"

"He can't write, and if he did I mebbe couldn't read it."

"But what's that thing?"

"Tenker's string. Reckon I can part make it out." She touched here a twig, there a bit of cloth, again a spill of paper, and counted some knots. "Somebody's hiding in a pine thicket, one- two- three mile to the west'ard. Gerundigut Cut, likely."

"Looby!"

"Looby, sure as Satan's in hell!" confirmed the interpreter. She returned to a study of the tenker's code, that loose ritual of the un-lettered. "He's hungry. Here's more figgers. Four knots."

"Four o'clock?" suggested Durie. "That would be before dawn."

Gypsy nodded. "He'll be coming in."

"Here?"

"Yup. We gotta hide him some way."

"And feed him."

"If we had a side-show we could paint him up and take him along as the Wild Woops of Timbuctoo."

"Don't forget the hundred dollars on his head, Gypsy."

"It's fetched out the black-hunters already. I seen one at the show. Well, let's get our snooksy-snorum while we can."

Breakfast was hardly over when Jans came to the tent.

"Boxes ready at ten, Miss Amour," he announced.

Gypsy thrust her small, sleek head through the flap. "What for?"

"Company's moving to the Exchange Hotel."

"Not Durie. We're staying here."

"In preference to a sumptuous chamber with mirrors?" Jans asked, looking hard at Durie.

"Who's to look after the bestial if I leave?" she propounded.

"The animals go with us." He was staring at the canvas which showed plainly the outline of a human shoulder. "Who's in that tent?" he demanded.

Gypsy bared her teeth at him. "Keep your eyes where they belong if you don't want 'em scratched out."

"It wouldn't be Looby?" he said softly.

"Mind your goddamn business."

He turned to Durie. "You can't do that," he warned. "It's against the law."

"We're not doing anything," Gypsy retorted. "So be on your way, Mister Nosey." She changed her tone. "Oh, Quinny! You wouldn't split on us!"

"You're a brace of precious idiots. But I'll do what I can with Passerow about letting Dur—Miss Amour stay."

Though puzzled, the manager made no objection. The girl's unaccountable preference for tent life saved him just so much in hotel charges.

21

Having a high opinion of Bassford Pilkington's resourcefulness, Jans went to him for counsel about Looby.

"And the wenches have got him now?" Pilk asked.

"Yes. In their tent."

"That's harborin'," said his friend. "They could get into bad trouble for that."

"So I told them. I wish I knew how much Lucky Seven Smith knows."

"I heard of him chasin' a fellow, down Gerundigut way yesterday. Fired a charge at him outa that foolck he carries, but the lad 'vaded into a thicket. He'll get him."

"Maybe he won't."

"Lucky Seven always gets 'em."

"Not if someone else gets him first."

"Who?"

"You and I."

Pilk's jaw dropped so abruptly that his pipe fell to earth. He stood, staring, and let it lie.

"Turn in that poor bastard for a hundred dollars?" he said slowly. "Not me!"

"Would you rather we'd get him, or Smith?"

"Smith," said Pilk, and spat.

"Listen, Pilk. You don't know Looby. He hasn't got enough brains to fill a teacup. There isn't a chance of his keeping out of the hands of Lucky Seven or some other black-hunter. Not with a hundred dollars on him."

Mr. Pilkington gathered up his pipe and thrust it in his pocket. "You can have it," he said. "I wouldn't wipe the snot from my nose with that kinda money."

He turned away. Jans collared him. "Let me finish, you old fool. Do you know what I'm going to do with the reward?"

Pilk told him what he could do with it.

"How would that help Looby?" said Jans reasonably. "I'm going to hire the best lawyer in Albany to lay the case before the Governor. And if Mr. Throop is the man I think he is, we'll get a pardon."

"Oh!" Pilk grunted. "That's different."

As an apology it was the most to be expected from him. It satisfied Jans.

"The next thing is to get him," he said.

"We go up there and grab him now, huh?"

"Not unless you want your throat cut."

Pilk bristled. "Who'll do it? Not Lucky Seven."

"Two active young damsels with wicked, sharp knives," grinned Jans.

"Could Lucky Seven suspicion where he is?"

"I don't know. He's worth watching. Wait for me at the Pole after the show."

Another consultation was in progress contemporaneously on the same subject. The two girls were agreed upon the impracticability of keeping the fugitive indefinitely in their tent. What disposal to make of him, then?

"We'd oughta have help," Gypsy reflected.

"I think I know someone who'll help us," said Durie.

"Who?"

"Mr. Macel Ayrault."

"That big hunk? Where does he figger?"

"He told me he'd move heaven and earth to serve my smallest wish."

"Sweetie-talk," Gypsy disparaged. "Says little and means less."

"It will do no harm to try. Will you take a note for me?"

Yes, Gypsy would do that, though she doubted that much would come of it. The note, elegantly penned and discreetly worded, requested the pleasure of a brief interview with Mr. Ayrault in the tavern parlor.

The recipient's emotions were mixed upon reading the missive. An assignation with the wife of a friend? That wasn't in the cards.

Yet, she might have her sound reasons; perhaps she had learned of the betrayal of her secret and wished to secure his silence. Curiosity prevailed; Mr. Ayrault presented himself on the minute.

"This is very private, Mr. Ayrault," she began.

"At your service, ma'am," he said cautiously.

"I bespeak your aid on behalf of an unfortunate friend." She outlined the dilemma while he listened with growing astonishment and distaste.

"Why come to me?" he inquired at the finish of her recital.

"To whom else could I appeal?"

"Your husband," he blurted.

"My *what?* Are you making a jest of me?"

"No. Nor you're not going to make one of me, neither," he returned bluntly. "I have it on authority that you are secretly wedded to Jans Quintard."

Her eyes widened. She gave a little gasp. "To Ja——! On what authority?"

"The best," he replied doggedly. "But I've said too much."

"Did he tell you that?"

"Yes." Ayrault was honestly under the impression that this was truth.

"I can't believe it."

"He bound me to secrecy," he admitted. "I didn't mean to let it slip."

"It's as well that you did," she assured him. She bent forward, laid her hand upon his arm, looked up at him with her serene and luminous gaze. "I swear to you that there is no truth in it; that I am a maid—a spinster," she amended with a flush.

In his eagerness, he missed the sense of this. "Then there is no impediment?"

"Impediment to what?"

"My hopes."

She smiled at him not without coquetry. "Aren't we forgetting poor Looby?"

"Damn poor Looby! What do you ask me to do with him?"

"Hide him aboard your boat until we can spirit him away."

He towered over her. "And my reward? Will you come with him?"

226

"You mean will I fetch him myself?"

"I mean will you come with him and stay."

"On the boat?"

"You shall have a cabin more elegant than the inn. Silken hangings."

"Is that the price of your help?" she asked composedly.

"If I am to run afoul of the law, you ought to be there to countenance me," said he, with what he considered a seductive smile, and she an ogreish leer.

"It's your only condition? That I remain on the boat with Looby?"

"And me. I'll send the others packing."

"Very well."

"When will you come? Tonight?" he pressed.

"Not tonight. There are arrangements to be made. Tomorrow night."

In anticipation of success, Gypsy had made up Looby as a blackamoor and dressed him in livery filched from the costume box. It was a simple matter for Macel Ayrault, tooling a borrowed tandem, to drive to the encampment and return with a handsomely outfitted black behind him. At the Clinton Avenue corner he almost ran down Lucky Seven Smith who, having had a hard night, was languid on his feet. The mantracker cursed him and was wholeheartedly damned in return. Looby sat, quaking and unnoticed through the episode. He was presently stowed away in the hold, to the satisfaction of the two girls who had met the equipage at the wharf.

Together they inspected the superb cabin which was to be Durie's habitat for the last half of the week.

"I reckon you know your feed-bag," observed Gypsy to her friend as they climbed the bank.

"Yes," was the placid reply.

"Do you aim to trick the big ape or not?"

Durie smiled, "Did you notice the door?"

"What of it?"

"It opens outward. I can rope it so that General Jackson at the head of the army couldn't get in."

"There's the porthole as big as a window."

"And there's my flax-knife as sharp as a razor."

Gypsy scratched her ear. "You're mighty cockahoop for your age, wench. But some day you're going to get your comeuppance."

The evening's offering was the good old standby, *Sweethearts and Wives*. The house was comfortably filled, but, in spite of the determined efforts of the pleasure boaters, disturbingly cold. Mr. Tim Baggo came off after his "excruciatingly risible scene" (as stated in advertisements), somber as the First Gravedigger.

"What a pit!" he grumbled. "Getting a laugh out of 'em is like trying to skin a louse with a toothpick."

"They got no sense of art," said Fair Luna Wayne with a malevolent glance at La Jeune Amour, who had enjoyed a generous meed of applause for her own brief side, though it came from the center of the house alone.

Only the manager was cheerful. "We're getting the money, aren't we?" he said.

There was no question as to the receipts. But Jans had his misgivings as to their disposal. He had surprised Mr. Passerow making calculations on a slate. Mathematics with that gentleman meant but one thing. If further proof were needed, a list of lottery figures lay handy. Jans hoped that the hotel had received a sufficient advance.

Instead of remaining after the show to tidy up for next day, as was his custom, he slipped out after the final curtain. Pilk was waiting. His middle bulged queerly.

"I don't like this, lad," he mumbled.

"Can you think of any other way?"

"No-o-o," conceded the other reluctantly. "If we don't get him, Lucky Seven will."

"What's under your jacket, Pilk?"

"Ropes."

Jans winced. "He won't fight. I'm sure he won't. Not if I can get it through his poor, thick head that we mean him well."

"I don't like it anyways," Pilk insisted.

They made the Liberty Pole at a trot. The girls' tent was dark. Jans edged up to the rear and spoke cautiously.

"Looby! Do you hear me?"

No answer.

"We're friends. We've come to save you."

228

The tent remained as silent as it was dark.

"We're coming in. Don't make any move."

He parted the flaps. Pilk struck a locofoco. They peered under the cots and back of the hanging garments. There was nobody in the place. They came out into the night.

"Gone," said Jans.

"If he ever was here."

"He's been here." Jans stirred with his feet a discarded quid of coarsest plug.

"The wenches must have taken him somewhere else."

"Where would they take him? Steady," he added in a lower tone. "Someone's coming."

"It's the puke," said Pilk.

Lucky Seven Smith sauntered up and gave them a view of jagged teeth in the moonlight. The smile, if such it were, was less suave than the tone in which he addressed them.

"Bammed, and be poxed to you!"

"We're not the only ones," retorted Pilk.

"My meat," snarled the manhunter. "Keep off."

"It's a free country," Pilk reminded him.

"For them that can keep their freedom."

"The luckiest of us can't always do that, Mr. Lucky Seven," Jans said blandly. It was a shot in the dark, but the Missourian reddened as he thrust his face forward to peer at the speaker.

"It's the handy-actor. Where have I seen you before, though?"

"Along the Black Snake. You were plying your trade."

"Which you and your pal are taking up, it seems."

"We came here to see the ladies," Jans said smoothly.

"Oh? I'll wait and have a word with 'em, myself."

The three sat on the hitch rail and swung their feet until Durie and Gypsy appeared. Lucky Seven's presence complicated the situation to the extent of preventing the conspirators from making any inquiries. Mr. Smith was not thus inhibited.

"Ladies, your servant. Smith from Missouri, known as Lucky Seven."

"I've heard of you," said Gypsy.

He made her a graceful bow. "I trust to improve your impression. May we proceed to business?"

"What is your business?" asked Durie. "And what has it to do with us at this hour of the night?"

"We're all here on the same trail," he answered with a sweep of his head toward the other men.

Durie's steady look shifted to Pilkington and then to Jans.

"Don't answer any of his questions," advised Jans.

"Your tongue will get you into trouble yet, my young friend," warned Lucky Seven. He addressed Durie. "What have you done with your guest?"

"I have no guest."

"I know that. I know also that you have had. Where is he?"

"I do not recognize your right to question me."

He said softly, regretfully, "Youth and beauty like yours, to languish in jail. A melancholy thought. Deal with me frankly and I will not lay an information against you for harboring."

"Going back to town?" Jans rose and faced him. "I should, if I were you."

Lucky Seven's hand crept to his breast. Pilk moved in on him, the anchor peg of a tent in his grip. The prospect looked unfavorable to the Missourian.

"Two against one," he remarked, "and that one already vanquished by beauty." He swept a bow to the girls. "We shall meet again."

Gypsy marched up to Pilk. "What's those ropes for?" she demanded.

"Stray hosses," said Pilk with great presence of mind.

Her opinion of that was expressed in a strident gardaloo. "Prr-rr-rrt! Git! All of you. We need our sleep."

The two amateurs of the chase were about to follow the professional out of the lot when Durie spoke up.

"Mr. Quinn!"

"Yes, Miss Amour?"

"May I have a word with you?"

"Yours to command," he said with a flourish and followed her aside.

"Did you tell Mr. Macel Ayrault that I—that you—that we are man and wife?"

"No."

"He believes so."

"Can I help what Ayrault believes?"

"He announced it to me on your authority. You must have connived."

"Very well, if you will have it. I had my reasons."

"For a lie? I can't conceive what they would be."

"To protect you."

"I can assure my own protection," she retorted with a curl of the lip.

"Can you? Always?"

"That is a cowardly taunt—from you to me. And you now presume . . ."

"I am considering the good repute of the company which you are compromitting by your light conduct," he defended himself.

"Who are you to judge my conduct? Your own requires more explanation."

"When did you see Ayrault?" he asked uneasily.

"This afternoon at the tavern. I told him what he had heard was wholly false. And," she added, her brows contracting, "if you think to shelter my reputation by rumors of wedlock between you and me, public or private, I am not of your opinion."

"Thank you," said Jans, unable at the moment to fabricate a more satisfactory retort.

She swept past him into the tent without another glance. Gypsy raised her head from her cot.

"Lovey-doveying again?"

"No."

"You better not. Know what those two are up to?"

"I heard what Mr. Smith said. I don't believe it."

"It's a fact. They're after Looby and the hundred dollars."

"Oh, no!"

"Didn't you see the ropes?"

Durie shuddered, but said stoutly, "I can believe much of Jans Quintard but never that."

"D'you know what I think of that young blade?" pronounced Gypsy with chill deliberation. "I think he's a leather-hatted, double-vatted, slippery-slatted, up-and-downstairs son-of-a-bitch and a mauser. Put that under your pillow and sleep on it."

22

AMOUR! Amour!" chorused the pit. "Jeune Amour! Belle Amour! Amour *exquise!*"

They waved scented handkerchiefs and made osculatory noises. The gallery, thinly patronized, responded with loud and vulgar gardaloos, also produced through the lips, but to a different purport.

The Merry Moments were in fullest fig to do honor to the occasion. Though the air still preserved something of its summer warmth, all carried Taglionis, those new and elegant short coats and very tall flare-brimmed hats of drab, springtime-green, or jonquil-yellow. Collars and ruffles were Fashion's latest display: delicately frilled paper, plaited to perfection with hot irons. The array of neckcloths ran the gamut of the rainbow, and the brooch pins outglittered the show window of the Dame's Delight Jewelry Emporium on State Street.

"Ain't it dicty!" breathed Gypsy Vilas in vast admiration, peeping out between the dark curtains.

It was, indeed, an impressive sight. But, with the exception of unruffled Durie, the Thalians were in no appreciative mood. For the *Genesee Farmer* had appeared upon the streets that afternoon without the pleasant puff from Mr. John Quinn's pen. In its stead was a contribution straight from the editorial font of gall and wormwood. Mr. Peck, one of the most outspoken of the printing confraternity, had not liked the Thalian offerings and made no bones about saying so.

No more fustian performance (wrote the printer) has ever been proffered for the consideration of our cultured and discriminating populace. It would have been dear as three-penny barn-loft entertainment. In such a welter of ineptitudes it is difficult to apportion censure justly. Suffice it, then, to say that Mr. Passerow's *Admiral Cass* was a mumble-jumble of indistinguishable phrases, Mr. Crosbie's *Fleming* could more fittingly have been spelled *Phlegming,* since he wheezed like a victim of the tizzick, while Mr. Baggo's "comical" (God save the mark!) rendition of *Sam Chockablock* moved to tears rather than laughter.

Nor are the fair members of the troupe more praiseworthy. Mrs. Passerow piped; Mrs. Alwyn gurgled, and a comely damsel with wooden legs, designated as La Jeune Amour, gesticulated through her insignificant scenes with all the freedom and grace of Mailzell's chess-playing Turk about to advance a pawn. As for Miss Wayne, her all-too palpably mammalian interpretation of the coquettish *Caresse* would have more agitated the breasts of her audience had she less agitated her own. Over the performance of the minor roles let Charity draw the veil of Silence. Only the forbearance and courtesy for which our City is justly famed, withheld a long-suffering audience from demanding the return of its money.

Out front sat the author of this outrage, looking so grimly amused with himself that Jans wondered how much it would cost in fines and imprisonment to punch an eminent printer in the nose.

Fair Luna Wayne came to Durie. "You're all a-twitch," she said malevolently.

"Am I? I don't feel it."

"You ought to. Didn't you read today's journal?"

"Yes."

"And you pretend not to care?"

"My dad used to quote an old saw. 'They say? What say they? Let them say!'"

Fair Luna snorted. "All I got to say to you, Miss Puckerface, is please not to spoil our second-act scene by speaking your lines like you had a rotten pawpaw between your teeth."

"Give over, Miss!" Old Archbold drew her aside and received her elbow in the ribs for his trouble. "Don't let her fusticate you," he advised Durie kindly, and went on in soothing tones to give her an old-timer's counsel to a tyro. Let her take her first entry slow; be sure not to rush her cues, keep cool, and above all maintain a level. Excited and uplifted, Durie was prepared to maintain her own level and it should be a high one.

At her cue she minced on and was greeted by a tremendous outburst, far more fervid than anything she had experienced before, from the massed youth in the pit.

"How lovely the moon," she began, and was stopped by thunders of applause.

"How lovely the moon," she repeated, to noises of stamping and clapping, which she acknowledged with smile, swish of skirt, and curtsey. Very gratifying, but she did wish they'd let her get on with it.

"How lovely the moon." Then, with a resolute shout, "tonight." (Cheers, lasting a full minute.) "But where is my husband, the Count?"

What ensued was misery and distraction for the cast but apparently a pleasure to the young star. After five minutes of it, Tim Baggo whispered to Mr. Passerow, "You gotta give her éclat for being a cool 'un."

"If she wouldn't strut," groaned the manager. "Look at those elbows."

"Look at that face!" retorted the buffo.

La Jeune Amour was, indeed, radiant in her exultation. It was tempered little, if at all, by a low, insistent voice from the wings, repeating at intervals, "Play down! Play down!"

She scorned Jans' ill-timed advice. Why should she play down? They liked it, didn't they, out front? Like it? They loved it! She tossed her head and gave them all she had. The act ended, upborne on waves of acclaim.

The testimonial presentation was timed to follow the second-act curtain. Murmurs of admiration accompanied the rite; no more elegant and costly tributes had ever been seen on that stage. Durie's acceptance was gracious and quiet, inspiring Jans with the hope that she would hold that key in her recitation. As she came off, he expressed his expectation in curt, professional tones. Durie said coldly, "Why this sudden personal interest in poor me?"

"Far from personal, I assure you. I speak as being responsible for the poem."

"I shall render it according to my own taste."

She passed him, humming happily, to make some slight change of costume. When she came back, with Mr. Passerow making his ornate acknowledgment on behalf of star and troupe, Jans was seated with a leathern bucket beside him inscribed "Fire" in red letters.

"See that?" he said.

"Yes."

"One wriggle, one squeal, and you get it."

"You wouldn't dare!"

Scanning his face, she knew that he would. The calls from out front were impatient. She walked on, a slender and supple maiden in virginal blue, the straight, suave lines of the frock bringing out the gracious curves of bust and thigh. Her lips were a bow of delicate amusement. In her eyes was the sparkle of mischief. One little foot tapped the floor as she stood composedly awaiting silence. The calm voice with its seductive undertones took up the lines:

> *"The leading of apes is a story*
> *Of days and of dames that have vanished."*

Something dire happened to Jans' heart. That child a harpy, an avaricious money-grubber, a whorish trafficker in her own beauty? Could any art counterfeit that innocency? He listened, shaken, entranced, through the five stanzas. He hung upon the last pause, the musing, delicately scornful half-smile, the slow shake of the poised head preceding the final:

> *"So I'll love you no longer, oh, no!"*

Durie came off, eyes sparkling, breath quickened, to meet the comments of her fellows.

"Very commendable, my child," patronized old Archbold.

"You got 'em, girlie," said Mr. Baggo.

"Not without promise," Mr. Passerow said.

"Spiritless," observed Mr. Crosbie to Miss Wayne. "No fire. No come-you-hither."

"Dumb," agreed Fair Luna.

"Amour! Amour! La Jeune Amour!" vociferated the Merry Moments, and she must go out to take another bow.

In the five-minute entr'acte Jans got her aside for a private word.

"Durie, I want to see you."

"Is it about Looby?" she asked quickly.

"Looby? No. Looby isn't important. It's about you and me."

"Is that so important?"

"It might be the most important thing in the world to me."

She shook her head. "Looby is important to me. Gypsy says that you are after him—after the reward. It isn't true, is it, Jans?" she pleaded. "It can't be true."

"I can explain all that," he said impatiently. "There isn't time now. Meet me after the show."

"Not tonight."

"Why not?"

"I have another rendezvous."

"Oh, yes! Ayrault's supper party. I'll wait for you afterward at the Liberty Pole."

"No, Jans." Her eyes were troubled, but they did not evade his by so much as the flicker of a moment.

"You're not coming back?" he said slowly.

"You mustn't wait."

"Answer me! Are you coming back or not?"

"Act Three. Ready. Music!" Mr. Passerow called.

Jans caught up Laus Deo and struck a muted chord.

"Love will find out the way," he hummed savagely.

Durie gave him a queer, hurt look and brushed past, her head high. A moment later he heard her voice, strained and false with artificial emotion.

"What bodes this missive? A letter privately rendered under cloak of darkness!"

Counterfeit, bogus, wholly spurious in her art as in her character, thought Jans. There could be no further doubt. Uproot her from his heart and his thoughts, that was the only course for any man of sense and spirit.

That night Jans' sleep was fitful. The solemn, spaced chime of three o'clock brought him upright in bed, as if the voice of irrevocable time carried a special portent for him.

Crash!

The spurtle of fire momentarily outlined his window. A cannon-shot; the two-pounder on the deck of the *Merry Moments*. The signal for the winning and losing of the foul bet? *What'll be the signal? A blast from Black Betty . . . The lady's silk stocking at masthead.* He could hear the hateful exchange now.

He staggered to the window. Loud talk and snatches of song rose from the street. He identified the uproar; the Merry Momenters had been evicted from the boat to leave Durie and Macel Ayrault in a lovers' solitude. And he, Jans, poor sentimental fool that he had been that night at Geneva, had denied his passion and cheated himself of a plaicer who was now laughing at him with her paramour. Well, she'd make Macel pay through the nose; some comfort in that. Jans cursed the comfort.

The voices neared his window.

"Who primed the gun?"

"Wilgus Sybrandt."

"And a thumping charge I put in, well rammed down," guffawed Sybrandt. "It should have been a volley."

"Let's go back and sing 'em an epithalamium."

"Leave 'em to their play. Who's for bed?"

"What! In the prime o' night? Forward to the Fair Grounds. We'll rout out the sideshows."

Sleep was not for Jans after that. The four walls of his chamber stifled him. He dressed and went out into the night, plunging ahead blindly, aimlessly, out as far as the Wide Waters, up the heights and back, through wood and stream and meadow. A night-prowling rattlesnake warned him. The rhythm of the thunderpump in a swamp was like the pulse of an overburdened heart. Entering the Third Ward Park he sat down beneath a young tulip tree, leaning his back against the bole and trying to doze.

Had his eyes been open he might have seen a bulky figure pause at the Spring Street entrance and then lurch on. Macel Ayrault had been drowning his woes, his indignities, his intolerably wounded male pride in the solace of liquor. Never in his conquering life had he been so repulsed, so humiliated. And by this slip of a Thespian! Bargain? she had said coolly through the roped door. There had been no bargain except that she would come aboard and remain at his pleasure. Pleasure! Damn her for a dangerous vixen. She might have ruined him for life with that cursed little sickle of hers when he tried to break in.

He rolled back to a lonely berth.

Sunrise found Jans skirting the wharves. There was the *Merry Moments*. And there, at staffhead, a length of silk filled and fluttered in the brisk breeze of morning. His fevered eyes ranged the portholes. His feverish brain pulsed with the anguish of a question. Behind which one . . . ?

A sash slid in one of them. A cropped head appeared. Catching up a rock, Jans let fly. It missed by a scant foot. The head ducked back.

"Under cover, you fool!" growled Jans.

He went back to rout out Pilk and tell him that Looby was found.

They decided to wait until Durie was safely off the boat before attempting the capture.

"What about the young bloods?" asked the cautious Pilkington. "We might have trouble with them."

"We'll have to chance it," Jans replied.

Luck was with them in this respect. After their early-morning departure from the boat, the Merry Momenters, on pleasure and riot bent, repaired to the Liberty Pole lot, raided the shows, fought the constabulary, and landed, one and all, in jail. Being still far from sober when arraigned before the magistrate in the morning, they were remanded back for twenty-four hours, after which they were to be released upon their promise of leaving town at once. Thus were the Thalians deprived of their chief support.

The same magistrate who so summarily dealt with the rioters had another disturber of the peace before him shortly after. The testimony of the constable was that the young female, one Gypsy Vilas, who purported to be an apprentice midwife, had attempted to effect the rescue of a notorious Auburn jailbreak known as Looby. To this end she had rushed upon Looby's two captors, shouting and blaspheming in injurious language, painfully kicked one and feloniously bitten the other, and on being apprehended had addressed the constable in terms unfit for His Honor's ears.

As the assaulted citizens, Messrs. Quinn and Pilkington, declined to press a charge, she was reprimanded, fined a shilling and released. The captive who had sobbed brokenly throughout the hearing was remanded to jail, and the hundred-dollar reward ordered paid to the captors over the objections of a man named Smith. Several onlookers who murmured and hissed were expelled from the court room.

Still seething with fury, Gypsy went to the theatre to find Durie and told her story.

"Now, what d'you think of that son-of-a-burnt-bitch!" she demanded.

"The same as you do," said Durie through tight lips.

"I knew he was a wrong un. A gentleman pretending to be an actor!"

"Think of poor Looby, back in that awful prison! I could kill Jans Quintard."

"False to one, false to other," Gypsy sang. "He tricked you finely."

"This is worse." Durie would always feel another's wrongs more than her own. "This was for money. The other was my fault as much as his."

"Prr-rr-rrt!"

"Well, partly mine. It wasn't planned treachery like this. I'd rather be Lucky Seven Smith." She shuddered. "I can't forget poor Looby's back."

"Think of your fifty dollars, too," said the more practical Gypsy.

"I wish I had it back," Durie sighed.

"I'll never get back my share," her confederate said with a reminiscent grin. "That jail-keeper wasted no time in sleep. Oh-oh!"

Thirty-nine people made up the audience that night, of whom four adopted Printer Peck's hint and demanded their money back after the first curtain. The game was up for the Thalians.

Mr. Tim Baggo marched across the inn yard, whistling merrily and dangling by their laces a pair of boots that looked as if they had just been shot. A pot of bear's grease stood by the watering trough. Dipping out a slather on a bit of stick he carefully anointed the foot-gear, then applied some blacking of his own composition. When the broad toes reflected his face, he desisted and shod himself. He was about setting forth, presumably for conquest, when the approach of a fellow Thespian delayed him.

"Have a vapor?"

"Thanks, Quinny. Don't care if I do." He took the two-penny Elmoro with a nod of acknowledgment.

"Tim, have you got any money?"

"What! On a Friday? Not a bowel." He turned out empty pockets in guarantee.

"We've got to have some."

"Get it from Passerow."

"Passerow's skipped. Vamosed. Evaded."

"With the money-box?" The buffo's jaw sagged.

"Four bits left in it. Mrs. Passerow's upstairs, crying and moaning something about three-five-ought in letters of fire."

"What's that mean? Has he quit her?"

"Some of his damned lottery dinkums, I suppose. No, he hasn't quit her. Wants us to meet him at East Bloomfield. How in hell does he think we're to get out of here without money? Is anything paid on the hotel bill?"

"Not a stiver. The theatre's closed to us, too."

"Ain't life hell!" said Mr. Baggo philosophically.

23

THREE nights at East Bloomfield replenished the money-box. The fund was at once depleted by the necessary purchase of an ox, one of their team having eaten a poison-weed and succumbed. The transaction was conducted by Mr. John Quinn after a lively debate with Manager Passerow who had other designs for the money. The outcome was a deputation of Messrs. Quinn, Baggo, Crosbie and Archbold, who notified the manager that, unless the treasury moneys were henceforth put in charge of Mr. Quinn, there would be a turn-out,* the scenery and rolling stock would be impounded for overdue salaries, and the company reorganized on a co-operative basis. For good measure, the athletic Mr. Baggo offered to punch the manager's nose into a pimple if he tried on any more of his quacksalvery. Deeply wounded, Manager Passerow protested that his motives were of the purest but the luck had always been against him. He was sent ahead on the spare horse to carry the flag.

The shift threw more work upon Jans than any one person could perform. Help was needed with both animals and scenery. Jans had observed how handy Gypsy Vilas was. He went to her.

"Want a job?"

"With you?" she said distrustfully.

"With the company."

She hesitated. Her birthdames had planned to part company with the Thalians as a losing venture, which would involve her separating from Durie. That was a powerful consideration.

"How much?" she asked.

"Ten shillings," he replied. "If you get it," he added with a wry grin.

*Turn-out: strike.

"And my keep?"

"That part of it you can be sure of."

"I'll take it. But I think you're a stinking mauser, just the same," she added conscientiously.

"Think what you like as long as you do your job."

Hard luck was so normal a condition of theatrical road life, that the deterioration in their fortunes was accepted without repining by the Thalians. It seemed to pursue them with something like malevolence from now on. A horse fell lame, causing them to miss engagements. A wheel dropped off the scenery wagon, plunging it into a ditch and ruining a Rhenish castle, convertible into a bank lobby and a fashionable parlor set. Mrs. Passerow's throat grew worse. Fair Luna garnered poison ivy for a chaplet and coquetted painfully through her roles like a schoolgirl with the mumps, to the derision of even a backwoods audience. She wept, on-stage and off, and despatched piteous letters to the Honorable Vryling Lovatt which went unanswered, that statesman being on a business voyage to the Indies.

At Watercure the romantic Flavel Crosbie inspired amorous passions in the widowed and mature breast of an opulent lady, under whose solicitations he deserted the outfit without the formality of a resignation. Mr. Passerow, with a lamentably juvenile make-up, substituted for him, and Jans went in to fill the hiatus. A gifted amateur named Johnson was picked up at Phelps and inducted as responsible utility. He was terrible, but his twenty-dollar fee, the savings of a laborious year in a woodyard, was the first considerable cash that the troupe had seen for three weeks. He fell in love with Mrs. Alwyn and, his tri-weekly offer of honorable marriage being discourteously rejected, mooned about, forgot his lines, missed his cues, and lurked in corners making calf's eyes at the object of his adoration until the performances were threatened with disruption.

The troupers were now so reduced that they lacked scenery for any but the simplest productions. The same set, with such alterations as Jans and Gypsy could contrive, must suffice for a bank, an inn, a millionaire-man's residence and a royal palace. Rural audiences were, fortunately, undiscriminating in such matters; they would trustingly accept what was set before them up to the verge of the simple Elizabethan stage averment, "This is a Tree."

Finding themselves stuck in Waterloo on a week-end, they ventured a Sabbath-day performance, resulting in the arrest of the entire troupe. Only the fact that they had offered an unimpeachable Morality saved them from jail at the hands of outraged justice, represented by a whiskey distiller on the bench. Twelve shillings and costs. It left them without avails to cross the Longest Bridge in the World spanning the marshes to Cayuga Village. Therefore they rounded the foot of the lake and went up the west side where, according to Jans' information, no show had been for a year. They played crossroads engagements to fair, but almost cashless houses, until they reached Ovid where they hopefully expected real money.

They were now in a no-cash territory where receipts were in kind, ranging from such negotiable staples as flaxseed, whiskey and homespun, to buffalo robes, beaver pelts, and one proffer of a tame raccoon as admission money. As provender was always forthcoming, they were assured of their daily sustenance, but there was small margin for salaries.

Mr. Passerow had flown the flag, gathering a capacity house of sixty-five patrons in the country-store loft. Scenery was hoisted into place, the lights adjusted and the curtain rigged when ominous word was brought by a townsman. Four bits was too much. The circus had charged only two bits and it had a sea-serpent and a band in uniform. Either the Thalians must meet that rate, or the assembled citizenry would disperse to their homes and the company could play to the storekeeper's cat.

Jans proved a strategist. He accosted the local spokesman. The circus had been on a cash basis, had it not? Yes, that was so. Very good! Cash admittance, two bits: produce or exchange, four-bits worth. There was a consultation. The compromise was accepted. The company played to capacity. As keeper of the funds, Jans was able to count enough money for passage to the other shore by King Ferry.

There Durie had her first experience of show business at its most desperate. A starveling dog-and-monkey troupe, run by a miserable little humpback and his imminently pregnant wife was stranded in the town. The monkey had been arrested for filching an apple from the grocery counter and was now shivering in the pound. The proprietor had been going from selectman to selectman, pleading for

243

the release of the animal before it coughed itself to death. The authorities were stony; the fine must be paid or Jocko held in custody. As a last resort the man appealed to the Thalians. Without authorization, Jans offered to give half of the evening's cash receipts to the unfortunate pair. It was a futile gesture; the total specie turned in was less than two shillings.

That night the monkey died. Going out early in the morning, Durie saw a group of townsfolk talking excitedly. They were angrily discussing a problem in town economics. What was to be done with the woman, in labor at the jail, there being no other place for her? Were she and her child to become charges at the public expense? Durie met Jans and Tim Baggo bringing up the tiny show-wagon. The dogs were howling.

"Where is the showman?" she asked Baggo.

"Hanged himself," he gulped.

Durie gave a little cry of pity and dismay.

"For want of ten shillings," Jans muttered.

"And you let him," she accused.

"What was I to do?" he demanded angrily.

"Nothing, naturally. With your blood-money snug in your pocket."

He turned white. "Blood-money! And what of your hoard? Does harlotry pay so ill? Not to mention black mail."

"Steady, boy," Tim Baggo warned.

In the grip of the black Quintard wrath, Jans paid no heed to him. He kept his hot eyes fixed upon Durie.

"You are as vile and cruel as you are treacherous," she said evenly. "If you were a man, I'd choke that down your throat."

"Doubted. Cowardice usually goes with falsity." She spoke with an infuriating effect of indifference, as if the personal element mattered nothing.

"You're going to be sorry for that. And you're going to tell me so."

"I'd bite my tongue out first."

"You're going to tell me so," he repeated.

Her anger mounted to match his. "Jans Quintard, I swear to you on my honor . . ."

He laughed.

". . . on my honor, that I would not degrade myself to ask your pardon under torture. Never, never, never!"

"Save it for rehearsal," interposed Tim Baggo.

The tragedy left Durie with a sense of insecurity, the first that her self-reliant soul had ever known, a frightening doubt of the future. . . . Where would she be when, like the pregnant widow, she was thirty years old? What would she be?

Frost came the next evening, ominous sign of an early season, as they slanted down the hillside road to Cayuga Lake and the town of Union Springs. It was Saturday.

"It's a rough town," Mr. Passerow said. "But they've got money."

Only one hall in town was large enough to accommodate the prospective crowd and that was undergoing repairs. But in the oak grove beside the grist mill a medicine show had adapted an ancient shed to its purposes, leaving behind it a rickety but still available stage. By six o'clock what little serviceable scenery they had left was set, the curtain was rigged, the patent lamps purchased by Mr. Passerow were ranged along the front, and Jans was praying for a windless evening. At best he did not trust that touchy mixture of turpentine and alcohol. Drafts sweeping through the open-ended shed might bring about disaster.

The skies had cleared, though a sharp chill hung in the air. The audience gathered early, many of them showing evidences of having stopped at the tavern. A solid block of quarrymen occupied the left side of the front. They wore heavy jackets and bright scarves, and applied themselves to green-glass eagle flasks. Opposite them was a group from the boatyards who spat tobacco juice and bellowed rough songs. Three woodcutters had brought their axes upon which they leaned, affecting the attitude of a dandy with his cane.

Ten minutes before curtain time, a grizzled old trapper in an unseasonable and unsavory bearskin jacket appeared before the window and extended toward Jans a small dark, hairy object.

"What's this?" asked Jans.

"Scalp," said the woodsman. "Prime."

"We don't take scalps," Jans explained politely.

"Ain't you a four-bit show?"

"Yes. But . . ."

"Ain't that a four-bit scalp?"

"Undoubtedly, but we don't have any use for it."

The trapper withdrew, grumbling in his beard. Presently he was back with a bag full of rutabagas.

"Six bits' worth," he said, plumping it down before the window.

"Cash only," Jans said. "Sorry."

The rejected patron sat down upon a fallen maple, produced a flask and applied himself to that violently alcoholic ferment of honey called metheglyn, cursing the outfit from hell to breakfast. He'd be even with 'em!

Nobody asked for his money back in the intermission, a matter of mingled surprise and relief to Jans. The Union Springs clientele might be rough but it was not uncharitable in its judgments.

Hardly had the curtain parted on Act Two, when there was an interpolated bit. Durie, Gypsy, Jans and Mr. Passerow were on in a sparkling scene of parlor persiflage. Durie was inquiring with her prettiest simper:

"Who will sit in judgment upon an issue involving feminine vanity?"

"Me," answered a wild, thin, infuriated squeak from the rear.

The scalp-and-turnip-bearer had found or forced an entry and brought with him a portion of his rejected produce. Gypsy ducked as a large rutabaga whizzed past her head. Her next speech, not from the text, delighted the house, which roared its approval.

"Here's your dad-blasted entrance fee," shrilled the old boy, and let go with another vegetable.

It went low. There was a hiss and a flare as one of the explosive lights toppled and rolled, setting another atilt. A wall of flame rose between pit and stage. The curtain caught and withered in the blast. The two meager water buckets which Jans emptied were nothing of a check. The billowing audience stampeded for the exits, except for a goodly few quarrymen and boat builders who braved the fire to help the trapped performers at the risk of their own lives.

Exit would have been easy had not some scenery fallen, blocking the rear door. Jans turned to look for Durie. A huge mechanic had her around the waist and was valiantly kicking at the obstruction with hobnailed boots. Another was shielding Gypsy from the blast. Fair Luna writhed in a heap, uttering yelp upon yelp. The others, on all fours to avoid the swirl of the fumes, had crept into the blistering flies. In that desperate moment Jans wondered whether any of them would get out alive.

A terrific crash at his back startled him into a swift leap.

"Way-o! Stand clear!" yelled a harsh voice.

Other crashes followed. Jans, half-stifled with smoke, saw the bright gleam of an ax blade, and a whole section of wall toppled and sank as the three mighty woodsmen dashed in to the rescue. The last one got Fair Luna by the ankle and dragged her, shrieking and bucking, into the open air. All the rest had poured through the opening, and none too soon. Three minutes later the roof crashed.

A nose count showed all saved. A stonecutter had a badly burned arm, two of the boatees had been cut by flying glass, and there was temporary anxiety over Mrs. Passerow who had inhaled too much smoke for her lung capacity.

The scenery was gone; the extra costumes were gone. The props were burned, and the money-box was somewhere in the wreckage. It was ruin. One grim satisfaction was afforded to Jans. The scalp-hunter passed him at a frantic gallop, pursued by Miss Gypsy Vilas, flax-hook in hand, voicing an explicit intention of doing him an irreparable if not mortal injury.

Exploration among the ashes turned up three hot but unmelted shillings in the remains of the money-box. As treasurer, Jans called a roster of the private funds. A little over two dollars was reported. The new treasurer made a little speech setting forth their financial status. They had better stick together on a communal basis until they could raise enough money to divide and go on their separate ways. If anyone had a better suggestion, now was the time to offer it. Nobody had, though Mr. and Mrs. Passerow were observed conferring, aside.

"Professionally, I'm inexperienced," pursued Jans. "What do we do?"

Old Mr. Archbold spoke up. "Go on the streets," he said grimly.

"Open-air performances?" Jans looked dubious.

"Not performances. Olio."

"A raree-show? Me?" put in young Rapalje, "Rather would I starve."

"Wouldja!" said Gypsy Vilas. "Try it once. I have. It's paltry."

"I have held multitudes entranced with 'The Great Soliloquy'," said Mr. Archbold.

"I can do wonders with a bit of string and three walnuts," offered Mr. Tim Baggo.

"Has anybody seen my shoes?" asked Fair Luna Wayne. "Maybe I could perform a simple hornpipe without 'em."

"Miss Amour can render a recitation," suggested Gypsy. "I can sell medicine—if I had any to sell."

The little circle glanced furtively, one at another, balking at the unsavory essential. Rapalje blurted it out.

"Who'll pass the hat?"

"Draw straws for it." This was from Mr. Baggo.

"Ladies, too?" asked Mrs. Alwyn in a die-away voice.

"Why not?" said Durie quietly.

Jans swallowed hard and audibly. "That's the treasurer's job," he stated.

"Good old Quinny!" chuckled Gypsy. "Oh! I forgot." And she gave him a savage glare.

Jans addressed the old actor. "You've experienced this before, Mr. Archbold?"

"I have. It's hell."

"Do we start in here?"

The old fellow shook his head. "Cash is too scarce in a small town. We must strike for the cities. Auburn is but ten miles across the hills."

"We've played Auburn," objected Mrs. Alwyn.

"Not on the street corners," he retorted.

Jans suppressed a gulp of distaste. He tried to keep his voice cheerful as he made his announcement. "We may as well get an early start. Breakfast at six. What there is of it," he added under his breath.

They did not do so badly. Up at sunrise, Gypsy Vilas had caught a stray fowl (she said it was a stray), and they had the turnips abandoned by the swift and fugitive trapper. Durie was at the cooking pot before Jans was about. She did not speak to him when he approached, but her curiosity followed his movements as he peered out over the lake from shaded eyes, and muttered something that sounded like a curse, followed by "Good riddance." Then she sighted the small boat with two figures, one of which pumped jerkily at the oars. Already it was too far out for her to identify the Passerows. At breakfast call the whole troupe learned of the desertion.

A thin drizzle ushered them into Auburn. They pitched camp on the edge of the tamarack bog where a cold, clear, sulphur spring welled up, fortified themselves with a hot meal, and footed it up North Street, seeking a propitious spot. Their hopes that there would be no other show in town were at once dashed. Not only was Fingle's Traveling Museum of World Wonders advertised for that evening but, worst of all competition, a charity exhibit for the Infant School was scheduled.

"We'll have to exhibit at six o'clock," said Mr. Archbold. "That will catch the show crowds on their way."

He selected the corner outside the Bank Coffee House. No progamme had been arranged. It was to be hit-or-miss, with Mr. Tim Baggo as Master of Revels. For reasons of professional pride, Mr. Baggo advised that none of them use their programme names. He, himself, would appear as The Great Trickamungo, King of Deceptions. With his best humorous appeal, he gathered a crowd of two dozen and opened the entertainment with an abstruse manipulation of his mystifying string and walnuts. But at the critical moment, the cord slipped from his chilled fingers, ruining the mystification and the illusionist's technique. Covering his embarrassment with a merry quip (coldly received by the audience), he presented for their intelligent and cultured consideration, Sebastian Smith, the distinguished tragedian, who would move their sensibilities with his notorious rendition of *Hamlet.* Mr. Archbold's thunderous rhetoric reduced the audience by several departures. Mlle. Dotty Dainty (Fair Luna Wayne) recited "Miss Deborah Diddle of Daisymead Square" with such archness and so many seductive flouncings that she received several invitations for the night, one of which embodied a cash guarantee. Under the name of Percival Jones, Mr. Rapalje delivered "Barney, Leave the Girls Alone" and got a laugh from a half-witted boy in the front row. Midway through her special selection, Miss Jones, the Tuneful Linnet (Mrs. Alwyn), broke down into hysterical sobs, and the master of ceremonies rushed into the breach with an antic dance to which he merrily trolled:

> *"With my ti-lol tweedle-tum,*
> *Likewise fol-lol feeddle-fum,*
> *Not forgetting diderum hi,*
> *Also tweedle deedle dum."*

Durie (Miss Euphrasia Duval) could have wept for shame. But it was now her turn. She delivered Jans' poem and three more spectators melted unobtrusively away.

"Pass the hat! Pass the hat!" Mr. Baggo urgently whispered to Jans.

Much as she despised him (the blood-money grubber!), Durie felt a pang at her heart for Jans. His mouth was twisted into a wry grin as he advanced holding Mr. Archbold's battered beaver, the most dignified receptacle in the troupe, at a stiff arm's length.

"Do not leave! Do not leave!" urged Mr. Baggo, as a backward move of patrons gathered momentum. "More entertainment is to come."

A shawled housewife dropped a copper into the hat. Jans thanked her in a voice that might appropiately have emanated from a corpse. A couple of mechanics matched coins. The loser contributed a fip. Jans bowed and called him "Sir." Two young bloods strolled out of the coffee house, singing. One of them stumbled into the alms-gatherer.

"Watch where you are treading, you unchancy lout!" he began. "God Almighty! Jans Quintard!"

Jans stood frozen. The hat was extended at the end of his rigid arm.

"What masquerade is this?" demanded the other in utter amazement.

"We solicit your kind attention to the continuance of our entertainment," droned Mr. Baggo.

The second diner, soberer than the first, plucked the companion by the elbow.

"Let him alone, you fool!"

Fingering in his waistcoat pocket, he delicately extracted a bill. Another fluttered after it into the hat, from Jans' acquaintance. The pair locked arms and passed on their way.

"Luck-o!" said Tim Baggo exultantly.

"Charity!" said Jans. His face was gray.

"Lay-dees *and* Gentlemen," intoned Mr. Baggo, "we bespeak your kind consideration of our next number."

He was speaking to a remnant, consisting of four grownups and an urchin. These turned and dashed for cover as a spurtle of rain swept the street.

The bedraggled Thalians hurried back to the shelter of tent and wagon. Left behind, as having nothing to contribute to the street show, Gypsy had a roaring fire to welcome and comfort them. After supper she listened to Durie's painful account of the street scene.

"Wanta quit?" she asked.

"What could we do?"

"There's a medic show in town. Hunter's Debilitated Female Pills."

"I couldn't sell pills, Gypsy. Wouldn't know how."

"It's simple. We sit on the platform. I'm the debilitated female, before taking the pill. You're after taking. We get our ten per-centum."

"Anything is better than the street corners," said Durie with a shudder.

"Shall I give Quinny our notice?"

"Wait a moment, Gypsy."

Into Durie's head had popped a passage from *The Maze of Marriage*.

Quit an associate, if needs must, for due and proper cause, but never in his hour of adversity.

"Gypsy, we can't do it."

"Why can't we?"

"Leave them when they're down? What would they think of us?"

"Who? Quinny?" said Gypsy bluntly.

"No! All of them. What would we think of ourselves?"

"That's different. All right, gal. I guess we stick."

24

BEDRAGGLED but undaunted, the troupe limped into Syracuse. That veteran peripatetic, Old Archbold, remembered that Andy Van Patten, an aged and merry Dutch innkeeper, was noted for his partiality for show folk. Andy had lost his tavern, lock, stock and barrel, with all equipment including stables and bar, by betting on Francis Granger's election in the previous fall. A year of drinking having assuaged his grief, he raised some capital and built the Old Line House kitticornered from his original property. Let John Quinn try Andy.

Accordingly, Jans repaired to the Old Line bar where he found the proprietor quaffing his morning eye-opener, though it was nearly eleven o'clock. Upon learning that his visitor was in the show business, Mine Host Van Patten rolled his bulk behind the bar to mix a second toddy. Jans put his anxious question.

"Show biznizz? No, sir. We're an unaffording town for show biznizz."

"What's amiss?"

"The clergy. May they fry on their own griddles, Methodist, Baptist, Presbyterian and Papist."

"Have they closed the theatres?" asked Jans eagerly.

"Not closed. But scairt their congregations so they don't dare show their noses in pit or gallery."

"The people must be hungry for entertainment," suggested Jans.

"They are so."

"How's your custom at the bar?"

"Tol-lollish, I got my reggalars."

"I can double it for you."

Mr. Van Patten was kindly but he was also Dutch. The wary gleam of the trader lighted his bilious eye.

"How much does it cost me?"

"Not a cent."

"No, no young fella!" objected the tavern-keeper earnestly. "There's a weevil in that nosebag somewhere. Offer me something for nothing, and I look to the hasp on my purse."

"Would the offer of worthy talent for a show scare you?"

"I got no ballroom."

"This bar will serve."

"When you've strung your curtain and set your scenery, where'll my patrons sit to their ale?"

"Neither curtains, scenery nor props. We're reduced to the bare bones of our trade. But we offer sterling entertainment."

"I see. Moosical?"

"There are musical numbers."

"My patrons like moosic. Some are Germans. They are the tear-in-the-eye sort. Others are canallers. They are for the rollicky, bust-your-gut choruses. Get 'em going and they'll sing all night. *And* drink!" he added with satisfaction.

"Just so. And there's your profit of it."

"Where's yours?"

"Accommodations for the troupe and half what you take across the bar above your average."

Mr. Van Patten scratched his head. "A half?" he said. "No, a quarter."

"A third," said Jans.

"Fetch your troupe," said Mine Host.

Pleased at the prospect of a roof over their heads again and regular meals assured to their stomachs, the troupe set to work upon a programme chiefly musical under the leadership of Jans and Laus Deo. This was for Jans no glee club divertissement, but hard labor for a living. With the aid of Durie a passable ensemble was achieved which made up in volume what it lacked in finesse. Now that they were under cover again and the shameful hat no longer to be passed, they resumed their professional names and became the Thalian Galaxy of Song and Merrymaking.

They were a hit, instantly and emphatically. Word spread on

the wind that entertainment was to be had free at the Old Line. The spacious tap filled up. Chairs were fetched from the dining room. Benches from the store room supplemented them. At ten o'clock the outer door was closed just too late to exclude a constable who forced his way in to demand a cessation of the unseemly noise, a deputation from the canal basins having joined the choruses. Invited to nominate his choice in song and liquor, he exhibited a cavernous basso and a taste for rumbullion. There was no further trouble from the authorities.

Exhausted, but happy, Mr. Van Patten and Jans faced one another across a coin-littered table at one A.M. Outside, an improvised choral association was singing German lieder. Across the street some canallers were fighting the watch. Half a dozen patrons were asleep in the hall. Standee charges of ten cents could be collected in the morning, so why disturb them? The host said to Jans, "You are bespoken. For a week. Two weeks. Mebbe a month."

Jans shook his head, smiling. "We couldn't stay that long."

"Next week we charge admission. Sixpence after seven o'clock."

"And divide the gate," suggested Jans.

"Slick fella," chuckled Mr. Van Patten. "You'll all get so rich you'll want to stay a year."

The Thalians took on the status of an institution. As such, they built up a clientele of repeaters. Gratifying though this was, it entailed extra work by calling for frequent change of programme. Mr. Van Patten's patronage was avid of novelty. Through the grilling task of learning and practicing new numbers, Jans found Durie a stout pillar of reliability. Her sole concern seemed to be for the best interests of the company.

He assumed a new manner toward her, treating her with an elaborate and derisive deference which, to his discomfiture, moved her not at all. Once she did ask, though with an air of curiosity rather than protest, "Why are you pestering me so?"

"Am I?" he returned in pretended surprise. "It would be a great pity that you should be annoyed. I'm sorry."

"You are not sorry. And I am not annoyed."

That exchange caused Jans to take himself under consideration. He decided that he was a weak-spirited fool. Honest with himself, he admitted that her mere proximity still had power beyond his resistance to stir him. If there were any response in her, it was not to be discerned in the level glance of those grave eyes with the topaz lights in them, in the measured sweetness of her husky-soft speech.

There was but one course for him; to go away as soon as he could liquidate the company's affairs and apportion enough money to set them comfortably on their way. Meanwhile he would maintain a resolute reserve.

His good resolution lasted hardly twenty-four hours. Mr. Tim Baggo was responsible. Too much Saturday afternoon hospitality from a group of his admirers had inspired him to volunteer a solo concert which left him hoarse as a bull podunker. By the time of the evening diversion, he was totally voiceless and hardly able to croak out his announcements as Master of the Revels. This was unfortunate, as it threw the performers back upon old material. Mr. Archbold recited. Tim Baggo juggled. The audience evinced signs of restlessness. Jans took a quick resolution, fostered partly by necessity, partly by a reckless desire to test Durie's resistance.

"Announce a new feature to follow Mark Antony's Oration," he directed the Master. "Andrews and Quinn."

Mr. Baggo did so with extra empressement and received a flash from La Jeune Amour's eyes fit to scorch the nap from his neckcloth. She hurried to Jans.

"What is this?" she demanded breathlessly.

"'The Great Adventurer'."

"I can't. I won't," she exclaimed in panic.

"You must. It's announced."

"You're taking advantage." She was quivering.

"Folderol! It can't mean anything now."

"No," she said dully.

"Unless you've forgotten."

"Forgotten!" she whispered, and suddenly he was sorry and ashamed and kind.

"It won't be hard, Durie. I'll take the first stanza. Just think of the music. Never mind anything else."

Through the fervid Shakespearean periods by Mr. Archbold,

Jans could see her struggling to get control of herself. The perfunctory applause died out.

Mr. Baggo announced, "A duet, the esteemed and tender old ballad, 'The Great Adventurer.' Alto, La Jeune Amour; baritone, Mr. Quinn. Guitar accompaniment, Mr. Quinn."

Her hand was clammy-cold in Jans' as he led her on. He struck the preliminary chords. He was going to sing better than he knew, and he was going to sing to her as if there were only the two of them in the world.

> *"Over the fountain*
> *And over the waves.*
> *Under the mountains*
> *And under the graves."*

He saw her lips quiver, her eyes soften to a memory, the slow, rich color rise beneath the skin.

> *"Over floods that are deepest,*
> *That Neptune obey,*
> *Over rocks that are steepest,*
> *Love will find out the way."*

It was he who was shaken now. He looked away lest he should impart his emotional tumult to her. Mechanically his fingers produced the stringed interlude; he prolonged it to give her more time. Could she do it? He was not sure. She made a single step toward him and her voice rose, assured and lovely, with that strange seductiveness which moved him to a sort of exultation.

> *"You may tame the eagle*
> *To stoop to your fist."*

Was there just the slightest stress on the last word to tell him that she remembered what he could never forget, that song in the darkness of Harvard Yard when she had amended the line?

> *"Or you may inveigle*
> *The Phoenix of the East."*

Somehow he must keep his heart in place lest it thicken his throat so that he could not join her in his cue line. He braced himself

with an effort, striving for steadiness of tone, lest he betray himself—and her—to the vulgar crowd.

> *"The tigress, you may move her*
> *To give over her prey.*
> *You shall ne'er move a lover*
> *Love will find out the way."*

The vulgar crowd was applauding wildly. What was this?
Durie was taking a bow. She must have forgotten her lines.

"Some think to lose him," he prompted in a quick whisper.
His fingers slipped into place, but her own, pressed over them,
muted the chord. Again she bowed. She moved off to the left.
There was nothing to be done but follow. They were in the small,
curtained alcove, alone, secluded from sight.

"I couldn't go on," she said. "I couldn't, Jans!" Her eyes sought
his, bewildered, imploring. Laus Deo fell into a corner with a
disharmonious thrill of strings. Out front the people were applauding and calling.

They drew together, breast to breast, mouth to mouth, clasped
and throbbing. Outside, the applause mounted. Durie forced herself back from him.

"Oh, cruel!" she breathed.

"You love me," he gloated. "You can't pretend any more, Durie.
You love me."

"I hate myself," she muttered.

"More! More! Again!" called the crowd.

"We've got to go back."

"I can't. I won't."

"Durie! You must! Listen to them. We can't break up the
show."

He caught up Laus Deo, plucked out two ringing chords.
The tumult subsided.

"Now!" he urged.

She said, through her lips pressed white, "I'll do it this time.
I'll never sing again. Never! Never!"

All zest was gone from her when they responded to the encore.
She was accurate enough in rendition, but as spiritless as Dr.
Balcom's Gentlemanly Automaton. Jans did his valiant best with

string and voice to carry the burden. Once he caught a faint flicker of his partner's lids, and thought that he might again rouse her to an echo of his own fervor. The hope came to nothing. Due chiefly to his efforts the audience sought another recall. Durie flatly refused.

"It is with deep regret," announced Mr. Tim Baggo to an impatient audience, "that the fair and tuneful Miss Amour finds herself unable, through a temporary indisposition, to respond further to your vastly appreciated plaudits. I shall endeavor to fill the hiatus, however unworthily, with a few mystifying illusions, aided by a yard of string and three walnuts." (Grumblings.)

That evening marked the beginning of the decline of the Thalian heyday.

Any day now Captain Bassford Pilkington was due on his Rochester-Albany run. Jans encountered him, resplendent in a new uniform, on the canal front. Both gave the same greeting:

"How's trade?"

"Sagging," Jans answered.

"Whooping," Pilk said. "Books is the ticket. Coming in with me, lad?"

"Can't, Pilk. I've got to see this thing through. We're splitting up soon. Pilk, do you know anything about Looby?"

"Back in Auburn."

"Did you get a lawyer?"

"Best in Albany. He laid it before the Governor. Thinks he'll have him out by spring."

"Poor Looby! He'll be just as well off, though, in a warm cell, with winter coming on."

A grin overspread Mr. Pilkington's rugged countenance. "Heard from our friend, the puke?"

"Lucky Seven? Who's he hunting now?"

"Me and you. Says he's going to nail our ears to his gunstock."

"Think we'd better leave the country, Pilk?" asked Jans with a grin. "I'm all of a quiver."

"I kinda like this York State," Pilk said. "But that puke is certes talking bigmouth in the taps. Wouldn't want to have him behind me in the dark."

"I'll keep an eye out," Jans said.

Upon parting they made an appointment to meet in Albany when the canal opened in the spring. Pilk had no special plans for the winter. Jans thought that he might try the New York theatres again.

The day of dissolution came and Jans had not had a private word with Durie. Why should he wish to, he asked himself. She was second-hand, a damaged piece of goods. She had gone to Macel Ayrault of her own free will. What if Ayrault came back for her? He, Jans, had no grounds for interference. Yet he could not bear the thought of losing her to Ayrault. What did he want, then? Was he going to take another man's love-leavings? Everyone in the troupe knew of her relations with Ayrault. He'd be a laughing-stock.

No, by God! That wasn't for Jans Quintard. He would take his leave of her kindly, but she must understand that this was the end between them. There would be no protest from her; he could be sure of that. But the assurance brought him no satisfaction. At least he must say good-bye, and he would like to say it privately. But that damned Gypsy was always in the way.

There she was in the chamber that she shared with Durie when Jans went there. Durie was busy shortening a gown for the road while her roommate pottered about.

"Are you all right?" he asked inanely.

"Yes, why not?"

"I never get a chance to see you alone," he complained with a malevolent glance at the other girl.

"Shall I go out?" Gypsy asked her friend.

"I suppose you may as well," Durie said indifferently.

Gypsy pointed a finger at their visitor. "I'll be right in the hallway, Cocky."

"This is good-bye, Durie," Jans said.

"Yes."

"Shall we ever meet again, do you think?"

"I don't know."

At that his self-control broke.

"Durie, come with me."

"Where?" she asked wonderingly.

"What does it matter! Anywhere. Over the mountains and over the waves."

"Why should I?"

"Because we love each other."

"Not I."

He marveled at her, remembering her, distraught with passion in his arms, and now so composed, so unmoved.

"Not when we sang together?"

"You took advantage."

"Or that night at Geneva?"

"That was accident." But her color had deepened.

"And of no importance, I suppose."

She made no reply. He shook himself angrily. "Oh, well! You're probably right. You can do better elsewhere. Shall you pursue your career on the stage?"

"I don't know."

"What concern is it of mine, you mean. But twenty-five dollars will hardly carry you through a winter." (Of course she had much more than that unless she had squandered the emoluments of her successful operations.)

"I shall make do."

"But how are you going to get along?" he persisted. "Where are you going to go?"

She raised her head from the sewing that occupied her, and looked him steadily in the eyes.

"Not into any more stable-lofts," she said.

"Or upon rich young men's pleasure boats, I hope," he retorted. Her eyes did not shift nor did she change color.

"That comes with an ill grace from you," she said calmly.

"I don't know why." Anger tightened his throat.

"Has anything that passed between us given you the right to call me to account?"

"At least, I've got an investment in you," he blurted.

For a moment she regarded him wonderingly. Then she smiled. It was not a pleasant smile.

"I'm my own property, Mr. Jans Quintard," she said with calm emphasis. "Not yours or another's."

"Time up!" Gypsy called from the hall. She entered, her arms akimbo. "Come on, Bucky, you've talked enough."

"Too much," muttered Jans unhappily.

"Follow your snoot, then, and don't stop to blow it."

"Good-bye, Gypsy."

"Good-bye and good riddance." Gypsy was implacable.

"Good-bye, Durie."

"Good-bye."

She did not look up again from her sewing. She did not dare.

25

Tang of threatening winter was in the air as the two girls swung along the road. Every farmhouse exhaled its plume of smoke. For variety they had taken the road rather than the towpath. When they grew footsore it would be time enough to seek the canal level and work a passage by cooking and cleaning on some respectable raft or Durham. Or, being now moneyed gentry, they could pay their way on a packet.

Durie was for Albany where she thought that she might winter at the museum. Gypsy was eastbound, also, but was reticent about a plan which, she hinted, was still under consideration. She had rejected a flattering offer from a medical show in Troy; her experience in the higher areas of the drama had spoiled her for lesser standards. She was through with midwifery, too: all work and no play.

Ten miles out they were overtaken by a singular-looking vehicle, a huge vat on high, sturdy wheels, drawn by two slow and powerful horses. A patriarchal figure occupied the driver's seat. From the meshes of a vast beard, a thin voice issued in pious song:

> *"Broad is the path*
> *That leads to death*
> *And thousands walk together there*
> *But there's a straight and narrow path*
> *With here and there a trav-vel-lai-aire."*

"That must be Whiskey Hersey," said Gypsy.

"Who's he?" asked Durie.

"Freights out of Cazenovia with his own corn. Twenty cents a gallon. Everybody knows Hersey."

"Maybe he'd give us a lift," said Durie whose left heel was exhibiting premonitory symptoms of a blister.

"Hi, Elder!" Gypsy hailed.

The old fellow pulled up with a flourish of his whip for response.

"How much passage to where you're going?"

"Mohawk. The pleasure of your company and conversation is my charge," said he kindly.

He moved aside. The wayfarers clambered up and stowed their packs.

"Where you bound?"

"Points east."

"Travelin' for pleasure or jobs?"

"Know of any good jobs?" countered Gypsy. "No mill tricks, though."

Hersey pondered. He was known to be a compendium of local information and prided himself on it. He scanned his passengers.

"Dairy-malkin?" he asked tentatively, and answered himself with a shake of the head. "Hen-hussy? No. Tavern-help? Mebbe." He eyed them expectantly. "Tavern-help?" he repeated.

"Sleep cold, eat leavings, and wait your pay," objected Gypsy.

He considered further. "Can you read'n write?"

"My friend, here, she's book-larned," boasted Gypsy.

"A schoolmarm?"

"I've never taught," said Durie. "I suppose I could."

"There's a whoobub over the Manheim School. Was you ever to Manheim?"

"Oh, Gawd!" from Gypsy. "What a hole! Can't hardly speak English. All Palatinate Doichers."

"It's an English-spoken school, though. Might be a steady job."

"A dame-school?" asked Durie.

"Never has been. It's closed now. Reckon they'd take most anybody who'd have it."

"What closed it?"

"The teacher feller wanted a raise to twenty-five dollars a month from twenty. They wouldn't pay it an' I don't blame 'em."

"Could I get twenty a month?" asked Durie.

"What! A female? Twelve'n a half, if you're lucky."

"I wancha to understand," said Gypsy perkily, "that Miss Amour don't work for no such mouse-money."

"The committee'll set you out to board and lodge if you please 'em," explained Elder Hersey.

After a night's sleep at the Mohawk inn, Durie decided to try for the place.

"It'll carry me through the winter," she told her companion. "I might not find anything as good in Albany."

"Suppose you miss it?"

"Then I'll come on by the path and join you. Where?"

"Ah!" said Gypsy. "That's it. Where?"

"You must have some idea where you're going."

"Brr-rr!" wheezed the other. "I got blains in my bones from that cold bed." She reached out to pour herself a hooker of rum from the decanter which was part of the regular breakfast set-out. "I don't aim to sleep cold this winter. I can tell you that, gal. I'm notional it might be Schenectady for me."

"It's a live town. Think you'll find something there?"

Gypsy smirked. "Tim Baggo," she said.

"Oh, I see!"

"He's been after me since Rochester, but there hasn't been much chance," continued the frank Miss Vilas.

"So next spring I may be calling you Mrs. Baggo."

"It might come to that," Gypsy admitted. "Again, it mightn't. We ain't got that far yet."

"Good luck, Gypsy."

"You don't believe in it, though."

"What? Wedlock? Not for myself."

"You better," said Gypsy.

"Why?"

"You're getting too old to go boguin' around the country alone."

"I can take care of myself."

"Can you, though! What about Geneva?"

Durie reddened. "That will never happen again."

Gypsy delivered herself of a roadside proverb. "If it ain't the hay, it's the straw! Other lads besides Quinny has got fetching ways."

"Don't, Gypsy. It makes me sick to think of."

"Listen to me, gal. You get married first good chance you get; that's my last word to you. Marry rich and solid. You can do it with your looks and learning."

As they parted, Gypsy reflected with satisfaction that she had put a bug in *that* ear.

The committee was meeting in the unheated schoolhouse. Clerk Shaver read in his heavy Palatinate accent.

"Present, dis November fift, Chairman Semple und die Herren —er—Misters Snell, Bookstober, Klee und Adles."

Committeeman Bookstober stated the problem in a dull, discontented voice.

"Ve haf sold de tigguts und ve haf no school."

"Ve haf a school," corrected Committeeman Klee. "Plenty of school. Twenty-seven paid-up pupils bud no teejer."

"No teejer, no school," insisted Mr. Bookstober.

"Mr. Mantell was a sound teacher," said the chairman.

"Twendy-fife dollars! Pfui!" snorted Mr. Adles.

"Ve haf an abbligant, Mr. Chairman, yes?" inquired Mr. Snell.

"Yes. A young woman has applied."

"A dame-school! Pfui!" contributed Mr. Adles from the seat of the scorner.

"If we do not choose to pay for a man, we must be content with a woman," Chairman Semple pointed out.

"I moof de candidate be summoned before us," offered Mr. Bookstober.

It was put and carried. Mr. Semple left the chair and returned with Durie. Though she had put on her severest frock and stripped that down to the extreme of simplicity, the committee blinked in surprise. Clerk Shaver recovered his equilibrium first, opened his ledger and prepared to make entries.

"Name?" he inquired with an ingratiating smile.

"Endurance Andrews."

"Condition?"

"Spinster."

"Age?"

"Twenty-one," lied Durie brashly.

"Education?"

She stated her acquirements from the two young ladies' seminaries.

"Eggsperience?"

"None."

"Former oggupation or oggupations?"

"I have been traveling for the betterment of my intellect," replied the candidate, not too untruthfully.

"Church connegtions?" asked the clerk weightily.

"Baptist."

There was a slight murmur. All present were good Lutherans except the Chairman, who was a Congregationalist.

Clerk Shaver made the entry, poised his quill, then lifted his meager visage and scowled at Durie in a manner calculated (though incorrectly) to daunt.

"Wages expegted by the applicant?"

"Twenty dollars."

"Too much!" cried the members in full chorus.

"It is what you paid the former teacher."

"He vas a man. A dame-school pays half vot a reckler school pays," Mr. Bookstober informed her.

"Do you expect me to do only half his work?"

"An inbrober observation," said Mr. Klee sternly. "Ve might go to twelf und a half if abbligant iss found suidable."

"Pass the matter of wage, for the present," put in the chairman. "The board may now examine for fitness."

They went at her, hammer and tongs.

"Reckon twelf percentum on two hundred dollars hire-money," from Mr. Snell.

"Twenty-four dollars."

"Who is der greatest American?" from Mr. Shaver.

"George Washington."

"Who is der greatest Cherman?"

Answering by inspiration, Durie responded, "Martin Luther," and observed nods of approval.

"Two und two und two und four multiplied by ten. Quick!" cried Mr. Adles.

"One hundred."

"Recite an improving verse," prescribed the chairman.

Upon thought, she summoned one up from her childhood:

> *"Attend to what I tell you.*
> *My exercise I'll show,*
> *And then you may inform me*
> *If it be so with you."*

She was equally glib with a hymn—all four stanzas. She gave correctly the capital of Sweden, the largest city in Maryland, and the source and flow of the Nile. Only in the quick-fire spelling test did she miss, and then but one word, through inability to interpret the richly accented "gadderpillar" of Clerk Shaver's posing. Notwithstanding the slip, she sensed a generally favorable reaction on the part of the members when the chairman informed her that she might withdraw. All voted aye on the question of employing her, except Mr. Adles.

"Too priddy and too dickoepfig," he said. "Ve shall haf trupples."

He was over-persuaded and withdrew his opposition, still grumbling. On the wage question, however, he stood firm. Twelve and a half a month and her keep was all any schoolmarm was worth. How much did they take in at the school? Only six shillings a term per pupil. If Miss Andrews wished a refreshment of wage, let her go out and sell more "tigguts" to possible pupils. But, "Ve shall have trupples," he repeated darkly.

Pedagogy, as Durie at once discovered, involved more than merely teaching an assortment of juvenile intellects, ranging from seven to seventeen years of age. That was easy except for the fact that the younger children spoke little or no English. Besides instruction, she was expected to clear the path of snow, fetch in faggots to light the morning fires, provide drinking water, appease complaining parents, treat minor ailments, peddle the term-tickets which entitled the pupils to schooling, and bear herself with becoming meekness.

She was luxuriously lodged with a Welsh widow who allowed her a fire when the mercury touched zero. Three meals a day, beginning with a breakfast of oatmeal, eggs, sausage, turnips, johnny-cake with molasses and butter, salt-raised biscuits and two kinds of bread, washed down with coffee; and concluding with light evening supper of chicken, roast meat, three vegetables, preserves, pie or pudding and tea, were her bulwark against malnutrition. The only drawback to the young boarder's satisfaction was that Mrs. Owens tried to mother her, something of a gall to Durie's independent spirit. Another annoyance was that the schoolmarm was expected to attend church—all sessions—as well as prayer meeting and sociables, and to be at all times circumspect in speech and demeanor.

Trouble had been Trustee Adles' prediction for the new teacher. It was fulfilled at the first meeting after Schoolmarm Andrews' installation. These monthly gatherings were pleasurable occasions. for the board members, being devoted to an unfavorable appraisal of the incumbent's shortcomings, with suggestions for improvement, which the teacher was expected to accept with submissive gratitude. Durie listened politely and at the close of a comprehensive indictment in which all the members except the chairman took part, said, "We need a new stove."

A stunned silence followed. Committeeman Snell found voice to utter an incontrovertible statement.

"Stoves cost money."

He looked around for confirmation and received it from an unexpected source.

"They do," said Durie. "Twenty dollars will purchase a prime Franklin heater."

"You say twendy dollars like it was a York shilling," said Mr. Klee plaintively.

"The children are cold. Their poor little noses are running half the time."

"Vipe 'em," said Committeeman Adles brightly.

"Attend to de subject, if you blease, Miss," Mr. Bookstober rebuked her. "You haff heard our gomblaints dat de progress of de school iss unsatisfagterry."

"I want lower benches. How can they study when their poor little feet are all chilled from hanging in the air?"

"Answer, don't ask," said Clerk Shaver with a formidable scowl. "Are you hiring dis board or iss dis board hiring you?"

"I told you." A triumphant murmur from Committeeman Adles.

"I want a clean water firkin with spigot," continued the determined schoolmarm. "Melted snow water gives them wind on their stomachs."

"Pleass, no bad langwich," protested Committeeman Snell.

Durie observed a pained expression on the face of the chairman who had hitherto encouraged her with an occasional quiet smile. Well, perhaps she had gone a little far. Yet, compared to what she had in reserve, this was nothing.

"Iss dot all, Miss Andrews?" inquired the clerk with grim politeness.

She nodded.

"So, gut! Haf you any answer to de charches against your gonduct of the school?"

"Who makes the charges?"

"Who makes?" In his exasperation, Clerk Shaver hammered on the table. "Diss respectable board iss who makes."

The schoolmarm appeared regrettably unimpressed.

"What am I supposed to do?" she asked the chairman.

"An apology would be in order."

Durie's expressive face assumed its most persuasive appearance of candor.

"I'll do anything, if you'll give me the stove and cut down the benches," she offered.

"Should ve bargain with diss young berson?" inquired the sour Mr. Shaver.

They were, it appeared, in no mood to bargain. Requesting the teacher to withdraw, they went into private session and emerged with a decision which the clerk sternly imparted to the culprit. For her recalcitrance, her salary was to be reduced to ten dollars per month. Durie looked thoughtful.

"And if I do not choose to accept?"

"You loose your chob," said Clerk Shaver. "As soon as ve find another teejer."

Durie pounced upon the qualification. "You expect me to wait until then?"

"Ve allow you to remain. At ten dollars."

"Suppose I don't?" said Durie equably. "You can't find another teacher at the price and you know it. Closing got you into trouble before. You've taken the people's money, and you don't dare close again. Either you give me an indenture to April at the same wage, or I quit you now and you may whistle Yankee Doodle for your supply. And I *want* this schoolhouse made fit for my children to study in." For once in her self-controlled life, Durie was vehement.

She marched out like an army with banners.

Over six-o'clock breakfast in the kitchen, Mrs. Owens already had the news.

"Got your box packed, Miss Andrews?" she perkily asked.

"No. It won't take me long. I'd as lief go." But the wolf howl of the wind in the outer blackness caused her a shudder. "I don't like that board," averred the schoolmarm. "Not any of 'em."

"Not even Mr. Adrian Semple?"

"He's the only one that's human."

"He saved your fry in the committee." Mrs. Owens looked arch. "I think he's making the sheep-eye at you."

"What! That old man?"

"No more'n middle-aged," corrected her landlady. "I doubt he's thirty-five."

"He's so solemn."

"He's a weighty man. Six run of stone to his mill. Since his Mehitabel died, there ain't a girl in town but what would take him like a snap-turtle takes a gnat."

"Let 'em have him," said the schoolmarm. "I don't want him."

Being, nevertheless, human and woman, she was flattered when the great man terminated a call—on school business, naturally—by inviting her to attend a church sociable with him. She was sufficiently versed in local customs to know that this was portentous, though not definitive. She accepted and had an extremely dull time. The next approach was more serious. Would Miss Andrews accept his escort to Sunday evening service?

Miss Andrews evaded. She was not of the Congregational persuasion. And she had some leftover work to do. Such a spasm of shock and pain was manifested upon the austere Semple countenance that she hastened to explain, not quite truthfully, that the Sabbath-day task concerned New Testament exercises. Mrs. Owens was equally shocked, not at the proposed Sabbath violation but at Miss Andrews' failure to appreciate her opportunity.

"What would people think?" said Durie.

"They'd think you were going to marry him."

"I'm not."

"The more fool, you. What ails you about him? He's a sightly man."

Durie had to admit that, in his way, Mr. Semple was handsome enough.

"And a provider. Mehitabel lacked for nothing."

"Neither do I," returned Durie. "And I earn it, myself."

Mr. Semple possessed the admirable but uninviting virtue of patience. After several evasions Durie accepted the Sunday invitation. It was an error. This she realized as they entered the aisle. Their arrival was signalized by such a stir and craning of necks that Dominie Hawkes was moved to rebuke his congregation. Throughout the evening, Mr. Semple held the hymn book which they shared with a proprietary effect of clasping her hand.

Manheim men, being concerned chiefly with vital matters of business, naturally relegated courtship to a secondary place. Time was too valuable to be wasted on it. The course of true love might or might not run smooth; it did run short. A fortnight after the church visit had set tongues a-buzz, Mr. Semple called at the Owens house. Beaver hat, skin gloves, cameo brooch and gold-headed cane proclaimed the nature of his errand as plainly as published banns. Any exhibition of maidenly surprise on Durie's part would have been mere play-acting. The caller, invited to be seated in the parlor (temperature 45 degrees Fahrenheit), leaned his cane in a corner, placed his hat upon the floor, draped his gloves elegantly upon the rim, adjusted his neckcloth, cleared his throat and said, "Miss Andrews, will you marry me?"

Durie said with frank gravity, "I'd rather teach school."

He cleared his throat. "May I without offense point out that you are no longer in the first prime of youth?"

Durie blinked. She refrained from the obvious retort.

"I offer you an honorable name and state in life, and security."

Security! It was a more potent argument than he realized.

"I like my freedom," Durie said.

"Have you no better reason than that?" It was spoken indulgently.

"I could never think of you any way but as Mr. Semple."

"I prefer that form of address."

"Even from your wife?"

"Certainly. It is fitting, proper and dignified."

"So are you."

"I thank you." He bowed.

"I'm not."

"With the responsibilities of wifehood and motherhood . . ."

"Oh!" said Durie, as if something had just occurred to her and she did not like it.

"With new responsibilities, as I was saying, you would doubtless experience a change of mind and demeanor."

"What ails my demeanor?"

"Nothing that is not permissible to a spinster still young (Durie winced). But as the head of my household . . ." He left that in the air.

A spirit of exasperated and outrageous coquetry invaded Durie. "You haven't even said that you love me," she murmured.

Mr. Semple's fine gray eyes glazed. "I must protest against this light-mindedness," he said. "We are discussing a subject of grave import."

"But I am light-minded," she pointed out. "Not even you could cure me of that."

He drew the deep sigh of long-suffering patience. "May I bespeak your careful consideration of my offer?"

"I don't want to marry you. I don't want to marry anybody."

"I am a man not easily discouraged from my purpose," he stated.

"Oh, dear!" said Durie.

"Hence I shall not permit this—er—maidenly sensibility to divert me from an enterprise of which the advantages are patent. To both parties," he supplemented in generous afterthought.

An absurd and ribald fancy came to Durie's mind. If Gypsy were in her place, she knew what the answer to Mr. Semple's argument would be. It would be a loud, labial gardaloo. Durie was obliged to remind herself sternly that she was a schoolteacher with ladylike standards to maintain.

"I shall repeat my offer at some future and fitting occasion," said Mr. Semple, rising and reassuming the formal splendors of hat, gloves, and walking stick. "I bid you good evening, Miss Andrews."

Mrs. Owens, who had all but frozen her ear to the door, scuttled away and was awaiting Durie at the kitchen stove.

"Dumb! Dumb! Mortal dumb!" she upbraided her boarder. "You'll be sorry."

"I shan't," said Durie.

"No, likely you won't. I'm notional he won't give you the chance. The Semples always get what they want."

"I'd better run away," said Durie in discouragement.

But it was a particularly cold and blizzardy winter. Something of her hardiness had been corrupted by the ease of the life pedagogic. She found herself musing voluptuously upon the new steam-heating plant which Mr. Semple had installed in his mansion. What a pompous existence, merely to move a lever and flood one's bedroom with warmth! But—Mr. Semple would be sharing the bedroom. Oh, dear!

All was going well in school. The new Franklin was installed. A carpenter had lowered the benches. Fresh drinking water was kept on hand, to the disgust of Trustees Klee and Adles who gloomily foresaw a decadence of scholarship as the result of such cossetting. It did not work out that way. The pupils went at their lessons with an enthusiasm bred of their awakened affection for Teacher. Even the most captious parents were obliged to admit that the dubious experiment of a dame-school was turning out well.

Though personally more and more tender toward Durie—discouragingly so, in fact—Mr. Semple was developing an official tendency to put questions and offer suggestions. After fending them off for a time, she took the offensive.

"You'd better let me run my school my own way."

He contemplated her uneasily. "You have hinted at new projects."

"One of them is a school exhibition. Will you honor it with your presence? I shall, myself, contribute a recitation."

"Scriptural, I trust."

"Poetical."

He winced. "May I express a hope that it will be suitable to your position?"

"Come and judge for yourself."

Manheim best remembered its first school entertainment not from the gratifying performance of the pupils, but from the poem rendered by the teacher. And the memorable feature of the poem was that, at the close of the second stanza, Mr. Adrian Semple rose from his seat and with an expression of pain upon his handsome visage left the schoolhouse.

For Durie's choice had been "A Dismissal," and when she had come to the line that ended each stanza, "So, I'll love you no longer, oh, no!" sheer, defiant mischief had inspired her to look straight and teasingly at her suitor. Her audience loved it, all but a few. There was an area of silence in the fervent applause, where sat the sour-faced committee. Durie took bow after bow, and retired in profound depression of spirit. For, throughout the recital she had heard, off-stage, a voice that, however sardonic and critical, still was potent to move her as no other could.

"Don't bridle. Don't wriggle. Keep your voice down. You're not Lady Macbeth."

If she married Mr. Semple would it help her forget that voice?

She went home and found her suitor waiting in the parlor.

"I must protest," he began. The line of his lips, she noticed, was uncompromisingly flat.

"I'm sorry," she said, sounding not the least bit so.

"It was a most unbecoming exhibition."

Durie's chin went up. Her eyes steadied and became watchful. "What is unbecoming about it?"

"Frivolous," he said. "I might say meretricious. I might even say ry-bold."

"The correct pronunciation is rib-bald." She could not resist that. He was such an old sobersides.

"You remind me that you are a teacher," he said hollowly. "I would that you had remembered it before this unhappy exhibit."

"It didn't seem to make anyone else unhappy."

"I fear, Miss Andrews, that a person capable of choosing such a selection is unfit to instruct our youth."

"Is this, too, a dismissal?"

He frowned. "I shall feel compelled to bring it before the board."

"Why not go further?" she suggested maliciously. "If I'm unfit to instruct youth, I must be equally unfit to be your wife."

He received this shot with gloom. "I have not said so. On the contrary, I harbor the hope that the responsibilities of such a position would exert a sobering influence."

"They won't. Put that out of your mind."

He groaned. "Then I must accept you for what you are."

Suddenly she was sorry for him. "I'd be a calamitous wife for you," she warned.

"I cannot concur in that view, Miss Andrews."

"You can and you do," she smiled. "But you won't face it. Let me stick to my schoolteaching," she went on persuasively. "I'll promise to be good. Otherwise I'll run away and you'll never see me again."

He shook his head morosely. "I will use my good offices," he promised and left.

Durie said morosely to Mrs. Owens, "I wish the board would discharge me. Then I'd have to decide."

Mrs. Owens told the ladies at the sewing bee, "He's as good as got her."

The board did not discharge her. It satisfied its conscience with a recommendation that in the future she display a more circumspect conduct. Trustee Adles renewed his dismal prophecy of "more drupples," if they kept her on. The proceedings were duly reported to the schoolmarm.

She could have told the board that Mr. Adles was right.

Troubles or no troubles, she was determined to fight for the kind of school she wanted. But the time was not yet. Wait till the spring, when birds and men could build again.

AN IMPROVING lecture was offered at Fairfield. The March weather being moderate, a select party was composed in Manheim to make the five-mile trip by sleigh and hear what the Islands missionary had to tell of his adventures and successes among the cannibalistic heathen. It was Durie's idea that she might induce the Reverend Santley to come and speak to her schoolchildren. For once Chairman Semple approved a scheme of hers.

The hall of the Fairfield Medical School was well filled. After the lecture, which Durie found long and edifying, there was a social reception at the local clergyman's manse. Here was the opportunity to broach the subject of the Manheim visit. With her escort Durie moved slowly forward through the crowds to the bow-window where the distinguished visitor was reaching forward across several shoulders to grasp the hand of a man whose back was toward Durie. That made no difference. She knew him instantly.

"Well, well!" the missionary was saying in his hearty, pleasant voice. "My old pupil! How goes Harvard?"

"I am out, sir," said Jans.

"What is it?" said Mr. Semple. Durie had stopped dead.

"Nothing. I was dizzy for the moment."

"And where have you been, Quintard?" pursued the ex-Harvard instructor. "You're as brown as one of my savages."

"The sun is harsh in the Indies."

"Ah! The Indies. What have you been doing there?"

Durie's straining ears caught the answer plainly. "Learning the truth of an ancient saw, sir."

"A singular diversion. Which one?"

Jans half turned to look into Durie's paling face. *"Coelum non animum mutant qui trans mare currunt,"* he quoted slowly.

Durie closed her eyes.

"Ah, yes!" the missionary smiled. "In the words of the pious hymnologist, 'We change the place, but keep the pain'."

"Do you think, sir, he was one who had traveled to dull the pangs of thwarted love?"

"Who? Mr. Watts? Earthly love?" Dr. Santley was shocked. "Surely not!"

"Are you ailing, Miss Andrews?" her escort asked solicitously.

"No, no, I'm perfectly well. Pay no heed to me."

"There's young Quintard from Little Falls. I must inquire about his respectable uncle. Will you come and be presented to Dr. Santley?"

"Not now, please. Later." She slipped away.

Mr. Semple greeted the missionary and turned to Jans.

"What fetches you to these parts, young man?"

"My uncle has been ill."

"I regret to hear it and trust that he is improved."

"He is, thank you."

A certain shortness in the Quintard manner annoyed the older man, who now felt it incumbent upon him to express his disapprobation. "I understand that Senator Lovatt has had reason to regret your eccentric pursuits."

"Oh, as for that," Jans returned with deliberate flippancy, "Uncle Vryling cut me off with the jagged edge of a shilling, but we are still on terms of kinship."

"Then you are back in the mills?"

"I am not. Any further questions?"

Mr. Semple blinked.

"If not, I'll be off. Good night, Dr. Santley."

"Good night, my boy. My respects to the Senator."

"A very assumptive young man. He will come to no good end," pronounced Mr. Semple solemnly. He then addressed the missionary upon the subject of the lecture. Dr. Santley regretted that his schedule was, for the present, filled. Mr. Semple wandered about, vainly looking for Durie.

Pressing through the jam, Durie had found Mrs. Owens in the hall.

"Dearie me! You do look peaked," exclaimed the Welshwoman. "Whatever's the matter?"

"Too many people. I want to get away."

"Where can you get to? You'd freeze outside."

"I'd rather," said Durie savagely.

Mrs. Owens took thought. "There's a glassed porch. I don't know whether this dominie uses it. You could go there if the bolt isn't shot."

She led the way beneath the staircase to a small door. Durie crept through into chilly semi-darkness. She called back in a low voice, "Don't tell Mr. Semple where I am."

"Do you want anything?"

"Only to be alone."

It was not true. She wanted Jans Quintard, but feared him more than she wanted him.

An oblong of light was outlined on the wall beyond her, and was blotted into darkness as the low door closed behind the entering figure. She could not distinguish his face. It made no difference. She felt his nearness through every nerve of her body; had she supposed him a thousand miles distant, she would still have known.

He said, "Durie."

"Who told you I was here?"

"Nobody."

"How did you find me?"

"Did you think I shouldn't find you?"

"No," she said dully. Then, with sad decisiveness, "Jans, this is no good for either of us."

"I had to know."

"What?"

"How it is with you. Are you well and happy?"

"Yes." It was a spiritless affirmative.

"Married?" He brought it out with an effort.

"No."

"About to be?"

She was silent for a space before she said, "Let me alone, Jans."

"Fortunate people—light people—do change their hearts in absence," he said. "I wish I were of them."

"Yes, I heard your proverb."

"*Forsan et haec olim meminisse nec juvabit,*" he murmured.

"More Latin. That's a sure sign you've been drinking, isn't it?"

"Drink and dreams are the Quintard curse. Though, indeed, I'm sober enough now. And you've forgotten all that doubtless."

"I haven't forgotten anything. But I shall."

"Light come, light go. I suppose it's as true of dreams as of everything else."

Again she said resolutely, "This is no good, Jans. It leads nowhere."

"Durie, I've heard that you're to be married."

"How can I honorably marry?"

"Why can't you?"

"You should know."

"You mean Macel Ayrault?"

"I mean you."

"Still keeping up the farce?"

"It was no more than that to you, I know without any reminder."

"Must I remind you that you were never the worse for me?"

"You need not fear responsibility," she said contemptuously.

"Why should I? I don't admit it."

"No, you wouldn't. Not that I blame you more than myself. We were equally at fault."

"Fault?" he retorted impatiently. "What fault? I suppose I might have taken you. I forbore—and how you and Mace Ayrault must have laughed together at the poor gull!"

There was a brief silence. Her voice came, weak, bewildered. "You forbore?"

"As you well know."

"Then you didn't—we didn't—there was nothing—that night in the loft?"

"Spare me this pretense of ignorance."

"Pretense!"

"Do you wish a certificate of intaction at my hands?"

She moved closer to him, peering up into his eyes. "How do I know that you are not trying to—to spare my sensibilities?"

"Why should I? You took your profit on the situation."

That, in the tumult of her mind, she ignored. Later it came back to trouble and anger her. She stood up. She wanted to get away where she could think.

"Wait, Durie," he said. "There's another matter to be settled between us."

"Not now, Jans."

"Yes, now. It's Looby."

She gave a little moan. "I was trying to forget."

"I don't want you to forget. I want you to listen."

She stiffened. "Where is Looby?"

"In Auburn."

"And you took the reward? You and your friend, Pilkington?"

"Yes. But . . ."

"That's enough, I don't want to hear any more."

"You're going to hear it, though."

She covered her ears with her hands. He pulled them down. There was a discreet tap on the panel. A voice said warningly, "Miss Andrews, you're sought for."

She moved toward the door.

"You're going to be sorry, Durie," Jans said.

"I shan't. Not ever."

"I'll write."

"I won't read it."

"I'll write just the same. Remember my proverb."

"I wish only to forget it. And you."

The door closed behind her.

In the middle of the night an appalling thought struck Jans Quintard. Suppose it were not pretense on Durie's part? Suppose she had been as innocent as she appeared? Suppose that dim murmur which still struck to his heart with its appeal "I don't know anything about this, Jans" had been the truth? Suppose in the stress and confusion of drink and passion and exhaustion she had truly believed herself to have surrendered to him, and him to have taken her? And, as the ugly sequel, she had recklessly yielded to Macel Ayrault, believing her virginity already lost. Upon what hedgerows thereafter she had left the tatters of virtue was something that did not bear thinking about. If all this were true, how could he absolve himself from responsibility? That he was actually guiltless of despoiling her was not enough. It was her mistaken belief in her guilt that had brought her to catastrophe, and for that situation he was responsible. Assuming that she had been virtuous. . . .

Nonsense! What maggot was gnawing his brain? Would a pure girl have demanded the price of her virtue and carried through as cold-blooded a bargain as was ever struck at the door of a brothel? Would she have passed so lightly from one lover's arms to another? And that other, Macel Ayrault, who had doubtless been made to pay through the nose but, at least, had got what he paid for! The boom of the two-pounder in the night had left no room for doubt on the point.

She did not look like a strumpet. She did not act like a strumpet. Further proof of her artfulness, he violently assured himself. Once and for all he would so clearly establish his position toward her that there could be no further possibility of error.

He found quill, ink and paper and in the dead of the shivering night wrote:

To exculpate myself and reassure you, in case you need such substantiation, I would recall to you one episode which may have been erased or blotted in your memory. You said to me, "I don't know anything about this, Jans." There was an interruption from across the inn yard. You may have been already asleep when I belatedly answered you, "You shall not learn from me." It may have been in good faith—God save the mark!—that you exacted the blackmail from my uncle the next day. But, in case there might be any doubt in your mind, which I can still hardly credit, this will assure you on my honor as a gentleman, that, for all the harm that came to you through me, you might still be a maiden.   J. Q.

The matter of Looby he left until he could face her with it. Having duly wafered and sealed the message, he committed the letter to the Little Falls postmaster, paid the fee, and learned that it would be sent out not later than the second afternoon following. As he was not leaving his uncle's house until the end of the week, there would be ample time for reply. He thought of what it might be with trepidation. If Durie claimed that her assumed seduction and Jans' subsequent neglect had driven her to accept Ayrault as a paramour, what amends could he make? Was he laying himself open to further extortions? No, that he could not believe. At least Durie was now leading a decent life. He had detected in her no deterioration of demeanor or of self-respect. Curious! Once more doubt invaded his mind. Well, her reply would clear it up. Impossible for her to evade the issue of his letter.

The revelation made by Jans had set Durie's mind in a turmoil. Relief was her first response. Presently she discovered, however, that the knowledge had in no wise altered her attitude toward herself. She felt no different. The reason was that she had never in any degree forfeited her self-respect. Did that argue a lack of moral perception on her part? Very likely. What of it!

Marriage! An obstacle had been removed. For in case of her deciding to accept Mr. Semple's honorable offer she had, as a matter of course, intended to inform him of her lapse. That this would be followed by a prompt withdrawal of his candidacy, had occurred to her as a strong probability. In fact, she had been unconsciously relying upon it. The only reason for her not having revealed the derogatory fact earlier was her fear that it would compromise her situation in the school. Now that fear was removed. With it went her bulwark against the marital pressure of Mr. Semple. Dismay lurked in the thought. Yet she had decided to accept him. It was this that she had in mind when she told Jans Quintard of making sure that they would not meet again. It was her only defense.

Returning from market, Mrs. Owens had been hailed by Postmaster Bye. There was a letter for the schoolmarm. It was on pale blue, prime quality paper, five cents prepaid, posted in Little Falls, sealed with a carven stone, and, if Mr. Bye was any judge of handwriting, from a young gentleman. Would Mrs. Owens take it? Mrs. Owens would.

She was waiting for Durie, letter in hand. At sight of the writing, the girl blanched.

"You know it?" said the landlady.

"Yes." She stretched out a hesitant hand.

"Wait a bit."

Mrs. Owens put the square behind her back. Active Durie could have broken her in two and possessed herself of it. She made no move.

"It's from Little Falls," said the landlady.

"Yes."

"From that scapegrace nephew of rich old Senator Lovatt?"

Durie nodded.

"I ask no questions, but was he with you in the dark of Dominie Bowen's glass-in?"

"Yes."

"What did you talk of?"

"Things that are past."

"Are they past?"

"Yes."

"Then d'you know what I'd say to me, if I was you? I'd say, 'Burn it.'" As Durie hesitated, she added, "Not but what I'm just as piny as you be to know what's in it."

Durie said, "Burn it."

She followed her landlady into the kitchen to overlook the operation, which was hard on Mrs. Owens. She had hoped for a private peek at the contents.

Mr. Semple called that evening, with his eighth proposal.

Durie returned a desperate, "Yes."

27

L ONG betrothals were not in order. Mr. Semple was quite within the social scheme in pressing for an early marriage.

"Am I to go on with the school?" asked Durie.

"My wife a schoolteacher? Certainly not."

"Have you anyone else for the place?"

"Well, no. Not yet."

"Then I think I'd better continue until the board finds some-one."

It was the best excuse she could muster, but it would not serve for long.

At the April meeting, the teacher was summoned as usual to appear before the board to answer the accumulated criticisms by the members. Since Miss Andrews' accession this sport had lost its zest. It was unprofitable. It was even risky, since, for every charge brought against her conduct, the schoolmarm was more than likely to adduce a retort impugning the management of the board. Worse, she was always demanding improvements. Improvements cost money. Clerk Shaver had prepared a list showing that under Miss Andrews, the sum of $36.15 had been expended upon fandangos. He was about to present his argument when she forestalled him.

"Spring is coming," she began briskly, "and soon the children will be playing outdoors." She paused. "They have no place to play."

"Vot for dey vant to blay?" inquired Mr. Snell. "Do they gome to school to blay? Leddem study."

"There is recess."

"Reezess!" from the scornful Mr. Klee.

"A fandango!" from the resentful Mr. Snell.

"If the lot back of the schoolhouse were cleared, it would make a very nice playground."

"Blayground? Wass fur a blayground?" demanded Messrs. Klee and Snell in a breath.

"With a swing and a trapezium and a teeter-tawter," continued Durie in her most seductive voice.

"Iss diss a circus or a school?" thundered Clerk Shaver.

"Iss what you ged for a dame-school!" piped Mr. Adles in a tone of one whose dire prophecy had been gratifyingly vindicated.

"Idees!" snorted Mr. Bookstober.

"I believe that I express the sentiments of this meeting," the chairman said, "in holding that Miss Andrews' proposals require more contemplation than we have time to accord them at present."

"Anyhow, I'd like the back yard cleared," Durie said.

"I can see no burbose," Clerk Shaver objected.

"I'm coming to that," Durie said, keeping her voice and manner carefully commonplace. "As it is now, the children have no place to go."

"Go?" said Trustee Snell to Trustee Bookstober.

"Go?" said Clerk Shaver to Trustee Adles.

"Go?" echoed Trustee Klee, appealing to the chairman. "Vot iss dis go?"

"I think," began the chairman with a slightly flushed face, "that this is not the suitable time and place . . ."

"And so," the schoolmarm broke in brightly, "I have sketched out a rough plan."

She put the sheet of paper into Mr. Semple's hand. From his flaccid grasp it passed to the other members. Mr. Klee, who had forgotten his glasses, looked at it upside down.

"It is a building, *nicht wahr?*" he inquired distrustfully.

"Yes, Mr. Klee. A building. Nice but inexpensive."

"Ve haf here vere ve sid a fine building cost four hundret dollars. Vot for should ve haf anodder building?"

Durie's patience began to wear thin. "Oh, don't be so dumb!" she cried.

"Order! Order!" The protest was unanimous.

"Dot iss not a way to address a member of dis respeggtable body," admonished Mr. Shaver.

Mr. Klee poked at the drawing. "I moof she eggsplains." He applied to the schoolmarm. "Vot iss it you vant?"

"A privy," Durie said.

At this enormity the clerk of the board belched so explosively that it left his jaw pendent.

"Mr. Clerk! Mr. Clerk!" vociferated Trustee Bookstober. "Strike out dot vort from de record."

"It iss stricken," said the clerk solemnly.

"Such a vort!" proceeded the outraged trustee. "Nobody uses such a vort, led alone a young female."

"If you know a prettier one I'll use it," said Durie. "You may call it the town hall or the Leaning Tower of Pisa, for all I care. I want a privy for my children. Two privies—one for the boys, the other for the girls."

Chairman Semple spoke with calm austerity.

"Since this distasteful subject has been regrettably forced upon the attention of the board, I may state that I have, myself, served on a committee of that honorable body, the State Legislature, in which capacity I visited no less than thirty-two schools. Not one of them possessed a—er—a structure such as has been proposed to us."

"Then they ought to be ashamed of themselves," Durie declared.

"Silence!" "Order!"

She swept the board with an undaunted eye. "How would you like it, yourselves?" she shot at them.

The *argumentum ad hominem* struck them into scandalized silence. A weak voice was heard.

"Moof ve adchourn."

The meeting broke up in confusion.

A week later in special session, the board unanimously voted down a proposition, couched in carefully guarded terms which could not have offended the most delicate sensibility. An amendment was added which embodied a stinging rebuke to the teacher.

Nevertheless her efforts were not wasted. The subject continued one of subterranean discussion and came to fruition five years later when a serviceable edifice of this sort was erected by the private effort and at the private cost of an irascible Scotch carpenter with seven children. Having had his humane plea rejected by the board, he punched the Clerk's nose—twelve shillings fine—cut the timber from his own woodlot and put up a weatherproof pile. Other schools followed the pioneer example. Thus was the little red schoolhouse augmented by the little white outhouse.*

In no time at all it was all over Manheim that the schoolmarm had scandalized the trustees in open meeting. She had used that word! Before all those men. How could she keep her position after such conduct? And what about Widower Semple?

"He can't. Not now." It was the unanimous opinion of the feminine populace.

That her affianced did not come to escort her to church the next Sunday should have been sufficient warning to Durie. She supported the neglect with Christian meekness, or what might have passed for that admirable quality in the minds of those who did not know her. When Mr. Semple did arrive, his brow was dark with rebuke.

"This," he began, "is indeed an afflictive occasion."

"Am I out of my chob, as Mr. Klee calls it?" she asked lightly.

"I am referring to my personal feelings, Endurance."

"Are they hurt?"

"Deeply."

"So are mine." (She did not look it.)

"Do you consider that you have cause of complaint against me?" he asked.

"All things considered, you might have supported my position in the meeting."

"Whatever the merits of your position and, mark you, I do not concede them, your method of presentation was deplorable. It lacked respectability."

"I am not respectable?"

"In this instance, Endurance, I must reluctantly answer in the negative."

"Then you cannot afford to marry me."

"Cannot afford is hardly the term I should choose."

*My Great-aunt Sarah recalls that, as late as the middle of the century this type of architecture was known in the northern counties as an "Andy," whence the juvenile euphemism, "Going to the Andes." This she surmises to have been a belated recognition of Endurance Andrews' missionary work in hygiene. "Surely," wrote Aunt Sarah to my grandmother, *"aes triplex* itself never more suitably memorialized the services of a humble and forgotten educatrix."

"Drat the terms!" replied Durie with unschoolmarmish vigor. "You wish to be released?"

"I have not said so," he answered in a hollow voice.

"What do you want, then?"

"If there were some evidence of a chastened spirit," he began hopefully, only to be cut short by Durie's positive, "I'd do it again."

He sighed. "You understand that by your unbridled speech you have made it impossible for me to support your status any longer."

"Good-bye, job." Durie blew a kiss into Mr. Semple's shocked face. "I'm sorry for my children."

"The children," he retorted stiffly, "will be safely and properly cared for by the board. But you, Endurance, what will you do?"

"Oh, I shall thrive along."

"My heart misgives me for you."

"Your heart, did you say?" She started to laugh; but the spasm of pain that passed over his stolid face wiped the mirth from hers. She put out an impulsive hand to rest on his arm. "Oh, Adrian! I'm sorry. I didn't understand. I'm truly sorry."

"It will pass," he said with an effort.

"It would never have done, anyway. You know that."

"Yes, I know that. I could never have engaged your affections. Only your loyalty."

She said, "If only I'd caught you earlier! Oh, forgive me! I oughtn't to have said that."

The ghost of a difficult smile answered her. "Perhaps one day I shall be glad to remember it. Good-bye, Endurance."

"Good-bye, Adrian."

She would have lifted her face to him in charity and pity. But already he had grasped his gloves and hat, set his neckcloth, retrieved his gold-topped cane from the corner and marched resolutely out the door.

28

Boots," said the mellifluous voice. "Good as bespoken ones, and cheaper. Medicaments. Cure anything. Books to read. All tastes. Dandy shirts. Make your girl love you. Zany-caps. Laugh fit to kill. Trusses for the gut-sprung. Good licker for the down-hearted." The pace of the utterance accelerated sharply. "Playing cards, toy colors, spit-boxes, finger bowls, silvery blunts with thread strong enough to hang yourself, castor hats, Rogers' patent knives, corsets, pickled sturgeon, Shaker brooms and shaving soap. Little Falls needs my goods and I need your trade. Step aboard and see. It costs you nothing to look."

The orator stood with one foot on the boat's coaming and made invitational gestures. A hail from an adjoining warehouse brought his head around with a jerk.

"Hallo, Pilk."

"Eh? May I be lathered with vitriol and shaved with a handsaw if it ain't my college lad! We'll have a guzzle on this. Come to the skipper's cabin in an hour."

"How's trade?" Jans asked when he came aboard at sundown.

"Too good for one man. I need help. And I need capital funds."

"You're not running this show alone, surely!"

"Got a lunkhead 'prentice. He can't read a price mark."

Extracting liquor from a special jug, he compounded two jorums with corn, Jamaica ginger and fresh mint. He removed his quid, lifted his glass, and intoned:

> *"Prosit, Bruder, du sollst leben*
> *So viel Tage, so viel Jahre . . ."*

"That'll be enough, Pilk," Jans broke in with a grin. "There are ladies within earshot."

"Let 'em plug their ears," retorted the Captain, drinking. "The sight of you would gladden a glass eye. You're browner than my bay mare's rump. Where you been?"

"Touring the Indies."

"Business or pleasure?"

"Business. For Senator Lovatt."

"That old chunk of tripe! I thought you was well quit of him."

"Of the mills. Not of my revered uncle." Jans hesitated. "There was a debt. Some money he had to pay out for me. I satisfied it by shipping supercargo on a venture of his."

"So you're even with him?"

Jans nodded.

"Got any ready rhino?"

"Pocket funds only."

"Couldn't raise the wind to the tune of a couple hundred?"

"How badly do you need it, Pilk?"

"With that and what I got I could buy plural interest in the boat, and be full boss."

"What's the security if I get you a loan?"

"Security, hell! You get a partnership. Supercargo? I'll show you supercargoing!"

"It's worth considering."

They made a tour of the craft. All was shipshape, but Jans' inherited commercial talent devised several improvements in the merchandising layout. He suggested abandoning the bottled nostrums as quacksalverish and low-class and using the space for a layout of the popular greenish glassware from the Saratoga factory and the boldly designed flasks of the Albany Glassworks. Book space, he thought, might be enlarged, and an art corner contrived for the colored lithographs just beginning to make their way into the public appreciation. At the mention of art, Captain Pilkington swelled perceptibly.

"Lemme show you," said he, and led the way forward to a closed-off space, placarded: "Entrance 1 sh.: Children, Half Price."

"More Le Sueur?" asked Jans.

"Better, and quicker returns." He lighted two sidelamps, drew a curtain, and made a showman's gesture.

Where the Frenchman's pigs had disported themselves in wanton

play, the heroic-size oil by Mr. David, of Cain meditating the murder of Abel, now stood forth in all its sour impressiveness.

"Catches the church custom," said the Captain proudly. "Parson
Brownson preached on it in Utica. Said every pious family oughta
take warning by it. I had to stay three days to satisfy the trade.
Open on Sundays, too, when the canal regelations won't leave me
do no other business. Whaddya say, lad? Will you come in?"

"Give me time, Pilk. When do you come back?"

"I'm Albany-bound to restock with notions. Say this day week."

Jans plodded up the hill to the Lovatt mansion where he found
his uncle in the library, julep at elbow, swearing gutturally over a
chess problem.

"Go away," he growled. "Can't you see that I'm busy? What do
you want?"

"A loan," said Jans. With Uncle Lovatt it was best to come to the
point at once.

"How much?"

"Two hundred dollars."

"Humph! More woman foolishness?" The Senator persisted in
regarding Jans' theatrical ventures in the light of a plaicer-chase.

"No, sir. A commercial venture."

"Be more affording with your information if you expect to touch
my money."

"It's a partnership in a Durham."

"Who's your partner?"

"Bassford Pilkington."

"Four-Skate Pilkington? I've heard of him. Smart trader. But the
man's not a gentleman. His repute is calumnious. What do you
know of him?"

Explaining Pilk was not easy. There was too much that was
better left unsaid. But Jans did his best.

"You make a poor fist of it," commented the Senator. "Patently,
the man's a shady character."

"He's been a good friend to me, sir."

"So have I, though it's little you appreciate it," returned the
Senator with pathos.

Lacking any response that would have suited his uncle's mood, Jans let this pass.

"Well, anything's better than your poxy, stagestruck gallivantings," continued Uncle Vryling. "Let's look into this freighting business. I might arrange some charters from the mills."

"It isn't freighting, Uncle." He outlined the plan.

"Huckstering by canal, eh? Not a bad notion." He drained his long glass. "Fetch me my pad and pencil." Thrusting aside the chessboard, he fell to figuring. "This is a commercial proposal, eh?" he presently said, looking up with his sharp little wren's eyes. "Strictly business."

"Yes, sir."

"I'll hire you five hundred dollars at a reasonable twelve-and-a-half-percentum."

"Two hundred is all I need, sir."

"Take five hundred, buy your sixty percent share from the owner, and send Mr. Packington pilking."

"Do what? Oh! Cross-deal old Pilk? I couldn't do that, sir."

"Then get out of my sight and be damned to you!" Uncle Vryling was reacting as he always did to any opposition.

"Yes, sir," replied Jans with his customary amenity.

"Wait a bit." The young man turned, with his hand on the door-knob. "That girl," said his uncle.

Jans' face became blank.

"Wipe that damned Quintard mulishness off your damned Quintard phiz. Well enough you know who I mean. Or have you been about seducing other wenches?"

"I've seduced no one."

"So much the better, if true. I had a letter from her."

"From Dur—— Miss Amour?"

"From your Miss Amourette. Why does she seek your post address?"

"I have no notion, sir."

"Hope of more black mail, doubtless. Perhaps you want this sum of money for her. Eh?"

"When did I last lie to you, Uncle Vryling?"

"No, that's true. You Quintards don't lie. Part of your poxy pride.

Well, there it is. She demands your address in a single line and is, very respectfully, Endurance Andrews."

"Andrews?" Jans said quickly.

"Yes. Why not?"

"Then she didn't marry."

"And what of that?"

"Nothing."

"The prey escaped the springe," Uncle Vryling said with relish. "A fine catch he would have been for her, Adrian Semple. But that sterling citizen . . . Eh? What's that?"

For Jans had muttered, "A stockfish," under his breath.

"I wish you possessed his firmness of character," the Senator said with severity. "He, at least, found her out in time. So she lost her swain and her position at one stroke."

"Her position?"

"In the school. For foul speech in public."

"That, at least, is untrue," said Jans calmly.

"What! You doubt my word, sirrah?" Uncle Vryling roared.

"No, sir. Your information."

"Go look at the school record at Manheim."

"If it were in the Bible I still would not believe it."

"You're a besotted young fool."

"Have you her letter, sir?"

"I burned it."

"Unanswered?"

"Unanswered."

"But she may be in trouble," the young man said, more to himself than to his companion.

"And designing to foist it upon you," said the Honorable Vryling viciously. "Must you be Don Quixote de la Mancha for every pretty adventuress who casts a languishing eye in your direction? Set your lance in couch and so to the rescue, eh?"

"No, sir. I have no wish to see her again. But if she were in need or distress what would you have me do?"

"Oh! Ah! A very proper spirit," allowed the Old Corinthian, his disgust and anxiety both mollified. "As for that, I daresay you're as deep in the mud as she in the mire. The five hundred dollars is at your draught."

"Thank you, sir. I can't take it on your terms." He went out, leaving his uncle to the problem of checkmate in three moves.

The crash came half an hour later. Unable to fix his mind upon the chess combination, Senator Lovatt hurled board and men against the wall, yelled for old Nicodemus to pick up the wreckage, and went abovestairs to find his nephew. Noises from the spacious attic guided him. There Jans had heaped at the stairhead a collection of miscellany representing the accumulation of ten years.

"What are you doing there?" demanded the owner of the house.

"Collecting my property, sir."

"To what purport?"

"Sale at the best terms I can get. Could I borrow a two-wheeled cart from the mills?"

Senator Vryling sat down and conned over the heap. There were two guns, a fowling piece and a musket; three fishing rods, one a very fine greenheart, a flute, a chased-silver flask, a brass-studded trunk of beautifully embossed leather, a long mink greatcoat done up in spices against the moth, three outmoded hats, a Chinese tea-chest full of toys, a pair of silver-finished skates, a fortified hickory sled, seven neckcloths, a very elegant meerschaum pipe, a stuffed hawk, and a harmonicum. The rest was odds and ends.

"How much do you hope to realize from such an offal heap?" inquired the Senator disparagingly.

Jans cast a knowing eye upon it. "From one seventy-five up, sir."

"Don't be a fool, Jans."

"Well, say one-sixty. Not a cent under, unless I lose my voice."

"Five hundred dollars, my boy," said the uncle seductively.

"Two hundred and a free hand."

"Go and find your damned cart and try to keep out of jail this time. Oh!" the Senator clapped a hand to his forehead. "That half-wit canal boy of yours—what's his name? Looby. The Governor's signed a full pardon for him and he's free by now. You'll be taking up with him again, I presume. I wish you joy of your choice associates."

"Thank you, Uncle."

"Damn you, Jans! Come back when you're strapped. I shall miss you, my boy."

Off went the cart, with Laus Deo riding atop the junk-pile, and

Jans singing at the push-bar. A week of happy salesmanship cleared up the lot, ending with a street vendu in Amsterdam, total takings $208.30. Jans went fishing in the Mohawk with one eye on the canal for the approach of the *Barter Boat*.

It arrived with eleven deck passengers, and an itinerant automaton in charge of the inventor. A melancholy voice issued from below, where languished a yearling calf taken in trade by Pilk for a wind-sprung harmonium. The stock of books had been replenished and there were some strikingly garish toys. The array of glassware was impressive. Pilk informed Jans that he had taken on the commission agency for a line of printer's inks, a small-prize lottery, and a church bell, of which there was a sample forward. Trade was brisk. Things couldn't look brighter. The boat was a dandy.

"We'll have side-splashers and steam on her yet," bragged Pilk.

Meanwhile the Durham ploughed the main at a reliable four miles an hour. Jans slung a dragnet out behind which kept them supplied with fresh fish: eels, pike, bass, and once in a while a blue trout or a young sturgeon. At each trade stop Captain Pilkington blew his ball-whistle for announcement, and expatiated to the collected throng upon the diversity, novelty and quality of his wares, ending his oration with the unvarying formula:

"And believe me, friends, patrons and customers, when I tell you this truth: an open purse makes glad the hearthside and a nimble ninepence fetches more than a sulky shilling."

Then the people would swarm aboard and Jans would handle the trade with urbanity, tact, and profit. Evenings, the partners set the lamps and did a steady business with the saturnine Cain.

On a moonlit July night, Pilk danced upon the deck.

"We'll be millionaire-men yet," he gloated.

"We're doing well," admitted his partner.

"What'll we do with it all?"

"Re-invest it and make more."

"Gor, lad! Ain't you never satisfied?"

"There is plenty of new trade untapped. And Cain is going stale on us. No preacher has painted a moral lesson from him for a month."

"I always did prefer the pigs," said Pilk. "Maybe I could find that Frenchy."

Jans shook his head. "Not for our route. I've got a better idea. Get rid of Cain and put a little stage in."

Pilk stared. "Ain't you got shut of that bug yet? And where would you get your actors?"

"Buy 'em."

"Huh?"

"Or have 'em made. Marionettes. Puppets. There's a mechanic in Albany that can build me a troupe, and I'll write the drama."

"It sounds spoopsy to me," said Pilk. "But if you're notional thataway I reckon there's no stopping you. But we gotta buy out Byles first."

"The money's ready. I'm sending off the draft from Schenectady."

Pilk executed another exultant shuffle. "Lad, we gotta celebrate. We gotta have a good, ole red-eye scale when we get to Albany. I ain't been properly slubbered since Uncle laid the chunk. How long since you been, boy?"

"You ought to know," answered Jans quietly.

Pilk shivered. "Oh, God!" he wheezed. "Whaddya wanta fetch that up for? It's pretty much spilt my taste for licker, too. But we might have a leetle kantikoy," he pleaded. "Nothing to rouse the watch. Nothing but what we could make our own way back to the boat. Have dinner at a coffee house and supper at a tavern, and visit two or three taps, to finish off. You fetch along your feedle-deedle"—thus disrespectfully did he refer to Laus Deo—"and we'll give 'em a song."

Within the meaning of the Minister's Oath, both celebrants were sober when they emerged from Goodrich's Inn upon Albany's streets at one o'clock of a warm July morning, bound for the Great Erie Basin where their craft was moored. They could walk steadily. They could sing harmoniously, and did. A constable addressed them in reprobation, his accents thickly Dutch. They stood him on his head, appeased his dignity with a shilling and proceeded, singing louder than before.

Descending to the waterfront, they were checked in their music by a shriek of shocking intensity. At the foot of an elm, a man's figure writhed and twitched. They ran to him. Jans knelt down to lift his head.

"What's the matter?"

"I been stabbed," mumbled the man uncertainly. He pressed both hands upon his belly.

Pilk got out a flask, opened it and held it to the sufferer's lips. "Who done it?"

"I dunno. I never seen him." His face was ghastly and bewildered.

"Why, it's Pig Baker!" Jans exclaimed. He ran his hands over the man's body. There was no gash to be found.

"I can't find anything. What happened?"

"I was having a bit of a snooze under the tree," answered the swine-warden in a lifeless half-whisper. "He musta snuck up on me."

"You dreamed it," said Jans.

Baker's eyes turned back in his head. His lips stiffened, parted and loosed a shriek that was the very essence of agony. His body jerked in a spasm and a froth of vomit spurted from him.

Pilk recalled having passed the mortar-and-pestle sign of a compounding physician halfway up Pinkster Hill. They lugged the writhing patient to the place and roused the elderly Dr. Townsend. After a swift inspection he bled the sufferer and administered opium.

"Wash your hands at this basin," he directed the two men, pouring some vinegar into it. "Thoroughly."

"What is it?" Jans asked.

Dr. Townsend considered him thoughtfully. "You're Senator Lovatt's nephew, aren't you?"

"Yes, sir."

"Are you with him in the mills?"

"No. I'm canalling."

"Mm-mm! Business or pleasure?"

"Business. This is my partner."

"Open for a westward charter?"

"Yes, sir."

"Come in tomorrow evening. I'll look after this fellow."

Trying to find a man who was adept at the facture of manageable figures took up much of the next day for Jans. The artisans who had kept the Mailzell panorama's supply of androids up to requirements had left town. A wood-carver to whom Jans was directed had his own notions of art and refused to conform to a layman's wishes. An assortment of second-hand manikins in a warehouse proved, on inspection, to be too shopworn. For the time, the intending puppeteer was obliged to give up his project. He and Pilk replenished stock for the westbound voyage.

At the appointed hour he found Dr. Townsend smoking his pipe over a neatly draughted map of the canal with all towns listed. Would Jans, the physician asked, be willing to deliver a note to a designated doctor or official in each community and bring back a reply under seal? There would be a small fee and Jans would be, in a measure, of service to the state whose interests Dr. Townsend represented as member of a special committee. Parcels of drugs would be awaiting them in a specified warehouse, to be freighted at top rates in consideration of speed. Jans accepted both commissions.

"How is Pig Baker, sir?" he inquired.

"Dead."

"Dead? Wasn't it very quick? What was his ailment?"

"Can you keep your mouth shut?"

"Yes, sir."

"Do you know of the great epidemy raging in New York?"

"I've heard something of it."

"This is it. Cholera Asiatica."

29

As a dutiful nephew, Jans stopped off on the way through Little Falls to pay his respects to Senator Lovatt. There was news waiting for him.

"I heard of your little plaicer, Jans."

"Where?" The involuntary eagerness of the question raised the Senatorial brows.

"In Philadelphia. Through stage-folk acquaintances."

"What was she doing?"

The Honorable Vryling shrugged. "Oddments."

"Was she—was she all right, sir?"

"So far as I learned." He sensed an unasked question. "And alone, I believe."

"It's nothing to me, of course," Jans said stoutly. "Just curiosity."

"Exactly," said his uncle.

Durie had, in fact, not done badly. Washington and then Richmond had provided theatrical employment, such as it was, and she came back to New York with funds enough to afford her a week of leisure in which to think matters over. There were no stage jobs there. She must do something.

School teaching? Dull, but respectable and safe. Being a schoolmarm was all very well for winter; but this was full spring, as a chorus of birds overhead vociferously informed her. The Book, Stationary & Notions trade? No better. She would rather sleep under a tree than a counter. Somewhere upstate the banner of a road company would be flaunting—Mr. Passerow's or another's. How could she be sure that Jans Quintard would not be with it? A voice sang in her memory.

> *There is no striving*
> *To foil his intent.*

She shook herself angrily. Was she still bound in that numbing enchantment? Someone had once told her of a wise woman who brewed a philter to exorcise love-thoughts. Gypsy Vilas! She felt suddenly hungry for the easy, warm companionship of the little vagrant.

Would Gypsy still be in Schenectady? Not likely, now that winter was over. More probably she and Tim Baggo would have taken the road, assuming that they were still together. That was no safe assumption. Gypsy was a volatile creature. Wherever she was, she would have left word for Durie somewhere by tow-rope channels of news.

Durie took passage for Albany on Messrs. Livingston & Fulton's steam packet, *Clermont,* and had a very genteel trip. Thereafter it was less genteel. She warehoused her box of fine clothing and hit the path with an economical pack and her staff.

At the sign of the Hungry Pike she struck Gypsy's trail.

"That little slewer!" said the surly barkeep. He had not forgotten the play of Gypsy's knife that had discouraged his ardor. "Last I heard, she was a factory wiper over to Scotio."

Poor Gypsy! She must have fallen upon evil fortunes indeed to have taken a low-grade mechanic's job paying no more than five shillings a week, and found. Evidently Tim Baggo had quit her, or she him. Durie crossed the river to pursue her inquiries.

Yes, the overlooker remembered the Vilas wench very well. A limb of Satan. She won a five-dollar draw in the lottery and was off by westbound packet to seek a job with the circus, preferring (so she injuriously told him) the company of apes and elephants to his.

Westward went the searcher, enjoying the freedom of the road more and more every day. The circus was at Utica, but no Gypsy. She had gone on. Durie ran her to earth at Rome, settling into a job as milk-malkin in a cattle barn. After greetings were over, Durie asked, "Why did you quit the circus?"

Gypsy reached around behind and rubbed herself gingerly. "Did you ever curry a giraffe?"

"No."

"You have to climb a platform with a sponge on a pole. If the giraffe don't like our ways, he waggles his neck and knocks you off. The painted clown came around to laugh at me one day and I jabbed him with the pole and knocked out a couple of teeth. He was the boss's wife's fancy-man. So I got the run-out. I guess I just ain't a stayer, Durie. I couldn't even stick by Tim, and I liked Tim. Sleeping under a roof is all very fine, but a gal can't keep it up forever."

"Where is Tim?"

"Back with the show, I reckon."

"What show?"

"Passerow's, of course."

"Are the Passerows back in business?"

"He is. She ran away with Penmaster Robinson. They're traveling the Great South Pike by gig, giving lessons in plain, fancy, and round."

"Where's the company?"

"Out west somewhere, Buffalo way. Durie, would you like to go back?"

"Yes, I would, but . . ." Doubt darkened her eyes.

"He ain't with 'em any more. If that's what's hindering."

"Where is he?"

"Gone back to his rich uncle, I hear," said Gypsy carelessly. "I think no more of him than a pint of pukeweed, him and his lovesickly caterwauls."

"They weren't." The contradiction was involuntary.

Gypsy frowned. "You've still got him in your gizzard? Wasn't once enough for you?"

"There wasn't any once, Gypsy."

"Anan?"

"Oh, I don't expect you to believe it. It doesn't matter," said Durie wearily.

"You going back to join, gal?"

"I will if you will."

"All the coined money I got wouldn't wear a hole in a stocking heel."

"I've enough for both of us."

"We're eating dust tomorrow," said Gypsy joyously.

They took the trail in the morning, making inquiries as they went, followed several false reports, and eventually sighted the flag with its fancy border and central T flying from the ballroom window of the Bath Inn. The announcement on the front-hall hoarding was *Mother and Child Are Doing Well.* Durie felt the old tingle in her veins.

"I could step right in there and say Dolly's lines now," she exclaimed.

"I'm notional we're a couple of ninkums to work for that old sharpshooter again," reflected Gypsy.

"Mr. Passerow? He isn't so bad." Durie had absorbed the tolerant theatrical tradition of letting bygones be bygones. "Besides, what other chance is there? I'm going to make a try anyway."

"So do," said her friend. "Me, I want to smell his money on the first pay day."

That there was money to be smelled was apparent when the two Thalia wagons rolled into the village. They were freshly painted in resplendent design. The scenery was refurbished, the costumes new, the whole outfit had an air of prosperity.

"Dicty!" said Gypsy. "Where'd they get the dibbs, I wonder."

Manager Passerow, wearing a gold watch-chain that would have tethered an ox, received them graciously. His eye kindled with an extra-professional interest as it rested upon Durie's slenderly ripening figure.

"An opening for you, my dear?" he said. "There will always be an opening for you in any production of mine."

Durie was not sure that she quite liked that "my dear." She said, "And Miss Vilas? We go together, Mr. Passerow."

"In that case—yes. We can make her useful in utility. Report to Mrs. Gorman, Miss Vilas. She has taken my—er—late wife's place, and is in charge of wardrobe. I will ask you to remain for a few minutes, Miss Amour."

He fussed importantly with some papers on the traveling desk. Departing, Gypsy signaled over his shoulder with derisive eyebrows a message which her chum readily interpreted as "Look out for the old goat."

"Miss Amour," he began. "I have had a bit of a windfall."

"I am gratified to hear of that, Mr. Passerow," returned Durie primly.

"Yes, Dame Fortune has at last smiled at me."

"The lottery?"

"The Mint and Mine. Not the Grand Prize, to be sure. But a thousand-dollar draw cannot be regarded as despicable. Our tour, too, shows a modest profit. We will talk of this again. Meantime your salary begins at ten dollars."

Surprised at this munificence, Durie thanked him. "And Miss Vilas'?" she asked again.

He frowned. "At your request. She shall have five dollars. But only so long as she offers no interference."

"To what?" asked Durie bluntly.

"To our projects—my projects for you."

"I am sure," returned Durie with deceptive urbanity, "that Miss Vilas would never seek to interfere with any of my professional interests."

"Umph!" said Mr. Passerow discontentedly. The interview closed upon that note of indeterminacy.

The two girls slipped back into the routine of the road life with no effort of adjustment. Flavel Crosbie's place had been taken by a fatly handsome young fellow named Locke who played with a chronic smirk. Ripley Rapalje's leprous overlay had worn off during the winter; he was once more his cheerful, shallow self. It seemed to Durie that Tim Baggo had aged sadly, his features gone slack from dissipation. She was relieved to note that he and Gypsy greeted one another with ready camaraderie; no breakage of emotional bones there. Old Mr. Archbold welcomed them affectionately; Fair Luna Wayne, less than affectionately. She was still pretty in her over-blown way, still hardly vivacious, but her waistline was gaining upon her, and there was a slight puffiness beneath the wide, violet eyes.

The advent of the two girls, particularly Durie, struck her as a possibly unfavorable omen for her own preferment. She accosted the younger girl with jocose negligence.

"How's your leg?"

"My leg?" repeated Durie.

"Since you broke it above the knee?"*

"I don't understand you."

Fair Luna guffawed. "Had it mended many a time since, I'll warrant. Like cures like, they say."

*A contemporary vulgarity, meaning to be seduced.

303

Gypsy sidled up. "Doing much in the tin-cup line, Miss Wayne?" she inquired.

The reference to her testimonial trophies was not lost upon the other. "You keep your remarks to yourself until called for," she retorted with angry dignity.

"Then don't try and come the uppity-duck over us," warned Gypsy, "unless you want trouble."

"I make nought and less than nought of your threats," said Fair Luna, borrowing an effective line from one of her roles.

It failed to impress Miss Vilas. "I seen Grandpa," she said, with less regard to truth than desire to stir trouble.

"I fail to take your meaning."

"Your old whistlebone. The prime old buck. 'Bitch me! Bitch my bones,' " she piped in outrageous mimicry.

"Do you refer to the Honorable Vryling Lovatt?" inquired Miss Wayne with fine hauteur, somewhat impaired by her appended phrase, "you dirty little slewer!"

Pleased at having drawn blood, Gypsy let the offense pass. "Watch the old punk," she advised. "He's got the boguing eye for a gal. I could finger him away from you like a yokel's fip."

"I'll report you to Mr. Passerow. I'll have you jounced out on your hunkers," raged the insulted Miss Wayne.

"Ah, go crawl through a maltworm's gut," said Gypsy cheerfully. "Come on, Durie. You'll get spluttered on if you stay here."

Later Tim Baggo told the girls that Gypsy's taunt about the benefits had gone home. For the Honorable Vryling, though he had not withdrawn his personal patronage, had cut off all professional emoluments.

"Some kind of turn-up with Old Passover," the buffo explained. "Something about money last year in Geneva." He glanced covertly at Durie.

Money? thought **Durie**. Hadn't Jans hinted at something of the sort in that wounding, bewildering interview, the day after that night in the loft? Well, it was beyond her.

"Where did you see old Fuss-and-Feathers?" Mr. Baggo asked Gypsy. He had overheard the passage-at-tongues.

"Haven't seen him at all."

"Oh! Just giving Fair Luna a scare? You may see him soon. By the way the wench is prinking up her clothes, she's looking forward to a reunion."

"I wish her joy of it," said Gypsy grimly.

The adventure, the changefulness, the excitement of the road took a new hold on Durie's spirit. Nightly she was warmed by the delight of the small-town folk, still of the frontier in their isolation and their artlessness. The eager wonder with which they turned from their harsh lives to the contrived glamors of the plays, the repeated thrill of dispensing enchantment was, reflexively, a spell laid upon her soul.

Better parts were coming her way now. So, as Gypsy Vilas mischievously pointed out, was the manager. Durie needed no confirmation on this point. She lived the parts, and worked hard on them; she disliked the attentions and the intentions that went with the parts, and worked equally hard to evade those. As Mr. Passerow graciously insisted upon rehearsing her himself, avoidance was increasingly difficult.

"I wisht I had your chance," Gypsy sighed.

"I only want to be let alone," said Durie.

"Then you better black your face and go in for cork parts," grinned her chum.

"Fair Luna has been hinting about being set up in a company of her own. Is it just her fancy?"

"Might be the old Senator."

"That's what I thought. Perhaps we could get in there."

"The pullet dodged the fox, and met the weasel," quoth Gypsy.

"Wouldn't you go?"

"If the hay is soft, why shift to straw?" Gypsy was feeling aphoristic. "Aren't we comfortable here?"

"I thought I was done with flax-knives."

"Old Pass playing the goat, huh?"

Durie nodded. "I'm going to apply to Senator Lovatt first chance."

Opportunity seemed to offer when the Thalians reached Ithaca. The smart gig drove in with the Lovatt henchman in attendance. But the formerly hospitable Senator was austere. He gave no festal suppers. He made no advances to members of the troupe. When he encountered Mr. Passerow, he passed the embarrassed manager with a stiff nod. He confined his attentions exclusively to Miss Wayne, chiefly after hours. That vigilant damsel was always in the way when Durie might have had a word with him. At the close of the engagement the pair took the road in the gig, Fair Luna very ladified in a new pink hat with agate danglers.

With prosperity, Miss Wayne's arrogance came to the top. It was said, afterward, though unconfirmed, that she made demands upon her elderly lover for a New York production, hoping to compromise on Albany. In any case, they drove into Cortlandville on frigid terms, and when the caravan arrived Senator Lovatt was in the inn parlor glumly soothing his spirit with a tumbler of switchel. There Durie found him. She entered, dropped him a curtsey, and stood serene, poised, and almost childishly lovely before him. He looked up, but did not rise.

"May I have a moment's conversation with you, Senator Lovatt?"

"You may not," he snapped.

"Have you a reason for refusing me so slight a consideration?"

"Oh, hell!" he broke out. "Sit down. Never could say no to a pretty female. Have a drink."

"No, I thank you. I trust you will not deem me forward."

The frown returned to his forehead. "If it's about my scapegrace nephew, I shall."

"I have no interest in your nephew, sir," she said primly.

"Squeezed the lemon dry, eh?" He suggested with jovial familiarity.

"I have no conception of your meaning."

"Innocence and dignity. A very pretty play. Sets well upon your style of comeliness. But hark you, my prettykin, there's no more blood to be squeezed out of that turnip. Do you take my meaning now?"

"Not a word of it." The candor and steadiness of her gaze disconcerted him.

"The money."

"Money?"

"One hundred and fifty dollars, notes current, duly receipted for. Will you deny your own hand-of-write?"

She gasped once. But her eyes did not waver.

"I know nothing of money or receipt."

He studied her face. "Bitch me, if I am not almost constrained to believe the girl," he growled. "Or are you a better actress off than on the stage? There is something to be explained here. You claim that you know nothing of any payment? Very well. I refer you to your manager. Ask Mr. Passerow."

"What shall I ask him?"

"Ask him about the moneys paid into his hands to satisfy your claim against my nephew, Jans Quintard."

"I advanced a claim against Ja—— your nephew?"

"Ask Passerow."

"On what grounds?"

"Loss of your virtue. But ask Passerow."

"My virtue made a subject of barter?"

"Ask Passerow."

"No wonder he despised me," she said, speaking like a mazed person. "Mr. Passerow asked a price? And you paid it?"

"Certainly, I paid it! Through the nose. Though, to do him justice, my haylofting young spark refunded it, every cent. I ask myself," he concluded brutally, "whether we did not pay for prime and get shelf-worn goods."

She said clearly, "I think you are a very vile old man."

"Hoity-toity! At least, I am no easy young gull. I know the sex."

"Every cent shall be paid back."

"Eh? What's this?" He rubbed his bald spot. What would the girl be at? The Old Corinthian spirit reared its head. "Call it the price of a young fool's experience and cross it off the books, my dear." He spoke the fine sentiment with benign assurance, and was wholly at a loss to understand the look of contempt with which she favored him as she bowed and left the room.

Gypsy met Durie in the hallway and grabbed her arm.

"Whose throat are *you* going to cut?"

"Where is Mr. Passerow?"

"Gone out like Old Scratch was after him. But I can tell you where he was."

"Where?"

"Ear-tapping the inside door, while you was palavering Old Ruffleshirt inside. What about the new company?"

"I don't know."

"You don't know? Didn't you ask him?"

"No. I forgot about it. I must find Mr. Passerow."

She left Gypsy staring and perturbed.

Finding Mr. Passerow was not easy. That astute gentleman was playing for time. He had his little preparations to make. With all her determination, Durie was unable to corner him before the next evening. By that time Senator Lovatt had departed in the high gig, leaving Fair Luna furious and alarmed.

Manager Passerow had not been in the theatrical business for a quarter of a century without developing adroitness and assurance. Both were at call when he faced La Jeune Amour, who justified only part of the title he had bestowed upon her. She looked young, indeed, but by no means loving.

"How can I serve you, Miss Amour?" He deemed it good strategy to conduct the matter on a formal basis.

"Did you take one hundred and fifty dollars from Jans Quintard?"

His eyebrows went up. "I don't know any such person."

"John Quinn, then," she amended.

"There was a financial accommodation," he answered easily.

"With me as basis?"

"You entered into it. I considered myself morally your guardian."

"Morally!"

"You had been grossly wronged. It was my place to see that reparation was made."

"Black mail," she said.

"Let us refrain from vituperous terms." The manager was lofty and pained.

"Where is the money?"

Ah! This was better. If she was interested in cash, he could handle her. He said, "It has been put aside for you," extending a sealed envelope with her stage name inscribed on it.

She took it. "After a year," she commented.

"I had a pressing use for it," he explained, "in furthering the common interests of the troupe. At the moment I was out of funds."

Durie opened the envelope and counted the notes.

"Fifty dollars. Where is the balance?"

"My commission," said Mr. Passerow blandly.

The sheer impudence of it left her speechless. The manager assumed a brisk, now-we-can-turn-to-business mien.

"Shall we take up the question of a new medium for your talents, my dear?"

"No," said Durie and walked out.

She would have liked to walk out of the troupe, as well. It could not be done. Her one burning desire was to discharge that shameful debt. At whatever cost to her feelings, she must stay with the Thalians until she had saved out of her salary the sum necessary to make up the balance due. It was characteristic of Durie's pride that this debt humiliated her far more than the loss of her reputation. For the shabby transaction put her in the light of having exacted a price for her good name. And from Jans Quintard, who might have been her lover and was not! The burden was intolerable.

It was then that she wrote to Senator Lovatt for Jans' address.

30

TRADE was not as brisk on the *Barter Boat's* return trip as the partner-owners had anticipated. There was an abnormal amount of summer-sickness along the canal route. People even died of it. In Oneida County it was attributed to pickled oysters. Along the Black Snake it was said that last winter's potatoes had bloated, causing disease in those who ate them. Tomatoes were blamed by those who still believed them poisonous. Injurious miasmas were reported from many localities. People became fearful. Business suffered.

Early one morning, Captain Pilkington came on deck at Weedsport to cool a brow fevered by consequence of having met some old waterways friends on the previous evening. He leaned overside and gave a startled yelp. A face was staring up at him from the water. It was dark and foreign and bushy with hair, and the wide eyes looked even deader than the surrounding flesh. Pilk cast a hasty glance around. Fifty yards away another body undulated gently among the rushes. A cent-a-miler redemptioner craft, moored in the neighboring basin had evidently been discharging cargo. Pilk called Jans.

"Think it's the cholery?" he asked. "I hear there's some about."

"I know there is."

"Why'n't you say so?"

"Didn't want to scare you."

"I ain't scairt—exactly. What a dummergung I was not to stock the gut-ease medicine again! D'you reckon folks'd buy that ginger pain-killer for it?" Pilk was ever the man of business.

"Not from me. I'm for getting back to Albany."

"And giving up the trade?" His partner's jaw dropped.

"We're doing no business. This thing might be serious. I've an idea they could use me in Albany." He was thinking of his collected medical reports.

Pilk brightened. "We could lay in medicine and almanachs. Almanachs sell good in a sick spell."

Dull though the store-trade was, the boat partly made up for it in passenger traffic. Every town produced its quota, most of them with traveling boxes and bulging bags. There seemed to be an uneasy feeling on the part of the well-to-do populace wherever they were, that somewhere else was more healthful. They were on the move.

Pilk raised deck fares to two cents per mile. At worst they were paying expenses.

Coming into Little Falls, Jans received a sealed note from the lock-keeper, addressed in Senator Lovatt's spidery writing. It requested in the formal terms of Uncle Vryling's displeasure that the nephew report at the mansion upon receipt. Jans found him in his library, looking worn.

"Can't you keep your females from invading your home?" he began petulantly.

"I have no females, sir."

"Very well, female, then. God knows, one is enough."

"She came here? What for?"

"To demand why I had not supplied her with your post-address. I told her the less communication between you, the better."

"I'm afraid that I agree, sir."

"So did she. Bitch my bones, Jans! The child has spirit."

"Anything else?"

"A letter. Fair, genteel writing, too, the cover. Told me she trusted to my honor to deliver it. Damn her!" A reluctant grin livened the florid face. "She's as sharp as she is spirited."

He fumbled in a pigeonhole of the desk and brought out an oblong, neatly waxed. Jans took it.

"You will excuse me, sir," he said, and withdrew to the balcony where he opened it. Three banknotes protruded. Putting them aside, he read:

Herewith fifty dollars in notes negotiable. I have but recently learned of Mr. Passerow's perfidy, which gives you the right to think as meanly of me as I of you. But I, at least, can and will purge myself of the shame. The balance shall be paid at my earliest capacity. When I encounter you, it is difficult for me to believe you treacherous, cruel, and avaricious. Then the figure of poor Looby, beating his head against the jail bars, rises to confute my weakness of heart. It is the dearest wish of my life that I may never set eyes upon you again.   E. A.

Jans rejoined his uncle, the letter and notes in his hand.

"Well?" from the Senator.

"She accuses me of being cruel and treacherous," Jans said dully.

Uncle Vryling, leaning upon the high mantel, tapped snuff from the pornographic box, ministered daintily to his nose, and brushed away the flecks of powder.

"You told me that you had not tampered with her virtue," he observed.

"And you doubted me. But that is not what she has in mind. . . . Uncle Vryling, I don't know what to do."

"Do? Do? Act according to the precepts of gentlemanly behavior, sir. What else is there for one of our blood to do? Noblesse oblige." He was austere and impressive.

"It isn't so clear," Jans returned moodily. "Let me state a hypothetical case, sir."

"Proceed, my boy."

"Suppose a young girl . . ."

"Girl? Maiden? Chaste?"

"Yes. But—well, sir, suppose her to believe herself to have yielded her virtue to a lover . . ."

"Wait a moment! 'Believe herself'? You wish me to understand that she was in a state of uncertainty after the fact?"

"There wasn't any fact," Jans said hastily.

"By what persuasion should she misinterpret a basic physical condition?" demanded the uncle.

"Hot rum upon champagne."

The Senatorial countenance twisted into a grimace of displeasure. "Am I to believe you—er—the young man in hypothesis—the sort of scoundrel to ply an unsuspecting girl with ardent spirits prefatory to seducing her?"

"No, sir. That part was accidental."

"We are to assume that the girl was a virgin before the event or lack of event?"

"So I firmly believe."

"And that, after whatever the devil did occur, she was actually ignorant of what did happen?"

"Yes, sir."

"Then she was no virgin. That, my boy, is the harsh logic of the situation."

"I know it must seem so. But in this instance it isn't."

"Bitch and damme!" cried Uncle Vryling in the exasperation of bewilderment. "What sort of Sphinx's riddle is this?"

"There is more to come. A matter of conscience."

"Conscience! I should think so, indeed," grumbled the uncle.

"Suppose further that the young lady, believing herself to have been despoiled, yields through recklessness or desperation to a real seducer."

"Leaving no doubt in her mind this time, I assume," said the sardonic Senator.

Jans winced. "I suppose not, sir."

"Then where is the difficulty of conscience?"

"Put yourself in the young man's place. Though innocent of actual seduction, how far could he exonerate himself from moral responsibility for the girl's subsequent downfall?"

"Pooh! Hairsplitting! Matter for long-haired metaphysicians." But he began to caress his bald spot, a sure sign of doubt. "It is perhaps not so simple as it seems," he conceded. "Let's have done with this harrying the hare around the bush. Who was the successful Lothario that cuckolded you *ante factum?*"

Jans said painfully, "Within a week Maçel Ayrault had her on his boat for the night."

The Honorable Vryling helped himself to more of Brown's Superior. "Yes, I can perceive your sense of responsibility which does you honor. You owe her consideration. But not marriage. Let's have no thought of marriage."

"She neither demands nor wishes it. In fact, she professes nothing but contempt for me."

"Bitch my soul!" Uncle Vryling vociferated. "Does this little play-doxy pretend to despise an honorable offer from a source so superior?"

"There was no direct offer made. Though I would gladly have

313

made her my wife until I believed her involved in the enterprise of black mail."

"So she was."

"No, sir. It was trickery on Passerow's part. She is refunding the money."

The Senator was shaken. "She told me that such was her intention. I didn't believe her. You can't accept it, Jans."

"I'm afraid I must."

"Take that poor child's savings?" Uncle Vryling cried with an abrupt change of front.

"Can't you see, sir, that she is buying back her own self-respect?"

"Perhaps you're right." He brightened. "We owe her restitution, no doubt of that. Suppose I establish her in her own play, give her a fair start, such as Fair Luna would give her eye teeth . . . Never mind that. Give her her start and then—*Spongia!* as the learned Erasmus hath it. Wipe it out and say no more about it."

"A very pretty plan, but it has a weak spot. She wouldn't accept it."

"Eh? What? Well, I daresay you're right. She seemed a very determined young person. Not without character. Of a sort," he added testily, "of a sort. It's a kittle business. Let it rest for the time. There's another matter for our consideration. I have had word from Dr. Townsend of Albany."

"On the chol—— the sickness?"

"You needn't boggle at the word with me. I'm not afraid of it."

"Of course not, sir. But it is becoming prevalent. Wouldn't it be wise for you to go away for a time?"

"Where would you have me go?"

"To the high country. The vapors do not rise far."

"What of my mills?"

"They can continue for a time without your supervision, surely."

"You'd have me run away?"

"Not run away. Take a vacation. Consider your years."

"Hell to my soul! What does the young fool mean, my years! I'm as hale as ever I was. D'you take me for a deserter? Let's have no more of this nonsense."

"Very well, sir. Since you feel that way."

"I do. Dr. Townsend wishes you to make all haste to report to him. From his message, I take it that he holds a grave view of the onset."

"With reason," said Jans.

All their passengers left the *Barter Boat* before Schenectady was reached. The region around Albany was suspect.

Albany they found a city divided against itself. Many citizens of importance denounced as "scareheads" the doctors who prated of the Plague and warned against contagion. Such wild talk! It needlessly alarmed the timid. It roused distrust. It was bad for business. The citizenry was leaving in large numbers. Theatres and stores were closing. Stages arrived empty and departed full. All this Pilk learned as he visited the warehouses to inquire into prices and supply while Jans called upon Dr. Townsend.

The gaunt old gentleman was angry.

"Goddamn fools!" he fumed. "Mustn't frighten folk by saying it's contagious. Mustn't disturb trade. Stink-barrels on street corners! Days of fasting and prayer! That Whig whoremaster, Henry Clay, calling for a national day of penance to stop the contagion. But does anybody watch over people's food to see that it's clean? Or ask what water they're drinking? Or pay any heed to the stinking sewage that floods the streets after a rain? Hell, no! Tell me what you found, young man."

Jans reported. The grizzled physician nodded.

"It's spreading. From the sick to the well."

"It is contagious, then?"

"Is fire in dry flax contagious? Of course it's contagious! Don't let any fool, be he doctor or preacher, persuade you otherwise. Are you open to a charter? The commission will pay."

"Yes, sir. Where to?"

"Back westward. I'll give you a list. There's a meeting at the Medical College. Like to accompany me?"

Jans assented. As they entered, a professor was engaged upon a clinical exposition of the disease. There were two familiar forms, he said: the frigid or creeping, and the spasmodic. He gave some highly realistic details of each. The disease was curable if caught early before the chill set in. After that there was little hope, though

315

bleeding was always useful, and packing in warm salt was recommended.

"Coma supervenes," he stated with scientific exactitude, "from exhaustion of the grand constituents of the blood, soda, and farina. The heart feebly essays a last onward impulse; the muscles, like dying worms, wreathe upon themselves and the patient suffers an afflictive and melancholy death."

"How would you like that, my young friend?" said Dr. Townsend's rasping voice in Jans' ear.

Jans shuddered.

"Then put nothing in your mouth that unclean hands have touched. Be sparing of the bottle but mingle a little whiskey in your water. Keep upwind of any case you may encounter. Prayer won't cure you, but your evenings are better spent in a church than a tap. No charge for the advice. See you take it."

The invoice was a heavy one. Special handlers were at the warehouses, sent by the commission to expedite loading. The implication was that haste was required to meet an emergency. With an official representative, Jans checked the items.

There was barrel upon barrel of chloride of lime. There were hogsheads of salt; there was lye in stout kegs; a large consignment of brandies and Jamaica ginger was stowed under lock below. Four nitrous oxide manufacturing machines were marked "Handle with Precaution." Knowing the gas only as a medium of entertaining, Jans expressed his curiosity, and learned that it was effective against noxious vapors. A considerable order of sick-room dainties, jellies, spices and wines came in late. Over all, floated the pervasive odor of camphor.

Coming up from below, all a-sweat from the hard labor of stowage, Pilk sniffed the air.

"Whew! How much camphor we carrying?"

Jans showed him the list.

"Glory! We musta gutted the market." He fell thoughtful. "What's the state of the till?"

"Oh, forty dollars. Maybe fifty."

"I'm notional we can use that to a profit. What'd the shippers pay per pound?"

316

"They didn't give prices. All this is for free distribution. About thirty cents, I'd assume."

Pilk went overside and was presently seen entering a warehouse door. When he vaulted aboard again, the light of commercial excitement was in his shrewd, blue eyes.

"D'you know what they ask for camphor now?"

"No," said Jans. "How much?"

"Six shillings."

"Too high."

"Too high, hell! Gimme the key, lad."

"You're going to buy at that price?"

"Yes, and give our note for what's over. There ain't a week's supply in all Dutch Albany. We can double our money along the route."

The deal was quickly consummated. In twenty minutes Pilk was back, exhibiting a handsomely discolored eye and a triumphant smile.

"Met another bidder," he explained. "He was going to eighty cents but he never got there. There's seventy-five dollars' worth coming aboard. Thirty on credit. Sign here, Jans."

They cast off. A committee, advised by post, met them at Schenectady. With magical speed the deck load was transferred to the dock, the freightage charge paid, and the boat ready to proceed. But Captain Pilkington was not to be found. As speed had been made a condition of the charter, Jans prepared to go on without him when he appeared after sunset, directing the operations of a handbarrow trundled by a young blackamoor, and looking disgusted.

"Where the devil have you been?" Jans demanded.

"Little private traffic," mumbled Pilk.

"This isn't a private cruise."

"No reason for not turning an honest penny."

"Where's the penny?" Jans looked significantly at the burdened cart.

"Damn this town! I've freighted the damn camphor all over the place, and nobody buys."

"Small wonder! We've just delivered a full consignment for

free distribution. You can't sell goods that are being given away on the next corner. Did you ever stop to think of that, Mr. Slick Commercant?"

"I'll sell the poxy stuff yet," growled Pilk. "Cast off!"

Rotterdam needed no camphor. Tar was its desire, tar in barrels to counteract the miasmas. For Rotterdam, by resolution of its Board of Trustees, had formally declared cholera to be born of atmospheric impurities, and black smoke hung over the village like a pall. The supply of clarifying combustible was almost gone. Why, demanded the village fathers angrily, had the *Barter Boat* not brought them tar? Because, Jans explained, Dr. Townsend of the Committee did not hold with tar. Chloride of lime was recommended.

Pilk urgently nudged his partner. "Shut your silly clam. Lemme talk to 'em."

He stood upon the coaming and addressed the locals in a passion of salesmanship offering his camphor at the low price of ten shillings a pound, and they'd better take it before another town bid higher. It was an effort, Jans admitted to himself, worthy of Uncle Vryling Lovatt. But it was wasted.

Rotterdam, through its elected representatives, replied coldly that it wanted tar. If the *Barter Boat* had no tar it had better move on and give wharf room to somebody else.

To Jans' sardonic congratulations upon his partner's business acumen, Pilk retorted that he could go to hell. The atmosphere on the boat became murky.

Their experience at Amsterdam, the next stop, did nothing to improve relations between the partners. This was their last port of call. After unloading, they were to return, light, to Albany for another charter. To Jans' surprise, there was no preparation at the basin for unloading when they pulled in quite early in the morning. With the help of their hoggee, a runagate apprentice named Bowk, he tied up. Pilk staggered on deck. He had been sampling the medical supplies the night before, and now looked upon the world with a cankered eye. A church bell pealed and was joined by a second and a third.

"Good Lord, it's Sunday!" Jans ejaculated.

"Anybody but a fool'd know that," growled Pilk.

Jans did not like being called a fool and so informed his partner. Pilk snorted. Throwing off his coat, he rigged a plank and rolled a barrel to the wharf.

"You can't do that," protested Jans.

"Why can't I?" He sent a second barrel expertly spinning to its place.

He discovered why, through the agency of the local pathmaster who emerged from an adjacent warehouse.

"Five dollars fine for discharging cargo on the Sabbath," that functionary pointed out.

"Go stick your head in a swill-piggin," Pilk retorted.

The official left and returned with a constable. Pilk was haled to the lock-up.

A night in durance did nothing to improve his temper. It did, however, rally the town authorities to his support. Captain Bassford Pilkington was nothing to them, but the supplies on the *Barter Boat* were sorely needed, and the Captain's aid in discharging cargo was essential. This alone got him off with a light penalty: $5.00 for violation of the canal rules, plus $10.00 for assaulting the pathmaster.

Jans settled from the money-box, but with very ill grace. They unloaded, pocketed the fee, and set back for Albany, light and high, and making their four and a half miles an hour. There was little talk between the two, and that little no more than perfunctory exchanges on the conduct of the trip. Jans gloomed. Pilk sulked. Drawing into Schenectady, Pilk shouted to the hoggee to pull up.

"What's that for?" demanded Jans.

"Business."

"Our business is to get back to Albany and pick up another load."

"Who's captain of this craft?"

"You are, when you're aboard. But I'll remind you that I'm a full partner."

"Don't you play the boccarorra with me, my lad," warned Pilk, openly truculent now.

"You're going ashore to peddle your damned camphor," Jans charged.

"What if I am?"

"Just this! You've wasted seventy-five dollars of our funds in your silly speculation. You've mulcted us fifteen dollars more by your foolishness at Amsterdam. How much more of this do you think I'm going to stand?"

"You know what you can do, if you don't like it. Shove off."

Jans lips tightened; a livid line appeared above them. It was what Uncle Vryling used to call "that damned black Quintard look."

"I'll shove off when I get the money owing me, not before."

Pilk pursed his mouth. "Prr-rr-rr-oop!" he went in a raucous and insulting gardaloo.

He leaped to the wharf, Bowk, the hoggee, following with a dollar of his wages in his pocket. Disdaining to address his partner, Jans called to the lad.

"You've got just an hour."

The Captain was back in less than that. No words were needed to tell Jans that his errand had been futile; his sour face was enough. Several minutes later young Bowk appeared in a new shilling hat. He was pale, sweaty and breathing heavily. Instead of fetching out his tandem, he sat upon an up-ended keg and groaned.

"What's the matter of you?" snarled Pilk.

"Cholery," said Bowk. "I'm dyin'." He was volcanically sick.

Pilk examined the evidence with a cold and cynical eye. "Potted cherries, smoked beef chips, ice cream," he recounted. "What else?"

"Honeyparch.* Just one drink," wept the lad.

Pilk cuffed him. "Get aboard."

"I ain't goin' no furder. Gimme my arnin's."

When Pilk tried to force him, he groveled, threw both arms around the keg and yelled like a maniac. By the rough, towpath custom he forfeited all accrued wages. But Jans counted out four dollars, while Pilk looked on with a wooden face. He turned to the waterfront crowd which had been attracted by Bowk's lamentations.

"Who'll ship? Good grub. Monthly pay. Fair treatment. Who'll ship?"

*Probably meth▓▓▓▓▓▓▓▓▓▓▓

Nobody came forward. A whisper ran. "Cholery boat." The crowd edged away. By that evil word the partners knew that they could hire no help along the waterfront.

Pilk said grimly, not looking at Jans, "Turn and turn about. Take the tiller."

This was all very well for the all-day journey to Albany. But if the *Barter Boat* took another load and could find no help, it would be hard with the two who must share the total labor between them. Jans would have split up the partnership at Albany but for old Dr. Townsend's urgency.

"There's big money in it," he said to Pilk, and to Jans. "You can't quit now. Medicines are giving out and people are dying like flies."

"Is it as bad as that?"

"They're making cholera refuges of the almshouses in some towns. Warehouses, too. There's where the supplies are most needed. I've got 'em under tarpaulins, ready for you." He paused, glancing from one frowning face to the other. "You ain't afraid, are you?" he asked Captain Pilkington sharply.

"Certes, I'm afraid. What d'you take me for, a goddamn fool?"

The old physician studied him. "But you'll go?"

"Get me a hoggee and I'll go."

Jans merely nodded his agreement.

They had to leave without the needed towpath driver. Not for any inducement would a single person on all the waterfront sign up for service on board. Those who at first seemed tempted by the offer of a double wage, would approach, glance at the prow, and sheer hastily off. It was Pilk who discovered the reason. Someone had indelibly branded a small letter c beneath the coaming. The Captain accosted his partner sourly.

"That bitches it. Now's your time to quit."

"What makes you think I want to quit?"

"Oh, you'll quit, all right! Know what this means?" He pointed to the burned-in letter.

"Of course. Cholera-boat."

"That ain't the half of it. It means you and me to work the boat alone. You on the path and me at the helm; and then me on the path and you at the helm. Eat? You'll eat with one h and drive with the other. Sleep? You'll sleep with the tiller lashed and wake with some fancy packet captain damning your gut for not giving him three-quarters of the waterway. You'll bless every lock you come to because you can stretch your five minutes on the deck. How long will you last at that, my dandy college-bred softy?"

"As long as you will."

Pilk spat a stream overside. "I hear you say it."

There were times in the next few days when Jans could not remember the day of the week, the pocket in which he kept his pipe, or the destination of the voyage. Towns loomed. Pilk feebly cursed his tandem to a stop. Clamorous citizens swarmed aboard with requisitions for items which his dazed brain refused to check. Whenever he saw Pilk near at hand, Pilk seemed to be drunk. But that might have been his own confusion of sight and mind. Or it might have been simple exhaustion on Pilk's part. At least the horses retained their respect for him, whereas when Jans stumbled and fell, they did not even look around, but dragged him until he shouted "Whoa!" It had not occurred to him before, but maybe they too needed their sleep.

There was the evening when, after a drink, he was moved to song. Pilk cursed him and he cursed back. He decided to fight Pilk as soon as he got rested; if he killed him, he wouldn't care. Pilk was a sharp-shooter, a bounetter, a bilk. Pilk and his sixty-cent camphor! He'd take it out of the filthy bastard's hide. . . . Fifty hours to Utica and sleep—Fifty hours.—Fifty—fiff-fiff-fiff— Oh, God!

Little Falls, Herkimer, Frankfort, finally Utica. Utica and tolling bells. Black smudge against brazen skies. Men praying in the streets. Calls for grave-diggers, two dollars per corpse. Calls for nurses, for doctors' aides; calls for bedside watchers; calls for volunteers to distribute medicine.

Citizens in castor hats and broadcloth mingled on the wharf with rough mechanics, waiting to unload the boat. There was no time to check invoices, even had Jans not been too dazed to hold the dancing numerals in focus. Everything was cleared except their own camphor. An offer was made for that: seventy-five cents a pound. Jans couldn't believe his ears. Pilk set his jaw and rejected the offer. Crazy! But Jans was too bone-weary to quarrel further.

A gray-faced, dignified, anxious-looking doctor came aboard with messages for Albany. The epidemy was all through the Black Snake. Syracuse was in dire straits. There was a shortage of all medical necessities. Traffic had been stopped to the west of the city, released, stopped again. How quickly could the *Barter Boat* get back to Albany, reload, and deliver at wharf-end in Syracuse?

"Six days," said Jans, wondering whether his arithmetic was right.

"Shall I send word by courier that you can be counted upon?"

"Get me a hoggee."

Dr. Clarke shook his head. "You've had a case aboard, haven't you?"

"No. It's a damn lie."

"You're marked for it."

Jans cursed again. They would get no help from path or berm. Indeed, the canal side was strangely depopulated. Rumor said that the Plague spread by canal. The human tide, diverted from its proper channel, had taken to the pikes.

Water traffic, too, had thinned out, which was fortunate for the *Barter Boat*. Manned by two insomniacs and headed back to the terminus, it yawed wildly from bank to bank, scraping lordly packets, overrunning lowly rafts, failing to drop the rope and so tangling with adverse traffic, howled at, cursed, and threatened by thunderous captains and piping hoggees alike, and eventually, making Albany.

Five days, by Jans' reckoning, had passed since their previous docking. From the looks of Dr. Townsend when he came to the basin, it might have been ten years. The virile old physician looked and moved like ⁓ galvanized corpse. Jans regarded him, aghast.

"Have you . . . ?"

"No. Two of my best colleagues have gone. I've had to take over their work. That's all."

"What are our orders?"

"Syracuse."

"When will she be loaded?"

"By sunset."

"I'm dead for sleep."

The old man pointed to a warehouse fronting them. Jans reeled over to it, found a pile of coarse crocus bags in a corner, and dropped into the nest. Before sleep engulfed him, he was conscious of his partner staggering toward the hill that led uptown. Going to fuddle himself with liquor, probably. Let him! How he kept going was more than Jans could fathom. As soon as this emergency was over, he'd be well rid of Pilk and all his ways.

It did not seem an hour when a bellow wakened him. There stood Pilk, legs straddled, an evil grin on his silly face.

"Wake up, you punk."

"Go away." Jans was too spent and listless to be angry any more. He was conscious of no emotion more active than a dull distaste for his partner.

"I have been doing business while you snoozed."

"I don't care."

"D'you know what camphor is selling at?"

"I don't give a damn."

"Three-fifty a pound." It was a triumphal croak.

"I don't care! I don't care! I don't care!"

"Mebbe you don't care whether we sell or hold."

"No."

"Well, we're holding, whatever you say. So save your breath."

"Go away!"

"I'd admire to kick your teeth in."

But Jans was asleep again. His next summons back to the world was not to be disregarded. Dr. Townsend and a neat little man were standing over him. The little man held out a letter.

"From the Governor of the Sovereign State of New York."

"For me?" asked Jans stupidly.

"To whom it may concern."

"It's your warrant to go through obstructions," Dr. Townsend explained.

"What obstructions?" mumbled Jans. Had the canal breached its bank again? And, if so, how would a gubernatorial message help a grounded craft off bottom?

"Committees, health boards, pathmasters, lock-keepers, anybody who tries to block the traffic."

Jans' sleep-muddled brain struggled with a memory. Something that had been told him on the last trip. The doctor at Utica!

"Are they holding up the boats?"

"We don't know. There hasn't been a packet in today. There is trouble about the redemptioner boats."

"There ought to be." Jans thought of the two bodies at Weedsport.

"That's neither here nor there," continued the doctor's positive voice. "This cargo has to go through to Syracuse at any cost. Do you understand that?"

"Yes."

"Even if you have to fight your way."

Jans nodded. He was not precisely in fighting form. Now, if he could get about ten hours more sleep . . .

"Will your partner stand by you?"

"Yes." Whatever Pilk's demerits or shortcomings, he would never shirk a fight in a good cause. Or, for that matter, a bad one.

"Stop nowhere. According to my advices from the west, they're dying like flies on a treadle spread. Every hour counts. I've got you a fresh horse."

"No driver?"

"No. You'll have to sweat it through between you. I'll expect you back this day week. *Au revoir.*"

Albany to Schenectady took nearly all day. Several of the lock-keepers had deserted their posts, and the partners had to work the gates, themselves. It was off Scotio that Jans got the shock of his life.

By the spell-and-spell arangement, it was Pilk's turn on the path while Jans snoozed at the tiller. An impassioned inquiry dead ahead as to where the flaming hell he thought he was going roused him to action barely in time to sheer off from a dingy Durham. He answered in the Erie tradition with a curse or two and was about to doze off again when a sound from between decks brought him up, all standing. It was a snore; not an ordinary snore, but such a raucous rasp of inhalation as could be achieved only through the goiterous passage of the Pilkington neck.

Yet there, fifty yards ahead, was Pilk, driving the tandem. Pilk or Pilk's poltergeist. Jans had heard of canal-haunts but had never seen one. He leaned over the side, scooped some water, dashed it in his face, and took another look. No, that lunking figure was never the compact Pilk. Yet it was familiar.

A thin wafer of song drifted back on the breeze:

> *"Oolie-oolie-aylie-oo.*
> *Oolie-aylie-oo."*

Jans gave a great shout. "Looby!"

31

STRAIGHT, heavy and black the column of smoke rose into the July air, a portent of evil. Cazenovia, Pompey and now Lafayette. Manager Passerow cursed his luck. Where the reek of burned tar rose, it was not worthwhile to draw the curtains; they would play at a loss. What damnable mischance! Just when the little troupe was enjoying a run of modest prosperity this epidemy must descend. It was time to furl the flag.

He called the company together. They were one short. Old Archbold had sickened at Lennox and died on the road, thirty hours later, of an "ague." The others knew what that blue chill was. They set their chins and said nothing of the fear in their hearts. Only Fair Luna collapsed in hysterics at rehearsal, and could not play that evening. One day's receipts forfeited. It could not go on. The manager told them so.

"Passage money?" suggested Tim Baggo.

Mr. Passerow's arms spread wide, his fingers splayed in an eloquent gesture.

"How much in the money-wagon?" demanded young Locke.

"Nothing. A few shillings."

Mrs. Gorham began to cry affrightedly. Tim Baggo jogged Rapalje with his arm. "Come on. We'll take a look."

"Look as far as you like," granted the manager. "Here's the key."

The split amounted to less than a shilling apiece. Equipment and stock belonged to Passerow. Nothing to be hoped from that source.

The manager drew Durie aside. "I'm going to New York."

"How?"

"In the small wagon. There's room for two," he added insinuatingly.

Durie refused to understand him. "Is there room for three? I can't leave Gypsy Vilas."

"Now, Amour! Sweetheart!" protested the manager in a languishing whisper. "I can make a future for you on the New York stage, with my weighty connections. Don't be a little bluenose. What can you do without me?"

"Take to the road."

"You're still hankering for that wastrel paramour of yours, I warrant," snarled the manager, balked and furious. "Don't think to catch him twice. He's a cut above the likes of you, my girl."

"You remind me that you owe me fifty dollars still," she returned coolly.

"Whistle for it, doxy." He added a surpassing vulgarity and stamped away.

"What you been doing to old Passover?" asked Gypsy, coming up.

"Trying to get you a gratis passage to New York."

"Nothing's gratis to that billygoat. What's in the pocket, Durie?"

"Three shillings. A little more." While the weekly envelope came in, she had made her faithful payments against the debt of honor. The drain had left her without much reserve.

"I got twice that. Let's strike for the Big Ditch."

"They say the cholera runs with Erie Water."

"Either you get it or you don't," said the fatalistic Miss Vilas. "The plucked bird flies light. Let's make our packs."

They bade good-bye to a glum company. Durie observed with interest the leavetaking between Gypsy and the buffo, cheerful and comradely.

"Good luck, gal."

"Meet you up Salt River, old boggle-de-botch."

Durie marveled. How could two who had once been lovers dismiss so airily the memory of past intimacies and kindnesses? Was love between man and woman, indeed, so light a thing? Why could not she, who had never known its culmination, rid herself as easily of its claims? Personius Andrews, she was sure, would have approved Gypsy's philosophy above hers.

The two girls struck northward in the glow of a spring morning. Durie's tackle provided them with lunch from a wayside creek, though Gypsy grumbled at the trout as being less flavorsome than her favorite stickle-back. At Fayetteville, Gypsy made for the tavern. Her more frugal companion hung back.

"Two pence for ale? We can't afford it," she protested.

"You know the woods but I know the towns," retorted Gypsy. "We'll share the pot and read the walls. You never can tell what you'll find."

"What do we want to find?"

"Jobs, ninny. D'you wanta sing on street corners again?"

Durie returned a vehement negative.

While Gypsy was explaining to the barkeeper that an *honest* tapman did not spade the froth until the ale seethed over the brim, Durie consulted the literature which covered the four walls. An immense crop of cholera cures, plague panaceas and painkillers had blossomed forth. Itinerant quacksalvers offered their services on a no-cure, no-pay basis. Interspersed with these hopeful presentments were grimmer reminders of the pestilence: bargain coffins, plain or lined; grave sheets; quicklime for safe and healthy interments; mourners' blacks, cheap and handsome, for sale or daily rental. And, in handwriting that testified to haste and urgency:

HOSPITAL HELP WANTED
Nurses, Experienced Male, 16 Shil. Female, 12 Shil.
Night Watchers, $1.00; Helpers, Messangers, Cleaners; Affluent Pay.
Apply B'd of Health Com^{tee}, Syracuse Hotel.

Bearing the ale to her partner, Gypsy listened to the reading, with her sagacious little head cocked sparrow-wise.

"Only fools say education don't pay," she observed. "Twelve shilling a day. Gor!"

"For experienced nurses," Durie pointed out.

"We'll get the experience with the job."

"And maybe the Plague."

"Better die in a bed than a ditch," said cheerful Gypsy.

"It's liberal pay," conceded Durie, figuring that she could save enough in a month to clear the arrears of her debt and face Jans Quintard with a scorn that he could not return. (Not that she ever wanted to see him again!) "We can try it anyway."

The rich, soggy odor of tar met their nostrils a mile out of town.

When they entered the limits, it was complicated by the effluvium from vats on the street corners, working and bubbling with chloride of lime. It was a lucky nostril that got a breath of untainted air within the precincts of Syracuse.

At the hotel a weary man in octagonal spectacles received them.

"You're very young," he objected, upon learning of their mission.

"Twenty-one last month," returned Gypsy.

"Any experience?"

"Two years of midwifery," she lied glibly.

"We're taking what we can get," he sighed. "Have you seen the Institute?"

"No, sir," Durie answered.

"It's been converted into a cholera refuge. You'd better look at it. It might lead you to reconsider."

He gave them directions, supplemented with cotton plugs for the nose and ears, two vials apiece, one containing hartshorn, the other vinegar, and cards of admission.

They had no difficulty in finding the building, a long, narrow frame edifice on a small rise above Fayette Street. "Thompson's Herbalist Institute," an ornate sign above the entrance proclaimed.

Durie opened the front door. A gush of sultry air, fetid with the odor of corruption before death, met them. Gypsy turned green.

"I'm going to puke," she gasped.

"Sniff your hartshorn," said Durie, reaching for her own.

A dull clamor from above met their ears, dominated by a high, thin monotone of anguish.

"Let's get the hell out of here," Gypsy gurgled.

A door opened opposite the entrance. A young man with a grim, gray face stared at them.

"Dr. Thompson?" Durie inquired.

"Ran away. Like the prudent man he is."

"Are you in charge, sir?"

"Yes. Dr. Colvin."

"We're nurses."

"You!" He stared.

"Don't you need us? . . ."

"Need you! We'll take anything. But you couldn't stand it a day. Want to look?"

330

He led them upstairs and threw open a double door. A fetor more powerful than that below overwhelmed them like a wave of filth. The high wail pierced their ears, with an undertone of groans and retchings.

"How do you like it?" said the grim young man.

The lecture room, seventy by twenty-four feet, had been cleared and a double row of deal boxes, filled with straw for bedding, set out. The boxes were four feet wide. All but half a dozen accommodated two persons each. Men and women were distributed indiscriminately. What little bedding there was, consisting at best of a coarse coverlet or blanket over the straw, was indescribably defiled. The floor was a sludge.

Durie swallowed hard. "Can't the windows be opened?" she asked.

"Against regulations."

"Better go to jail than die of stink," said the practical Gypsy and thrust her stout boot through a pane of glass.

Dr. Colvin burst into nervous laughter which he seemed unable to control. Durie considered the lines etched deep from brow to chin. "How long since you have slept?" she asked gently.

He made a vague gesture. "Two days. Three days. I've lost count."

"Have they left you here all alone?"

"My assistant died last week."

"Cholera?"

He shook his head. "Fright."

"Where are the nurses?"

"At their supper. They're always eating or drinking." He lifted a hand for attention. A sound of shrill singing was audible for the moment above the sickroom lamentations. "Swine!" he said venomously.

Durie surveyed the sickroom. "Tell me what to do."

"There isn't much. Opium when the pains come on. Iodine for the collapsed cases. They mostly die anyway." He set out the drugs. "Keep the nitrous-oxide machine going to allay the miasmas. You're really going to stay?"

"Yes."

He fetched a deep sigh. "You've got vinegar. Keep your hands

331

and arms moistened. Call me in three hours. No, in two," he amended lamentably.

"Yes, sir," said Durie, inwardly resolving to make it four.

The two girls drew water with the well sweep in the side yard, and sluiced out the room. It was the most nauseous task ever undertaken by either of them. Birthing, Gypsy informed her partner, was coffee-and-comfits-in-the-parlor beside this. They looked for clean bedding; there was none. Some of the convalescents were whimpering with hunger. No food was discoverable except coarse rye bread and pickled fish from a keg that had stood too long in the torpid heat. The sick were tormented with thirst, but orders were to give the tepid water sparingly lest it bring on retching. There was brandy for the "chilled" cases, but it lacked the normal effect. Gypsy tasted and reported; it had been liberally watered.

An emaciated woman beckoned feebly to Durie.

"I'm cold," she whispered.

"I'll try to find a blanket," said the amateur nurse doubtfully.

The woman's hands and feet were marble-bluish. Her fingers were shriveled; her tongue was coated as if it had been dusted with chalk. But the face was peaceful. Evidently she was suffering no pain.

"Hot water," she murmured, feebly shivering. "I'm cold."

A great, roly-poly of a woman, with a red jovial face and an apron tied above her exuberant busts, ambled across the room and bent over the patient who had sunk back.

"Wha'd she say to you?" she asked Durie.

"She said she was cold."

"That's a good one, that is!" bellowed the heavyweight, slapping a thigh that jellied under the impact. "Cold, huh! Haw!"

"What's so funny about it?" Durie eyed her with distaste.

"Cold, huh? Haw! She's got a warrant to be cold. Cancha see she's dead?"

Durie closed her eyes and opened them slowly. "What shall I do now?"

"Come and have a drink. There's two other stout wenches and a bottle of port wine in the hall room."

Durie realized by what agency the brandy had been watered.

"Is that all the nurses there are?"

"Yup. Unless you and the little slewer over there stay. But you won't."

"Why not?"

"Because you're a couple of lily-livers. I can tell it by the looks of you. I saw your snoot go up when I ast you, civil-like to share a bottle."

"It's medical supply, isn't it?"

"What if it is? D'you think you can keep up in this stink on water? Try it!"

"We're new here," Durie explained pacifically. "We don't know our way around yet."

"You'll learn," returned the other, mollified. "If you don't die first. A couple of 'em has. They were spindly chits." She yawned. "I'll go back and get my bit o' sleep. You and your chum can take over. Nothin' like work to learn you what to do."

Neither of the girls feared work. But here their labors appeared futile. They could not keep the big, bare room clean, though a full two hours a day were spent toilfully bearing water buckets up the steep stair. They could not attend to all the forty patients. For every one that died—and they died fast—another was carried or carted in, adjudged in the category of "collapsed," "frigid," or "spasmodic" by the exhausted young doctor, and dumped into a box, to recover or not, according to his luck. The cries of the sufferers when their anguish set upon them, tore the nerves.

Gypsy wanted to quit. So did Durie. But some reserve of pride and ruggedness in her spirit held her to the sickening routine. That and her growing admiration for Dr. Colvin. After the third day, he called the two tyros into his makeshift office where he kept records, compounded drugs and snatched at odd hours of sleep.

"Any complaints?" he asked hollowly.

"No," from Durie.

"What's the use!" from Gypsy.

"Are you getting enough food and rest?"

"No," from both.

He shrugged. "I suppose not. The other nurses . . ."

"Bitches," said Gypsy.

"Don't let them put upon you. Let them do their share of the work."

"It'll never get done if we wait for them to do it."

"I have to take what the committee sends me. You two are a godsend. I don't know what you do it for. I don't know what I'd do without you. And I don't know that the three of us together are doing any good. But we have to try, don't we?"

Durie answered with a reassuring smile.

Gypsy said mournfully, "If I could stop being sick to my stomach, I wouldn't give a damn."

One of the three regulars appeared at the door. A faint reek of brandy hung about her.

"Hey, Doc!" she said.

"Get back to your work."

"And leave you canoodlin with your two little punkies?" jeered the woman.

Gypsy bristled up to her. "Who're you calling a little punkie, you corpse-robber?"

Dr. Colvin thrust between them. "What brings you here, Loakes?"

"There's an old cockaloo askin' for you in the big room."

"Stricken?"

"No, loony in the head, I guess. He's preachin' to the beds."

All went to the ward. A gaunt, bearded, elderly man stood within the door, one arm upflung in a gesture of threat and warning. A deep voice boomed out his message: The Almighty had visited this scourge upon the city for its impiety in fostering a line of Sabbath-violating stagecoaches, and permitting Godless theatre-shows to flourish. Let the inhabitants repent their sin in sackcloth and ashes. Dr. Colvin touched his arm. The exhorter turned.

"I am Elder Symes from Pompey, sir, humbly striving to do the work of the Master."

"Would the Master have talked or helped?" asked the young physician mildly.

"I have spoken my word as in conscience bounden. Command me."

Dr. Colvin scrutinized the man who towered above him. His was an ascetic face; the lips joined in a harsh level; the cheeks parchment-shriveled upon the craggy bones; but the eyes were lambent with zeal and compassion. The doctor's expression brightened.

"A volunteer? What can you do?"

"Whatever I am bidden."

"Tell um to lug out that cad," said Nurse Loakes contemptuously, pointing to a pallet where stretched a corpse which, ten minutes earlier, had been a girl.

Without a word, the lank Elder reverently gathered up the body and bore it to the dead-room.

"He'll do," Dr. Colvin said. "You girls can work with him. Never mind the others."

The applied partnership, they promptly ascertained, was a regimen in which the Elder took the heaviest burdens upon himself. There was nothing too onerous or dangerous for his zeal. After an all-night watch, he would supply an outside shortage by volunteering as a grave-digger. He had an unerring instinct for knowing where his comfort was needed; more than one patient died peacefully in his arms. Once when he surprised Gypsy throwing up into a slop-pail, he tucked her beneath a sinewy arm, carried her out into the open, and peremptorily bade her go take a swim in the creek and not come back until evening was cool. He then took over her mop and finished her floor job. At lamp-lighting hour he would station himself in the doorway and sing stern Presbyterian hymns, mainly damnational, in a singularly rich and moving basso.

Durie's respect was soon tempered with affection. The fact that, over their scanty meals, the Elder, who had learned of his helpers' professional connections, conscientiously labored to wean them from a career of levity and sin, did not alienate their regard. Gypsy joked at and adored him.

Inevitably the staff split into two factions. The older nurses took and held jealous possession of the ante-room where there was a cooking oven. They shirked every possible job, invariably left the ward in filthy condition for the relief to clear up, and openly flaunted Elder Symes. Lacking eminent authority, which was centered in the Health Committee, young Colvin exercised what diplomacy he could command. The "shrews from hell" were amenable to only one threat: that of mulcting their pay.

Though the hospital was habitually short on food and stimulants, there was always a smell of cookery from the den and generally a whiff of liquor on the breaths of the trio. No adequate watch could be maintained over the supplies as they came in. Gypsy more than once expressed the conviction that pilfering was going on, and took no pains to moderate her voice. Relations between the two factions worsened daily. The shrews took special delight in baiting the Reverend, as they called him, with gutter-words and snatches of ribald song.

As he was giving directions to Gypsy one rainy morning, the door of the den opened slowly and a liquorish voice chanted:

> *"Answer, answer, my girl Nelly,*
> *Who got you that bloated belly?*
> *Listen, father, if I tell 'ee . . ."*

The Elder angrily slammed the door and strode away. It was opened again to a cackle of shrill laughter. An odor of rich cooking floated out. It offended the nostrils of Miss Vilas who had break-fasted meagerly on porridge and parched-rye coffee. She stood in the entrance, viewing a scene of luxury. The gaunt Loakes was seated in an arm chair with the youngest nurse, a fat and rosy creature known as Medory, cradled on her knees. The third member was dishing up a savory stew.

"Take the ward, one of you," Gypsy said.

"Take it yourself," retorted Mrs. Gaines, stirring her dish. "I been on since midnight."

"Well, keep on."

"It's your trick," insisted Gypsy.

The plump Medory twisted her head languidly and smiled, exhibiting snuff-browned teeth. "Go away, Mith Nathty," she lisped.

The provocation was too much for patience. A tempting curve of rump lopped over the lap which supported Medory. Gypsy's kick landed full and fair.

"You damn lallygaggers!" she shouted.

Medory squalled. Loakes grabbed for the assailant's hair. Gaines joined in. The breakfast stand was overturned. A bottle popped out from someone's clothing to add the reek of gin. Gypsy went down, fighting like a fury.

"Help! Murder! Durie!" she yelled.

Durie came flying down the ward, with her implement at the

ready. A shaker broom is no quarterstaff, but in competent hands its hickory handle can be an effective weapon. Durie poked tentatively at the whirl of clawing, kicking bodies, located a jaw and jabbed it so powerfully that its owner stiffened. A swinging thwack on the head temporarily discouraged Loakes. Gypsy, her blood streaming from a dozen nail furrows, was hanging with bulldog tenacity to the gagging throat of Mrs. Gaines. Murder would have been done had not her chum pried her loose.

Recovered from her momentary dizziness, the sinewy Loakes scrabbled for a knife that had fallen to the floor. Durie kicked it away from her grasp, and the battle was on again, with weight and numbers on the side of the old guard pitted against the youth and agility of the invading force. The five bodies were a writhing tangle when a new element was introduced. Durie's first thought was that a bear had gripped her. She was rolled into a corner like a keg. Medory spun against a wall and collapsed. Only the interposition of the table saved Mrs. Gaines from hurtling through the door and probably down the stairflight.

"What means this unseemly tumult?" the great rich voice of Elder Symes demanded. He was holding Loakes in one mighty hand and Gypsy in the other, and shaking them rebukingly when they struggled to get at each other.

Four voices blended in explanation, charge and countercharge. Durie had gone out for ointment and bandages. Despairing of enlightenment from that Babel, the man of God surveyed the den, identified the gin bottle with a frown, explored a corner cabinet richly stocked with viands and liquors and reached his judgment.

The three, he informed them in measured terms, were limbs of Satan. Hell's hottest fires yawned for them in a future life. As for the present, he proposed to denounce them to the Health Committee and to see to it personally that not only their pay was stopped, but that they should be whipped out of town, bare-backed and at a cart-tail. One day would be allowed them for demonstrated repentance and reform.

"You could smell sulphur sizzle when he told 'em what he thought of 'em," the charmed Gypsy reported to Dr. Colvin. "He shriveled 'em like spiders on a hot grid."

The three were actually cowed into promises of good behavior.

337

Only the flabby-fair Medory bore malice. Between whimperings she averred that the Vilas wench had "tore two hankth of hair outa my very head and I'll make her thorry she ever come here. Jutht let her wait!"

On his own motion Elder Symes took semi-military charge of the trio. It may well be that they were awed more by his physical prowess than his spiritual authority. The result was the same. They stood their tricks and did their work and though they did not attain the standard of cleanliness and efficiency set by the younger girls, Dr. Colvin was well satisfied. It was little short of a miracle to his mind. He gave daily thanks for the Elder.

Pay-day came around. Dr. Colvin delivered the envelopes to the two girls. Ten shillings bonus had been added to the stipulated wage. There was a larger envelope for Elder Symes which he refused.

"Buy food for the ward with it," he said.

For supplies were running low. The hospital was living from hand to mouth.

"The *Barter Boat* ought to be in this week," said Dr. Colvin.

"What's that?" asked Durie.

"The Pilkington-Quintard Durham. They're freighting medical aid, special, from Albany."

Durie changed color. "Will they be coming here to the hospital?"

"No. We'll transfer at wharf and send 'em back for more."

That evening Durie surprised Medory mousing around the general kitchen where she did not belong. Civilly asking if she could help, Durie received a muttered and indefinite reply. Shortly after, Gypsy entered and brewed her pot of mock-tea preparatory to going on the ward for the night trick. A bad night was in prospect. There were three moribund cases, and two more in which the premonitory chill had set in.

Later there would be no respite for the physician. Dr. Colvin was hopefully trying for an hour's rest, when Nurse Durie burst in.

"Oh, Doctor! Come!"

He struggled to a sitting position. "Which one is it? Twenty-four? Or seventeen?"

"Gypsy."

He was on his feet in a bound. The girl had fallen at the head of the stairs, and lay, convulsed and dazed. He felt her brow—cool. Forcing her jaws he looked at her tongue—clear.

"Hot water, mustard, white of egg. Quick!"

Durie darted away. The kettle was already on. Three minutes had not elapsed when she was back. Already a ghastly change had come over the sick girl's face. Her eyes were averted; her lips drawn back. At first it seemed impossible to make her take the steaming draught. But the young physician was skillful. Gypsy's throat worked. She swallowed. The blessed retching set in. Between them they got her to the study couch. A faint color appeared in her cheeks.

"Is it the collapsed cholera?" whispered Durie in anguish.

He shook his head, frowning. "What did she eat?"

"Nothing. She drank some willow tea."

"Fetch me the pot."

"Doctor, is she going to . . . ?"

"No. It was touch and go, though."

Durie ran for the teapot. Shaking it out, the physician picked at some bark shreds and scowled.

"That's never willow-bark."

"What is it?" Durie's eyes were wide and scared.

"Looks like mountain ashberry."

"Poison?"

"That wench used to bed with an herbalist," he muttered.

"Medory? She was in the kitchen this evening."

"I'll fix her!"

Shrieking and fighting, the poisoner was lugged off to jail. The lock-up had already contributed seven cases to the hospital. She became the eighth, returning in three days. Hers was a slow case. She lingered on between spasms of anguish and spells of unconsciousness. There was one onset when she shrieked through a whole night, tearing nerves to a frazzle and robbing of sleep the unhappy convalescents who so sorely needed it. She would not die and she could not recover.

Concerned for her other cases, Durie applied to Dr. Colvin.

"Isn't that gas-box on the shelf a pleasure-machine?"

"It's a facture of nitrous oxide."

Durie nodded. "We had one at Mailzell's in Albany. Six pence a trial."

"It counteracts the cholera miasmas. So they say." His expression indicated skepticism.

"Ours used to be advertised 'Breathe deep and forget your irks and troubles.' I was wondering . . ."

He smiled wearily. "Try, if you choose."

"It might keep her quiet. At worst . . ."

"And if it kills her, it's small loss," concluded the case-hardened doctor.

Medory responded magically to the soothing gases; so much so that Durie applied the method to other "spasmodic" cases. It could not cure, but at least it reduced the total of suffering in that tragic enclosure. Dr. Colvin inclined to the belief that, taken early, it might even save the lighter cases. He meant to write a report on it for a medical journal, if ever he could find leisure, "Ameliorative and Possible Curative Effects of Nitrous Oxide (N_2O) in Spasmodic Cholera."*

August came in with furious rains. The town was flooded with filth. Cholera increased at a terrifying pace. The emergency Institute overflowed and the Health Committee diverted its attention long enough from the pleasures of learned debate—whether the cholera was miasmic, telluric, meteorastic, or fomitic of origin—to make an inspection of the plant. Though officially stolid of nerve, they were shocked by their findings. The purpose of all inspective committees being to lay the blame upon someone other than themselves, Chairman Kennedy called the entire hospital staff together and reprimanded them (nasally, by reason of the cotton plugs in his nostrils) for laxness, inattention and lack of system, with a special rebuke for Dr. Adam Colvin in charge. Was there anything they wished to say in extenuation?

Dr. Colvin said, "No," in the exhausted voice of discouragement.

Nurse Vilas whose six-hour off-duty spell for rest had been cut in two by the Committee summons, piped, "Yes." Had the Chairman ever mopped slops three times a day?

"The question is improper, impudent and inadmissible," returned Dr. Kennedy.

"You're an old bastard," said Nurse Vilas with conviction.

*Either the Colvin brochure was never published, or it was unknown to or ignored by the later experimenters in anesthesia.

"And you'd better get the hell out of here," supplemented Nurse Loakes.

"The likes of you tellin' off the likes of our Doctor!" added Nurse Gaines.

A clout of foul cloth hit the wall beyond him. Nurse Loakes brandished a mop. The three committeemen withdrew to the yard to draw up an exeat discharging without pay the entire personnel as of date.

A formidable apparition descended upon them. Elder Symes was gaunt, sweat-drenched and unshaven, but there was a holy fire in his eye. With the sole aid of a decrepit half-breed, he had that morning excavated the steaming earth for three bodies, whose souls he had reverently committed to a merciful God by number, the record of their names having been lost or, more probably, never entered. His labors had kept him from the hearing indoors, but he had learned its import.

One after another the committeemen protested his intrusion. Amidst the sound waves of that sonorous voice, their feeble objections were swept away like straws. He gave them a brief outline of the work. He sketched the characters of his fellow workers, glossing nothing, but indicating plainly that the least of them was more worthy than any deputation of visiting Pharisees. His Scriptural texts were full of a rich though uncomplimentary allusiveness. Thoroughly chastened after ten minutes of this, they listened meekly to his practical suggestions.

The outcome was a report to the full committee reluctantly endorsing Dr. Colvin, enlarging his authority, and appropriating for the overflow patients a file of "shantees" on the flat below the Institute. These were assigned to the female sick, and nurses Andrews and Vilas were transferred to them, aided by a callow but stout-hearted medical student named Whitney. Their last day in the hospital proper lost Gypsy the only patient in whom she had a personal interest. The redoubtable Medory made a good fight for life. But her blood was vitiated by old disease. In her last conscious spell, with Gypsy and the gas-box in attendance, the dying woman piously forgave her enemies and imparted to her benefactress a herbal recipe for removing undesirable persons with dispatch and safety from detection.

32

SLEEP and an easier routine relaxed the pressure on Jans' temper. He was more ashamed of himself than he would admit in the matter of the quarrel. Pilk was uncompromising. His pride had been hurt; his business acumen impugned. What little speech now passed between the partners was no more than the gruff exchange of navigational essentials. Looby seemed unconscious of anything amiss. He was happily absorbed in the simple routine of the towpath and would stretch his shift at the tandem any time that the others overslept their off-watch.

Traffic became thinner and thinner as they moved west. Few of the locks now were tended; they must lock themselves through, an unwelcome imposition of extra labor. Pilk was in a smoldering rage. Let him but get rid of this cargo and no goddamn fool was going to whimwham him into any further ventures. Jans remained silent. He was done with argument. Also with Pilk as soon as accounts could be settled. And with it, the friendship. That hurt.

Approaching Syracuse, Looby was on the rope, Jans at the wheel, and Captain Pilkington below. Both path and berm were lined with boats of all descriptions: packets, freighters, pleasure craft, immigrant cent-a-milers, pegged in or moored to trees. On some a single figure kept disconsolate guard. Others seemed abandoned. But for a few boats headed east, the traffic would have been wholly stagnant.

Jans hailed the Captain of the *Bonnie Lass,* a tavern acquaintance of earlier days.

"What's amiss?"

"You'll find out soon enough," was the sour reply.

Short of Teal's Lock, an official on horseback halted Looby, rode on, and imperiously waved the *Barter Boat* to the shore. He was dressed in a shining white linen suit and puce castor hat, and carried a sword. He looked important.

"Bear in," he ordered.

"What for?" said Jans.

"By authority of the Freeholders of Syracuse in me vested."

"This is state property," Jans pointed out.

"You can't enter the city."

Captain Pilkington emerged from the hatch. "Who's the cockatoo?" he demanded.

Jans shushed him.

The official said, "Any passengers?"

"No."

"Sickness?"

"No."

"I'll come aboard and examine."

"You set foot on my deck and I'll kick your poddle overside," from Captain Pilkington.

"Keep quiet, Pilk. Let me handle this."

"Pick up, Looby," bellowed the Captain. He seized the horn from its brackets on the rail and blew furiously for the lock.

"You'll get no locking," warned the official. "If your driver moves, I'll arrest him and impound your horses."

"Lay off, Looby," Jans called. "For God's sake, Pilk!" he added, as his partner thrust forward a purpling face. To the official, he said pacifically, "We're laden with supplies for the hospital."

"I don't know anything about that. Orders are to let nothing through from the east."

"Will you take this letter to the authorities?"

The official looked at the signature. "Governor Troop don't run Syracuse," he snarled.

"Who does?"

"The Committee of Freeholders and Inhabitants."

"Will they send conveyances to transfer our cargo?"

"You can't land barrel, bale or bundle," put in a second official, coming up on foot. He was gaudily attired in the uniform of a Captain of Light Horse Artillery. "How do we know it ain't pizened with Plague?"

343

"Too much goddamn palaver going on here," Captain Pilkington contributed.

"You must excuse my partner," Jans said suavely. "He's a little overdone. Suppose you inspect. How long before we can go through?"

"Might be five days, might be fifteen," answered White Suit airily. "Quarantine."

"Backed with powder," added the artillery captain, jerking his head sidewise toward the lock where lounged two rough-looking fellows with fowling pieces.

"Very well, gentlemen," Jans said. "Captain Pilkington does not recognize your authority to board his boat. I bid you good day."

He called in Looby. The horses were set to graze in a low meadow. Jans addressed his partner.

"Pilk?"

"Anan?"

"I want to talk with you."

"Talk, then."

"They've no authority to stop us."

"They've got the guns."

"How many boats do you recognize, held up here?"

"*Canada Carrier, Bluebell of the Forest, Mary Jane, Seaman's Fancy, Herkimer Hearty,*" Pilk rattled off. "Can't quite make out that red-striper, but she looks like the *Erie Sweetheart,* and beyond her, I reckon that's *Smith's Sons' Stalwart.* Mebbe twelve, fourteen, in all."

"How many will fight?"

Pilk's pale eyes lighted up. "Didja ever see a canawler wouldn't fight?"

"Pilk, we're going to run that quarantine."

"When?"

"Tomorrow night."

He laid out his plan, to which his partner assented with silent nods. Pilk was to make the rounds of such captains as he knew, swear them to secrecy and invite them to join. There was no incentive except their proclivity for battle and their resentment against the local officials. That would be enough, in Pilk's opinion.

The *Barter Boat* became a center of covert activity. Burly men

344

in painted hats and brass buttons came, spoke low, with heads close-converged, and went. Some deposited weapons, ranging from horse-pistols through sword-canes to a Tuscarora bow with arrows from a three-penny museum boat. At midnight Pilk staggered aboard with a small brass cannon in his arms, which he deposited on the deck with a solid chunk. At sight of it, Jans' eyes dilated.

"What's that?"

"A two-pounder," said Pilk. "Charged," he added, patting its flank affectionately.

"Where did it come from?"

"A fancy boat, back in the reeds. Cap'n's a fine, big young buck. Said he was a friend of yours."

"Ayrault?"

"Yup. That's the fella."

"He lies. He's no friend of mine," said Jans harshly. The sound of that dull boom in the dead of night at Rochester, advertising Macel Ayrault's triumph, still beat on his brain. He kicked the small cannon.

"Take it away," he said hoarsely.

"Go to hell," said his partner.

A visiting captain interposed. "Leave her lay as she is, mister," he advised. "Cram her up with bolts and nails and you can shoot your way through hell with her."

Jans bestowed a malevolent glance upon the neat little artillery piece. "Cover it up then," he said. "We don't want the guard to see it."

Jans hunted up the pathmaster. Didn't the Governor's warrant give their boat the right of passage through the locks? The official examined the paper and said that it did. Very well, then; would he help them go through? Not him! He had a family to consider, he had, and them quarantiners had hired a lot of tough cusses to back them up, marshmen from Montezuma, knife-casters, jackeroo men, gunners; pink you as soon as look at you. No, sir! The best he would do was to bid the lock-keepers not to stop the boat.

Sometime that night Captain Pilkington quietly slipped ashore. So far as individuals were concerned, the quarantine was a leaky net. He had little difficulty in reaching town and less in doing business. When he returned to the boat the comparative good humor inspired by the prospect of battle had given place to a recurrent sense of his wrongs at the hands of his partner.

He slapped a piece of paper violently down upon the galley table.

"Read that."

Jans read. It bore the imprint of a local supply house which agreed to take all the camphor delivered at wharf by freighter *Barter Boat* within forty-eight hours, cash on delivery. The price made Jans' eyes bulge.

"Five dollars a pound!"

"Five dollars a pound," confirmed Pilk in a triumphant squeak. "Stick that up your snoot and see how you like the smell of it."

The nostrils on the offended "snoot" worked. Jans said with cold restraint, "Pay in the cost of the shipment to the till, and I'm satisfied. And I wish you well of your profits," he concluded with acid emphasis.

"My profit?" Pilk stared at him.

"Yes. Outside of the expenses you've tapped the till for, I wouldn't touch a penny of it with a pike-pole."

It was the complete repudiation. Pilk's goiter swelled and purpled. "You're a poxy son-of-a-bitch."

"I'll pass that—for the present," Jans said.

"You can take it up any time you're ready," retorted the other, leering.

Jans' temper was still in an evil ferment when a robust shout from the deck afflicted his ears.

"Quinny! Ho, Quinny! Jans Quintard!"

"I'm busy."

If there was one person on earth whom he did not want to see, it was Macel Ayrault.

"Busy be damn! I'm coming down."

The great bulk, descending, shut out the light. "Hi, Quinny!"

"What do you want with me?"

The big fellow's lip drooped. "What ails you, Quinny? You might give a chap a decent word," he complained.

"I'll keep my decent words for decent folk."

"What have I done to you?" Ayrault asked, aggrieved as a mis-accused schoolboy.

346

"You're taking up my time. I wish you'd get off my boat. You and your damned cannon. As soon as we've run the guard, I'm going to throw it in the canal."

He knew that he was acting like a petulant child. He did not care. The apparition of Durie Andrews, the beauty and innocence of her face, the allure of her low voice had tortured him in his dreams, and the end of all dreams was the dull boom of the piece, blowing the pure vision to fragments.

Macel Ayrault was regarding him in bewilderment. "The cannon? What's about my little Brass Betsy? I believe the lad's exalted in the head."

Jans' restraint broke. He stood up. His voice was cold and thick.

"You're a fool, Macel. You always were a fool, and you always will be. You can't help that. But you could help being a braggart scoundrel and advertising a young girl's shame to all the world."

The vacuous face across the table took on a certain dignity. "I think you'd better explain that, Quintard."

"The cannon. The shot in the night."

"At Rochester? What of it?"

"It was the signal, wasn't it? Damn you! To advertise your victory and the winning of your bet to the world?"

"Victory? Bet?" Enlightenment dawned upon the broad face. "About the little Amour? I never fired the shot."

"Don't lie to me," Jans said fiercely. "I heard it. I—I can hear it still." He raised his hands to his head.

"It was those drunken ninnywits. They let off the cannon."

"What difference does it make who let it off!"

"Jans, I never won that bet."

Jans sat down heavily. "You—never—won . . ." he repeated. "She stayed on your boat with you."

"She did stay on the *Merry Moment*."

"With you," insisted Jans.

"With the damnedest, sharpest, wickedest little knife ever you set eyes on." He shuddered. "That active wildcat has no respect for manhood," he said grievously.

Jans laughed, then sobered. "She may have thought you had no respect for womanhood," he pointed out.

"I got it now. You know, Quinny"—his eyes grew round with

speculation—"I wouldn't wonder but what that girl was virginous."

"Would that surprise you so much?"

"Well! A Thespian! I dunno." He shook his head ponderously. "It's a queer world, Quinny."

"It's a better world than ever I thought it before," exulted Jans. "Did you ever hear of a gentleman marrying a Thespian, Quinny?"

"It's been done, I believe. Were you thinking of it?"

The big fellow sighed. "She's mortal hard to forget."

"God knows!"

There was a long pause. The two young men regarded one another across the table.

"Where is she now?" Jans asked, at length.

"Haven't a notion. Last news I had she was going South."

Jans shook himself. "You'll report at ten, Mace?"

"Right, my lad! Have Betty ready."

Mysteriously there appeared at Teal's Lock, as the sun sank among thunderheads, a demijohn of keg-ripened peachy. It met with the instant approval of the three armed guards. Their capture, two hours later, was easy and bloodless. Neatly trussed, they were stowed away in the hold of the *Seaman's Fancy*. One of them, however, had freed his neck long enough to let out a yell. A dark figure leaped up from back of the lock-keeper's shanty and scurried, hare-like, toward the city. Pilk cursed.

"He'll rouse the town on us," he growled.

They locked the *Barter Boat* through in record time. Pilk was at the helm. Jans was stationed in the bow with a horse-pistol. Mace Ayrault had established Brass Betty on the coaming of the cabin where she could be readily swung to cover any quarter. No lights were shown. The vulnerable point was the draught power, where the tremulous Looby handled his tandem. There seven tough captains escorted the hoggee and two substitutes in case he were shot or ran away. These cheerful mercenaries, variously armed, would have come along for the mere exhilaration of combat; but Jans had promised a bounty of ten shillings each on condition that they stay to guard the consignment of supplies until morning brought about their safe delivery.

Nobody threatened interference until they approached the Salina

Street bridge where a crowd of perhaps fifty or sixty persons was massed. Captain Pilkington tooted his horn once for a halt. The mercenaries were all for a charge and a merry mix-up; the high command was more prudent. Captains and hoggees were called in and distributed at strategic points for defense. The horses were stowed below.

"The object of this trip," Jans explained to the fretting canalmen, "is to get our cargo through. We can fight tomorrow, or any time. Business first, pleasure later."

The craft crept along under pole-power. A stab of light thrust upward from a bridge abutment, followed by a sudden *Blump!*

"Looks as ef we might have the pleasure now," commented Captain Smith of *Smith's Sons' Stalwart* appreciatively.

"Tell 'em, Mace," called Jans.

Ayrault's great voice boomed through the darkness, plagiarizing an aged watchman of Cambridge Town.

"Disperse, all ye lawless folk and disturbers of the peace! Or," he added from his own vocabulary, "I'll blow your guts to tatters with my pretty little cannon."

A yell of defiance answered him. He struck his match and applied it to the touch-hole. A belch of flame and a quite respectable roar split the night. The captains discharged their weapons in unison. Howls, objurgations and shrieks for mercy answered as the crowd melted away. The land forces rushed out to explore, but found no casualties, as was to have been expected, since all had fired in the air. It promised to be a disappointing excursion for the canallers.

Some rods beyond the bridge, Jans discerned by a flicker of lightning a loose group of half a dozen men carrying muskets. He dropped.

"Take cover," he yelled, Captain Pilkington supplementing it with the more familiar, "Low bridge!" to which boatmen respond instinctively and instantly.

Not quite soon enough, however. Three shots, Jans counted. A bullet thugged into the woodwork aloft of him. A voice cried out harshly, then said in a surprised tone, "Grained, begod!"

The wound was superficial. All Jans' and Pilk's persuasion barely availed to prevent what could have been a suicidal sally by the infuriated captains. Passing the lumber piles whence the shots had come, Jans fired once, a light charge, intended only to sting, but was sure he had missed. A twanging voice at his ear was followed by a grunt from the dark shore.

"Got 'em!" said the hoggee from the museum boat.

A figure hobbled for cover, limping and cursing the arrow protruding from his thigh.

There was no further trouble. By midnight the *Barter Boat* was snugged up in Salinas Basin, her private militia, with generous allowances of grog beneath their belts, sleeping where they fell at their posts.

Weighing the chances of arrest, if he went ashore, Jans decided that he must venture it. On the coldly impersonal note of shared business interests, he broached to his partner the subject of legal advice. Pilk ungraciously replied that he could hire all the damn pettifoggers he liked at his own damn expense, but that he, Captain Pilkington, would have none of it. He was going to deliver his camphor and get drunk and Mr. Quintard had better keep out of his path, for there was no telling what he might not be moved to do in reprisal of his wrongs. He departed, and with him the captains.

With five dollars from the till, Jans consulted Lawyer Fabricius Hawley, an ornament of the local bar who confirmed the *Barter Boat's* right to accomplish its passage to its appointed destination.

Jans returned to the basin and put in a busy day superintending the transfer of cargo to the dock where carts picked it up for the hospital. Having received the stipulated price of freightage from the committee, he locked it in the strong-box and fell asleep. In his activities he had no help from his partner. Captain Pilkington was occupied downtown with his own private and profitable transactions.

Rhythmic footsteps above his head awakened the sleeper. Somebody was dancing in the moonlight; two people, Jans judged. A voice trolled a song—Pilk's voice, jovial and thick. Pilk spoke.

"Captain Smith, I gotta foot like a feather."

Mumble in agreement from Captain Smith.

"Captain Smith, I gotta hand like a hammer."

Another acquiescent mumble.

"Captain Smith, I'm a rich man."

An appreciative grunt.

"My partner's a rich man. Who made him rich? I did, Captain Bassford Pilkington. Five dollars a pound."

"Thassa lotta money," said Captain Smith respectfully.

"And what do I get for it? Scorn an' contempt. From my own partner. Thinks hisself a ruffleshirt. Mister Jans Quintard, the ruffleshirt."

"Punch um in the nose," suggested Captain Smith.

"D'you know what I said to Lucky Seven?"

"The marsher? Hefty fellers, the marshers."

"Fight 'em or drink with 'em, I can best 'em both ways. Didja see their eyes bung out when I clapped my money-bag down on the bar?"

Jans sat up sharply in his bunk.

"Lucky Seven says he's going to cut my partner's ears off," continued Pilk.

After giving this due consideration, Captain Smith asked, "What's he want his ears for?"

"Keepsakes. I told him he could have 'em for all of my hindrance. So, young feller"—this to Jans whose form had appeared in the hatchway—"you'd better wear your head in a bag when the marshers come around."

"Where's that money?" asked Jans sharply.

"Five hundred dollars and more. Five hundred lovely shining dibs. Where you'll never see it, you cheap ingler."

"Hand it over."

"Whaffor?"

"To put in the strong-box."

"Black drink on that. You wouldn't have it when you could. Now you don't get it."

"Don't be a fool, Pilk, you're drunk."

"Who's got a better right? G'night, Captain Smith. See you in the morning." He stumbled forward and disappeared between decks.

While Looby was cooking breakfast, heavy steps sounded on the planks of the wharf. Jans heard the steps, but did not discern the silent approach of two men who crept to the hatchway and stood, waiting. A voice ponderous with authority called:

"Sheriff's warrant for Jans Quintard."

"Your warrant does not run on state territory."

"State warrant. Come forth, Jans Quintard, in the name of the law."

"Get to Lawyer Hawley and tell him I'm arrested," Jans said to Looby under his breath.

Looby opened the porthole and plunked into the canal like an alarmed frog.

Unsuspecting, Jans started for the deck. A jackeroo in the grip of one of the waiting marshmen thudded on his skull. He passed out quickly. The marshmen who, in cahoots with the sheriff had prepared the fake warrant, went below to loot. They were still at this congenial occupation when Captain Pilkington awoke boozily. Considering the handicap of his condition, he put up a good battle, but the odds were too heavy against him. A crack with an axe-helve ended the argument.

When he painfully opened his eyes, it was upon a scene only too familiar in his long and varied career. What surprised him was not that he was in jail but that Jans Quintard also was. Without taking the trouble to reason about it he realized that his grievance against his partner had dissipated. He said hoarsely, "Hey, lad."

"That you, Pilk?"

"Yes. Can't you see me?"

Jans blinked. "I—I guess so."

"Well, here we are again," said Pilk with hollow cheer.

"Can we get out?" Jans recalled the other's adroitness in an earlier dilemma.

"Not this box," answered Pilk, evidently speaking from experience.

"Got any money?"

"Not a bowel."

"My head feels queer."

"Lad?"

"What?"

"I guess I been a goddamn fool."

"You aren't the only one."

352

As mutual apologetics the interchange lacked form. Nevertheless it was the complete composition of their quarrel.

In those days of panic and confusion, nobody paid much attention to such a minor matter as a couple of strangers in the lock-up. They might get a prompt hearing, more likely not. If they had no money, their chances diminished to zero.

Looby's hysterical report to Lawyer Hawley (whom he did not find for four days) indicated that the *Barter Boat* had been the object of a piratical attack, and that young Quintard had probably been finished off by the assailants who knocked him on the head. When no corpse answering to the young man's description turned up, Mr. Hawley revised his opinion, despatched a note to the Honorable Vryling Lovatt, and conducted a search. Once the missing client was found there was no difficulty in securing his release and that of his companion.

The change of environment was hardly for the better. Jans was taken to the hospital burning with fever.

Pilk went along to care for him.

33

W<small>ILL</small> he die, Doc?"

Captain Bassford Pilkington, gaunt, unshaven and shabby, anxiously scanned the seamed face of young Dr. Colvin.

"Who? Number Eighty? Probably."

"Ain't there anything can be done?"

Dr. Colvin shrugged. "We can ease the spasms with gas if they come on again. He's stopped trying to live."

"Why?"

"Who can say? Worn out with the pain, perhaps."

Pilk sighed. "I reckon I better take the cart and rustle some prog."

Conditions in the refuge had bettered with the arrival of the *Barter Boat.* Medicines were replenished. Cots were set out in the hallways, to be filled as soon as set up. Improvised vats gave forth vapors of lime to mingle with and, at times, half neutralize the overpowering sickroom stench. They did little to discourage the insect swarms which visited bed, sink, offal-pail, kitchen, and back again to the beds, unhampered.

The Institute had further benefited by the unpaid services of Captain Pilkington who, in the intervals of watching beside his friend and partner, acted as general almoner and collector of provisions. In this capacity it was his duty to solicit food for the patients, from door to door, the official supply from the overworked and undermanned Board of Health being both uncertain and inadequate. A two-wheeled cart with a somnolent ox in the shafts was his medium of collection. The convalescent patients were expected to take turns as operatives. Since they prudently ran away from that place as soon as their legs would carry them, the work devolved upon the faithful Pilk.

Hardly had he started on his rounds when the ox, discerning a patch of edible weeds in a corner lot, mutinied. Too exhausted to argue, Pilk grubbed among his meager gatherings, extracted a loaf of soured salt-bread, a grudging contribution from the Mansion House cook, and sat munching with his stubby legs dangling. A female voice accosted him.

"Hello, Turnipneck."

Life had inured Pilk against undue sensitiveness, but this gratuitous reference to his goiter annoyed him.

"You go to hell, whoever you are," he retorted, not even turning.

"Miss Vilas, to you. What kind of rig-out is that? A cad-wagon?"

"No, it ain't," Pilk returned with dignity. "It's a prog-cart, if you want to know."

"Who you collecting for?"

"The cholery refuge."

"You working there? I thought you was a boatee."

"So I am. My partner's got the plague."

"Who? Quinny?"

"Yes."

"Is he bad?"

"Dying."

Gypsy tried to tell herself that it would be small loss, but Pilk looked so miserable that her heart, at worst an impressionable organ, softened.

"Some of 'em get well," she said encouragingly. "He's young and tough. I'll take a look at him when I get time. Durie and me are working in the shantees. What are you stopping here for?"

"My ox won't go."

"Gimme that goad. What does a canawler know about oxes!"

Her skilled operations speedily persuaded the balky animal of the error of his ways. As the equipage lumbered away, she conned over in her shrewd little mind the information about Jans and decided to keep it to herself. If Jans died, she could tell Durie later. If he lived, he would go away with Pilk and no harm done. There was no likelihood of Durie's coming upon her ex-lover unawares, Gypsy reckoned, since both girls were kept too busy in their own department to visit the main refuge.

On pretext of improving their medical supplies she got away

from her chum that afternoon and climbed the hill to see Dr. Colvin.

"Quintard? The *Barter Boat* fellow?" the physician said. "I'd do anything I can if only for the good turn he's done us here."

"Can't you save him?"

"The choleroid coma has already set in."

"Could I see him?"

"It can do no harm, I suppose."

Gypsy tiptoed to bedbox eighty. "Quinny!"

The eyes did not open. The head rolled once and back.

"It's Gypsy. Gypsy Vilas."

The leaden lips stirred. A wisp of sound issued. "Durie."

"Not Durie. Gypsy."

"Durie," breathed the lips.

"Who's Durie?" the doctor asked.

"Oh, a girl he used to know," she replied casually. She was not going to have her friend subjected to that grim and hopeless spectacle. If she was done with her infatuation for Jans, there was no sense in it. If the embers of her passion still smoldered, why take a chance of letting pity stir them up?

"Any orders for the shantees?" she inquired.

"No. Just report your deaths."

As she reached the gate, a stylish gig drove in and discharged a familiar figure. The Honorable Vryling Lovatt, hurrying up the steps, did not give her so much as a glance. His mind was concentrated upon the hope that he might be in time.

The doctor met him with a caution. "It may be contagious. Authorities differ."

"Fiddle-dee-dee!" snorted the Senator. The sturdy autocrat who had tended his own operatives through a short-lived but severe outbreak of the pestilence, was not to be daunted by considerations of personal danger. "Where's my nephew?"

A moment later he was saying in awed tones, "Is—is that Jans? I shouldn't have known him."

"The pain brings about strange alterations," Dr. Colvin explained.

"Can he be roused?"

"You may try. I doubt that he'll know you."

"Jans! Jans, my boy. It's Uncle Vryling."

The head rolled. The eyes flickered and closed indifferently.

"He's lost his grip on life," the physician said.

"You mean he doesn't want to live?" gulped the Senator.

"He's given up trying. Living has come to be identified in his mind with the agony. He won't return to it. If we could reconstitute his interest and give the *vix medicatrix naturae,* the natural healing force of the system, a chance to assert itself he might still pull through. But," he finished with a gesture eloquent of despair, "so many go out that way!"

"*Quae nunc abibis in loca?*" the voice whispered. "I spoke that line once to a girl, a loved girl. *Quae nunc abibis in loca?*" Then with shocking animation from that deathly visage, "Lost! Durie!"

The doctor's expression became intent. "He called that name before. Do you know any such girl?"

"No. None."

"Wait!" He clapped his hand to his forehead. "Where have I . . . ? Surely I heard Nurse Vilas call the other nurse by that name only yesterday. Senator, I can't leave my patients. Will you be my messenger?"

"For what?"

"Go to the shantees. You'll find the direction post outside. Ask there for . . ."

The Honorable Vryling was out of the door before the sentence was finished and sprinting down the slope.

Durie was busy setting out her medicines for the day when she heard the urgent question for her name.

"I'm Durie Andrews. What is it?"

In his excitement and distress Senator Lovatt took no note of the surname.

"You're to come to the ward at once."

"Who wants me?" She opened the door.

"Dr. Colv—— Why, bitch my soul! It's Jans' little plaicer!" cried the uncle, stupefied.

"Did Dr. Colvin send you, Senator Lovatt?"

"Yes. It's for my nephew."

"Jans?"

"He's dying."

Her hand went to her heart. "Where?"

"Back in the ward. He's been calling for you."

She had become ghastly pale. "Here? At the refuge?"

"For God's sake, don't waste time! I'll give you any sum of money. One hundred dollars. Two hundred. Five hundred. Anything!" he cried.

"I don't want your money," she wailed. "Gypsy!"

She roused her associate, angrily tearful at this trespass upon her sleeping period, and left her in charge. On the way up the hill the Senator attempted to apologize for his earlier expressions. Durie hardly heard him. She was suffering an inner turmoil. Jans in the refuge and dying! How long had he been there? Why had she not been told? What was it that Dr. Colvin expected of her?

The prospect of seeing Jans filled her with dread. What could be the result but an awakening of the old pain, the old, poignant conflict of passion and disillusionment? Yet incongruously the thought that she might never again see him in life was intolerable. Somehow this muddled and pathetic old dandy at her side seemed to be deluding himself that she could save Jans; a chimera born of his grief and fear. There was nothing within her power that Dr. Colvin could not perform more competently. Had the doctor really sent for her? Or was it a subterfuge on the part of the distraught uncle?

At the ward entrance she was met by the physician.

"Go back. There is nothing you can do now."

Senator Lovatt cried out lamentably.

Durie whispered, "Is he . . . ?"

"No. I've had to give him a draught. You'll be summoned later if you're needed."

The summons came before midnight. The patient was conscious, or as nearly so as he was likely to be. Dr. Colvin had joined the watching Senator at the bedside.

"Speak to him," he bade the girl.

"Jans," she whispered.

"Louder."

She found her voice. "Jans. It's Durie."

The eyes, burning from their hollows, opened, and stared at the ceiling. The lips formed words:

"The leading of apes is a story . . ."

"Apes?" broke in Senator Lovatt. "What's this gibberish? His mind is wandering."

"No. Quiet! He's coming back."

> "... a story
> Of days and of dames that have vanished."

"Jans! Jans!"

"Don't wriggle. Don't prance. You're not Lady Macbeth. You're a young damsel. Try again. Keep your feet still."

She looked helplessly at the doctor. He frowned.

"There's a response. But you aren't reaching his mind."

> "Animula, vagula, blandula,
> Hospes comesque corporis ..."

Jans intoned. "Drunk again, Quintard?" he questioned and answered himself, "Lapsing into Latinity; that means you're drunk. Drink and dreams are the Quintard curse. What was the voice I heard? Was that drink? Or dreams? Or Durie?"

Dr. Colvin caught the girl's arm. "Try again."

"What? How?"

"The poem. Is it something you've shared with him?"

"Yes."

"Render it, then. Exactly as you used to."

She recited:

> "The leading of apes is a story
> Of days and of dames that have vanished.
> A damsel is ne'er ..."

"Have a care! The stuff's explosive. I told that fool, Passerow ... Get the women out! Quick! Get the ... Durie! Where's Durie?"

Dr. Colvin pressed back the heaving shoulder. "This won't do. He'll wear out what little life he has left."

Jans' head rolled. He breathed heavily.

"What can I *do?*" Durie implored.

"Isn't there something else? Some reminder that might call him back without so exciting him?"

She shook her head, discouraged.

The sick man drew a throbbing breath. Strange sounds issued from his lips.

"He's trying to sing," said the Senator, appalled.

The words became faintly articulate.

> *"You may esteem him*
> *A child for his might . . ."*

The voice blurred, wavered, ceased. Durie was shaken by an over-mastering dread. It seemed to her that if she let the song die, the singer would die with it. She pressed her clenched fists to her breast, struggling for command, forcing the faltering notes to take on form and resonance from her throat.

> *"Or you may deem him*
> *A coward for his flight."*

Jans' eyes opened, but no longer in that fixed, insensate stare. There was wonder in them. His hand moved feebly.

"Go on! Go on!" the physician urged, for Durie was wavering on her feet. At the word, she straightened. The constriction in her throat eased. She gave forth her pent emotion in the full splendor of her voice.

> *"But if once the message greet him*
> *That his True Love doth stay,*
> *Though Death come forth to meet him*
> *Love will find out the way."*

"Durie!" said Jans and smiled.

34

NEITHER by temperament, training, nor inclination was the Honorable Vryling Lovatt suited to the towpath. But it was that or nothing if Jans was to be gotten home with speed and comfort. Looby had been found, but he and the bone-weary Pilkington could not run the boat between them. The ageing dandy must take his turn on the rope and at the tiller. He had no difficulty with the tandem, being a thorough horseman, and his costume of tall beaver and pearl-buttoned broadcoat was greatly admired among his fellow hoggees. As a steersman, after a few minor collisions, he achieved reasonable skill and a notably enriched vocabulary.

Carefully considering all the circumstances, the Honorable Vryling had mapped his course. In the interests of all concerned his nephew and the too-attractive Thespian must be kept apart. He could not understand that Andrews female. She seemed to be enamored of Jans, which was comprehensible enough. Why, then, should she disclaim any intention of seeing him again? Trickery? She had not acted like a trickster. That business of insisting upon a refund of the money, for instance. How explain that? Women were the devil!

No protest had been offered by Jans over his transfer to the boat. In his great weakness, he had slept through the trip and was so vague when he awoke that his uncle hopefully promulgated a strategy and enlisted Pilk as an accomplice. While dubious as to the feasibility of fooling Jans, the Captain agreed to play along.

They were nearing the home port when Jans opened the subject.

"Uncle Vryling, how can I reach Miss Andrews?"

"Who?"

"Endurance Andrews."

"Oh! That girl! How should I know?"

"What was she doing in the refuge?"

"My poor Jans! That was your delirium."

"I didn't see Durie Andrews there? And speak to her? And hear her singing?"

"One of the nurses was singing one day, I believe."

Jans raised his voice. "Oh, Pilk!"

"Here, lad." Captain Pilkington's rubicund face appeared.

"Was Durie Andrews—La Jeune Amour, you know—in the sick-ward or wasn't she?"

"The play-girl? Now what would she be doing there, lad?"

"That's what I'm trying to find out. Who was it singing, then?"

"Singing? Nobody was singing. It wouldn't be allowed there."

"You two had better come to better terms about your clumsy lies," Jans said grimly. "D'you think I can't tell flesh and blood from a phantasm?"

"Too well," Uncle Vryling muttered.

"Then tell me what she was doing there? Had she been stricken?"

"No. She was nursing."

"Is she there still?" he demanded eagerly.

"She was when we left."

"Was there no message for me?"

Uncle Vryling blinked. "Not exactly for you, Jans. There was a——settlement."

"Money?"

"Yes. Before we got away from the refuge, she caught me up and insisted on paying over the balance of what Passerow extorted from me. That girl has her pride," he concluded reluctantly.

"Too much," Jans breathed.

"So that account is squared."

"Yes. Well—wasn't there any word for me, sir?"

"Only that she was now discharged of her debt and nothing remained between you and her."

"Did she say that? She's wrong. There's one matter yet to be cleared up between us."

"Let her alone, boy," his uncle advised. "She's been badly hurt, I'm afraid."

Jans stared. "Have you become a partisan of hers, sir? Let me tell you, she can hurt as well as be hurt. I must get a letter to her at Syracuse."

"You would waste your time."

"Why? You think she has left?"

"No. But she will accept no communications from you."

"You exacted that promise from her," Jans accused angrily.

"No exaction was necessary. It was her own wish."

"Then I must go to her."

"When?" The Senator's smile was indulgent, but confident.

Jans, who had sat up in bed, sank back, discouraged. "It's true. I'm fit for nothing. But this weakness won't last forever."

"Nor will the plague. Already it abates. And your bird will be flown."

"I'll go after her."

The Lovatt temper flared. "Bitch-and-damme, sir! Have you no pride? The girl wants none of you." Then, with a change of voice, "Bear with me, my boy. I am worn with past anxieties and forget that you are still less than yourself. I'll leave you to your sleep."

The verdict of the Little Falls doctor was that Jans must rest for a month. It was received with very ill grace. A month! Where would Durie be in a month? Jans chafed and cursed. Notwithstanding his discomfiture, he mended steadily in body and spirit.

"What will you do now?" asked Uncle Vryling, compounding with his own hand the first julep permitted to the invalid.

"Finish my play."

"That poxy fabrication!"

"Never mind, Uncle." Jans' smile was deprecatory. "I doubt it will ever reach the footlights."

"Not by furtherance of my money," said the old stiffneck with emphasis. He swallowed his drink in a gulp to give point to his assertion and stalked out. His place was presently taken by Captain Pilkington.

"How's your gizzard, lad?"

"Working again." A pause. "Pilk."

"Anan?"

"I've got to find Durie."

"The more fool you!"

"Will you look for her?"

"Where?"

"I suppose she'll go back to the stage."

"They always do," said the sapient Pilk.

"If you could get track of the Thalians."

"They've bust up."

"Passerow would keep tally of them."

"He mought. Then again he moughtn't."

"You're not going to help me, Pilk?"

"Certes. I'd help you if I knew how."

"There's always tow-rope news," Jans said hopefully, borrowing Gypsy's phrase.

"I'll keep my ear cocked. Are you coming back to the boat, Jans?"

"Freighting? We're stony, aren't we? And no stock left."

Pilk caressed his goiter, a sign of embarrassment. "Not exactly as you might say quite stony," he mumbled.

"How's that?"

"I got squirrel blood."

"Talk straight, Pilk."

"I don't hold with banks, private nor Biddlebanks."

"What's Emperor Biddle to do with us? Or your squirrel blood?"

"I'm notional about money," explained his partner. "When it's hid, it's safe. That's my fancy."

"Hid where?" Jans demanded.

"Where the squirrel hides it. In a hole. Everytime you put the rhino in the strong-box, I took some out and stuck it under the floorboards in a hollow rib."

"That's why my accounts would never balance. Damn your eyes, Pilk!"

"Damn away, lad. Lucky Seven and the marshers got your box but they didn't get my little lot," said Pilk complacently.

"How much?"

"Seventy-eight dollars. Enough to stock up with. And we still got old *Cain*. We could raise the ante on *Cain*. Folks are going to be mortal pious after the chastening effects of this visitation of wrath. I got that from a parson. Do you reckon you could talk the Honorable into a charter or two for us, lad?"

Jans laughed, "I'll try."

"Then you'll keep on with the boat!"

"What else is there for me? Yes, I'm sticking, Pilk."

He went back to his writing. Little by little his drama had reduced itself to its simplest terms. Now there were but three characters, a bold innovation, indeed. What of it? The whole conception
was new, revolutionary. He concerned himself specially with the
feminine lead. Remodel it as he might, it was still Durie.

"Damn it all! I'm haunted," he snarled.

The population of the cholera shantees had thinned down. Half
of the entries had been discharged, cured. The other half had gone
out by the dead-wagon. With only five convalescents left in their
care, the two girls were transferred on part time to the hospital
proper. Mrs. Gaines having caught the Plague and died in harness,
and Mrs. Loakes having drunk herself into delirium tremens.

The two specials still slept in their tiny shack by the streamside.
There Gypsy, whose turn it was to prepare breakfast that morning,
addressed her later-sleeping friend.

"What you been crying about?"

"I never cry."

"Look at your face! All swole."

"I suppose I've been sleeping on it."

"Crying in your sleep," pursued the relentless Gypsy. "For that
worthless mauser, I'll be bound."

"He isn't," Durie's indignation died and with it her spirit. "I
suppose he is."

"Damn well you know he is."

"Oh, Gypsy! I ought to. But when I saw him lying there so weak
and helpless I couldn't help thinking, 'If he dies I shall never be
certain.'"

Gypsy's face became grim. "You want to be certain? I'll make
you certain."

"How?"

"Remember the Missouri puke?"

"Lucky Seven Smith? Yes."

"He came in last night."

"Cholera?"

"No. Shot wounds. Taproom fight. Go and talk to him."

"Why should I?"

"He can tell you about Looby and your fancy man."

Reluctantly Durie allowed herself to be taken to the wounded man. Weak as he was, he kept twisting his head about, looking from cot to cot, quivering at every groan of the stricken around him. The hardy fighting man was gray-faced with panic, the kind of fear that renders its possessed helpless to resist contagion. He gulped the medicine that Gypsy handed to him.

"I feel queer," he quavered.

"Cocker up!" Gypsy exhorted him. "Here's my friend, wants to ask you about Jans Quintard."

"You his doxy?" he inquired of Durie.

She shook her head.

"I'll send you his ears by post, when I get out of here."

"Suppose you don't get out?" snapped Gypsy.

"Then I'll wait for him in hell," said the puke with feeble malevolence.

"Tell her what Jans done to you, Lucky," said Gypsy.

"Stole my marked meat right out from under my dukes."

"That was the jailbreak? Looby?"

"Yes."

"You'da sent him back, yourself, wouldn't you?"

"Look, wench," said the patient earnestly. "I'm a manhunter—a blackbirder, if you like. I'll take a runagate for the reward just like I'll shoot a buffalo for the pelt. But there's one thing I don't do. I never yet sold out a poor bastard that trusted me."

"Is that what Quinny did?" Gypsy nudged her companion to attention.

"Him and his partner, Pilkington."

"Do you know that, Mr. Lucky Seven?" Durie asked.

"Did I see them claim the money or didn't I?" In his evil intent he now indulged in a flight of fancy. "And did I take another jail delivery back to Auburn and see Looby battering his head against the bars and bleating like a sheep?"

"Don't!" cried Durie and covered her ears.

She stumbled to the door. Gypsy followed her.

"Now you know."

"Yes."

"Feel better?"

"No."

"What a mush!" said Gypsy in despair.

There came a day when no new cases entered the Institute, and there was but one death. Dr. Colvin announced his intention of going home to sleep the clock around, leaving the two girls in temporary charge with Elder Symes. When Gypsy entered for the early clean-up a petulant voice whined, "No mornin' prayers?"

"Where's the Elder?" Gypsy asked with a heart suddenly chilled.

"He ain't been here to see us."

Murmurings from the other straw-boxes confirmed the complaint. The ward had come to depend upon and find comfort in the gaunt, old bluenose's stern adjurations. Lucky Seven Smith clutched at the girl's skirt as she passed him on her way to investigate.

"Ain't he coming?" he gasped. "Ain't the Elder coming?"

"Not for the likes of you." She shook herself loose as a moan of despair issued from the sick man's mouth.

Elder Symes lay across his cot, fully dressed in his blacks, even to his austere bow-tie. His face was greenish gray and strangely peaceful. It was one of those merciful cases where the disease strikes swiftly and painlessly at the very center of life. Gypsy bent over him. His eyes opened slowly.

"I must go to my sick," he said anxiously.

He straightened and fell back.

Gypsy ran to get the hot salt-pack, the mustard sinapism, the other desperate and useless devices. She got him stripped and between the covers.

"Weary, weary!" he muttered. "An unprofitable servant."

She took his stone-cold hand between her rough, warm ones. She knew the coming of death when she saw it.

"Go to sleep, Dominie," she said gently.

Two hours later, stiff and haggard from the enforced immobility of her watch, she staggered down to tell Durie. Durie tried to comfort her.

"There goes the best of 'em," Gypsy mourned. She perked up. "And he's taken the worst with him."

"The worst? Lucky Seven?" Durie asked.

Gypsy nodded and dried her eyes. "Lost his holt when the old man didn't come 'round to pray for him. Give a squeak and off he popped."

"I'm glad he told me about Jans," Durie said through clenched teeth.

"I think you're a liar, gal."

"I'm not. It's settled my mind for me."

"Just the same, I wish he'd lived to post you those ears."

"Why?"

"It's hard to be mushy over a face between a couple of stumps."

"Gypsy, I hate you!"

"Hate's easier to get over than love. We're through here. We got the dibbs." She patted her skirt. "Let's hit the path."

"Dr. Colvin has asked me to stay until they close."

"Little Hilda, the Helping Hand! Then what?"

"I don't know."

"Back to the banner?"

"I suppose so."

"Old Passover, he'll be forming up again." Gypsy reflected upon the prospects. "See you in a week or so, then."

Never in all her life had Durie so craved untainted air as toward the end of her stay. That charnel stench had become the aura of daily existence. Walls, floors, ceilings had grown intolerable; they exhaled the unseen fumes of pestilence and corruption. If ever she was to feel clean again, the forces of nature must restore her; sunlight and dew and the healing winds of heaven.

A great, bright gale blew from out the west on the morning of her release. She could not leave with one farewell unbidden. Close-ranged beneath the brow of the hillock, the graves of the hospital dead were shaded by a willow coppice. Durie had marked the mound that covered Elder Symes with shallow coverage.

Now she garnered with her flax-knife sheaves of the various autumn flowers, sunshine gold and imperial purple, and spread them, a panoply of splendor, upon the earth. There lay the best man she had known. She recalled Personius Andrews' apothegm:

"Could I enlist Death as my adviser, I should affect the Lotteries. Death picks the gold and spares the dross."

Better for the world had death spared Elder Symes and taken Jans Quintard. Yet she could not rid heart and memory of Jans. Strive as she might, she was still committed to an unworthy love by no higher bond—she shook herself angrily—than that of the ignoble flesh.

The traitorous pulse of youth and sex. Again the echo of Personius Andrews. He knew!

The spice of autumn was in the air when, pack on staff and staff on shoulder as of old, she took the towpath. A faint haze of smoke from the burning reeds of the Montezuma Marshes brought a tang to the nostrils. Presently, as she strode, she found herself singing. Life was good. Earth and heaven were young. One could learn to forget.

All along path and berm, abandoned craft bore melancholy testimony to the ravages of the past, now spent. Once she saw a corpse barely moving in the torpid current. Near Salinas a lost or deserted child crouched on a bridge, whimpering from hunger. She fed him out of her thin store, and would have found a refuge for him, but he clung to the railing and shrieked like a wild thing when she tried to lead him. The first night she slept in a haymow outside Manlius—Manlius, where her life-current and Jans Quintard's had met again. She must not think of that!

Up betimes, she found a band of the six-centers just breaking camp. From the scent of their fire she could tell that their cooking was deplorable; so, out of the kindness of her heart, she took over pot and kettle and dished up a proper breakfast. They were a scrawny lot, spiritless and without leadership. Farmers, fearing them as probable vehicles of the pest, refused them shelter or food. Half of their original quota were gone. By ones and twos they had dropped, crawled into the bushes and, so far as their companions knew, died there. A hulking apprentice with a broken nose reported having seen Gypsy Vilas flaunting it on the foredeck of a Durham as the boat was locking through. To shouted inquiries about her destination she replied that she was on her way to Albany to run for Mayor.

Approval of Durie's cooking took practical form in an invitation to join the band. She politely declined. The pace, she knew, would be too slow for her swinging four miles an hour. All the vigor of the generous earth was flooding back into her limbs. She felt fifteen again and wished she were.

There were times that day when she overtook packet boats, exchanging blithe repartee with the more volatile of the deck passengers. A young blade leaped to the bank beyond Chittenango, doffed his castor, and solicited the honor of pacing her for a few miles, an offer graciously accepted. But when, emboldened, he offered to pay her night-fare on board, she demurely explained that, as the betrothed of President Martin Van Buren, she was forced to decline.

The weigh-lock, halfway along the Black Snake, stands shaded with overhanging elm and willow. In normal traffic there might have been fifteen or twenty boats lined up to wait their turn. Now, as the sun was near to setting, there were four—more than the lock-keeper had seen in file for two months. A curve of the old Furnace Road brought it close to the canal, furnishing a busy site for a coffee house. There Durie designed to sup on ale, cold roast, cheese and pie, and strike along the pike for a free lodging place. As she approached, a yodel, rendered with melancholy gusto from beneath an elm on the berm came to her ears.

> *"Oolie—oolie—aylie—oo.*
> *Oolie—aylie—oo!"*

"Looby!" Durie cried.

He sat up, waving away a swarm of mosquitoes. "Huh? Oh! What's your pleasure, lady?"

"Don't you know me, Looby?"

"Certes I know you. You got me outa jail."

"How did you get out this time?"

"Who? Me? Outa where, lady?"

"Auburn Prison."

"Oh, there!" He pondered the matter. "Bought out," he said.

"Then they'll catch you and put you back again," she cried distressfully.

"They can't. I gotta paper."

"Nonsense. You shouldn't be here at all. What are you doing?"

"I'm on the rope again. Them's my team in the medder. Good money. Prime prog. Clean bunk. Rum at the end of your trick.

Wouldn't want no fairer treatment," declared Looby complacently.

"But for whom are you working?"

"*Barter Boat.* Cap Pilkington and Mr. Quintard. Wassa matter, lady?"

"You're working for those two?" she said in a choking voice. "After they sold you back into jail?"

"They lawed me out again."

Durie's hands went to her temples. "How, *lawed* you . . . ?

"Wanna see my papers?" Brightening, he plunged his hand down his neck and brought forth, warm from his hairy hide, a pardon in full form with seal.

Durie took it with shaking hands.

"Wuth a hunnerd dollar ree-ward, I was," the ex-jailbird said proudly. "My two gennelmen took the hunnerd dollars an' give it to Governor Throop, an' he gimme this. They can't never take me back to Obbun no more."

Durie sat down heavily. The facts were falling into place in her mind with appalling significance.

"Think carefully, Looby. Jans and Pi—Mr. Quintard and Captain Pilkington took the reward and used it to get you a pardon. Is that it?"

"Yes, lady. That's it. You sick, lady? Would you wish a drink?"

It was the ingrained habit of Miss Endurance Andrews to move swiftly toward any given point or purpose. Now she advanced with clogged feet and feverishly working brain. The five-rod space to the *Barter Boat* seemed five miles.

She had sworn to Jans that she would never sue for his pardon. Thereupon the Quintard temper had flared—and why not!—and he had retorted that if she ever did, he would reject the olive branch. Personius Andrews had written: "Once a resolution is put into words, be it promise or challenge, it and the maker are dishonored by its revocation." That clashed in her ferment of thought with another Andrews apothegm: "Ask-your-pardon is a poor repairment for injury inflicted. Let your deed be your apologia." And again, further to complicate the confusion in her mind: "None can diminish you in your own esteem but yourself."

Where did it all leave her? In turmoil.

She was abreast of the boat. Nothing stirred aboard. She hailed in a voice that seemed to her to belong to somebody else of an unstable disposition.

"*Barter Boat,* ahoy!"

Jans Quintard's easy baritone answered from between decks, "Ahoy! Who hails?"

"It's me."

Jans Quintard's face appeared above the hatchway, rigid with amazement.

"I don't believe it."

"I want to see Captain Pilkington."

"What for?"

"To give him a message."

"Won't I do?"

"No, please."

"Pilk's away on a trade."

"When will he be back?"

"Not until tomorrow morning. You can write your message."

"It isn't that kind."

"What kind is it, Durie?"

"It—it's an apology."

"To *Pilk?* Why Pilk?"

"Because I've misjudged him."

"About Looby?"

"Yes."

"And you prefer dealing with him to . . ."

"To someone else. Pilk will understand. Pilk is kind. He hasn't an evil, uncharitable Quintard temper."

"You don't strike one as being in a specially apologetical frame of mind."

"I can explain to Pilk that—that I've found things out."

"So have I. Important things."

"Not as important as mine."

"More so, I think. About you and Mace Ayrault."

"There is nothing to find out."

"That's what makes it so important."

"Let's get back to Pilk."

"All right. We're back to Pilk. Prodigious fellow, old Pilk!"

"When one has misjudged someone, what does she do to make amends?"

He gave it careful consideration. "She might marry him."

"Would that be making proper amends?"

"It would, in my poor judgment."

"Marry Pilk?"

"Oh, Pilk! Are we still on Pilk?"

"Aren't we? I'm getting mixed up. Does this boat take passengers?"

"Sometimes."

"What's the fare?"

"To what port?"

"Wherever you're going."

"More than you'd want to pay, perhaps."

"I'm mortal rich," she said.

"Come aboard."

"You might have said that earlier."

"I was afraid you might refuse."

Setting her hands on the rail, she vaulted to the deck. "Here I am."

"You've been here all the time. Night and day."

Her raised brows and softly brooding eyes interrogated him.

"In the play I've been working on. You're in every line of it. You run through it like a melody, an enchantment, a passion. I couldn't rid it of you."

"Did you want to?"

"*I* wanted to. The play wouldn't let me."

"Where is it?"

"On my desk."

"Aren't I to see it?"

"If you'll come below."

She studied him, a smile tremulous upon her lips. "Do you think it safe for me?"

"You've always got that wicked little scimitar of yours, haven't you?"

"My flax-knife? Oh, yes."

"And your hand hasn't lost its cunning?"

"My heart has." She slipped her fingers into the bosom of her bodice. The bright curve of the blade glanced and vanished in a ripple of Erie Water. "I'll never want that again."

"Please God!" Jans said.

At the hatchway she stopped and laid her hand on his.

"Before we go down, Jans . . ."

"Yes, Durie?"

"I want you to know this: My heart never quite believed the evil of you."

"Nor mine of you. . . . Are you crying, my sweet?"

"I n-n-never c-c-c-cry," said Durie indignantly.

Afterword

My GREAT-AUNT Sarah remembered always the signal whistle from canalside and the children trooping down with welcoming shouts, "The *Book Boat!* The *Book Boat!*" and the hoards of their penny banks in hand. *Quintard's Folly,* the grown-ups called it. Often it stopped all day at a town to let the romance-hungry people read their fill of Scott and Cooper and Irving, of the copious Amelia Opie and the reliable Charles Brockden Browne; or, for the lighter-minded, the *Universal Jest Book* and the very comical *Thinks I to Myself—Who?,* while the pious found assurance in that font of edifying information, *Buck's Theological Dictionary* and in *English Mary, or the Happy Reward of Virtuous Fidelity,* and the hopeful consulted the *Dream Dictionary* and the almanach astrologies. It was notorious that the enterprise was conducted at a loss.

For ten cents one might read through the day, bringing a dinner pail to lose no precious time; an hour cost two cents. The children thronged the penny-counter where, to be sure, there was little for a penny except pipsissiway and licorice drops, but with the accumulation of their thrift they could buy toys, paintbox colors, Rogers Patent Pen-knives, playing cards (if no elder were looking), and the most fascinating paper-backed volumes, rich in colored pictures.

Perhaps, one or the other of the Quintards would be reading aloud in a circle of rapt, young faces. For this was the Quintard folly, to instil into eager minds the love of good reading and take no profit of it.

One end of the reading room was given over to a stage, narrow and shallow but with authentic footlights and draw curtains. Thereon the Quintards rendered at frequent intervals a contracted version of *Sunrise to Sunset* with themselves in the principal roles, aided by a seamed character called Pilk who played the wicked mill-owner with manifest reluctance.

Aunt Sarah knew of the original play with full cast having been hooted off the professional stage in Rochester, mainly at the instigation of Mr. Thurlow Weed, the printer, who editorialized to this stringent effect:

Here we observe the sort of injurious mischief that sets class against class, poor against rich, raises the twin specters of hatred and discontent, and breeds revolution. All good citizens should not only eschew but should actively reprehend such calculated malignancy.

So the Jans Quintard drama was withdrawn from professional presentment, and reduced to three characters in one act, and the limitations of family production. Aunt Sarah thought it a rather fustian play and La Jeune Amour an inept though earnest actress who, nevertheless, enjoyed an inalienable following. For, at the advanced age of thirty, when she should have retired into respectable middle age, flaccid and wrinkled with childbirth and housewifely drudgeries, she was still straight and lithe and lovely, the mistress of enchantments and the toast of Erie Water from Buffalo to Lock Number One.

When a very old lady, bedridden and in pain, Great-aunt Sarah's proudest recollection of authorship was having found in that floating library a copy of one of her own works, *Land of Milk and Honey; a Tale for Young Americans,* by Sarah Hopkins Bradford. But that was in the fifties, when towpath and berm were no longer free to wayfarers and the haughty, beribboned tandems had given place to a humbler breed, and the hoggees sang:

> *"I got a mule and her name is Sal,*
> *Fifteen miles on the Erie Canal . . .*

Schooling had become general and the Quintards were about quitting a trade that no longer needed them.

Only a memory of them remains. But what a memory! For it springs from the roots of mirth and happiness, of contempt for all things mean, of fervor for all things joyous and sane and kind, and its flowering is imperishable.